Too sweeping w/ aut
strong phone.
A help judge of
who — stores, really
what expect.

Becoming Bourgeois

NEW DIRECTIONS IN SOUTHERN HISTORY

SERIES EDITORS

Peter S. Carmichael, *University of North Carolina at Greensboro*
Michele Gillespie, *Wake Forest University*
William A. Link, *University of Florida*

Southern Farmers and Their Stories:
Memory and Meaning in Oral History
by Melissa Walker

The View from the Ground:
Experiences of Civil War Soldiers
Edited by Aaron Sheehan-Dean

Becoming Bourgeois

Merchant Culture in the
South, 1820–1865

Frank J. Byrne

THE UNIVERSITY PRESS OF KENTUCKY

Publication of this volume was made possible in part by a grant
from the National Endowment for the Humanities.

Editorial and Sales Offices: The University Press of Kentucky
663 South Limestone Street, Lexington, Kentucky 40508–4008
www.kentuckypress.com

06 07 08 09 10   5 4 3 2 1

Library of Congress Cataloging-in-Publication Data

Byrne, Frank J., 1968-
Becoming bourgeois : merchant culture in the South, 1820-1865 /
Frank J. Byrne.
p. cm. — (New directions in southern history)
Includes bibliographical references and index.
ISBN-13: 978-0-8131-2404-9 (hardcover : alk. paper)
ISBN-10: 0-8131-2404-2 (hardcover : alk. paper)
1. Merchants—Southern States—History. 2. Southern States—Social conditions—
History. 3. Southern States—Economic conditions—History. I. Title.
HF3153.B97 2006
381.0975'09034—dc22
2006019967

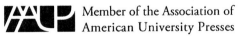

To my wife, Mary McCune,
my mother, Marilyn Byrne,
and to the memory of my father, Frank L. Byrne

Contents

Acknowledgments

This project started as a seminar paper at the University of Georgia, developed into a dissertation at Ohio State University, and is now a book. Over that time I had the good fortune to meet numerous individuals who encouraged my love of history while at the same time challenging many of my assumptions about the past. Numan V. Bartley, Emory M. Thomas, Peter Charles Hoffer, and John C. Inscoe proved to be wise teachers both in and out of the classroom. John, in particular, has assisted me more times than I care to admit and continues to be a generous scholar in a profession where too often such individuals are a *rara avis*. My dissertation committee, Mark Grimsley, Warren R. Van Tine, Randolph A. Roth, and the aforementioned John C. Inscoe, provided thoughtful analysis of my work and is responsible for much of the insight it may have. My adviser Mark Grimsley deserves special thanks for helping me complete my dissertation in the face of several obstacles and much personal drama. His scholarship and professionalism offered me a refreshing example of what is best about our vocation.

This study would not have been possible without the financial support of several institutions and the assistance of excellent people performing important work in numerous archives. I would like to thank the archivists from Texas to Virginia and from Massachusetts to Georgia who made this book possible. I am particularly grateful to the interlibrary loan librarians at the Ohio State University, the University of Akron, and the State University of New York at Oswego for their diligent work in tracking down the hundreds of requests I have submitted over the years. Research for this project was supported by grants from two Henry H. Simms Awards and a Graduate Student Alumni Research Award (Ohio State University); a research travel grant from the University of Texas at Austin; a Mellon Research Fellowship from the Virginia Historical Society; and a Faculty Enhancement Grant from the State University of New York at Oswego. A portion of the introduction and chapters 1 and 2 appeared in "The Merchant in Antebellum Southern Literature and Society," and I wish to thank *American Nineteenth Century History* for permission to reprint small portions of this article. I would like to thank Joyce Harrison at the University Press of Kentucky for her unfailing support in helping make this book possible. Suggestions and advice from the editors of the New Directions in Southern History series and the anonymous readers helped me strengthen my analysis. I would especially like to thank Michele Gillespie for her thoughtful comments. She made this a better book.

Numerous colleagues, friends, and family members helped me survive and occasionally thrive in graduate school and beyond. Lesley Gordon, Pat Breen, Wendy Wickham, Phil Adamo, Greg Wilson, Ken Wheeler, Greg Parsons, Dave McGee, Lori Cline, Karin Zipf, Febe Armanios, Mike Fronda, Bill Caraher, Charlotte Weber, and Dan Pappalardo helped me understand more about myself and, often indirectly, the South. Eugene Kadish, Ian Heisey, and Kermit Mangus once again showed me how often the friends you make as a child prove to be the most constant over time. More than once my sister, Anne Boyles, and her family provided relief and a psychological haven when my merchants seemed sure to overwhelm me. Colleagues in the History Department at the State University of New York at Oswego provided wise counsel and encouragement while I completed revisions of the manuscript. Geraldine Forbes, J. Douglas Deal, Mark Kulikowski, Tim Thurber, Gwen Kay, and Karl Davis deserve special thanks.

The best thing that happened to me while in graduate school was meeting my wife, Mary McCune. Her wit, kindness, intellect, and love bring meaning to my own journey. A journey made all the more delightful with the company of our two sons, Jack and Liam. In the same bargain I gained wonderful in-laws in Clare and Harry McCune. Finally, I would like to thank my parents, Frank and Marilyn Byrne. A professor from northern New Jersey and a teacher from Omaha, Nebraska, they instilled in my sister and me an appreciation for the past and a hope for the future. No words nor any dedication can express my appreciation for all that they have done for me. The example they set as parents, scholars, and friends continues to inspire me.

Introduction

In the summer of 1862 Jorantha Semmes wrote a letter expressing her war weariness to her husband Benedict Semmes, a Confederate officer. Responsible for the care of their five children in Federally occupied Memphis, Tennessee, Semmes told her husband, "I am tired of this separation." His absence had left her bereft of "all gaiety of heart." Caring for the children helped occupy Jorantha's mind during the day, but she missed her "better half" at night when "it is *so* lonely."[1] Jorantha Semmes increasingly questioned the romantic militarism of the Civil War. Others, we know, shared this sentiment. Historians have noted that the trials of war eroded the patriotism of many southern women. Semmes's anxiety over the fate of her family and the Confederate cause seems to conform to this pattern.[2]

What distinguishes Semmes's writing from that of other educated southern women is its commercial tone. The couple's letters reflect the concerns of their shared occupation, the mercantile trade. Benedict Semmes established his Memphis store shortly before the outbreak of the Civil War. His absence during the conflict forced Jorantha to assume responsibility for the store's operation, and their correspondence reveals her business skills. In June 1862 she wrote her husband that under Yankee occupation the boatloads of provisions arriving daily in the Mississippi River port sold "like lightning for specie." The money she made selling what stock remained from the store, combined with the rent she collected from boarders, led her to inquire whether he might need five hundred dollars sent to him. As a savvy wife and mother in a mercantile family, Jorantha also suggested that the family's earnings in Memphis should be invested in "a land purchase instead of letting it be idle." More than a year later her continued confidence in business matters is obvious as she wrote her husband that the "terms" of her recent business transactions "are such as you would approve." In 1864, Benedict openly acknowledged her acumen in financial matters when he asked her about collecting some debts: "I would like to have your own views, for you sometimes see things clearer than I."

1

This commercial discourse is not a historical aberration; rather it is the result of a southern merchant culture that experienced profound change during the Civil War. The war at once destroyed the southern merchant's financial world and opened new business opportunities in what would one day be termed a "New South."[3]

The ideology of antebellum and Confederate merchants contained a series of unresolved contradictions. These merchants embraced the South but were not of the South. They traded, haggled, and invested their wealth in a slaveholding South where a planter elite created an agrarian society seemingly hostile to industry and urbanization. At a time when most Southerners rarely traveled outside their surrounding environs, merchants annually sallied forth on buying junkets that took them to Baltimore, Philadelphia, and New York City. While most southern whites remained unlettered, merchant families frequently achieved a level of education rivaled by only the planter elite. These and other cultural differences created a gulf between merchant families and their southern neighbors that both sides recognized. The unique culture of the southern merchant family helps explain Jorantha Semmes's ability to operate her husband's store during the Civil War.[4]

The skills merchants needed in order to succeed in the South also left them open to attack. Criticized as "cunning fellows" who differed little from Yankee shopkeepers, southern merchants frequently found themselves defending their trade. Remarking on their sharp trading practices and undeserved social prominence, critics frequently charged merchants with gross opportunism. Characterizing his antebellum business career, Atlanta merchant Sidney Root offered the southern merchant's typical defense to such accusations when he declared, "I never loved money for its own sake." The Janus-faced southern merchant, at once the shrewd entrepreneur and obsequious apologist, is an image commonly found in antebellum southern culture; it appears even within the personal correspondence of the merchant community itself. Despite the convention of the storekeeper as a "southern Yankee," these merchants' deeply held Christian sensibility, joined with their support for slavery, made them distinctly southern.[5]

The present work investigates the culture of this segment of southern antebellum and Confederate society. It focuses on what historians have come to call the "middling sort," that group falling between the mass of yeoman farmers and the planter class that dominated the political economy of the antebellum South. This study explores the experiences of urban merchants, village storekeepers, and small-scale factors, as well as the roles these merchants and their families played within the southern political economy. It is essential to note that the southern merchant class was far from a coherent, unified community in the antebellum and Confederate South. It included poor street hucksters, respectable dry-goods storekeepers, and the merchant princes in such larger cities as Charleston and New Orleans. What bound these individuals into something approaching a class with distinct interests was the fact that their livelihoods depended on their ability to sell goods in a society that still honored, at least rhetorically, the republican pursuits of the farmer and mechanic. Furthermore, much like what Sven Beckert discovered in his analysis of a more influential bourgeoisie in nineteenth-century New York City, the social identity of southern merchants appeared most often when their interests conflicted with other social groups. Socially mobile in a boom-bust economy, retail businessmen belonged to a dynamic, self-identified community. Like members in other social groups, these individuals would enter and leave their chosen profession. The occasional merchant entered the ranks of the planter class or, more often, quit the profession to farm, but the evidence suggests that most saw their economic interests and cultural values as distinct from both groups. Unlike their planter neighbors, southern merchants did not produce a bourgeois version of a George Fitzhugh or James Henry Hammond to articulate a liberal capitalist ideology before the Civil War. It is my contention that such an ideology did not exist. Merchants, however, did share a broad, often unspoken worldview that shaped their daily lives. This work will attempt to comprehend the peculiar strains of modernist and conservative thought that imbued the culture of these merchants.[6]

Informed by much cultural history produced over the past thirty years, I emphasize social views and behavior as well as institutions and economic structures. Diaries, letters, newspapers, credit reports, and other sources are interpreted as records of social experience and as documents of beliefs. Through this process I have attempted to recover critical elements of the *Weltanschauung* that merchants and their families shared. The first half of this study compares their worldview and material well-being with popular representations of merchant culture that were conspicuous in nineteenth-century southern society. Depictions of merchants in newspapers and essays will be juxtaposed with the more personal images revealed in their own writings. As the title of this book suggests, I argue that merchants living in the antebellum South were still "becoming" bourgeois, meaning that the unique "formal manners" and "ethical standards" that made the bourgeois in Victorian Europe and in the northern United States "refined" did not reach consummation in the southern merchant class before the Civil War. These merchants defended the slave South and rejected many of the reformist currents found in the Protestant tradition of the ascending northern middle class. The political and economic changes wrought by the Civil War fundamentally altered the position of merchant families within southern society. The collapse of the slave order allowed them to embrace a free labor, market-oriented Anglo-American bourgeois ideology. The second half of this study explores the impact of the Civil War on merchants and how their changing ideals influenced life in the Confederacy.[7]

The merchant class has occupied an important, though often disruptive, economic and cultural position in the South. Certainly the work of early twentieth-century novelists testifies to a prevailing uneasiness with the rise of liberal capitalist values in a pastoral South. Creative writers have depicted the merchant and his store as malevolent agents within the social order, most famously in William Faulkner's novel *The Hamlet* (1940). After the Civil War, the merchant Flem Snopes moves to a small village in Faulkner's fictional Yoknapatawpha County, Mississippi, where he obtains a clerking position in the local store. Business cunning and a reputation as a dangerous barn burner enable Snopes to overwhelm the old order's feeble opposition to his rule. The stranger's mastery over the community is complete when the asexual Snopes marries the voluptuous Eula Varner, daughter of the richest man in town. Faulkner's story is one of the modernist impulse, represented by the merchant Snopes, destroying the traditions of a southern community. A similar theme is found in T. S. Stribling's novel *The Store* (1932). Here the lure of the wealth and prestige available through the retail trade causes the moral destruction of Colonel Miltiades Vaiden, a hero of the Civil War and Reconstruction. Vaiden, symbolizing the Confederate South, loses the respect of his community with the dishonorable means he employs to acquire a village store. Faulkner and Stribling both associate merchants with values hostile to the legacy of the antebellum and Confederate South.[8]

Popular depictions of the southern merchant consumed by greed and driven by a terrible ambition unknown to rural white Southerners did not first erupt in a conservative backlash to the commercial excesses of the post–Civil War New South or, later, its more successful twentieth-century descendent, the Sunbelt. Rather Faulkner, Stribling, and others fall within a much broader southern literary tradition that can be traced back to some of the region's earliest and most talented writers. For example, Augustus Baldwin Longstreet, William Gilmore Simms, and Edgar Allan Poe each contributed to the development of the merchant stereotype. Borrowing certain tropes from northern and British literature, the subject of commercially driven characters living alongside their more conservative neighbors, be it in rural or urban settings, offered these authors an excellent opportunity for social commentary.[9]

The antebellum judge, newspaper publisher, college president, and humorist Augustus Baldwin Longstreet ridiculed the pretensions of the mercantile class and its commercial values in several stories in his classic work *Georgia Scenes* (1835). Most notably, Longstreet's "The 'Charming Creature' as a Wife" lampoons a family that includes an "unlettered merchant," a vapid mother, and their beautiful daughter Evelina, who subsists on "admiration and flattery," "the only food which she could relish." William Gilmore Simms's novel *Guy Rivers: A Tale of Georgia* (1834) adds what would become a familiar twist to popular representations of storekeepers and peddlers working in the South by depicting them as Yankees. Simms's tale of adventure in frontier Georgia includes the character of Jared Bunce, an amoral peddler hailing from Connecticut. The author lets a hearty backwoodsman speak for all "true" Southerners when he has him denounce Bunce as a man whose "rascality ain't to be measured," a scoundrel that "kin walk through a man's pockets, jest as the devil goes through a crack or a keyhole, and the money will naterally stick to him, jest as ef he was made of gum turpentine." Edgar Allan Poe, the antebellum South's most original writer, devoted an entire story, appropriately entitled "The Business Man" (1840), to mocking the banality of commercial life. The protagonist, Peter Pendulum, is a "methodical man" who loves to speculate, willingly lives by the dictates of the clock, and hates men of true genius. The latter, according to the businessman, work "at variance with the 'fitness of things.'" Antebellum writers like Longstreet, Simms, and Poe helped construct the stereotypical merchant character that would continue to reappear in southern literature long after the Civil War. Revealingly, these authors depicted southern merchants as a particular social type, individuals who culturally and economically did not fit neatly within their communities, if at all. They and their fellow

Southerners, white and black, often viewed their merchant neighbors as outsiders, what cultural historians today would call "the Other." In several respects this assessment, though grounded in misunderstanding and prejudice, was essentially accurate.[10]

Despite the tremendous growth of interest in the antebellum and Confederate South, we still know relatively little about the role merchants played in either period. Don Doyle, one among a handful of recent scholars to give the urban business community in the Civil War and postwar South serious attention, concludes: "The new order of things that followed the war and Reconstruction magnified the role of an urban business class within the South. To be sure, this class had antecedents in the antebellum towns and cities. But its incarnation in the New South era was far more imposing in scale, in geographic breadth, and in ideological vigor."[11] This book will explore the world of the "antecedents" to which Doyle alludes and will reveal that while the financial horizons of the southern merchant were artificially limited by the planter regime before 1865, the subculture they fashioned prefigured the New South. As Doyle's work demonstrates, most of the leading businessmen in such New South boomtowns as Atlanta and Nashville came of age before and during the Civil War. Thus it is not enough to explore the changing world of the southern merchant class during and after the war. Rather, in order to understand the economic roots of the postwar South and to determine how new the period really was, it is necessary to examine the many roles merchants performed in the Old South. While they neither manufactured weapons nor grew produce, merchants served as financial linchpins in keeping the southern economy viable during peace and war. Yet most southern historians have overlooked their critical role in the Old South, a silence that is especially surprising when one considers the southern merchant's prominence in contemporary accounts from the period. Instead scholars have concentrated on merchants in the postwar South.[12]

A recent exception to this rule is Jonathan Daniel Wells's insightful study *The Origins of the Southern Middle Class, 1800–1861* (2004). Wells's analysis of the development of a southern middle class complicates the standard depiction of the Old South as seemingly inhabited by only farmers, planters, and their slaves. By describing the activities of manufacturers, teachers, doctors, merchants, and others, Wells makes a strong case that a vibrant middle class exerted influence within the antebellum South. On the subjects of personal mobility, educational experience, political values, and other issues regarding the merchant class, my findings in this work agree with Wells's. Additionally, both he and I maintain that, in terms of the experiences for many individuals within this class, a great deal of continuity existed between the Old and New South. This said, our works often diverge in their methodology and conclusions.

Wells depicts a rather ideologically homogenous urban "middle class" that includes manufacturers, artisans, merchants, lawyers, and doctors, among others. Certainly a practical and intellectual case can be made for such a broad categorization, but as I will suggest in the following chapters, it conflates the unique trading experience of commercial retailers and wholesalers with that of individuals who made goods (manufacturers) and of those whose profession enjoyed great prestige (doctors). During the antebellum period, the members of Wells's middle class, as well as most other observers, including the U.S. Department of the Census, recognized the economic and social distinctions between these occupations. Furthermore, by including manufacturers in his analysis, Wells tends to ascribe the ideological perspective of such individuals as the industrialist William Gregg to his defined middle class as a whole. This leads Wells to conclude that most merchants, professionals, and the rest, strongly supported the use of slaves within an industrial setting. Wells suggests that this view was held by so many influential middle-class Southerners that free labor advocates in the North felt threatened. Thus the timing of the Civil War is, in part, explained by the apparent vitality of industrial slavery in the South during the 1850s. Wells makes an excellent case that Gregg, James De Bow, and several other southern spokesmen made industrial slavery their mission, yet few if any merchants seem to have supported the cause. The records left by more average, hence more common, Southerners in the commercial trades reveal ambivalence regarding the South's dependence on the institution of slavery. Finally, the most obvious difference between our two works, which undoubtedly influences our conclusions, is that Wells's study ends in 1861, while the Civil War is central to the present work. As was true for all Southerners, white and black, the trial of war left its mark on southern merchants and their families. This crucible offers the historian a unique perspective into the behavior and worldview of a class that would come into its own when the violence ended in 1865.[13]

Several historians have examined the social and economic position of the merchant in the postbellum South. Lacy Ford, Paul Escott, and Allen Tullos have described the often ambivalent economic role of the southern merchant following the collapse of the Confederacy. The increasing economic importance of the southern merchant as a furnishing agent, due largely to the advent of the crop lien system, explains much of this interest. Historians have also identified the store as an agent promoting significant cultural change in the nineteenth century. This judgment is mirrored in the popular culture as well.[14]

The gap in the historiography on the merchant class, which has only begun to be filled in recent years, can be attributed in part to the political economy of the antebellum South. The small planter elite ideologically and economically dominated the Old South and marginalized the merchant's role. Like most regional elites, planters designed the financial structure of the South to serve their own interests. The system they imposed on their region inhibited the growth and power of southern entrepreneurs. Despite playing a critical role within world capitalism, the planter class infused its society with an agrarian ethos antagonistic to urbanization and free labor. The drive for self-sufficiency on their plantations and the dependence of poorer whites on this plantation economy effectively limited the penetration of the national consumer market. The plantation economy also barred most slaves from buying consumer goods. Indeed full market integration would not be completed in the South until well after the Civil War. Antebellum planters also gained political power disproportionate to their numbers and came to embody the social ideal within the South. Eugene Genovese, David Brion Davis, Peter Kolchin, and other historians describe the social, legal, and economic boundaries that American slavery created. Merchants needed considerable skill in order to succeed in such a society.[15]

The southern merchant community nevertheless promoted the kind of aggressive business practices both before and during the Civil War that proponents of the New South would later claim as their own. In communities of the antebellum and Confederate South, merchants managed to adopt the competitive business philosophy of the North with few fundamental changes. The skills (salesmanship, economy, etc.) needed to succeed in an increasingly complex regional economy profoundly shaped the culture of the southern merchant class. A combination of modern business capitalism with more traditional social custom manifested itself in the merchant family. The culture of the southern shopkeepers and their families exhibits this tenuous fusion of organic social relations with free market enterprise. The Civil War severely tested the ability of merchant families to maintain their position within the South.

The present work seeks to make several contributions to the field of nineteenth-century American history. First, it reveals the important economic role of the merchant class within the antebellum and Confederate South. Second, it adds to our understanding of the dynamics within the southern white family. Few historical examinations have attempted to describe the unique character of the southern merchant family. For example, this study delineates how merchants and their families across the South reconciled the occasionally contradictory impulses of a modern capitalist ethic with the conservative religious and social traditions of a fading agrarian South.

Becoming Bourgeois: Merchant Culture in the South, 1820–1865 both rests upon and attempts to place its subject within a large and ever increasing historical literature on the South. Among the few works before Jonathan Daniel Wells's that explore the world of storekeepers, factors, and commission merchants in any depth, Lewis E. Atherton's *The Southern Country Store, 1800–1860* remains a valuable study. Influenced by the work of Frank Owsley, Atherton views southern society as essentially rural and middle class. He concludes that yeoman farmers behaved economically like their planter neighbors. Only a larger scale of operation separated the planter and farmer. Thus the planter depended on his cotton factor to meet his needs, while the mass of southern society utilized the country store as its economic agent. Atherton describes how southern merchants bartered merchandise for farm crops and then disposed of the latter in meeting their own wholesale bills. He touches on the social profile and material culture of the southern storekeeper, but his primary focus is the merchant's middleman role within the region's political economy. His analysis is grounded in the manuscript and business records available to historians in the 1940s. Despite its virtues, Atherton's book is dated. Issues that historians have come to regard as crucial in southern society, such as gender and race relations, are absent from this early monograph. Atherton's examination also concludes before the outbreak of the Civil War—a critical period for southern merchants.[16]

Thomas D. Clark's monograph *Pills, Petticoats, and Plows: The Southern Country Store* focuses on the rise of the southern store during the postbellum period. The antebellum and Confederate merchant receives only cursory analysis. Contrary to Atherton's conclusions, Clark's study discounts the economic role of the antebellum merchant. He maintains that before the state legislative assistance they received after the Civil War (lien laws, etc.), southern storekeepers were of "minor significance." Clark utilizes the same types of sources Atherton later incorporated within his work. His description of the position of the country store within the southern political economy, particularly between 1890 and 1920, is useful. Clark's analysis of merchant culture and the impact of the Civil War is more superficial and, like Atherton's, does not address more recent historical questions.[17]

In comparison to the scholarship on southern merchants, literature on the broader economic, social, and political history of the nineteenth-century South is vast and continually increasing. By most any standard, be it subtlety of analysis, richness of intellectual debate, or sheer volume of publications, the past thirty years have been a productive, exciting time for historians of the American South. Some historians have plumbed the *mentalité* of the planter class and declared the region to be prebourgeois protocapitalist, capitalist, or somewhere in between the two. Others have argued that sweeping generalizations about the region's political economy and culture during the nineteenth century fail to account for vast differences across a geographical area larger than western Europe. Many scholars in this second group have sought answers to different questions by examining the daily lives of slaves, women, and other oft-ignored peoples and classes. Writing histories "from the bottom up," these works address wider economic, gender, and racial questions. Still other historians have attempted to synthesize the various strands of this apparently disparate historiography by delineating how everyday practices and particular rituals, for better or worse, bound Southerners together. Perhaps the only theme, certainly the most important one, that unifies this literature is the understanding that the Civil War profoundly changed every Southerner's life. The historians who have produced this literature, particularly those whose works highlight the social-cultural history of the antebellum and Confederate South, have laid the foundation for the present study.[18]

Two final points need to be addressed at the outset of this book. The first relates to its scope and the second to its sources. Since this is a broad social-cultural study of a single, albeit influential, class within nineteenth-century southern society, at times issues that distinguished members of this group from one another are not as fully developed as are their shared experiences. For example, in terms of the scale of their respective businesses and even their personal values, a small storekeeper in the Mississippi Delta and a large dry-goods merchant in urban Richmond, Virginia, would appear to have little in common. Perhaps a German merchant operating on the Texas frontier would seem to have even less in common with either one. Of course these distinctions tend to mirror similar differences within the ranks of planters, yeoman farmers, and slaves across the South as well. Nevertheless, it is my contention that individual merchants shared important practices and values that also served to distinguish them from the vast majority of their neighbors, white and black. Most apparent, in a republican society that rhetorically championed independent agrarianism, all merchants were by definition subject to the whims of their customers. I devote a large portion of this book to analyzing the effects that this dependence had on their values and reputations. Thus, while issues that divided merchants (regionalism, class, etc.) will be considered in the following pages, their collective experience will be highlighted.[19]

An extensive collection of primary sources gathered from numerous archives across the South provides the bricks and mortar for the analysis in this book. The source base for southern merchants, storekeepers, and hucksters is at once ubiquitous and fleeting. Newspaper advertisements and account books abound, yet they reveal little about the daily life of the merchant. In order to uncover the main themes of this changing subculture in an agrarian South, it is necessary to examine diaries, letters, credit reports, and government documents closely. When available, such records offer the historian a valuable perspective on the world of the merchant living in the antebellum and Confederate South. They must be read not only for their basic content but for their language—what is said and left unsaid.

The view of southern merchant culture that can be pieced together from material in the archives and secondary sources reveals individuals at once conservative and innovative. Storekeepers in the agrarian South had to husband their resources and follow social norms while at the same time be prepared to gamble their capital on commercial opportunities when they arose. Freewheeling businessmen with often only indirect ties to slavery and farming, most merchants in the antebellum South possessed business habits that were alien to the aristocratic attitude of the planter class. Their business activities functioned well within the slave-holding system but did not rely upon the "peculiar institution" for their success. At the same time, despite their bourgeois inclinations, southern merchants remained distinct from their business colleagues in the North. Dixie merchants traveled to the North, read northern publications, and consumed northern goods at rates far higher than most Southerners. The ties merchants maintained with the North, however, were bent through a prism of evangelicalism, kinship, and racism that compelled the region's merchant families to defend the slave South.

The Civil War altered relations within merchant families and fostered the unique business values that would serve these families once the war ended. Merchants served in the Confederate army and viewed the conflict as a business opportunity. The Civil War brought rising profits as well as dislocation. Merchants made deals and relied on their families, particularly their wives, in order for their businesses to survive the conflict. As the war turned against the Confederacy, merchants began planning for the postwar business environment. Those who survived the war generally recovered their antebellum economic standing well before their neighbors. It seems the culture of the antebellum merchant family offered excellent preparation for the world of the New South.[20]

1

Merchant Culture and the Political Economy of the Old South

This chapter explores how commerce distinguished southern merchant families and their culture in the antebellum South. In part, this comparative history examines the various social classes that composed southern society. The measure of merchant families' experience can be taken only in relation to that of their economic and political neighbors, particularly yeoman and planter families. Merchants and their families showed themselves to be atypical Southerners in both words and deeds. Many antebellum planter and artisan families similarly troubled themselves over personal financial and legal issues, but the degree to which the market enveloped merchant families made them unique. These men and women built their lives on their ability to conduct daily business transactions for material gain. This ethic became more apparent over the course of the antebellum period as both the size of the merchant community and the scale of the southern economy grew. Their deep involvement in the market, combined with their financial and political network across the South and the Atlantic Ocean, gave commercial southern families a distinctive worldview. To varying degrees they believed themselves to be, and typically were, more cosmopolitan and financially adventurous than their neighbors.

Though rarely disowning their southern identity, merchant families prided themselves on their cultural and personal ties to the urban North and Great Britain. Their shared outlook, their understanding of how things were and should be, originated in their identities as businessmen and women. Unlike the southern planter class, the mercantile profession never developed intellectual leaders akin to George Fitzhugh or Edmund Ruffin. Less embattled and in many ways more closely tied to the northern United States than their planter neighbors, southern merchants, not surprisingly, also failed to articulate a single coherent ideological position.

Instead, the worldview of these commercial families rested upon the social prestige and economic power they derived from trade. Their work radically defined them. The daily routines that merchants performed in their trade manifested the liberal capitalist gospel they and their families embraced.[1]

Most antebellum Southerners, like most Americans in general, produced agricultural or manufactured goods. Merchants and their families typically did neither, at least commercially. Because they acted as economic middlemen, critics claimed that merchants produced little of value. Thomas Jefferson, that most famous of American republican thinkers, declared the "mark of corruption" could be found on those classes of people whose subsistence rested upon the "casualties and caprice of customers." Independent productive farmers served as repositories of virtue, he believed, while merchants and their trade were "unsound." Yet their roles as importers, wholesalers, retailers, and investors made commercial families indispensable to the health of the southern economy. Once again the example set by the "Sage of Monticello" is instructive. Like many Americans of his class, Jefferson's extravagant consumer habits, including spending more than six thousand dollars on wine during his first term as president, depended on merchant enterprise. An examination of the southern business classes, particularly merchants, shopkeepers, and grocers, reveals common practices that made the region's commercial families culturally unique. Though Jefferson went too far in pronouncing the mercantile profession debased, trade did leave its mark upon the merchant class while they left their mark upon the South.[2]

Technically speaking, *merchants* were wholesalers in both foreign and domestic goods, while *shopkeepers* typically limited themselves to local retail trade, and *grocers* sold both domestic and imported foods at retail. These business classifications applied to varying degrees throughout the Old South, but the three categories nonetheless ignored a host of other commercial occupations, from the poorest hucksters to the wealthiest cotton factors, that also filled the ranks of the region's business classes. For example, factors, though typically living in urban centers, served almost exclusively the needs of the planter class. Typically the factor was responsible for marketing the planter's staple crops as well as for obtaining whatever provisions his client requested, such as seed, fertilizer, clothing, and luxury goods. Each of these jobs required different skills and responsibilities. More fundamentally, however, all of these business positions, scale notwithstanding, shared practices and habits that shaped the lives of commercial families.[3]

A drive to accumulate, invest, and rise up the social ladder characterized the lives of prosperous southern merchants. Their methods of earning and speculating their capital also distinguished the mercantile trades from the planter and yeoman classes. The close relationship between this economic activity and personal identity, for individual merchants and merchant families, is evident in their writing. The correspondence of the southern commercial class during the antebellum period abounds with themes of industry and economy. Whether writing to business partners or their own children, merchants repeatedly touched upon the close ties between appropriate behavior, both public and private, and good business. Yet more often than not this ethos had little to do with any preconceived notion of honor or gentility. Rather the commercial personality that southern merchants manifested during the antebellum period, incorporating the values of frugality, prudence, utility, and possessive individualism, served as the means and the end to enjoying success in the marketplace. Holding an influential but often tenuous position in southern society, men and women in the mercantile trade cultivated personal discipline not only to maximize profits but also in an effort to regulate emotional swings between overconfidence and helplessness. Like many Americans and western Europeans living within the growing commercial economy, uniting the mass of shopkeepers, grocers, and merchants was what the historian Peter Gay has called the "negative quality of being neither aristocrats nor laborers, and of being uneasy in their middle-class skins." Though not a coherent political community or an active economic class, these men and women represented the emergence of a southern bourgeoisie.[4]

In order to explore the business culture of merchant families, it is necessary to have some idea of their population and position in the antebellum South. Determining the number of businessmen and women employed at any given time is a difficult task. In 1860 the Federal Census Bureau placed the total number of merchants in the slave states and the District of Columbia over thirty-eight thousand. Excluding hardware dealers, booksellers, clerks, and furniture and commission merchants, this figure provides a deceptive estimate of those employed in the region's commercial trades. A closer examination of specific counties and towns throughout the antebellum period that includes more categories of trade offers a more realistic view of the southern business community's size.[5]

Even though most rural communities could boast at least one store, merchants and their families tended to establish themselves in more wealthy, settled regions of the South. Indeed, over the course of the antebellum period merchants were often instrumental in establishing and developing new communities across the South as the frontier moved into the Southwest. One historian of rural Louisiana claims that settlements generally contained only a store, saloon, and perhaps a church. The most depressed county seats in middle Tennessee had at least ten stores, while more successful communities boasted upwards of twenty.

The 1850 census reported that North Carolina's two thousand merchants constituted little more than 1 percent of the working male population as opposed to the state's eighty-four thousand farmers, who represented 60 percent of this group. These statistics correspond with the census returns for the same year from central Virginia, where those employed in the commercial trades in rural Buckingham County represented 1 percent of the free population. Circumstances apparently did not change in the short term, for ten years later the Alabama census reported one merchant for every 385 Alabama residents, including slaves, and a disproportionate number of these businessmen lived in the state's rich Black Belt counties. My own analysis of twenty-two counties from nine southern states found that the commercial population represented a slightly higher percentage of the overall free population, totaling approximately 2 percent (see appendix, table 1).[6] Of course southern towns and cities contained larger and more diverse business communities.[7]

Throughout much of the antebellum period the population of Charleston, South Carolina, fluctuated between thirty and forty thousand people, and in only one decade (1830–1839) did the merchant community drop below one thousand individuals in a white male workforce that never exceeded twelve thousand. In 1840, Savannah, Georgia, was home to well over 650 commercial tradespeople representing almost 7 percent of the city's overall population. Ten years later Petersburg, Virginia, that state's second-largest city, and surrounding Dinwiddie County contained 431 people employed in commercial fields, representing 3 percent of the total free population. With a population barely exceeding six thousand people, 444 men and women traded over a million dollars in goods during 1854 in Atlanta, Georgia.

Such evidence suggests that the size of the southern business community varied over time and from place to place. Clearly it grew throughout the region from the 1820s through the 1850s. Furthermore, these statistics fail to include the merchants' families, most of which depended upon commercial returns for their daily survival. If average family size is factored into calculations regarding the total commercial population in 1850 of Buckingham and Dinwiddie counties, the percentages of these communities more than double to 3 and 10 percent, respectively. Likewise, my twenty-two county sample of the 1850 census (see appendix, table 5) reveals that average commercial households had 4.5 members, increasing their proportion to 7.9 percent of the total free population. The relative stability of the merchant communities in both counties seems to correspond with the experience of other occupations in the antebellum South. Over the ten-year period between censuses, a typical merchant would as likely remain within his or her profession as would other professionals or planters. Nevertheless, persistence rates for all occupations, particularly in a Southeast in relative economic decline, remained low. A dynamic class led by often ambitious commercial traders who climbed and descended the economic ladder, merchants are especially difficult to track over time in the census records. Trade deeply affected this population, while in turn merchants and their families wielded power that exceeded their numbers.[8]

Historians have frequently ignored how the important economic roles that the commercial classes performed gave them and their families influence in southern communities. Merchants stocked goods from the local area and from regional towns, and staples and luxuries from the distant North and, even more exotic, from western Europe. The spread of the railroad and telegraph across the antebellum South further strengthened the financial position of these business intermediaries. In the South Carolina Piedmont, Lacy Ford has noted, once railroads arrived the value of goods annually sold between 1853 and 1859 increased by more than 100 percent to $1,477,300. From the Georgia coast to the Mississippi River Valley, railroads and steamboats wrought similar change in hundreds of southern communities. Despite the fact that consumption rates and capital investment in the South still languished behind those in the North, merchants reaped economic and political results during this transformation. Yet the debates that swirled around trade questions, and the merchants' role within that trade, suggest the significant influence the commercial classes wielded in the Old South.[9]

Town boosters and regional spokesmen alike realized that the commercial trades linked them to essential commodities and investment from the northern United States and western Europe. Indeed both groups expressed more anxiety regarding the strength of local merchants relative to those from rival cities or from northern businessmen than over any conflict between commercial and planter interests. As early as 1826, the editor of the *Nashville Whig* boasted that the wide variety of stock available in his town enabled the rural Tennessee merchant to "lay in his stock of goods on as reasonable terms here as he can in any one of our seaport cities." Southern nationalist and antitariff spokesman George McDuffie declared in a northern publication that the "staple-growing states can never be practically independent . . . until the commerce which is funded on their valuable productions shall be carried on by our own merchants permanently resident among us." An editorial written in 1852 by "King Street" in the *Charleston Mercury* declared commerce to be the "mainspring of healthful and vigorous general action" and warned the South Carolina city's residents that Baltimore and New Orleans increasingly dominated southern trade. The editorial writer, likely a merchant himself, maintained that Charleston's salvation depended upon trade.

Even when discord between planter and merchant interests did erupt, it was generally between rival cities. Defending the interests of Mississippi planters, the *Vicksburg Register* encouraged its readers to patronize local commission merchants rather than suffer from the "vindictive warfare" waged by the rapacious, interest-raising businessmen of New Orleans. Not surprisingly, such exhibitions of commercial jealousy only increased when southern newspapers attacked the national financial dominance of a Philadelphia or New York City. The *New Orleans Daily Picayune* merely voiced the opinion of most Southerners when it declared that the North was "wrestling with strong and resolute hands to compel commerce into artificial channels." These articles offered numerous, sometimes conflicting, remedies to make the southern economy more competitive. While disagreement existed over the efficacy of internal improvements, government intervention, and a host of other strategies, unanimity prevailed in the belief that without a strong, independent business community the South would forever be eclipsed by the North.[10]

The businessmen and women who newspaper editors and others hoped would strengthen their regional economy hailed overwhelmingly from the South. Rural counties typically exhibited the highest percentages of native-born southern merchants, but even cities, though boasting more diverse commercial populations, were dominated by those born locally or in neighboring slave states. Yet many northern merchants, on the lookout for economic opportunities, settled in the South. As Jonathan Daniel Wells contends, some may even have been inspired by the conceit that they "could also change the South itself." Whatever their motivations, by the late antebellum period, northern and foreign commercial traders found themselves a notable minority in the southern merchant class. The survey of the 1850 federal census reveals that almost 78 percent of individuals employed in the commercial trades were born in their home state or another slave state, while 11.7 percent immigrated from Europe and 9.3 percent hailed from a northern state (see appendix, table 4). With few exceptions, these results repeat themselves in counties with large and small commercial populations.

Men represented the vast majority of those employed in both rural and urban commercial settings. The same survey of the 1850 federal census discloses that men accounted for more than 99 percent of those listed as merchants, storekeepers, and grocers (see appendix, table 3). This census survey also found no merchant, only the occasional "huckster," listed as black or mulatto. Even including such female-dominated occupations as millinery and seamstress work, women constituted less than 10 percent of the commercial classes in late antebellum Atlanta. During the same period a Nashville, Tennessee, business directory reported that women, excluding those operating boardinghouses, represented little more than 8 percent of the commercial workforce. The 1860 federal census reported one woman, a clerk, employed in a commercial field in Buckingham County, Virginia, while 186 women constituted 27 percent of the commercial workforce in Dinwiddie County, Virginia. Of this latter number, however, only eleven women, hardly more than 1 percent, operated or worked in establishments outside such traditionally female enterprises as dressmaking or millinery work.

The implications this pattern had for merchants and their families will be examined later, but one factor remained a constant. Whether an isolated crossroads merchant or an urban storekeeper, male or female, Southerner, Northerner, or European, the marketplace and its liberal capitalist values directed the commercial classes of the Old South. In turn these merchants influenced their communities. While his diary deplored the absence of genuine Sabbatarianism in Mobile, Alabama, the Northerner Henry Benjamin Whipple also testified to the vigor of the southern commercial classes and their market. On Sunday mornings, the horrified Whipple reported, "All classes may be seen wending their way to the market. . . . All seem bent on making the Sabbath morning a day of toil, of merchandise, of money spending & money getting." Whipple described what many Southerners already understood: that theirs was an increasingly commercial society dominated by planters but heavily dependent upon merchants. Those embarking upon a career in the mercantile trades recognized this relationship and certainly anticipated social and economic returns.[11]

Few individuals opened a shop or entered into a business partnership without first gaining at least some commercial experience as a store clerk—often in a relative's business. In the 1850s, Thomas Aby, for example, left his parents' home in Middletown, Virginia, and migrated to Grand Gulf, Mississippi, where he learned bookkeeping and clerked in his younger brother Samuel's dry-goods store. The Biggs brothers, Kader, Asa, Joseph, and William, all learned the mercantile trade in and around their hometown, Williamston, North Carolina, from their merchant and sometime preacher father Joseph. At age sixteen Reuben Clark left his father's east Tennessee farm to learn the mercantile trade from his older half-brother Samuel, who enjoyed a position in a Rutledge, Tennessee, store. During the early 1850s, John F. Jefferson and his brother Lewis learned the retail trade in Louisville, Kentucky, from their father Thomas and uncle Henry. With his family's financial assistance, John operated a two-story dry-goods store in 1857. By clerking and performing miscellaneous jobs around a store, young men like these, and the occasional woman, could establish business connections and usually earn a modicum of capital.

Significant numbers of merchants and other retailers hailed from artisan, farming, and planting families as well. Charles Christopher Blacknall's grandfather and father had both been planters in North Carolina, but upon the early and unexpected death of the latter, Charles and his two brothers were raised by their mother, Caroline. Though the family's economic status fell, Caroline managed to send Charles to school in Beech Spring and later in Henderson, where he became a "Latin scholar" and excelled in mathematics. Upon completing his formal education, Charles taught school for a time and studied law but found more gainful employment as a clerk in Henderson, eventually using the experience he gained from this informal apprenticeship to open a store, C. C. & T. H. Blacknall, with his brother in Franklinton in 1853. Regardless of their particular backgrounds, most businessmen and their families confronted similar obstacles when entering the mercantile and retail trades in the antebellum South.

Two critical areas of concern for young would-be entrepreneurs were location and start-up capital. These issues preoccupied southern businessmen and distinguished them from most of their fellow Southerners throughout the antebellum period.[12]

The troubled relationship between the southern merchant's responsibilities to his family and base economic considerations frequently influenced decisions regarding store location. Savvy merchants desired stable locales populated with few business competitors and many regular customers. A reliable clientele with cash and assets, whether farmers or artisans who depended upon one or two merchants for their goods, represented the ideal business environment. Isham Howze believed his new store in Marshall County, Mississippi, would reap a limited but steady business because his initial survey of the neighborhood suggested limited start-up expense and a "good" customer base. His diary entry makes clear that the decision was quite rational: "good" in this instance described men who paid their bills. When George Shelton moved his family from Hyde County, North Carolina, to Greene County, Alabama, in order to establish a grocery and dry-goods store, he not only had to ensure that the building he purchased would be large enough for the store as well as for his family, but he also had to consider the small town's commercial possibilities. Writing a friend back in North Carolina during the winter of 1847, Shelton reported that, with a growing population and a fifty-student academy for boys and girls near his home, "the prospect is very fare for a small Business," though he remained anxious that low cotton prices would mean that farmers "will be hard run to pay their debts next *Spring*."

Many communities presented businessmen with even more challenges. Scouting economic opportunities in Brownsville, Tennessee, on behalf of a merchant friend, Thomas Potter declared, "In pecuniary matters the people here are generally extravagant. . . . Merchants do & have done a first rate business here often for a while at least"; but Potter predicted that, with the bills of many households exceeding a thousand dollars, officers of the court would do the best business. Such an environment, though plagued with credit problems, at least held out some promise of economic success and of eventual bill collections for the prospective storekeeper. Worse yet were frontier conditions in Mississippi, where one businessman declared that corruption and incompetence in the state judiciary prevented merchants from collecting any money owed to them. Competition from riverboat retailers made life more difficult for storekeepers along the

Mississippi River. One angry Vicksburger complained to the town council about such dealers who "lie here all winter, trade in all things, and to a large amount, without paying *once cent tax* [*sic*], either to the State or corporation." This broadside ignored the fact that the vast majority of peddlers and itinerant retailers had to purchase a license from the state. Such problems for merchants in the lower Mississippi Valley increased over the course of the antebellum period as the population swelled and competition grew.[13]

Economic considerations had to be balanced with family needs when merchants chose the locations of their stores. Parents often wanted merchant sons to live nearby; sibling bonds and business networks frequently overlapped; and at times an aging grocer looked to his or her children for daily assistance. Such family responsibilities occasionally ran counter to good business. Like many nineteenth-century Americans, southern merchants confronted tremendous emotional strain when they moved their families to the seemingly verdant commercial pastures beckoning in the West. The example of the merchant Christian Duerr reveals how business location and family relationships, in this case a marriage, influenced each other.

Born in Mecklingen, Württemberg, twenty-four-year-old Christian Duerr immigrated to Suwannee Springs, Florida, in 1839. Once settled in his new home, Duerr made a living as a merchant, auctioneer, and land speculator. His personal life kept pace with his growing business activities. In 1841, Duerr married Mary Standley Dell, the daughter of Colonel Bennett M. Dell, a Florida planter of some means. Before the year was over, however, the young couple's glow of marital bliss waned beneath the responsibilities of parenthood and the weight of business setbacks. Duerr's solution was to move to Harris County, Texas, located near the Gulf of Mexico. There he expected his store to thrive on regional trade and the proceeds from the state's growing cotton economy. Though the move was a wise business decision, it nearly destroyed the Duerr marriage. Removal from Suwannee Springs and her father left Mary Duerr distraught. She begged her husband to move the family back to Florida where her father would help him get established as a cotton planter. Her remonstrations failed to change her husband's mind, but she finally caught his attention after she returned to Florida in 1843 to have a child and proved reluctant to come back to Texas.

Minding the store in Texas, Duerr read his wife's letters with anxiety and puzzlement. It seemed clear to him that his family's economic future rested in Texas, yet the separation from his wife and children left him doubting his priorities. Duerr's notes at this time abound with self-pity and abandonment. He declared his wife essential to his happiness and "dearer to me than everything else," but he seems never to have seriously considered going back to Florida. The Texas store offered too much profit. Despite appeals from his wife and father-in-law and tribulations caused by an irresponsible clerk, Duerr told his wife that his pride—"to even *seem* to be dependent upon anybody for a subsistence"—and his hope for prosperity in Texas would never allow him to move. After eight months Mary relented and came back to Texas with the children. No personal documents remain of the Duerrs after 1845, making it impossible to determine what contentment they may have found in their marriage. The record does reveal that Christian Duerr's business acumen served him well. The 1850 census reported that he owned four thousand dollars in real estate, and the investment his store represented, including outstanding debts and stock, easily surpassed this figure.[14]

Other merchant families seem to have endured the ordeal of westward migration with more equanimity than the Duerrs did. Jorantha Semmes, who would do so much to provide for her family during the war, had already followed her husband, Benedict, from her New York City home to Georgetown where he operated a dry-goods store in Washington, D.C. When the vibrant commercial trade in Memphis, Tennessee, beckoned in 1859, the successful merchant uprooted his family and headed west. After ten years of marriage and the birth of four children, Jorantha appears to have accompanied her husband with few complaints. Indeed, as will be shown in later chapters, in many respects the family flourished along the banks of the Mississippi River. A failed farmer and a marginal storekeeper, Isham Howze, his siblings, and his parents moved from their North Carolina home in Franklin County to Hunstville, Alabama, where Howze met his future wife, Elizabeth Wilson. After eleven years Howze purchased farmland in Lincoln County, Tennessee, and relocated his family yet again. Over the course of the 1840s, Howze's family continued moving west across the state until 1853, when he opened a store in Marshall County, Mississippi. Until his death in 1857, Howze filled his diary with misgivings over his poor financial choices and complaints about his failing health, yet he praised his wife and children for their constancy through it all. The Semmes and Howze families joined thousands of other Southerners who moved west in search of economic opportunity.[15]

Of course promising business locations offered young merchants no advantage if they didn't have the capital to open a store. Many entering commercial trade in the antebellum South depended upon financial assistance from their families. Bertram Wyatt-Brown has suggested this to be the primary source of capital for southern businesses. He has also maintained that parental aid and wealth gained through advantageous marriage were peculiarly southern methods of financing a small business. There is no doubt that family loans, gifts, and legacies provided important means of building many small businesses across the antebellum South. Little evidence suggests, however, that family capital did not benefit merchants throughout the antebellum North with equal frequency. Sven Beckert's analysis of the bourgeoisie in New York City found that, for merchants in that city, "family ties gave access to business contracts, partnerships, and credit, thus making them central to business success." Credit reports compiled by R. G. Dun & Company, a major source for nineteenth-century business history in both the North and South, document the amount of financial support that merchants received from their families.[16]

Southern credit reports from an informal sample mention parental or marital financial support for approximately 10 percent of merchant businesses. Yet even these references can be misleading when a merchant placed property in his wife's name. After several business failures, the Vicksburg storekeeper William Biggs kept most of his property in his wife's name in order to have "little of his own the law could reach." Furthermore, credit reports rarely disclosed the ways parents and in-laws burdened merchants. Operating a store in Port Gibson, Mississippi, Horace Carpenter, who is described in one R. G. Dun report as a "trifling picayune," complained that his wife's undeserving family demanded his continual financial assistance. Like many storekeepers in the West, the Mississippian Samuel Aby regularly sent money to his parents. He explained to his father in one letter that the thirty dollars he enclosed represented all the funds left to him. He needed "every dollar" to meet his business obligations.

Family resources often provided critical start-up capital for southern businesses. As noted earlier in this chapter, John F. Jefferson's ability to open his considerable store in Louisville depended in large measure on the financial backing of his father, Thomas, a prominent merchant in the city. The same type of paternal financial support seems to have assisted Kader Biggs and his brothers to open their retail operations in North Carolina. Nevertheless, obligations to parents and kin could drain precious wealth

from merchants as well. When pressed by his brother-in-law for an immediate loan in order to fend off financial ruin during the winter of 1845,
Francis Levert, a storekeeper in Huntsville, Alabama, extended $3,500
and wrote with an air of resignation, "The prospect of realizing the fruits
of One's labor, in any department of business, I consider the most gloomy
that has ever come up in the history of the world."[17]

Most merchants supplemented, or avoided altogether, debt to their
families by obtaining start-up capital through credit and business partnerships. Virtually all commercial enterprises in the antebellum South,
from the nearly insolvent country store to the largest wholesale houses
in New Orleans or Charleston, depended upon northern credit for their
survival. This was true for even established, successful firms. When the
New Orleans firm of Norris Maull & Company established a branch in
Memphis, they depended on credit from the Philadelphia manufacturing/
retail firm of Thaddeus Norris & Company. Most merchants, including
those with few assets and little experience, could obtain six months' credit
from northern wholesalers. This practice seemed so commonplace that in
his whimsical *Flush Times of Alabama and Mississippi: A Series of Sketches*
(1853), the humorist Joseph G. Baldwin could claim, with some exaggera-
tion, that if a young southern man desired to become a storekeeper "all he
had to do was to go on to New-York, and present himself in Pearl-street
with a letter avouching his citizenship, and a clean shirt, and he was regularly given a through ticket to speedy bankruptcy."

The inherent risk of liberal terms of credit led wholesalers to charge
southern merchants exorbitant rates of interest, a cost that was passed
along to customers through inflated prices. Yet to acquire the necessary
credit to stock a minimally competitive store or grocery—usually at least
$2,500 worth of goods but preferably twice that—almost all business-
men entered into partnership agreements with one or more individuals.
Predictably, family members often went into business together. When in
1847 George Shelton moved his family into a "good two story house"
located in Havanna, Alabama, he expected the grocery business he opened
in the back rooms to gross between seven thousand and twelve thousand
dollars a year. Shelton had the capital necessary to house his family and
start his grocery because his uncle, Israel, was "equally concerned in the
Business." Many successful partnerships also grew from personal and economic alliances between young clerks who eventually saved enough capital to open their own store. Occasionally would-be merchants appealed

directly to established members of the mercantile trade they hardly knew for start-up funds. Two young men desiring to open a store in Texas proposed that the merchant John Adriance furnish them with stock and start-up capital for a shop to serve the country market. The men promised to pay Adriance back with interest, but they seemingly had few assets, only their belief that "thar can been some cash made at the business if Juditiously manedged." If Adriance refused to furnish the men with the goods they required, dozens of southern merchant wholesalers, and many more of their colleagues in Philadelphia and New York City, accepted the hazards of making such loans as part of the price of doing business in the undercapitalized South.[18]

The obstacles young clerks and farmers confronted when becoming merchants paralleled in some respects those faced by the planter class in the antebellum South. Attaining independence as a southern cotton planter certainly required occasional relocation and the capital necessary for purchasing land, supplies, and slaves. Closer examination, however, suggests the experience of the merchant and his or her family deviated in important ways from the standard historical model of the planter family. Customers, not fertile land, typically drew antebellum merchants to settle in the southern Black Belt and Mississippi Delta. Country and town merchants continued to rely upon a strong agricultural economy for their survival, but they viewed this dependence as an indirect one. Their separation from the soil, albeit inconsiderable, subtly influenced merchant culture. Founding a business represented only the formative stage in this cultural process. Once they were established, storekeepers and wholesalers came to embrace the changes that business demanded of them and their families. The daily business activities these merchants performed illustrate the close and unique relationship between commercial work and family values in the antebellum South. Issues that governed the public world of southern businessmen and women—credit, partnerships, purchasing trips, and employer-employee relations, among others—left their mark upon merchant family culture.

Credit and debt concerns plagued the everyday working lives of southern merchants. Many of their neighbors, particularly in the planter class, made loans and sought financial credit at local and national levels. Indeed, some businessmen complained that planters and slave traders drained southern communities of credit that could have been employed in building factories or large stores. The crucial difference between merchants and

wealthy planters rested in the assets and motivations the two groups possessed. For example, large planting families typically viewed the occasional
loans they made to neighbors not only as a means of building good will in
case they themselves should require financial assistance in the future, but
also as an effective way to strengthen political and social connections. As
the historian Kenneth S. Greenberg has noted, loans or the endorsement
of notes could serve as a means of "gift exchange" between honorable
gentlemen. Additionally, the debt that planters incurred while conducting business with cotton factors and eastern businessmen was backed by
their assets—cotton, land, and slaves—and, at least in theory, represented
an investment in their plantations. While typically planter and merchant
families depended upon lines of credit for their economic survival, the
latter had a very different experience with the practice. In the capital-poor
antebellum South, credit and debt represented the lifeblood to a successful
retail enterprise. The loans merchants made to their customers certainly
held social significance, but, more importantly, they formed an economic
relationship. Storekeepers expected their customers to pay their bills.
Likewise, few merchants, as opposed to their planter neighbors, expected
to obtain credit from northern wholesalers on the strength of their personal assets. Small and middling southern retail agents, like merchants
throughout America and western Europe, understood that a reputation
for sound business practices was essential to gaining access to credit. In the
antebellum South, a merchant's standing rested not only on his business
skills but on his moral character and family relations as well.[19]

Over the course of the antebellum period, several mercantile credit
rating agencies, the most influential being Arthur and Lewis Tappan's
R. G. Dun & Company, recruited hundreds of agents from across the
United States to evaluate the creditworthiness of merchants for New York
wholesalers and lenders. During the 1820s and 1830s merchants received
much less scrutiny from creditors and wholesalers than they would after
1840. Still, before the advent of national credit agencies, obtaining credit
in northern cities was much more difficult. In 1859 the southern business
community secured $131 million in credit from New York City alone.
Small-town lawyers, those most often chosen to be credit investigators,
could make or break a local merchant's credit rating in northern cities.
Aside from summarizing real and personal assets, investigators frequently
commented upon the character of particular merchants and their families.
Thus one investigator was shocked to learn that the Mississippi storekeeper

Samuel Aby proposed to pay only thirty cents on the dollar on his outstanding loans when his wife rode in a "splendid" new carriage. Another
R. G. Dun investigator described the Tennessee firm of Pryor & Pregmore
as "hardly safe" because one partner, Jackson Pryor, seemed increasingly
"dissipated." Though they railed against this invasion of their private lives,
successful retail agents learned to practice those personal habits most likely
to win favor with creditors and customers alike.[20]

Living in Thibodaux, Louisiana, the storekeeper Edward Murphy recognized the importance of reputation to a southern businessman. In the
spring of 1849 he procured on credit a large quantity of medicine and
numerous doctor's visits for his dying father-in-law. When his father-in-
law died and the bills came due, Murphy expected his mother-in-law to
help pay the debt. She initially refused to pay, and he had to borrow more
money to sustain his credit with wholesalers and keep his local standing in Thibodaux secure. Murphy berated the mother-in-law to his wife,
Josephine, complaining that she "keeps me back" and implying that he
would sue her if she were not family. Murphy claimed he asked only that
his mother-in-law "deal with us as she deals with *strangers*." Murphy's good
name—with his customers, business colleagues, and most importantly
with his creditors—could have been sullied by his mother-in-law's delinquent conduct. The seemingly ham-handed way that Murphy manipu-
lated his wife's emotions and shamed his mother-in-law into paying her
medical bills threatened to tear the family apart. He obviously believed
the future of his store was worth the risk. In time Murphy's mother-in-law
paid the bill, and peace was restored in the merchant's household. More
important to Murphy, his reputation did not suffer. Two years later a local
R. G. Dun investigator characterized Murphy as an industrious man possessing excellent business habits and a high standing in the neighborhood.
Murphy succeeded in part by compelling his family to structure their own
lives around his business ethics. His actions exemplified the commercial
worldview best articulated by the southern merchant Isham Howze, who
declared "the man who owes money which he cannot pay when called
upon for it, is not a free man"—nor a man who can obtain more credit.[21]

The possible tragic consequences of a merchant's reputation being
destroyed became quite clear to Thomas McDowell during the spring of
1848. Shortly after McDowell moved to Mobile, Alabama, where he had
entered into a partnership with a cotton factor, he found the pace of life in
the city unsettling. He wrote to Francis Levert back in his native Huntsville

that he missed the sociability of that city because Mobile had none. In his new home "every man is working himself to death to make as much as he can in as short a time as possible." His misgivings about commercial life in the city were confirmed when the business community was rocked by the suicide of one of its members, E. L. Andrews. Unable to raise twenty-seven thousand dollars that he needed to pay his creditors in New York City and, apparently, in England, Andrews drowned himself off the city's "Liverpool dock." Earlier in the day he had failed to hear back from a creditor in New Orleans who represented his last chance for a desperately needed loan. He then wrote a letter to his partner asking him to take his wife to her friends in New York City. He sent the letter and ended his own life rather than "live to see his name dishonored." In a melodramatic twist, the letter of credit from New Orleans arrived the morning after Andrews died. The shocking episode appalled McDowell. He acknowledged that a man with capital and business acumen could make money in Mobile, but the hectic tempo of the city's commercial life and its impact on his colleagues made him long for the "peace & quiet of Old Huntsville." In much the same way that gentlemen of the planter class felt compelled to protect their standing within their community, merchants had to main-tain unsullied reputations in the world of business. As Francis Levert back in Huntsville told his own brother, "*Never tarnish your honor—no, not for all the property of both Hemispheres*" and "*let all your acts be above even a suspicion of that sort. . . . Leave your children . . . a Father's good character, at least.*"[22]

Ironically, southern businessmen and women found themselves judg-ing the creditworthiness of their own neighbors just as northern mercan-tile agencies judged them. Debt and credit considerations altered the rela-tionships that southern merchants shared with their neighbors and cus-tomers. Few planters or yeoman farmers, if they even could, felt obligated to extend repeated loans to their neighbors. Planters in particular were guided by political and social considerations. As J. William Harris discov-ered in his study of the country surrounding Augusta, Georgia, planters like Alexander H. Stephens and David C. Barrow "not only were making investments, but also were helping neighbors and friends. Payment might come in many ways, including the casting of a ballot." The economic survival of the planter class did not hinge upon making and collecting small loans from their farmer neighbors. The principle motivation for these loans could be found in the widespread belief that "to give credit may display generosity or liberality—and power." Most retail operations in the antebellum South depended upon credit purchases for the bulk of their business. Lewis Atherton estimated that 60 to 75 percent of all merchandise purchased by farmers was obtained on credit for which store-keepers would collect payment once a year—usually on January 1. These circumstances inevitably affected the position of the merchant family in southern communities. Storekeepers and their kin scrutinized customers for signs of economic difficulties or moral lapses that could hinder the discharge of debt. When the lawyer and merchant Jonathan Worth had difficulty collecting money from one of his customers in North Carolina, he judged him "not an honest man" and consoled himself with the knowledge that "this fact is acquiring notoriety." Worth frequently looked to his family, particularly his brothers, for help in collecting bills or information regarding his customers. He also used his significant influence as a neighborhood creditor to encourage poor debtors to work on various building projects he conducted in and around Asheboro. Over the course of his career, Worth came to understand what all southern merchants learned in time, that fluctuating cotton prices and the vagaries of human nature ensured most retail operators would accumulate a certain amount of bad debt on their books.[23]

Attempts by merchants to collect from destitute or shirking customers, often through the courts, necessarily divided community sympathies and sustained the increasing cultural divide between merchant families and their neighbors (see chapters 2 and 3). Though distinguished by his adamant style, the Nashville merchant James H. Turner spoke for many of his colleagues when he ran a notice in the *Nashville Republican and State Gazette* declaring after six weeks of bill collecting, "I WANT MONEY!! . . . I am compelled to have CASH to pay my debts, and do not like to dun." Below a headline declaring "Punctuality THE LIFE OF BUSINESS," another Tennessee merchant "*earnestly*" solicited customers to pay their debts so he could "have a pretty good amount of the '*needful*'" with which to order more goods. Whether collecting from debtor customers or establishing their own creditworthiness to northern mercantile agencies, retail operators recognized the sundry ways family could influence their businesses. More fundamentally, the personal conduct required to gain access to credit meant that the practices and values these families embraced were cast in a commercial die.[24]

Partnership agreements proved to be another convention of nineteenth-century commercial trade that both transformed merchant families and distinguished them from most other Southerners. By enabling young men and women to pool their resources, business partnerships served as a cornerstone of the southern retail trade. To be sure, Southerners outside the mercantile trade also entered into partnership agreements. North Carolina Governor John M. Morehead and jurist Thomas Ruffin shared an interest in the development of that state's railroads, while planter James Henry Hammond invested in William Gregg's textile enterprise in Graniteville, South Carolina. Practicing lawyers frequently created partnerships as well. Yet both the regularity and character of mercantile partnerships made them unique.[25]

Most business partnership contracts were short-term. Single store agreements, the most prevalent type of contract in the antebellum South, outlined the economic duties expected from each partner. These contracts usually had to be renewed annually or at least no longer than every three years. Virtually every contract provided a terminal date whereupon adjustments could be made within the partnership or the business relationship could be dissolved and the accounts settled. A partnership agreement between two storekeepers in the southwest, James F. Perry and Alexander Somervell, reveals some possible variations in such contracts. As proprietors of the firm Perry & Somervell, located in San Felipe de Austin, Texas, Perry agreed to furnish all the stock, and Somervell would pay 10 percent on one-half of the goods per year. Somervell would also transact all the firm's business while profits would be split equally between the two men. The Kentucky merchants Edward S. Haydon and Haden E. Stone formed a more balanced partnership in which each agreed to furnish one thousand dollars capital and split profits and losses equally. They presumed that their clerk would perform most of the daily labor around the store. Shrewd mercantile partnerships could strengthen a firm's credit rating, increase store sales, and build economic alliances. These business relationships had a powerful influence on families as well. The mercantile partnership often represented the most important bond a retail operator had outside his or her family. Not surprisingly, their financial ties, combined with hours working together at the store, often led business partners to develop strong personal attachments.[26]

The evolution of the firm Howze, Brady, & Pace located in Marshall County, Mississippi, demonstrates how a business partnership could affect merchant households. Two of the three partners, Isham Howze and a Mr. Brady, had previous experience in the retail profession, while Pace provided much of the firm's start-up capital. Howze, who at the age of fifty-eight was the oldest of the three, had a clear vision of what each partner's roles were to be over the course of their three-year contract. Chronically ill, Howze would keep the store's financial records, while Brady and Pace would perform "all the selling and hard drudgery" of stocking and maintaining inventory. Thought to have "good taste, good judgment, and sufficient confidence in himself," Brady was also to make the annual trip to the East, where he would purchase the firm's goods. This business arrangement benefited all the partners, particularly Brady, who was finally able to make the leap to the ranks of the merchant class from a clerking position, in which he had shown "very good" business habits.

Soon after the store opened, Brady began spending considerable time with the Howze family. Indeed, for several weeks he boarded with Howze and his wife Elizabeth. Within a year Brady was attending local parties with the Howzes' eldest son, twenty-two-year-old Adrian. Howze hoped the camaraderie between his partner and his son would prove beneficial to both young men. Howze's confidence seems to have been well placed, for following his death in 1857 Brady remained in close contact with Elizabeth and the Howze children long after the business of the firm had been settled. Days they spent working behind the store counter, going over the books, and simply passing the time discussing politics and religion produced more than a mere business connection between the partners of Howze, Brady, & Pace. Their mercantile partnership generated a social network of dinners, revivals, and political meetings that included their families. As was true for many storekeepers in the antebellum South, their professional and personal lives melded into one another.[27]

Even those in the business community who enjoyed less than harmonious relations with their partners found that this connection encroached upon their personal lives. The North Carolina merchant Cushing B. Hassell hoped for the best when he entered into a partnership with William S. Williams, the younger brother of a trusted former partner, Henry Williams, but things did not turn out well. At the very least the arrangement seemed to answer the capital needs of his Williamston store, but less than a month after the contract had been signed the two businessmen were at odds over their finances and work responsibilities. Hassell claimed he would be dashing about the counter serving customers while Williams would be "looking on suspiciously or in the Counting Room scrutinizing his conduct & hinting his suspicions to his brother."

Additionally, Williams would hurt the store's business by dismissing the value of their goods in the presence of customers. Hassell offered no rationale for Williams's odd behavior aside from his partner's apparent jealous nature. Enmity between the two men quickly led to dissolution of the firm. During the financial turmoil of 1837, before the partnership was a year old, Williams fled Williamston, leaving Hassell with losses amounting to fifteen hundred dollars for the year and thirty thousand dollars of outstanding credit to customers.

Like many troubled partnerships during the antebellum period, this one ended up in court. After several years Hassell eventually collected at least some financial compensation from the suspicious Williams, but the experience left its mark upon his family. The "evil eye of his partner" had made the family, particularly the Hassell children, feel ridiculous and embarrassed publicly. In light of the travails his father encountered in the business world, Theodore Hassell came to view the mercantile trade with distrust and anger. During his youth only his home served as a haven from the chaotic business world. Theodore Hassell believed that the demands of trade and the involvement of individuals like Williams compelled good men like his father "to grind the faces of the poor" or suffer financial loss. The emotional toll that a failed partnership could have on a merchant family left a legacy that could not be measured in any business ledger.[28]

As parties to business partnerships, most southern merchants found the necessary time and resources to practice a third business convention that influenced their family culture—buying trips in the North. Over the course of the antebellum period, hundreds of southern merchants sallied forth annually from their homes to purchase dry goods, hardware, and even some kinds of groceries in Baltimore, Philadelphia, New York City, and Boston. Included in this group were the vast majority of medium- and large-scale general stores, those grossing at least five thousand dollars per year, and even some marginal firms. The business these merchants brought with them was a boon to seaboard cities. For example, in 1849 southern retail operators purchased $76 million of merchandise in New York City alone. Ten years later these sales had almost doubled to $131 million. As early as 1822 successful merchants like Horace Carpenter from Port Gibson, Mississippi, purchased more than seventeen thousand dollars worth of goods in New York City. Six years earlier Benjamin Smith, another Port Gibson storekeeper, brought home a "handsome assortment" of goods from Philadelphia worth at least twenty-five thousand dollars.

More typical was Cushing Hassell's commercial junket in 1848 to Gotham, where he spent eight thousand dollars on goods. Aside from the wholesale or auction price of their northern goods, southern merchants had to pay charges for freight and insurance as well. James Perry paid $23.26 in drayage fees simply to have his purchased goods placed on a packet ship in Philadelphia for removal to his Missouri store. He paid another $111.55 to the American Insurance Company to insure the goods. Overall the minimum cost for shipping from the East easily reached three hundred dollars. Business representatives to the Third Commercial Convention (1838) held in Augusta, Georgia, concluded that the expense of a New York City buying trip for a merchant from Montgomery, Alabama, covering everything but the cost of the goods themselves, totaled $1,383. These trips required southern merchants to sacrifice considerable time and money, yet most were able to make the journey. By the late antebellum period, southern nationalists opposed these trips on the grounds that they impaired the growth of a strong, independent mercantile trade below the Mason-Dixon Line. Despite these protests, the rationale for southern merchants to buy their goods in northern cities remained compelling.[29]

Southern merchants ventured to the North to purchase their wares because it was there that they found credit, selection, and prestige. Despite the vocal boosterism of financial and civic leaders in cities like Richmond and Charleston, no southern city could rival the capital reserves of the wholesale merchants in Philadelphia and New York City. Only New Orleans offered significant competition for the business of southern merchants, but even with its pivotal location at the mouth of the Mississippi and the low interest loans its banks could offer, the city split the business of southwestern merchants with the North. The politics of these purchasing trips to the North—for example, their role in perpetuating the South's dependence upon northern capital and its ensuing cultural subordination—is rarely touched upon in the personal records that southern merchants left behind. Newspaper editors and political leaders seemed more exercised on the subject than retailers. Storekeepers preferred to communicate how northern wholesalers offered the widest selection of merchandise. When the Louisville merchant George Meriwether wanted the latest styles of silk shawls or Liverpool ware, he went to Joseph Robard or Henry O'Neill & Co. in New York City.

The desire for New York goods among southern merchants and their customers hardly abated over distance. A typical advertisement in the

Raleigh Register declared New York City the "London of America" where could be found "an assortment of Goods that for quality and style never were surpassed." Only the finest eastern clothing and "pantaloon stuffs" could satisfy the patrons of Robert Crawford's store in Washington, Texas. The prestige associated with selling the latest goods from New York City, London, and Paris offered yet another reason for southern merchants to buy their merchandise in the North. Despite the obvious dangers associated with these buying trips, including shipwrecks, fluctuating interest rates, and theft, most southern storekeepers believed the trade's advantages outweighed its risks. Viewing these trips as crucial to business success, merchants considered the profound effect the practice had upon their families as regrettable but necessary.[30]

Separated families represented yet another price attending commercial business in the antebellum South. Over time the expanding transportation network of steamboats and railroads did decrease the amount of time merchants had to spend apart from their families. When his partner required only three weeks to complete a buying trip to the North in 1857, Isham Howze declared, "How swift the times are—steam has wrought wonders." In his diary, the storekeeper Eli Bonney expressed great satisfaction when his New York goods began arriving at his Camden, South Carolina, store only a month and a day after he first left on his buying trip. For most merchants such expeditious and trouble-free commercial trips were rare. Poor weather, mechanical breakdowns, and business upheavals in northern cities made for trips lasting from four to eight weeks. It is little wonder, then, that business colleagues and friends regularly expressed concern and "earnest petitions" over the welfare of a departing merchant. Likewise congratulations abounded when merchants and their goods safely returned.[31]

Such regular, prolonged absence of merchants from their homes influenced their families in numerous ways. Even apparently strong, affectionate relationships could suffer the strain business trips placed upon marriages. Lydia Adriance, wife of Texas merchant John Adriance, came to realize how trade bound her family. When her husband tended to his far-flung business interests in Missouri, Texas, and New York, Lydia frequently waited two or more months for one of his letters. John's repeated absences proved a trial for his family, but his wife and children remained steadfast in their support of his career. A letter she sent her husband in 1850 is telling. Staying with her family in Watertown, New York, while in the latter stages of pregnancy, a worried and lonely Lydia Adriance wrote, "I am satisfied to make the sacrifice that I know to be necessary to promote your business interests." Their daughter Kitty told her mother it would be better to have the baby before her father returned than to have him "neglect important business" and be "obliged to spend a week or two here in suspense." In this instance, little Kitty seemed more resigned to her father's absence than her mother. This practical-minded daughter understood the demands of the marketplace. Martha Carpenter could have commiserated with Lydia Adriance over the demands of being married to a merchant who was away from home for weeks at a time on purchasing trips. Once, when her husband Horace returned to their home in Port Gibson, Mississippi, after conducting business in New York City, Martha introduced him to their strapping six-week-old son. During family separations children were born, parents died, and marriages evolved.[32]

The long absences of merchant husbands and fathers inevitably weakened patriarchal authority in various small ways. Louisiana store-keeper Edward Murphy's experience is illustrative. Few prosperous merchants asked their wives to help behind the counter, because, at least in theory, partners and clerks performed such duties. Yet at times wives had to step in. Before leaving on a purchasing trip in 1852 to the North, Murphy acquainted his wife, Josephine, with the operation of their store. He seemed particularly concerned about the safety of his merchandise, telling Josephine "you cant be too careful of fire, make the people put out their lights before you go to bed and see that the fire is out in the store." Aside from raising their infant son, Josephine had the added responsibility of supervising the family's slaves and clerks while Edward scoured northern wholesale markets for bargains. The duties merchant wives discharged, especially when their husbands were away, left them living in a unique cultural middle ground between northern and southern women that will be explored in chapter 3. In the end many wives and children in these households had mixed feelings about the demands of the mercantile trade. The same commerce that provided families with a relatively high standard of living also required fathers, and on rare occasions mothers, to leave home for weeks at a time.[33]

The merchant-clerk relationship proved to be another critical feature of commercial trade that distinguished merchants and their families from the rest of southern society. On a daily basis grocers and store-keepers were among the few Southerners who worked alongside their employees. Though often tinged with paternalism, these merchant-clerk relationships more closely resembled the type of economic connections that thousands of Northerners had than they did the relationships that southern planters maintained with either their slaves or their white neighbors. Many clerks lived in rooms above or behind their employers' stores. During a prosperous year the modestly successful merchant Cushing Hassell hired three white clerks in addition to the two black slaves already working in his store. In 1859 the wealthy firm of Beach & Root employed at least nine different clerks in its large store in Atlanta. A sample of the 1850 federal census reveals that the vast majority of clerks were born in the South, that they were much younger than their merchant employers, and that they represented a significant proportion of the overall commercial population—approximately 30 percent.[34] Ten years later the 1860 federal census reported that 298 clerks worked in Dinwiddie County, Virginia, representing over 43 percent of the population involved in the retail trade. Even rural Buckingham County, Virginia, boasted sixteen clerks in a commercial population of fifty-nine people. Of course most storekeepers hired only one or two clerks per year, while a significant number of smaller establishments survived without any help at all. The ebb and flow of business, combined with the difficulty of finding a trusted assistant, could make a storekeeper reluctant to hire a clerk for an extended period of time. For example, in 1855 the Savannah hardware dealer James Sullivan hired Thomas McGrath for $25 per month "for the present time or about 3 mos." Within a few months Sullivan would learn whether McGrath was dependable and thus worth keeping at the store. Apparently such temporary agreements were not uncommon. As an extreme case, Reuben King paid both the white *and* black employees in his Darien, Georgia, store a flat rate of two dollars per day.[35]

The merchant-clerk relationship, in both a commercial and personal context, was unique in the antebellum South. A brief examination of the ties planters and overseers shared suggests the exceptional bond between southern merchants and clerks. Planters generally had wretched relations with their overseers. The impossible expectations of southern slaveholders could never be met by a class of employees deemed overwhelmingly illiterate and troublesome. Obtaining efficient work from slaves without resorting to severe violence, all the while maintaining a deferential attitude toward a demanding employer, proved beyond the ability of many southern overseers. Once again James

Henry Hammond spoke for many of his fellow planters when he scornfully remarked, "An overseer cant conform to routine more than twice."

The contempt that planters routinely heaped upon their overseers and the bitterness the latter felt for their employers were qualitatively different from the sentiment found in merchant-clerk relationships. The occasional merchant did criticize his clerk for laziness, stupidity, and perceived moral failings. On the other hand, Edwin J. Scott spoke for at least some clerks when he complained that as an apprentice clerk in South Carolina he was "completely tired out and disgusted by his [employer's] continued ill-treatment, notwithstanding my faithful and unrequited service." Yet most employers proved reluctant to make damning generalizations about their employees as a class. Many merchants had learned their trade as clerks. They frequently encouraged family and friends to enter the trade as clerks and work up through the ranks to attain an eventual proprietorship. Rather than a legacy of the southern agrarian tradition, this ideal of occupational achievement resembles the perspective of ambitious young men living in such places as Utica, New York, in the 1840s. A spirit of camaraderie tempered the hierarchy of the antebellum southern store.[36]

Clerks typically found work through newspaper advertisements and personal connections. The job ads that merchants ran sought clerks with steady habits, good penmanship, and experience with bookkeeping. Personal referrals offered an even more common and trusted procedure for merchants to obtain help. A letter of introduction from a former employer affirming a clerk to be a "gentleman" and in "every way worthy and steady" gave merchants some basis to judge a prospective employee. Once a clerk could confirm that he had experience working in a store, meaning that he had received a "commercial education," he usually found employment. Obviously family ties could effect the same ends. The income a clerk could earn varied over time and place. By the 1850s those employed in prosperous firms located in villages and larger towns made several hundred dollars a year. In 1851, B. W. MaCrae earned $450 in the Clarksville, Tennessee, firm of John S. Harts, while in 1859, the Richmond clerk Robert A. Grannis made $400 plus another $20 in store credit working at the firm of Kent, Paine, & Company. After a year of dependable service Grannis received a raise of $100 in 1860.[37]

Southern clerks carried out a wide range of duties for their pay.

Storekeepers expected their clerks to wait on customers, stock shelves, conduct regular inventories, and occasionally assist with the bookkeeping. While discharging these varied responsibilities, the clerk had to appease an often demanding clientele. It was not unheard of for a clerk to travel to competing stores in neighboring cities in order to find a single item for a favored customer. The hours spent in the store varied with the demands of a seasonal trade, but most clerks worked at least twelve hours a day. During rush periods, when the remnants of the previous year's stock had to be sold and new stock unpacked, clerks often worked eighteen-hour days. Describing the increased respect he had for his position at the Nashville firm of Shephard and Gordon, clerk George O'Bryan wrote his mother that, despite the fatigue attending his work, it hardened his muscles and benefited his health. When young O'Bryan entered his profession, the prospect of working consecutive twenty-hour days chilled him, but soon he claimed to be "daily waxing stronger." More importantly he believed the Nashville firm to be "the finest place in the world to acquire a knowledge of business." O'Bryan based this conclusion on the merit of the professional and personal attachments he had developed with his employers.[38]

The bond that developed between clerks such as O'Bryan and their merchant employers left its mark on commercial households. Frequently boarding with their employers' families, young men could find stability when living away from home for the first time. Likewise, such an arrangement gave merchants ample opportunity to supervise the personal habits of their young clerks. Even older clerks occasionally lived with their employers. When William Biggs, then in his midtwenties, relocated to New Orleans and assumed a clerking position in the W. Watts Commission Company, he and his family lived in the same house as the Watts family. Not surprisingly Biggs came to know a great deal about his employer's household. Time spent together in the store, as well as after hours, often created emotional ties between merchants and their clerks. George O'Bryan considered his employer and fellow clerks to be a "family" that provided him with "a good house, good companions, a good room, a good bed, a good servant that cleans up my room, in truth every thing *good*."

That O'Bryan's employer, the firm of Shephard and Gordon, provided someone to clean his room is telling. Some storekeepers came to regard their clerks as an important part of their own household. The

Richmond merchant Horace Kent routinely treated his clerks to sup-per at Layetelle's and had a select few over for Thanksgiving dinners. Despite the family's obvious wealth, a daughter, Emma Kent, courted several of her father's impecunious clerks and eventually married one after the Civil War. This peculiar amalgam of generosity and self-inter-est led the firm of Kent, Paine, & Company to purchase a company pew in a Richmond church for the religious edification of its employ-ees. Merchant wives came to depend upon their husbands' clerks for help around the home, while children often viewed these young men as companions. As a young woman living in Murfreesboro, Tennessee, Kate Carney enjoyed occasions when clerks who worked in her father's store would serenade her family. After the performance the Carney family would occasionally reward the young men with fruitcake and cordial. Arthur Smith, one of the clerks who visited the household on occasion, was so committed to his employer that he risked his life and "was very badly hurt" battling a fire that broke out in Carney's store. These and other cases reveal how in return for their obedience and hard work, young clerks acquired vital commercial experience and received standing within the merchant family and larger community. Such inti-macy could make the merchant-clerk relationship, and the values each embraced, unique in the antebellum South.[39]

Credit, debt, trade, and merchant-clerk relations ordered the lives of southern merchant families. Ranging from such mundane concerns as credit anxiety to the vital buying trips, conventions of the retail trade distinguished these Southerners from the majority of their neighbors. The region's farmers, planters, and artisans often viewed the merchant's commercial world—credit, sales, and trade—with suspicion or out-right hostility. The southern merchant's family came to view regular separations, paid employees, and partnership risk, as natural and even essential to their livelihood. These business practices, and the domes-tic changes they produced, enabled merchants and their families to prosper. Nevertheless, such commercial habits did exact a toll. The economic power that merchant families wielded in southern society could be great, but their social standing often remained tenuous. Even the most prominent southern merchants occasionally felt embattled by their critics in the agrarian South. Economic dislocation and jealousy led many of their neighbors in the Old South to challenge merchants and the liberal capitalist gospel that their trade presumably spread.

2

The Antebellum Merchant in Southern Society

The business activities that ordered the internal lives of merchant families also helped fashion their public identity. Buying, selling, and investing made merchant families conspicuous in the antebellum South. Every day merchants had to perform before an audience. Whether selling goods to a reluctant customer, mollifying a nervous creditor, or simply attending church, men and women in merchant families negotiated public roles determined by their trade. Moreover, the parts these commercial actors played in their communities fundamentally influenced how planters, farmers, and slaves perceived them. Successful merchants understood the sundry ways their public behavior could affect profits and made sure they and their families acted accordingly.

Many white Southerners viewed merchants with suspicion. Newspaper editors, politicians, and others who shaped public opinion fostered ambivalent and often critical opinions of shopkeepers, factors, and lowly hucksters. These groups appeared to love money too much, and their sharp business practices violated community standards. Some feared that virtuous planters and farmers, lured by the merchants' siren song of consumerism, would find themselves drowning in debt. Even more troubling was the prospect that other Southerners might embrace the servile behavior popularly associated with the commercial profession. The commonly held misconception that most merchants operating in the South hailed from Europe and the North—that they were "Jews" and "Yankees"—intensified the alarm. The editor of the *Richmond Enquirer* was hardly alone when he declared that excessive commercial activity threatened to become a "curse" upon the cotton kingdom. At the same time southern spokesmen had to acknowledge their region's dependence upon the business acumen of its commercial classes.[1]

Antebellum Southerners obtained large quantities of goods from local merchants. Not surprisingly, such dependence on shopkeepers for food-stuffs, medicine, and other necessities could produce tension in the community. Yeoman farmers needed and resented merchants at the same time. The same political leaders who denounced the influence of commercialism upon southern character often came to regard a lively retail trade as essential to the health of their towns and counties. Evidence suggests that a growing ambivalence prevailed where economic reality met cultural ideals. The competing image of the honest, thrifty merchant over against that of the grasping businessman represented part of the larger conflict between conservative and liberal capitalist thought in the antebellum economy. Cautious white Southerners regarded merchants as possibly dangerous interlopers in a stable and virtuous agrarian economy. Commercially oriented Southerners viewed the development of a growing mixed economy as a positive good and considered merchants essential to the financial and even the cultural development of their region. In the final analysis both positions had merit and revealed much about the larger truth of southern identity.

Merchants' professional lives and public identities centered around their role in selling merchandise to the public. While planters kept accounts of their crops, slaves, and other farming activities, shopkeepers tried to keep track of their daily, weekly, monthly, and yearly sales and expenditures. Dependent upon commerce for their livelihood, merchants naturally filled their public and personal writings with business information. Double-entry bookkeeping and other accounting techniques helped some merchants produce a rough estimate of their annual profits. Most retail and wholesale operators were more interested in, and better able to track, sales and stock accumulation than yearly profit. Figuring annual rates of capital depreciation and appreciation proved particularly troublesome. Many retail operators failed to distinguish between business capital and total assets or between business and household expenses. Southern merchants did understand that the crop season of cotton, tobacco, sugar, and rice largely dictated their sales. December and January, when farmers had the money to purchase yearly supplies and perhaps a few Christmas treats for their families, saw the highest sales, while the summer months were typically dull times. In an effort to offset slow sales periods, credit strain, and the cost of transporting goods, merchants typically priced their goods at twice what they paid for them wholesale. Clearly prices, along with geography, credit, and temperament, affected a merchant's ability to turn a profit. Sellers and buyers dwelled upon these factors at length in their writings.[2]

Fluctuating sales often framed how merchants viewed themselves. Funding an expanding debt and a growing family, poor sales always brought "the blues" to Atlanta shopkeeper Samuel Richards. Of course what constituted good sales depended upon such factors as the location of the store, its size, and its value. Successful merchants in Atlanta, Louisville, Charleston, and New Orleans typically exceeded several hundred dollars a day in sales. The largest firms could sell thousands of dollars in goods on a single day. By contrast, village shopkeepers in the rural South often tallied daily sales well below a hundred dollars. Recording strong sales and busy days in account books heartened ambitious southern businessmen, yet even proven merchants endured periods of sluggish trade. Only the wealthiest merchants in the antebellum South managed to avoid the kind of periodic business crises that shook the confidence of the typical shopkeeper.[3]

Financial anxiety echoes throughout the diaries and letters of the southern merchant class. For more than twenty years Thomas and John Jefferson ran a profitable father-son grocery store in Louisville. Its location in a growing western city, in addition to the business acumen of its owner, helps explain why this store made hefty annual profits, while dry-goods firms in more rural areas, particularly in the southeast, were often less profitable. R. G. Dun & Company variously described the firm as "thrifty, undoubted" and "perfectly good for any debt," but John Jefferson's diary remained fraught with anxiety over business. The young Kentuckian regularly bemoaned the dull months even if sales were good. When the store enjoyed "beautiful" sales days, the experience of his less fortunate colleagues still chastened Jefferson. He needed look no further than his uncle Henry Jefferson's new store, which opened in August of 1857 with a pitiful $1.15 in sales, a sum that horrified the entire family. Cushing Hassell's Williamston, North Carolina, firm Hassell & Biggs received strong credit ratings during the antebellum period, but still the merchant agonized over monthly sales of "only" one thousand dollars in July or seventeen hundred dollars in January.

Of course sluggish trade proved even more daunting for marginal retail businesses. One discouraged Texas shopkeeper described his fifty-dollar-a-week trade as "doing nothing or as nothing as possible." A southern merchant's self-esteem, indeed his very identity, rested heavily upon shifting sales. The diaries and correspondence left by successful business-men reveal a deep anxiety over the quantity and quality of sales. Proud to be members of the mercantile profession, merchants remained wary of their place in southern society. An uncertain commercial economy, sus-picion between retailers and their customers, and the public image of the merchant in the antebellum South helped place the region's commercial classes in a cultural middle ground between the North and South.[4]

Small profit margins and the boom-bust economy of antebellum America contributed to the southern merchant's gloomy obsession with sales figures. Once again John Jefferson's store was representative of the larger stores. In 1859 his grocery sold over sixty-five thousand dollars in goods, producing approximately three thousand dollars in profit. Likewise the firm of Hassell & Biggs regularly made between one thousand and four thousand dollars every year during the 1850s. Returns for both busi-nesses seem high when compared to the per capita annual income in the South, which barely exceeded a hundred dollars in 1860. In reality these figures represented only small returns, if any at all, on the capital these merchants had invested in their stores. Hassell and many other storekeep-ers found that, after factoring in taxes, rents, and growing families, their profits amounted to "scarcely anything." The end of the financial year saw many businessmen reexamining their store logs in the vain hope that they had made some accounting error. Only the prospect of a boom year or a steady upturn in business gave partners in marginal firms hope in their unpredictable economy.[5]

The antebellum experience of merchants in rural Dade County in northwest Georgia is suggestive. R. G. Dun kept records on nineteen firms in the county. Eleven (61 percent) of these firms received marginal or unsafe ratings, while eight of them (42 percent) were valued at a mod-est two thousand dollars or less. Similar to those slaveholders living at the margins of the planter class, Dade County storekeepers with limited means, as well as their colleagues throughout the region, fought to remain solvent. This anxious labor compelled a discipline and psychological cost that shaped merchant identity. Account books had to be kept, sharp deals made, and money employed wisely. The nature of retail economy gener-ated more than a preoccupation with sales on the part of the commercial classes. Fundamentally it helped govern the relationship between mer-chants and their customer neighbors.[6]

Questions surrounding different currencies, delivery dates, and insurance rates plagued the southern merchant, which in turn affected how storekeepers and their neighbors viewed each other. The balance between cash and credit sales was particularly troublesome. All merchants hoped for cash sales, though most eventually gave credit to cash-strapped customers, with the expectation that the debts would be paid after the year's cotton crop was sold. Like many optimistic merchants, John West believed his country store in Buckingham County, Virginia, would not have to rely upon significant credit business. The one great advantage he and his partners enjoyed was their location near the Female Collegiate Institute of Virginia. This Methodist academy housed between thirty-five and fifty young women who regularly purchased such items as hose, pins, lace, and ribbon with cash. Word of this favorable location gained the notice of R. G. Dun, which reported in 1850 that John S. West & Co. sold a great deal of goods to the "Institute girls at a very high price." Yet even this "close fisted business man" found himself forced to give credit to many customers. In addition to farmers from the surrounding countryside, dozens of students from the institute relied upon credit for even small expenditures, the primary difference between the two groups being that the young women needed the financial support of their families to obtain credit. At the close of 1860, John West's log book included 265 accounts with planters, yeoman farmers, and numerous students, totaling more than ten thousand dollars in sales, much of it uncollected. Even thrifty businessmen like West found themselves seeking payment from customers, occasionally in court, a year or more after the sale. Forced to rely on credit sales for their economic survival, it is not surprising that debt payment influenced how storekeepers related to their customers.[7]

Southern merchants viewed debt collection as unpleasant but necessary. Uncertain business conditions and a mobile clientele compelled most merchants to try to collect outstanding debts at least every twelve months. Obviously the price that farmers received for their crops affected most storekeepers directly. Typical was the plight of one Alabama storekeeper who wrote a friend, "My sales this year has been quite good . . . but I fear Collections will be pass [sic; passable] owing to the Shortness of the Crops." When B. J. Hobson decided to leave his neighborhood in rural Buckingham County, John West had his business partner hunt the former customer down and compel him to pay his debt to the store. Like most southern businessmen, West understood that the difference between success and failure in the mercantile trade could rest upon a handful of unpaid bills. Marshall County, Mississippi, storekeeper Thomas Webber spent the entire day of January 2, 1861, dunning customers who owed him money, without success. It seems local conditions had made it "impossible to collect any money." Fortunately for the twenty-six-year-old merchant, he was able to pay off the five thousand dollars he owed with the "helping hand" of several friends who loaned *him* the money.

A motivated storekeeper could resort to very public measures when collecting bills. One Nashville dry-goods merchant ran a newspaper advertisement that announced "I WANT MY MONEY," while a Lynchburg, Virginia, clothier quipped in his local newspaper that he had "not yet learned to do business [with wholesalers] without money." The Hertford, North Carolina, merchant Stephen Elliott and his partner would have appreciated the Nashville merchant's lament. Their firm owed money that they could not pay on time to a Norfolk, Virginia, wholesaler. This led Elliott's partner to avoid the wholesalers when in Norfolk and resulted in a pointed letter from the Virginia firm that noted the fact and scolded, "We are in want, and must have our due. We ask no more of any Man." Plying his trade in Huntsville, Alabama, the businessman Alexander A. Campbell declared that he was "hard pushed for cash" and that those indebted to him should pay or "expect to settle with an officer." Yet sometimes even court judgments failed to help merchants holding debt.[8]

The Virginian Robert Preston and his partners owned stores in Alabama and Tennessee, where they regularly won court decisions for back payment from debtor customers. By 1830 four years of mixed sales and court appearances left the firm holding over twenty thousand dollars of debt, half of which was considered uncollectible "bad debt." Occasionally mercantile firms confronted bizarre obstacles in collecting unpaid bills. The McMinn County, Tennessee, firm of Reeder, Dodson, and Dorsey sued Susan Carter for property belonging to her husband David, who owed the firm money before he "absconded." Susan Carter and her father testified that they had "greater cause than anyone else to complain of the fraudulent conduct of Carter," because he "ran off" with Susan's sister. To make matters worse, her scoundrel husband shot one of her brothers as he and the rest of her male kin chased him into North Carolina. Predictably Susan Carter ended her statement by testifying that she had nothing that belonged to her ex-husband. The kind of financial pressures this Tennessee business firm, Robert Preston, and other merchants felt in their daily experience with debt collection affected their ties with their customer neighbors. Merchants depended upon the financial discipline and personal scruples of their largely agrarian customer base for economic survival. They had to rely upon a clientele of yeoman farmers and planters who idealized self-reliance and often held merchants in contempt for their apparent servility. From the smallest huckster to the largest wholesaler, merchants found this position disconcerting.[9]

Bad debt, produced either by economic depression or unscrupulous customers, drove merchants to distraction. At the same time, "good debt," the income derived from prompt loan payments, provided the lifeblood for the mercantile trade and the foundation for commercial power in the antebellum South. This circumstance explains, in part, the often schizo-phrenic quality of the public and private correspondence of southern merchants. After economic dislocation and troublesome customers left him awash in bad debt following the Panic of 1837, Samuel Aby wrote his parents from Grand Gulf, Mississippi, "One thing I know that if ever I sell goods again, I must have the cash down this credit system has done me great injury." Aby was hardly alone. Eli Bonney, a storekeeper in Camden, South Carolina, who found himself still recovering from the same financial panic that staggered Aby, declared in his diary, "To all mer-chants doing business upon the customary but abominable 'credit system' I would say when your customer calls to settle his accounts, 'Be ready.'" Southern business correspondence is replete with such declarations, but few merchants could afford to turn away the bulk of their trade. During another commercial depression some twenty years later, Benedict Semmes wrote his wife Jorantha that bad debts and poor business led him to lose "all confidence in individuals as well as Banks." In a second letter sent a few weeks later Semmes pursued the subject further, revealing that he had "lost all confidence in every body and am in a constant state of fear." Despite such lamentations, Semmes, Bonney, and Aby all remained in the mercantile trade and continued to depend upon a sizable credit business. Certainly economic necessity dictated that most storekeepers accept at least a limited retail trade built upon credit. Furthermore, as one of the few sources of credit in an agrarian economy, merchants wielded power in their communities that few could resist.[10]

By denying credit to economically marginal customers and threat-ening to end its supply to defaulting neighbors, merchants made sure that most Southerners managed to pay their store debts. Evidence suggests some businessmen enjoyed this financial control. The merchant and lawyer Jonathan Worth was one such man who wielded this power and occasionally lorded it over his poorer neighbors. Regarding a particularly derelict customer Worth boasted, "Drake never paid a debt before that I know of on demand," but ultimately Drake would pay because "he is afraid of me." This businessman and later politician, described by one North Carolina newspaper as possessing a short body, short fingers, and stooped shoulders, understood how to employ his economic leverage to great effect. Commercial correspondence and public records indicate that storekeepers like Jonathan Worth were a distinct minority in their profession. Merchants tended to find their credit practices, including browbeating their customers to pay bills, an annoying necessity. Indeed the most articulate members of this commercial class came to view the loans they made to customers as a special burden they had to bear in order to build a prosperous regional economy. As one Kentucky country storekeeper described the southern condition, a cash-only business offered no inducement for the farmer to raise more than subsistence crops for his family, resulting in the merchant's selling few goods. Credit sales, even transactions conducted by barter, ultimately diversified and strengthened the local economy. As commercial agents in a cash-starved South, merchants came to view their role in the retail and credit markets as fundamentally virtuous. This conviction both influenced and evolved from the merchant class's understanding of its place within the antebellum South.[11]

As we have seen, fluctuations in the economy and difficulties associated with retail credit led many storekeepers and other commercial agents to cast a wary eye on the southern financial order. More fundamentally, the demands imposed by sales and debt practices encouraged merchants to view the political economy of their communities as underdeveloped and turbulent. This perception was strengthened by the boom-bust cycle of the national financial and manufacturing structure, a regional economic system dominated by capital-rich but cash-poor planters, and a growing but still nascent consumer base in a regional slave society. Merchants and others believed such instability could not promote the general well-being of southern society. In part this element of their worldview reflected their liberal capitalist ethic. As numerous historians have noted over the past thirty years, most white Southerners, particularly those involved in staple agriculture, participated in the market economy. This fact, however, tells us little about how these economic actors viewed their participation in the market or about their attitudes regarding the expanding capitalist system in America.

Some southern intellectuals, typically adherents to classic economic theory, supported a free market. Others, including Henry Clay, George Tucker, and Jacob Cardozo, favored a more organized economy where the government intervened in order to spur industrial development, urban growth, and improved transportation. Then there were those somewhere between these two poles, men like John C. Calhoun, whose theory of the South's political economy the historian Michael O'Brien describes as having "started with a sort of Hobbesianism" and "ended with a more sentimental liberalism." As we shall see, those merchants who left evidence of thinking about the political economy overwhelmingly supported a mixed economic system and a significant role for government. Furthermore, they typically rejected the atavistic judgments of free market advocates like John Taylor and found in the true conservatism of George Fitzhugh that social relations in the South were organic. To be sure, merchants supported white supremacy and the ideal of a hierarchy based upon virtue, but their personal experience in a political economy that did not always reward skill and hard work led them to support a Whiggish agenda. Social harmony had to rest on a strong diversified economy and vigorous civic involvement. Ambitious merchants made sure they would play a significant part in creating this social and economic order.[12]

The public roles southern merchants performed during the antebellum period show the influence of both liberal and republican thought. To varying degrees most storekeepers subscribed to the unarticulated liberal capitalist idea that guarding individual self-interest promoted the general good. They resented having to pay for mercantile and liquor licenses and the government's interference in the daily operation of their businesses. The credit and commodities that merchants supplied in return for cash or goods represented their contribution to a vibrant economy. At the same time, merchants often embraced a social ethic that called upon individuals to sacrifice their interests for the good of the community. Commercial interpretation of traditional agrarian republicanism prompted small storekeepers and large wholesalers to conflate their interests with those of their communities. This worldview led them to conclude that true freedom, for individuals as well as for societies, did not reside only in agrarian economic independence, if such a state existed, but in commercial entrepreneurial liberty as well. Their leadership and organizations would bring about greater social harmony while furthering their business interests. Those in the merchant class regarded themselves as leading citizens who were devoted to the South and its people. In return they expected a measure of the deference accorded to the region's planter class, but ironically the very traits and activities that allowed merchants to succeed in the marketplace clashed with certain southern values and produced popular criticism that only further confirmed their outsider status.[13]

Professional and religious organizations provided important arenas where public-spirited merchants and their families could develop southern communities while enhancing their own social position. For example, during the 1830s merchants and other businessmen in Nashville, Tennessee, formally met to discuss strategies for improving mail and transportation services. Along the same lines, in 1839 the Mercantile Library Association of Baltimore built a reading room open to both sexes and all classes. A decade later the Mercantile Library Association of Charleston raised more than seven hundred dollars for a reading room that would prove a monument to the commercial community's "intelligence, liberality and taste, a credit to their profession, and an honor to our city." Outlining the contributions of its city's merchant community and board of trade the *Richmond Enquirer* concluded, "In their enterprise, in their sagacity, and in their practical energy, consist the true elements of growth and progress in every commercial community." Fraternal orders such as the Druids, the Odd Fellows, the Society of Red Men, and the Masons claimed many members from the commercial classes. These groups raised money for charitable causes and brought lecturers to town, all the while underlining the respectability of their membership. Confirming the benefit of civic engagement, one scholar found that, for the middle class in Louisville, "service on these civic and social organizations brought them recognition not only in the eyes of the other middle-class Louisvillians, but also in the eyes of people below them in status."

The wives and older daughters of established merchants frequently participated in such organizations as well. The historians Jane and William Pease have found that in 1830 more than 20 percent of the leading women in secular or church-related charities in Charleston were wives or widows of merchants. Less than 10 percent of this female leadership was married to planters. That the merchant class was heavily involved in community organizations is consistent with what has already been noted regarding the worldview of southern merchants during the antebellum period. They hailed the rise of stable commercial markets but still saw the need for strong, even paternalistic, leadership by the region's "respectable" classes. Predictably the Whig Party offered the natural political home for these southern citizens.[14]

The same cultural values that the Whig Party publicly espoused during the 1840s—hard work, frugality, domesticity, gentility, and self-improvement—most southern merchants also held dear. Similarly businessmen and Whig leaders alike believed that such economic policies as the Bank of the United States and Federally funded internal improvements offered a political means to achieve their economic goals. A national bank offered the promise of easier credit and a stabilizing force behind state bank notes. Likewise, internal improvements appealed to merchants who generally transported their goods at great cost hundreds of miles from the eastern seaboard over primitive roads and hazardous rivers. Finally the Democratic Party itself, particularly under Andrew Jackson, alienated many retail and wholesale dealers across the South. The merchants' conservative faith in a social hierarchy based on merit clashed with a Jacksonian democratic ethic that celebrated egalitarianism and small government. The contempt most southern merchants felt for the Democratic Party was passionate but would fade before the growing sectional crisis of the 1850s.[15]

Correspondence between the dry-goods merchant Charles Jacocks in North Carolina and his brother Jonathan suggests the disdain southern merchants had for Democratic leaders and the party's values. Early in 1834, Jonathan wrote his brother from Washington, D.C., where he witnessed the proceedings of Congress and had an opportunity to meet Andrew Jackson. Clearly the encounter with the president did not leave Jacocks in awe, and he reported to his like-minded brother seeing "alarming manifestations of the final success of him who rules and has usurped so much *popularity*, and scattered with so much liberality among his followers 'the spoils of Victory.'" The letter ended with words of praise for Henry Clay and John C. Calhoun. Two weeks later Jonathan Jacocks penned another letter that made explicit the brothers' complaints with Jackson and captured the essence of the future Whig platform. The note related a discussion Jonathan had with several close, though unnamed associates of Jackson who declared: "Those who are in debt & all those who do business upon borrowed capital (and they generally embrace the most enterprising part of the community, and are generally truly the Diamond in its rough state,) must and deserve to fail—that he [Jackson] never will restore the Deposits if he can prevent it & that he never will sign a bill chartering or rechartering a National Bank."[16]

Such rhetoric made southern merchants suspicious, if not outright hostile, to the Democratic Party. To varying degrees most favored some type of national bank, but all businessmen understood that credit was essential to their way of life. Merchants could not compromise on the availability of borrowed capital. The vehemence of Jonathan and Charles Jacocks's hostility toward Democratic policies seems to have been exceptionally strong even by the standards of their class. Several years later in reference to Martin van Buren, a founder of the Democratic Party who assumed the presidency in 1837, Jonathan sarcastically remarked he would rather send his son to Germany than have him live under the rule of "King Martin." This said, the import of Jonathan Jacocks's denunciation of the Democrats generally reflected southern commercial opinion between 1835 and 1850.[17]

Combining Whig and southern principles, merchants worked to build a liberal capitalist economy with conservative republican social values. For example, as a Whig representative to the North Carolina state legislature during the 1840s, the dry-goods agent Jonathan Worth supported a strong and active state government while challenging the expansion of the suffrage on the grounds that it was politically unsound. Outside the halls of government, Whig merchants advanced their political agenda in a number of ways. Like dozens of others in his profession, John Burbidge, a storekeeper from Walterboro, South Carolina, attended one of the many commercial conventions held across the South during the antebellum period. These meetings offered a platform for southern commercial men to lobby for favorite Whig issues. Commercial conventions, state and local governments, and lyceum halls offered venues where southern merchants joined fellow Whigs and the occasional commercially oriented Democrat to push for liberal markets and conservative values. They promoted a benevolent, active role for government and the rule of law, two themes they hoped their fellow Southerners would rally around. Under the leadership of men like Henry Clay and William Henry Harrison, Whigs expected political glory, a virtual "Elysian fields," according to one merchant-farmer in 1840. The antebellum merchant community failed to achieve its political and social objectives. Sectionalism and rancor destroyed their party, while the mass of white Southerners, yeoman farmers and planters alike, never embraced the dissonant values they associated with the merchants working in their communities.[18]

Throughout the antebellum period the southern commercial classes tended to support Unionist, nationalist principles. Evidence suggests that most retail and wholesale businessmen opposed the protective tariffs of 1828 and 1832 but were at the same time quick to denounce John C. Calhoun's nullification doctrine. Twenty years later, amid the sectional political upheavals in 1850, merchants continued to strongly oppose fire-eating states' rights principles. Lacy Ford has found that, during the secession debates held in South Carolina, the vast majority of up-country merchants and entrepreneurs opposed secession and supported political compromise. The same crisis led Mississippi storekeeper Isham Howze, a self-described "union man" and "law-abiding man," to support political leaders who favored the Compromise of 1850. He remained confident that "God is on the side of union men, and will sustain their cause." At the close of 1852, Howze continued to bitterly denounce the avid secessionist in his diary as "an enemy of God and man," deserving to be "hung upon a gallows as high as that of Haman." As the Whig Party disappeared amid the decade's growing sectional discord, southern merchants often remained pragmatic, even fervent, Unionists.[19]

Feeling politically abandoned after their poor showing in the national elections of 1852, many Whig businessmen expressed frustration at the lack of alternatives in a South increasingly dominated by the Democratic Party. Merchants like North Carolinian Cushing Hassell condemned the Republicans as an "abolition party," while remaining cool to their Democratic neighbors. Such men defended slavery and attacked the apparent Republican threat to their region's institutions yet continued to seek an honorable compromise with the North. Evidence suggests that a majority of businessmen in 1860, if they voted at all, supported the Unionist platform of the Constitutional Union Party. After the election, when momentum for secession became irresistible, cultural ties and economic pragmatism led most in the southern mercantile class to accept the political reality of the Confederate States of America. By early 1861 some merchants had joined the front ranks of secessionists in their communities, while others had not, nor ever would, embrace fully the Confederacy. At this late date one of the few surviving bonds that held these disparate political factions together was the realization that their economic goals, the policies most associated with the Whig Party, failed to gain a strong foothold in the South. Commercial conventions and occasional Whig victories did not create a diversified economy in an antebellum South where cotton reigned as king, with its court the planter class. Equally troubling to the commercial classes, their social status within the agrarian South remained marginal.[20]

A few merchants, particularly in larger urban centers, gained positions of cultural authority within their communities, but most white Southerners felt sharply ambivalent about the mercantile trade. Ironically the very attributes that made a storekeeper successful, prudence and frugality, led many Southerners to regard merchants as cultural interlopers—individuals lacking those virtues essential to southern character. Most people recognized that the health of their communities depended on the activity of their commercial population, yet many refused to embrace this class of citizens as authentic Southerners. As one editor sarcastically remarked, the job of a dry-goods salesman required "the shrewdness of a politician, the persuasion of a lover, the politeness of a Chesterfield, the patience of Job, and the impudence of a pick-pocket." This clever recital of stereotypical characteristics suggests why many agrarian and self-styled Jeffersonian republicans held the mercantile trade in some contempt. An examination of the attitudes Southerners held toward merchants, particularly two prominent stereotypes of the profession, reveals why they remained on the cultural periphery in Dixie.[21]

Antebellum Southerners based their opinions of the mercantile trade mainly on personal experience. Dry-goods and grocery stores served as some of the few social centers in many communities, especially in the country, giving most individuals a basis for making a judgment. In much the same way that stores served as centers in economic exchange networks, they also provided hubs where Southerners, black and white, male and female, could socialize. People living relatively close to their neighborhood store often dropped by not to make a purchase but to exchange gossip, whittle sticks, and discuss horse racing and cockfighting. Not surprisingly, this led many people to view their local storekeeper as a neighbor and friend, while still condemning the trade in general.

Adolphus Williamson Mangum's store in Orange County, North Carolina, rivaled the local church as a communal focal point. There he and his customers shared long discussions about politics, religion, and temperance. In the South Carolina town where Edwin Scott lived as a young boy in the 1820s, "some of the villagers and neighbors met *every day* at a store, where the card table was brought out into the piazza soon after breakfast, and gambling went on till night." In addition to gambling and the occasional "ball" where young ladies were invited, the store also witnessed "feats of strength" and "an occasional fist fight." Some years later when Scott clerked for a merchant named Jacob Barrett in Columbia, South Carolina, Charles Young's Theatrical Company performed all winter in the back of the store. Court days, muster days, election days, and auctions in particular, found southern shops bustling with business and personal traffic. Cushing Hassell's store in Williamston, North Carolina, always benefited when his cousin Colonel Asa Biggs gave a political speech in town. Southern store culture also offered the chance for entertainment. According to one observer, "fair days" in a larger town like Natchez, Mississippi, meant an "extraordinary number of private carriages, clustered before the doors of the most fashionable stores, or millineries, rolling through the street, or crossing and recrossing it . . . nearly every moment, from eleven till two." James Wiggins, a slave in Anne Arundel County, Maryland, would accompany his master on trips to Annapolis where the young man would dance for customers in the town's stores. This work earned Wiggins enough money to buy extra clothes and shoes for himself. Like most white and even black Southerners, Wiggins and his master saw their trips to general stores in both economic and social terms. Personal and business relationships overlapped in southern stores. Friendships developed and pleasantries passed between salesman and customer.[22]

This space, however, was more complicated than many sentimental memoirs and novels would have us believe. Tensions flourished amid the communities that frequented antebellum stores. The social encounters in these stores reflected what has been true throughout the ages: routine interactions among friends and neighbors are generally absent from the historical record, while the bizarre and violent are plainly evident. Thus what was commonplace in stores and shops as public arenas must often be gleaned from unusual events that were reported in newspapers, court documents, and other public records. The following bloody accounts from southern newspapers reveal much about everyday store culture before the Civil War.

On January 4, 1828, a man named John Smith entered a Little Rock store in the Arkansas Territory carrying a rifle. Smith chatted with the proprietor for a few moments about "some trivial business." When the discussion ended he turned to leave. Upon reaching the door, without speaking a word Smith leveled his weapon and discharged its contents into the chest of one Isaac Watkins, who was seated about ten feet from where Smith stood. The ball entered Watkins's breast and lodged in his backbone. He died in "great agony" within an hour. Smith made his escape while the community, including the territorial governor, raised a $572 reward for his capture. In another example twelve years later, Drs. Vans Sullivane and B. W. Morehead settled a personal dispute between them during what the *Port Gibson Correspondent* called a "rencounter" in a store operated by the firm of Taylor & Ballard. During the "short but fierce" struggle, Morehead stabbed Sullivane repeatedly with a three-inch pocketknife blade. Perhaps Morehead applied knowledge from his profession in this affair of honor. When the fight concluded, Sullivane was dead from a wound in his chest and several that had severed major arteries in his neck as well as his tongue. Morehead later surrendered himself to the authorities and was released to await trial after paying ten thousand dollars for bail. In 1855 a Georgia man by the name of Orr reclaimed a runaway slave from a Carolina jail. Near the end of their trip back to Orr's "works" outside Savannah, his slave, who remained nameless in the newspaper account, killed his master. Sometime later the authorities captured the slave. He had taken refuge in a country store not far from Savannah.[23]

These dramatic anecdotes give only a glimpse of antebellum life, yet collectively they help provide a sense of the cultural interaction that took place within the physical confines of the southern store. All three of these newspaper stories attest to the critical role stores played as social centers in neighborhoods and towns. One newspaper account described Isaac Watkins as a "useful and enterprising citizen," while the official titles of Drs. Sullivane and Morehead suggest the education and high standing they enjoyed. All types of people, particularly men in these cases, whiled away a great deal of time in dry-goods stores, groceries, and other such establishments. The fact that some merchants sold alcohol, grocers for example, no doubt encouraged customers to linger. Indeed, this is why some Southerners heaped scorn upon grocers. It also seems clear that, at least in western regions like Arkansas, customers bringing weapons into stores was not unusual, much less cause for alarm. As the actions of the runaway slave indicate, not all in southern stores were white or free. It would seem very strange indeed for Orr's slave to stop by a store while on the run if his presence there would raise suspicions. Slaves, as well as free blacks, could be found in most mercantile establishments across the Old South. Orr's runaway slave probably realized that a country store would allow him to blend with a crowd. Of course as these violent stories also suggest, stores offered a natural space where neighbors could satisfy their taste for vengeance or justice.

One segment of the community had a unique vantage on the society found in retail businesses: the merchants themselves. They participated in the social give-and-take of their stores, yet smart business owners recognized that whatever claims of friendship neighbors may have had, they were also customers; and the relationship between merchant and customer could be tumultuous. Long hours and the continual threat of bankruptcy led some merchants to describe their clientele in rancorous language. The tightfisted patron is a ubiquitous figure in merchant diaries and letters. While clerking in his father's shop in Louisville, Kentucky, John Jefferson and his coworkers referred to their customers as "Russians" behind their backs and employed battle analogies when evaluating sales trends. During a busy day in April 1857, the Russians appeared "quite formidable," but after sales exceeding four hundred dollars they were "vanquished at last." Certainly Jorantha Jordan would have appreciated Jefferson's commercial spirit. In an 1848 letter to her fiancé, Benedict Semmes, then a struggling merchant in Washington, D.C., she reminded her beau that "there is no friendship in trade." Rather than complain about the harsh realities of the marketplace, this practical daughter of a New York congressman coolly told Semmes she "liked it" that way. A merchant in Columbia, Tennessee, groused that he spent "every day of his life measuring calicoes and Lasses[,] weighing nails and copperas, and talking to old women as old as Methusilah [sic], and as ugly as a Jackass, or quarrelling with some fellow about his account." Among the small number of actual Yankee merchants plying their trade in the antebellum South, Samuel L. Lewis did not lose his temper when prospective customers called him a "dam [sic] pedlar." He wrote his father back home in Connecticut that he never got "provoked" but would "laugh them out of it and tell them I will sell them something any how if but for pence worth so goes it." [24]

The daily struggle to survive economically as a merchant in the antebellum South certainly promoted such attitudes on the part of the commercial classes. In an attempt to incorporate traditional republican values within their liberal capitalist trade, retail and wholesale traders demanded a high degree of personal honor from customers and fellow businessmen. The sense of betrayal many felt when their standards were not met occasioned bitterness or personal detachment. Customers and observers of the mercantile trade typically had mutual feelings about the commercial classes.

Blanket condemnations of southern merchants filled antebellum newspapers, travel accounts, and memoirs. An 1846 edition of the *Caddo Gazette and De-Soto Intelligencer* (Shreveport, La.) described merchants as people who "worship and adore riches—that will seek the attainment of their object even among the ruins of their country." Commercial locusts, merchants were "insensible to the laws of the land, and reckless of the rights of the laboring portion of the community—they have not national attachments or patriotism—*their ledger is their bible and money their God.*" The authors of these attacks generally based their claims on personal experience or anecdotal evidence gleaned from local opinion. For example, when the Northerner Henry Whipple visited Macon, Georgia, in the early 1840s he learned, evidently from prominent town residents, that "everyone" regarded the town's businessmen as "shavers." Merchant business activities, particularly haggling and speculation, encouraged an agrarian southern population to look upon the transfer of commodities from producer to consumer as "a kind of swindling operation." Certainly the southern press bolstered such opinion. Decrying the rising number of young men entering upon mercantile pursuits, *The People's Press and Wilmington Advertiser* in Wilmington, North Carolina, urged its readers to count the number of successful merchants and compare them to the region's agricultural population and witness "the vast amount of ruin and disgrace attendant on the former, and of comfort and competence on the latter." A similar refrain in an 1851 edition of the *Richmond Enquirer* declared that without the power of the bank and ability to obtain credit, the "merchant prince" is ruined; he is "dishonored and his pride is crushed."[25]

Additional evidence suggests that slaves also assumed the mercantile trade to be unnatural and benighted. When Fred Bibble's master, I. D. Thomas, died after being crushed by a falling box of freight in a New Orleans wholesale house, the Texas slave and others concluded that the "accident" was actually murder. The ill-tempered, penurious merchant finally received his just deserts when some wronged party cut the rope holding the box in place while Thomas stood underneath it. Whether it was murder or an accident, this slave, like many white Southerners, assumed commercial activities could be so repugnant they might result in violence. Of course many Southerners believed such practices to be so far removed from their own traditional mores that they represented a malevolent Yankee influence. The widespread though mistaken belief that most merchants then hailed from the North (see appendix, table 4) completed this crude syllogism. The historian Grady McWhiney found evidence that at least for some Southerners the phrase "to Yankee" meant "to cheat." Northern periodicals even bolstered this stereotype on occasion, though they often blamed sharp bargaining on the typical southern customer. In an article in a series entitled "Sketches of South Carolina" that ran in the *Knickerbocker Magazine*, one Yankee writer concluded: "It was no meeting of Greek with Greek in the contest of wits, but a perfect inrush of shrewd, disciplined tacticians in the art of knavery, upon a stupid and ignorant population." The southern periodical the *Christian Index* offered a variation on this theme in the late 1820s when it ran articles criticizing the region's well-to-do ladies for being the "source and mirror of vanity" who were "flattered by fops" (clerks) as they spent their waking hours buying nonessential goods in stores. While white solidarity and social cohesion continued to be the norm in the antebellum South, undoubtedly class tensions, particularly between storekeepers and the planter class, helped foster popular contempt toward the southern commercial classes.[26]

A small percentage of the merchant community belonged to the wealthiest ranks of southern society. These individuals tended to reside in one of the handful of larger towns and cities. Most merchants, however, generally those of more limited means, worked and lived in the vast southern interior where they came into daily contact with yeoman farmers and wealthier planters. It was here that friction between busy storekeepers and their agrarian customers created the most ill will. Yeoman farmers, defending their world of harmony and independence, still relied upon country merchants for such necessities as coffee and sugar. This dependence bred resentment. Uneducated farmers questioned why merchants avoided speaking in local "dialect" and flaunted their relative wealth by purchasing expensive clothing and carriages. Likewise, members of the wealthier planter class joined yeoman farmers in challenging southern merchants over the price of their goods and the availability of credit. After a particularly frustrating trip into the nearby town of Bayou Sara, Louisiana, the planter Bennet Barrow wrote in his diary, "I believe there is but one or two strictly honest merchants at B Sara—they put an inferior article on you—and charge from 50 to 200 pr ct." Another planter vented his outrage against the high prices set for goods by the business community in Macon, Georgia. In a letter to the local paper, "O.K." lamented that local merchants, "instead of being honorable as they may have been useful, or as their calling is useful, have been guilty of gross malpractices, and the whole course of trade has been marked by acts of corruption and fraud, until in her sister cities Macon is used as a bye-word and a reproach." Even those planters who did not denounce the majority of their commercial neighbors as scoundrels exhibited a healthy respect for their business acumen. One Mississippi planter instructed his daughter to follow the advice of a few nearby merchants while away at school. When it came to exchanging currency or bartering goods, he reminded her that these "trading men" could make deals "to much better advantage than yourself." This planter and his daughter thought such trading men useful, if not wholly trustworthy. Planters also had reason to suspect that unscrupulous merchants proved willing customers to slaves trading in goods stolen from their masters.[27]

As the dominant political and economic class in the antebellum South, planters had complaints against storekeepers that often manifested themselves in displays of outright contempt. The case of the planter Basil Kiger illustrates this disposition. As a large plantation owner and family patriarch in Warren County, Mississippi, Kiger expected the members of his household to marry well. Predictably Kiger became angry upon hearing that his sister-in-law Bettie, a widow with a small child, planned to marry a poor boy she met while on vacation. He felt sure the match would fail and Bettie would be left penniless. When other family members sought to assuage Kiger's misgivings by telling him the boy was a partner in a country store the planter scoffed, an establishment "with a stock no doubt that might be carried in a mans coat Packet consisting of a Bag of shot 10 lbs of sugar as much coffee and a Bbl. of sweet cider flanked by a home mad[e] ginger cake." Most men of Kiger's wealth and standing would have agreed with his assessment of the situation. After six months of family turmoil Kiger emerged victorious, and the wedding was called off. Of course the pragmatic storekeeper would on occasion return the favor by ridiculing imperious, debt-ridden planters. Seeking more than ten thousand dollars in outstanding debts incurred largely by local planters, the merchant John Burbidge declared the lot so "dreadfully avaricious, that when they can get a fair value for their produce, they always expect and look for a greater price, there is no end to their avarice." Unified around the inviolability of slavery and the necessity for racial control in the South, antebellum white communities could still be divided by class conflicts, which ultimately weakened the social authority and prestige of the merchant class.[28]

The dominant political and economic class in the antebellum South, planters had complaints against storekeepers that often manifested themselves in displays of outright contempt. That opinion-makers and communities marginalized the commercial classes is powerfully illustrated in the way the mercantile trade as a whole was characterized as particularly Yankee, Jewish, or both. Southern newspapers, books, and letters often used such claims against successful storekeepers, whether true or not, as a means to cast opprobrium on the profession and its members. The humorists Augustus Baldwin Longstreet and George Washington Harris, as well as the novelists William Gilmore Simms and John Beauchamp Jones, among others, at times perpetuated these stereotypes in their work. Though all evidence suggests that a substantial majority of antebellum merchants were native-born Southerners, as is often the case, perception proved stronger than reality. The presence of a small number of northern and Jewish merchants living in the South provided all the license that some Southerners needed to depict the trade as dominated by alien interests. This practice and its implications for antebellum merchants can be better understood by examining a few southern states more closely. The example of Moses Cohen Mordecai and the lives of native-born, northern, and Jewish businessmen in North and South Carolina exemplify the social barriers that merchants confronted and their attempts to construct a more southern public identity.[29]

On October 7, 1854, a brief message to state senatorial candidate Moses Cohen Mordecai appeared in the columns of the *Charleston Mercury*. A resident of the city writing as "A SUFFERER" demanded to know Mordecai's position regarding unrestricted free trade between Charleston and the West Indies. Many believed the trade had brought disease into the port city. They advocated a more stringent quarantine to shield the local population. Two days later a writer in the *Charleston Daily Courier* declared Mordecai to be a city candidate who remained unknown to people and leaders in "remote portions" of the state. Editorials suggesting that Mordecai belonged to the anti-immigrant Know-Nothing Party also emerged in the pages of the *Mercury* and other Charleston papers during the fall of 1854. As a candidate for a contested seat to the South Carolina Senate, Mordecai recognized the politics behind these questions and aspersions. He replied in the *Mercury* that the reports had been intended to injure his chances in the upcoming election. To be sure, the conventions of local politics in an antebellum southern city explain much about these attacks. The peculiar nature of the criticism that Mordecai received, however, derived from his position as an established merchant.[30]

A merchant and a Jew in the antebellum South, Mordecai seemed especially vulnerable to the charge of being an outsider. During the 1854 campaign, his detractors avoided religious slurs. While the planter and politician James Henry Hammond described Mordecai as a "miserable Jew" in his diary, the public press in Charleston remained silent on such matters. His standing as an influential merchant proved more troublesome.[31] Mordecai's opponents claimed he represented the city's merchant class. Their newspaper attacks implied that the interests of the powerful merchant class rested outside the commonweal. The close ties among the city's merchants, and Mordecai's place within that community, raised suspicions. As early as 1842, Hammond believed "the secret is that [Mordecai] is a man of force and influence in Charleston." References to Mordecai as "the candidate of the merchants" characterized the campaign. Eventually friends of the candidate came to his defense. In a *Mercury* article entitled "Mr. Mordecai as a Merchant," a writer calling himself "Community" asserted Mordecai's election did not "*alone*" rest upon his brother merchants but on the "*general*" vote of the people. The editorial broadsides between the two factions continued until election day. When it was over Mordecai had achieved a resounding victory. He received more votes than those of his two rivals combined. This campaign provides further evidence of the ambivalence newspaper editors and many of their readers felt toward merchants. In part, this was a reflection of larger intellectual dissonance in a region where some elements championed industrialization and modernity, while others sought to protect an agrarian tradition that seemed increasingly endangered. Such divisions existed among and within the various classes that southern society comprised.[32]

The press wielded tremendous influence in the antebellum South, despite the fact that the expense and limited availability of newspapers restricted readership to the educationally and financially privileged. This class of people, however, disproportionately molded southern popular opinions of politics and the economy. The language that southern editors adopted when discussing merchants suggests how they and their audience understood them. The following examples will explore several "merchant themes" that emerged in newspapers in North and South Carolina during the antebellum period. The sweeping economic and regional diversity in these two states makes them excellent exemplars.[33]

In the antebellum Carolinas, men and women defined themselves by their ties to family, neighborhood, class, and race. Despite the political differences between up-country and low-country residents or the economic gulf between yeoman and planter, Carolina newspapers exhibited a consistent ambivalence regarding southern merchants. Generally the press described storekeepers as either greedy, malevolent interlopers or compassionate wealth producers who were essential forces for town building. As we shall see, that so many Carolinians held conflicting views about their merchant neighbors suggests how much the marketplace and the national economy were beginning to transform the region. Needless to say, such ambiguous popular images troubled individuals who depended upon their public reputation for economic survival. Carolina merchants responded to these broad stereotypes by attempting to depict themselves as industrious and sophisticated Southerners.[34]

The stereotype of the greedy merchant portrayed in antebellum Carolina newspapers reflected a popular sentiment that originated in colonial American society. Eighteenth-century Southerners believed merchants encouraged imprudent planter expenditures in order to reap increased commissions. Many, resenting Scottish and English domination of the colonial trade, condemned merchants as foreign agents in the South. Peter Earle and others have discovered that in England and her empire "merchants were singled out by contemporaries as a race apart from other members of the commercial world." This legacy continued, albeit in an altered form, in the antebellum South. Rather than covetous European merchants, it was the New England "Yankee" who became the exemplar of commercial greed. Daniel R. Hundley spoke for many Southerners when he described the majority of merchants as "unscrupulous Southern Yankees." A significant minority had been born and raised in New England, but even those who had not had seemingly adopted Yankee ways. This prejudice helped shape the merchant image in the Carolina press.[35]

Carolina newspapers frequently presumed trade to fall within the Yankee domain. In November 1832 the *Carolina Watchman* in Salisbury, North Carolina, printed an anecdote entitled "Profit and Loss" that related the story of a Boston shopkeeper who pretended to sell his goods at very low prices, telling his customers he sold at a loss. When asked why he continued in such a business the thrifty shopkeeper replied, "Oh, I couldn't stand it at all, only *I do so much of it.*" The story implies the depth of both Yankee business acumen and sophistry. The reader is amused at the merchant's strategy while realizing his base duplicity. Hundley imputed the same habits to southern merchants. According to the southern writer, they appeared "full of their own conceit, but prodigal of bows and compliments, and always smiling of countenance, yet, did one credit their own most solemn assertions, always selling every thing at a 'most tremendous sacrifice.'" The *Greenville Mountaineer* related a tale of a local sales clerk who tricked a "fashionable lady" into paying twenty-two shillings for five shillings' worth of discarded silk after convincing her it was the last piece in town. The editor of the *Mountaineer* found the clerk's élan amusing but warned his female readers to learn the moral of his anecdote: that southern merchants displayed the same rapacious capacity for making a dollar as Yankee traders. Distrust of Yankee mercantile practices led the Carolina press to censure local merchants with close commercial ties to the North.[36]

Critique of Yankee business practices and their influence upon southern merchants often merged with sectional political broadsides during the late antebellum period. In 1850 the radical *Charleston Mercury* denounced the close ties between local merchants and northern businesses. Following the course outlined by the paper's fire-eating leader, Robert Barnwell Rhett, *Mercury* editors lamented the fact that local merchants made their spring purchases in such northern cities as Philadelphia and New York, where, they claimed, leading journals never used "the word *South* without a sneer, except when it invites Southern trade, and asks Southern men to kiss the hand that smites them." The trade between shopkeepers from the Piedmont "interior" and New York City particularly vexed the Carolina press. The opprobrium placed upon a marketing system that seemingly benefited northern interests at the expense of the South helped perpetuate the popular image of the merchant as a "Southern Yankee."[37]

In addition to ascribing Yankee manners to practitioners of the mercantile trade, the antebellum Carolina press suggested that they belonged to an effete profession. Newspapers described how shopkeeping activities broke with the agrarian traditions of the South. In 1834 the editor of the *People's Press and Wilmington Advertiser*, printed in the growing seaport of Wilmington, North Carolina, wrote an editorial bemoaning how few young men were entering upon agricultural and mechanical pursuits. The editor witnessed Wilmington parents forcing their children into the learned professions, while looking with contempt upon the mechanical arts. He concluded that parents wished for their sons to hold a degraded rank in a class they esteemed rather than to enter upon the "useful arts."

The editor mocked the idea of a "dealer in tar, rum, and fat, looking upon the occupation of a farmer or mechanic . . . and thanking God, like the Pharisee [*sic*], that he is not like other men." The high failure rate among the city's merchant community belied its claims to business success. The editor predicted trouble for Wilmington and the nation if parents continued to encourage their children to enter upon the life of the "genteel vagabond"—the mercantile profession.[38]

A paper in the coastal town of Edenton, North Carolina, expressed a similar opinion in 1841, when the editor of the *Edenton Sentinel and Albemarle Intelligencer* wrote an article responding to a story in the *New York Sun* entitled "Profession vs. Trade." The story described how two advertisements had been placed in a New York City paper, one for a clerk in a store, the other for an apprentice to learn the blacksmith's trade. A day after the ads were printed the number of applicants for the clerking position had reached fifty while no one had inquired about the latter. The *Sun* compared this degradation of physical labor in the northern Atlantic states to that in the slave South. The *Sentinel and Albemarle Intelligencer* offered a different explanation. The rising prominence of the mercantile trade represented a larger break with agrarian tradition. Urban shopkeeping symbolized this change. According to the editor, the hundreds of young men "lounging about in our large towns" furnished "indisputable evidence that many of the rising generation are contracting habits which in after life, must cause a large amount of sorrow and wretchedness." The new generation of clerks lacked the industry of the southern farmer. Carolina newspapers asserted that the mercantile trade was less virtuous and masculine than agricultural or mechanical pursuits. The image of the effete merchant promoted by southern editors served to warn readers of the dangers inherent in a commercial life. Separated from the land and physical labor, the dissipated urban merchant presented "a melancholy picture." Yankee manners and degraded labor represented two critical elements in the Carolina press's representation of the greedy southern merchant.[39]

Antebellum papers in North and South Carolina further confirmed the stereotype of the grasping merchant with commentary in news stories. A writer in the *Wilmington Daily Journal* attacked local merchants for speculating in food. With the successful 1854 harvests in America and Europe, the writer believed the price in Wilmington for a barrel of flour ($13.50) to be 50 percent too high. The paper blamed the avarice of merchants. Later that year the same newspaper ran a story about a mechanic in a nearby village who had moved after his business failed. The mechanic departed without paying the account he owed the local merchant. After a few weeks the storekeeper located the man 115 miles away. The acquisitive merchant, who was, according to the paper, worth upward of seventy-five thousand dollars, hired an agent to obtain the debt from the mechanic. Eventually the account was settled. In the end the merchant paid ten dollars to recover thirty cents that the mechanic owed for a comb and some paper pins. The story concluded by mocking the merchant's "feelings of exultation" upon receiving the debt and eventual "deep gloom" when he realized his losses. The writer portrayed the storekeeper's greed as uncontrollable and irrational. While the veracity of the story is debatable, the *Daily Journal* presented it as fact.[40]

Other Carolina newspapers chose to lecture upon the evil of merchant greed in their editorials. One in the Salisbury, North Carolina, *Carolina Watchman* on November 25, 1847, asked why so many failed in the mercantile trade. The answer, according to the writer, could be found in work habits and avarice. The rising generation of merchants lacked steady work habits. More importantly, their appetite for luxuries and "excursions of pleasure" led them to neglect their business. The *Watchman* advised young merchants that the path to success required diligently working and preventing the "brightness of gold to dim your integrity, or seduce your honor." The editorial concluded that the future of Salisbury depended upon its young merchants, a theme that articles in the *Watchman* exemplified. In 1846 the paper reprinted a story from the *Richmond Observer* entitled "The Two Neighbors Reconciled" in which rival merchants become the best of friends after embracing religion. The "scandalous enmity" and jealous greed that existed between the neighboring storekeepers disintegrated before piety. Protestant order represented one answer to the growing dissipation of the merchant class. As one scholar has concluded more broadly, this message resounded from pulpits "in every decade of the antebellum era," as "ministers of every denomination in every corner of the South lamented and censured what they perceived to be the South's obsession with moneymaking and acquisition." Carolina newspapers presented greed among the region's merchants as a threat society must resist.[41]

The disparaging images of antebellum mercantile life found in North and South Carolina newspapers centered around three main themes. First, merchants subscribed to cunning Yankee practices in their trade. Second, their ability to turn a profit through artifice and the inherent nature of commercial trade combined to make storekeepers indolent. Third, merchant greed, particularly in the younger generation, threatened the virtue not just of the merchant but also of the community. Together these themes represented the retail businessman as a capricious force in southern communities. Storekeepers seemingly subscribed to values alien to Dixie, but the experience of Moses Mordecai in 1854 Charleston suggests that the relationship between the Carolina press and southern merchants was more complex. Indeed, while newspapers busily recounted stories of rapacious storekeepers, they simultaneously portrayed them as indispensable community builders for the region. The "better" class of merchants exhibited solicitude, produced needed wealth, and served as economic pillars in Carolina towns. This dichotomy was not unique to the antebellum South. Writers in Great Britain and the northern United States had long been torn between their contempt for the merchant's crass commercial values and society's dependence upon this same class for goods, urban development, and promotion of the arts. Anthony Trollope, Frederick Marryat, Charles Dickens, and such American writers as George Lippard and Charles Frederick Briggs, reflecting the influence of William Shakespeare's *Merchant of Venice* and other earlier works, often portrayed the merchant class in an unfavorable light. Though many causes produced this trend, chief among them were the tremendous commercial and industrial changes that the Anglo-American world was undergoing in the early nineteenth century. Social and economic upheaval threatened traditional values that bound small communities. Journalists and writers who observed these developments in the antebellum South assumed the same disparaging view of merchants. Ultimately, as with most western writers, the profound contradictions between the interpretation of the merchant class as a community builder and an avaricious exploiter seems to have eluded most journalists in North and South Carolina.[42]

Few Carolina newspapers printed stories about benevolent merchants. Articles that do reveal the gentler side of the southern merchant are remarkable for their maudlin didacticism. In 1838 the *Carolina Watchman* printed a story called "The Compassionate Merchant," which illustrates the typical characteristics of such narratives. The story recounts a merchant visiting a tenant in order to collect the rent. Upon entering the home the merchant found the tenant critically ill and his family hungry. The merchant choked down his grief at the sight of the "little urchins," while placing money on the kitchen table. He returned to his store and ordered his clerk to deliver provisions to the family. The journalist ends the account by noting how much better the merchant felt after accomplishing his good deeds. The *Charleston Mercury* expanded upon this theme by applying it to nation-states. Quoting *Hunt's Merchants' Magazine* the *Mercury* editor declared commerce to have a pacific influence upon foreign relations. The course of history led him to conclude that "all commercial communities have been the friends of peace, and the strongest opposers of war." Trade and its disciples, merchants, civilized the barbarian and enlightened the ignorant. The editor believed that as Christian sojourners, tradesmen would soon "make the policy of all nations pacific by sending them the Gospel of the Prince of Peace."[43]

When not charging merchants with avarice, the press in North and South Carolina thus hailed their essential role in southern economy. In 1843 the *Carolina Watchman* ran a story describing the merchant as a critical economic agent. Without this commercial middleman, agriculture and industry would reap few rewards. Quoting the *Southern Quarterly*, the article concluded that southern interests were served by merchants' accumulating vast amounts of capital, because "the richer the merchant . . . the more laborers are stimulated, and the better they are rewarded, the less fluctuation there will be in prices, the fewer revulsions in business, the greater certainty in all investments." The writer called for an end to prejudice against the merchant class. The following year the *Watchman* printed a "moral sketch" by T. S. Arthur entitled "The Merchant's Dream." The story related the plight of Algeroff the merchant. Weary of a tedious commercial life wasted in the pursuit of gold, Algeroff yearned for a life occupied with music and books. One night, after the unhappy merchant fell asleep, a "beautiful being" visited him. She called upon the store-keeper to take her hand and view the world with a "broader intelligence." The angelic guide in this Dickensian journey showed the merchant how his trade paid the artisan, textile weaver, and farmer for their products. Eventually the merchant realized he represented a "link in a great chain" between producer and consumer. Algeroff awoke a new man, cheered by the thought that he "ministered" in his sphere "to the good of all around him." Stories such as "The Merchant's Dream" not only depicted benefi-cent merchants but also helped teach Southerners the importance of commerce and highlighted the merchant's role in building towns and developing the region.[44]

Newspapers in the Carolinas often measured the growth of their communities by the size and energy of their mercantile establishments. They regularly boasted of their town's commercial gains over rival communities. Editors attributed this progress to thrifty merchants. An editorial in the *Wilmington Daily Journal* detailed the scale and practices of the town's wholesale stores. One of the largest china stores in North Carolina, operated by the firm of McRae & Harris, had recently moved into capacious new quarters in a granite-faced building with a depth of over a hundred feet front to back, stocked with imported china from Liverpool. The news story proclaimed the store to be "quite the equal to any in Charleston." The same editorial went on to list the most successful Wilmington shops and concluded that "their name is legion, and their proprietors gentlemen." Later the *Daily Journal* noted the improvements that a Mr. Munde had made in his bookstore, offering further evidence of the "spirit of progress which is abroad in our town." During periods of economic stagnation the press also looked to local merchants for relief. An 1852 editorial in the *Charleston Mercury* lamented that the rival cities of Baltimore and Savannah had begun to eclipse Charleston in the relative growth of import trade. The writer determined that the city could revive its sagging fortunes if it elected more merchants to the South Carolina legislature. It would be difficult to acknowledge more explicitly that the city's growth depended upon its merchant class. Some less obsequious stories in Carolina newspapers implicitly recognized the town-building capabilities of storekeepers. Whether protecting the reputation of a community's cotton harvest, helping the poor, or attracting trade, the press in North and South Carolina frequently presented merchants as community leaders.[45]

The odd juxtaposition of stories about the unseemly conduct of greedy merchants with paeans to their contributions delineates the Janus face of the southern merchant. Conflicting mercantile images become more complex when considering merchants' self-representations in the Carolina newspapers. Paid advertisements offered southern merchants the most direct means to influence their image in the press. As the editor of the *Weekly Raleigh Register* succinctly concluded in a January 1853 edition, "Good practical business men never neglect the department of Advertising; hence the almost (to some) unaccountable rise and progress of some establishments, while others, with apparently better chances, fail for want of even ordinary support." Regular advertisements in the antebellum United States ran without change for months at a time. What the ads lacked in variety they made up in quantity. Southern merchants purchased thousands of advertisements, most of which simply notified readers of the arrival of goods or the availability of new items. During the 1840s more successful mercantile firms experimented with visually appealing illustrated newspaper advertisements. Their content, however, like most written advertisements during the period, remained elementary. When Carolina merchants attempted to create more subtle representations of their profession in local newspapers, they resorted to editorials and the influence of their civic associations.[46]

Merchants viewed themselves as champions for orderly habits and sophistication in the South. Like their counterparts in the North, these businessmen sought "through an 'effect of accuracy' based on numerical precision, correctness, and detail" to "secure their morally dubious vocation a reputation for honesty and fairness." They believed in the adage that time is money. A strong work ethic, regular business competition, public education, travel, and white racial hegemony represented key elements of their nascent ideology, and many storekeepers attempted to publicly link themselves with these values. A smaller number of merchants sought to impress these ideals upon their neighbors. The press offered them an important tool for both these purposes.[47]

Reprinted articles from *Hunt's Merchants' Magazine and Commercial Review*, consistently expressing the virtues of orderly business habits, served as a mouthpiece for merchant interests in North and South Carolina newspapers. A January 8, 1850, editorial in the *Charleston Mercury* recommended the suggestions of one such article to local residents. The story compared the energy of the merchant possessing strong business habits to the "forest bred Indian." Each of these types of individual had "schooled his senses into unerring habits of nice and accurate observation." Success depended upon their ability to understand and react to changes in their respective environments. Publicly merchants honored the virtues of intelligence, hard work, and skill over luck in the volatile world of commerce. A merchant later suggested in the *Mercury* that "lucky fellows" are simply those who "know what they are doing, and how to do it the right way." The personal correspondence of Carolina merchants reflected these themes of morality and order.[48]

Merchants' business habits influenced not only their reputation in the community but also their standing with important creditors in the North. Firms that produced credit reports on southern merchants, R. G. Dun & Company being the most important, determined the financial health of a store by evaluating its yearly sales, capital investment, and business reputation. The local merchants and lawyers who wrote these reports paid special attention to the latter. A northern wholesale firm hired the Fayetteville, North Carolina, merchant Peter Mallett to write credit reports on the stores in his district of the state. Reports he wrote in 1846 reveal the importance placed upon a strong business ethic. Mallett recommended that the Greenville merchant W. K. Delaney receive a generous extension of credit. The brief report estimated Delaney's capital between twelve and fifteen thousand dollars and his yearly sales to be eight thousand. More importantly Mallett concluded that Delaney had good character and moderate business habits and that he was generally a "fine fellow." The Washington, North Carolina, firm Bernard & Sons boasted capital exceeding seventy-five thousand dollars. According to Mallett, Mr. Bernard served as the "Capitalist" rather than his son, a lawyer who seemed to be "no business man." Establishments with only "tolerable" business habits received more critical treatment in Mallett's reports. One such firm in Greenville, Cooper & Strong, had the added burden of being recent "Yankee" immigrants. The credit report bluntly concluded that it was "well enough to let them alone." Mallett held his fellow merchants to a high standard of public conduct in business, a level he seems to have achieved himself when in 1827 he assisted a Cheraw, South Carolina, storekeeper by carrying $3,390 in cash to his partner in Fayetteville. A strong business reputation proved critical in acquiring access to the credit in northern cities on which southern merchants depended. Not surprisingly many of them embraced respectable public rituals to improve their credit standings.[49]

Antebellum merchants in North and South Carolina expressed their opinions regarding the public role of the businessman in their personal writing. Shortly after his eighteenth birthday, the aspiring merchant Cushing B. Hassell adopted a lengthy list of resolutions. He wrote in his diary that henceforth he would follow temperance principles, quit gaming and using profane or silly language (e.g., "by granny" or "dog my cat"), and exhibit honesty on all occasions. These rules of conduct derived from Hassell's deeply held Protestant beliefs and prepared him to assume the expected public role of the southern merchant. A reputation for drinking, gambling, or any other kind of dissipation could ruin a Carolina storekeeper. Joseph Biggs and others in Williamston, North Carolina, were mortified when a merchant named Bayley left for a purchasing trip to New York City in an utterly drunken state. Biggs wrote his brother that the man appeared "hardly able to ride." Similarly, in 1837 John Burbidge wrote a friend that when he discovered an associate had been seen in "bad company" in a gambling house he pitied him. Like many businessmen, Burbidge assumed such behavior revealed a lack of integrity. Ultimately such conduct would impact business adversely. Burbidge declared himself too ambitious to meet such an end.[50]

While Carolina merchants like Burbidge and Hassell attempted to shape their public image in personal correspondence, it had limited influence upon their representation in the press. Membership in civic associations offered a more effective means of public self-construction for merchants. Forming active civic associations allowed Carolina merchants to garner favorable publicity as community leaders while simultaneously disseminating mercantile values. Southern merchants and the associations they supported became especially prominent in the field of education. Many storekeepers nurtured schools in their communities. Jonathan Worth, a Quaker merchant in Asheboro, North Carolina, invited coreligionists to teach in a local academy he financially supported. As a young merchant in Halifax, North Carolina, Cushing Hassell joined a debating club called the Philodemic Association. Later he and his brother paid a New Hampshire teacher $150 to teach female scholars in Williamston, North Carolina. By 1849 Hassell had been appointed a trustee to both the Williamston Academy and the University of North Carolina. In 1856 the merchant Joseph Cathey served as a representative from his hometown and county, Forks of Pigeon, Haywood County, to a general convention of the Friends of Education in North Carolina. Such activities imparted a prominent status to these businessmen. The cultural accomplishments of merchant clubs and associations gained even more recognition in North and South Carolina newspapers. The development of the Mercantile Library Association in Charleston provides one such example.[51]

Formed in 1844, the Charleston Mercantile Library Association sought the "improvement" of each member through the joint contributions and collective efforts of the membership. The association's board of directors believed merchants needed to learn the principles of their trade. The association's 1852 report declared that the businessman's "hazardous profession" required an education to shield him from consequences "against which no mere experience can ever effectually protect him." The report expressed hope that the instruction available through the association would continue until the "love of knowledge is stimulated, habits of industry encouraged, the taste refined, the standard of excellence elevated, and the mind enlarged beyond the limits of mere trade and profit." To achieve this end the association sponsored lectures and established a city library. Thus a Colonel Preston from Columbia, South Carolina, delivered a lecture on the dignity of modern commerce one evening, while the following week an engineer explained the operation of the "Caloric Engine." The association's reading room came complete with a course of study for members who wished to add method to their efforts at self-improvement. Charleston newspapers announced meetings of the Mercantile Library Association and reviewed its lecture series. These articles depicted an organization of professionals dedicated to personal and communal development. The reality behind the image presented in the newspapers was that the Mercantile Library Association had difficulty recruiting members and supporting its reading room. Its public relations success appeared more certain. The board of directors recognized that the association's efforts to refine public taste would "gain a strong hold upon public favor and sympathy, which would greatly redound to its reputation and prosperity."[52]

Social grace represented a second major theme in the self-construction of the merchant class in the antebellum Carolinas. Storekeepers employed newspapers to advance an image of refinement that reflected their own values. Careful to swear allegiance to the slave South, merchants did pass judgment on the coarser aspects of their society. The absence of civility in developing southern towns particularly galled antebellum merchants. The *Carolina Watchman* printed an extract from an 1839 letter written by a merchant recently settled in Vicksburg, Mississippi. As conditions in the western state looked "worse and worse," the merchant pitied his associates who "can't collect any thing—the only money collected is by foreigners in the U. States Court." Businessmen could not seek compensation through the courts, because the state's legal system busied itself arbitrarily enforcing brutal criminal laws. The merchant informed his friends back in North Carolina that without serious reforms Mississippi offered no future for the civilized merchant. Carolina merchants shared the perspective of one of their number who in 1845 described his neighbors in Columbus, Kentucky, as "rough in manners" but said, "I think I shall like them after getting a little accustomed to their ways." Shopkeepers who periodically moved their operation further west became especially interested in the cultural life of a region and the civility of its people. Well-traveled merchants wrote editorials in Carolina newspapers comparing the advantages of particular towns. These self-styled urbane gentlemen cared whether a community had a reading room or academy. Pronouncements in the press made their concerns and pretensions known.[53]

Business and cultural ties to northern cities also served to make southern merchants appear sophisticated. Carolina editors allowed local storekeepers to use their publications for describing recent purchasing trips or reporting the latest financial news from the North. Their familiarity with cultural and business trends in the North impressed even southern partisans. Editorials and advertisements for clothing publicized the socioeconomic ties between southern merchants and the North. Yet newspapers denounced local merchants for Yankee sympathies while filling their columns with advertisements for the "latest fashions" from New York City or Philadelphia. In announcements intended to lure women customers, merchants rhapsodized over the clothing they purchased from the "most fashionable" northern tailors. The occasional storekeeper promised to teach women the northern "art" of cutting garments. The firm of Hastie & Nicol in Greenville, South Carolina, made its ties to the North explicit by naming its shop the "New York Store." Carolina merchants used local newspapers to introduce the concept of annual fashion seasons, and advertisements declared that with the beginning of the spring, summer, or winter, smart dressers should purchase the latest clothing. Of course for the fashionable, last year's style was no longer suitable. Even stores serving poor farming families in rural communities advertised new designs for simple calico dresses. The manuscript record leaves no hint as to where storekeepers gained their knowledge of fashion and women's tastes, but undoubtedly many welcomed advice from their wives and daughters. It is not difficult to imagine that sophisticated women like Jorantha Semmes in Memphis or Barcia Norfleet Gordon O'Bryan in Franklin, Tennessee, influenced what their husbands and sons sold in their stores. It also seems likely that the same northern wholesalers who sold them their goods coached southern merchants about the latest European fashion trends. Carolina editors aided the retail enterprise of antebellum merchants by cultivating fashion sensibility among their readership. The *Charleston Mercury* kept its readers apprised of the latest bonnet styles and which one was appropriate for each occasion. The editor gave a typical fashion recommendation in 1853 when he declared the latest style of European bonnets a success because they appeared "light as a feather, transparent as gauze," and lay on the head like a "Neapolitan plateau." Editorials and advertisements thus confirmed merchants' status as arbiters of southern refinement.[54]

The self-image storekeepers advanced in the Carolina press involved a number of inventions. The merchants' orderly habits and work ethic did encourage them to accept the dictates of timed "work-discipline." This said, the nature of their labor required few merchants to work as long or hard as yeoman farmers in the South. Selling, trading, and purchasing goods exacted greater psychological than physical demands from the storekeeper. Merchant representations in newspapers also embellished their relative sophistication. They did travel and study more then most Southerners, but their cultural accomplishments rarely matched those of the region's wealthy planter class. Southern merchants projected a distorted image in the Carolina press, contrasting sharply with the equally misleading stereotype of the greedy, Yankeefied merchant. These divergent themes helped shape the public contours of merchant culture in antebellum North and South Carolina.[55]

Storekeepers in the Carolinas and across the antebellum South operated within a cultural and economic no-man's-land. They functioned as middlemen in a society that subscribed to the agrarian values articulated by the wealthy planter class. White Southerners depended upon merchants to sustain the agricultural economy, a relationship that fostered both popular contempt and admiration. The conflicting images of the grasping storekeeper and the civic-minded merchant found in the Carolina press reflected popular ambivalence regarding the mercantile trade. Merchants would continue to be subjected to ambivalent treatment in Carolina newspapers until war eventually changed the face of southern society. Merchants themselves further muddled the picture by offering their own self-constructions in Carolina newspapers. Their attempts to portray themselves as refined and industrious southern businessmen achieved limited success in assuaging public suspicion of their profession. A great number of opinion-makers and common folk viewed merchants as cultural interlopers in their idealized agrarian South.

3

The Merchant Family in the Antebellum South

The family was the center of southern merchant culture. The ties between husband and wife, parent and child, brother and sister provided the ultimate foundation for merchant values. While the political economy of the antebellum South circumscribed merchant culture, family defined it. Household relations affirmed the bourgeois and conservative ideals that combined to distinguish merchants from the mass of southern society. The dynamics of all nineteenth-century white families incorporated varying degrees of affection, materialism, paternalism, and racism, but the peculiar blend of these qualities within the merchant family made it unique. The families of neighboring yeoman farmers sought independence, political standing, and growing market return from the land's bounty. The planter family achieved great financial rewards and political prestige from the cotton economy of the slave South. The merchant family not only exhibited characteristics similar to those of both the yeoman and planter classes; its values spanned the growing sectional divide of antebellum America.[1]

Men and women in merchant families embraced a variety of bourgeois and conservative cultural ideals. Over the course of the antebellum period their households became more emotionally inward-looking than those of their southern neighbors. Well-read parents exposed their children to northern magazines and European literature before sending them to private academies or tutors. This emphasis upon education helped demarcate a cultural boundary between merchant families and most other white Southerners outside the planter class. Education and the dictates of the mercantile trade also transformed marital relations. Husbands and wives experienced the separate spheres of home and work long before most antebellum Southerners did. Few families lived adjacent to their store, and the presence of a merchant's wife behind the counter, although resorted to on occasion, provoked comment. Merchant households saw their economic self-sufficiency decline as wives and children produced fewer goods in the home. The same process began to recast the antebellum planter family.

The marital ideal for the majority of men and women in both classes seems to have been what historians have called the "companionate marriage." As described by Jane Turner Censer, within such relationships "husbands and wives should be linked by mutual attraction and should provide affectionate support for each other while rearing a family." This is not to suggest that men in planter or merchant families surrendered control in a rush to adopt northern gender roles. Rather they were "refining their understanding of domestic relations." Women and slaves still held inferior social positions, but the status of the former was in flux, particularly within merchant families. The type of paternalism that Elizabeth Fox-Genovese has asserted defined gender relations in planter families, characterized in part by a "peculiar combination of hierarchically sanctioned male dominance in the household and bourgeois egalitarianism among men in the public sphere," was breaking down in merchant households by the late antebellum period. Whether one is inclined, like Fox-Genovese, to view the notion of companionate marriage in the Old South as mere "bourgeois rhetoric" or is willing to accept the persuasive arguments made by Anya Jabour, Jane Turner Censer, and other historians that the changes in planter marriages were more substantive, there can be no question that domestic relations in merchant families of the antebellum South were evolving into something more akin to those found in northern homes. By the 1840s one driving force for this change was the expansion of the market economy. Some historians contend, however, that the market economy made a more superficial impression on the planter household. Indeed, many wealthy planters feared the social effect upon southern communities of unrestrained commercial relations. Far from feeling threatened, merchant families attempted to improve their material and intellectual lives by consuming the growing abundance of goods and ideas available in mid-nineteenth-century America. The unique role of merchant families as brokers and consumers of this material culture influenced directly the personal relationships within them.[2]

Economic ties to such commercial cities as Philadelphia and New York allowed merchant families to wear French fashions, read the latest English novels, and decorate their homes with goods produced in northern shops. When not spending store profits on family consumption, merchants invested their money and accumulated capital. These activities seem to correspond with the intellectual mores and liberal capitalist practices of the bourgeoisie in Victorian England and the northern free states, yet the cultural parallels remained incomplete. The antebellum merchant family followed too many tenets of a conservative southern ideology to be able to develop a comprehensive bourgeois identity like that found in the industrializing North.

Slavery, patriarchy, and evangelicalism profoundly influenced the intellectual and material ventures of the merchant family. Like many of their southern neighbors, merchants bought and sold slaves. Merchant families who did not have slaves residing in their households still defended the institution and subscribed to the racial codes of the antebellum South. Despite their education and national cultural ties, fathers, husbands, and brothers exhibited little interest in exchanging their accustomed prerogatives within the family for the presumably more equitable gender relations evolving in northern and English families. Evidence also suggests that men and women in merchant families viewed their world through the prism of southern evangelical Christianity. Their religious sensibility held preaching, Bible study, and the conversion experience as fundamental to proper Christian living. Over time this religious impulse alternately complemented and challenged the behavior of merchant families. Ultimately all of these factors tended to restrain the influence of northern bourgeois culture in southern merchant families.[3]

Unfolding the layers of antebellum merchant culture requires an examination of how competing liberal capitalist, even bourgeois, values on the one hand and traditional agrarian values on the other shaped daily family life. Doing so will also help to explain merchant family prestige within, and alienation from, southern society. These families were from the South but not of the South. Unlike most of their neighbors, they integrated bourgeois practices and values into their daily activities. Physical separation between home and work was the most distinctive feature of these households. Like many northern professionals and artisans, southern merchants—who were overwhelmingly men—left their wives and children each day to tend their stores. Most southern men, whether farmers or artisans, lived and worked near their families, often right there beside them. By contrast, husbands and wives in merchant families rarely saw each other during business hours. This was more true for large, well-established merchants than for small storekeepers and grocers. Passing the time on a lazy summer day, the Wall Hill, Mississippi, storekeeper Isham Howze wrote, "What can I do? I could find work to do at home, but here I must stay, whether I have any thing to do or not: I must be found at my post, whenever I am able to be there." Yet even Howze, in a small village with only an occasional customer, felt it necessary to follow a strict time and work discipline at his place of business, an urge that proved to be one of many responsibilities of business that would plague the hesitating merchant. Heavy sales periods increased a merchant's absence from home. Samuel Aby wrote his parents that the fall trade of 1847 kept him and his partners "up late & early all the time busy as bees."[4] To attract the business of distant farmers who might travel as much as several hours to buy goods, merchants like Aby typically opened their stores at dawn and conducted business till nearly dark or later. The physical separation between home and work created divergent worlds for husbands and wives—even in those rarer instances when it was the wife rather than the husband who worked at the store.[5]

As noted in chapter 1, the vast majority of women in the retail trade were, in fact, artisans. Though rarely appearing in the manuscript record, skilled women dominated the ranks of milliners, mantua makers, and seamstresses. Selling goods as well as their labor, these businesswomen, many of whom were widows supporting families, set prices, occasionally gave credit, and advertised in newspapers. It seems likely that they followed traditional labor patterns, not limiting their work to a business day nor enjoying separation between work and home. A relatively small number of women operated larger dry-goods and grocery stores that depended solely upon retail sales rather than on producing custom goods. For instance, by the 1850s women accounted for an estimated 5 percent of small grocers in Petersburg, Virginia. What record some of these women left behind suggests that, like their male counterparts, they understood the rule to be: stay behind the counter whenever possible. Timothy J. Lockley's study of antebellum Savannah offers a dramatic illustration. Over the course of the 1820s, 1830s, and 1840s, a number of women in the Georgia city received fines and other penalties for repeatedly violating Sabbath ordinances, as well as for selling liquor without a license and "entertaining Negroes." Some of these women probably broke all three laws. Deeper examination of such cases would undoubtedly reveal the social causes of their actions, but the economic imperative that prompted some women to keep their stores open in order to sell to all types of customers would have been well understood by merchants like Isham Howze, even if they deplored it.[6]

Operating a store required time discipline. Merchants measured time and attested to the veracity of platitudes that equated time with money. A closed store sold no goods. The minutes spent traveling to and from the store and the hours employed within its walls reflected their commitment to a commercial regimen. The Atlanta merchant and Civil War blockade-runner Sidney Root articulated the pervasive commercial spirit when he declared, "Among my rules, which became habits, were these: to retire early and rise early, to work hard and master the business." John Burbidge, operating a store in Walterboro, South Carolina, assured his New York cousin that personal and familial ambition demanded industry. At the end of one letter Burbidge confidently wrote, "You will not find in me a rolling stone which gathers no moss."[7] Time away from home, in the store came to be viewed as productive. Even a bored Isham Howze knew that the work he could have been accomplishing at home rather than languishing behind his counter would not improve his long-term economic condition or reputation.[8]

Time discipline and dependence upon the store also shaped the merchant household, which was regulated largely by women. Merchant husbands on occasion did employ the business skills of their wives and daughters in the family store, particularly if they wished to avoid having to hire a clerk. More typically husbands applied the money their wives brought to the marriage toward improving the operation of their businesses. Aside from these contributions, most women supported the merchant family at home. With their husbands away at the store or on purchasing junkets in eastern cities, wives held profound influence within the family. Over the course of the antebellum period they, like many plantation mistresses, produced fewer goods in their homes and became their families' primary consumers. They purchased food, medicine, clothing, and household goods for their families. The wife of a successful merchant, much like the plantation mistress, might also have the responsibility of overseeing the family's house slaves. John Fite, son of an Atlanta merchant, remembered his mother as a household "superintendent." She personally did little physical labor but supervised "the negro women" who performed "the spinning and weaving . . . and very often . . . would hire a white woman to make the clothes."[9]

More fundamental than securing the material wants of the family, child-raising remained the principal duty of merchant wives. Indeed as parents merchant husbands and wives both revealed a bourgeois mien.[10]

Like many parents in the antebellum South and in the wider Victorian world, merchants and their wives looked homeward to their children for personal happiness. Most could relate to the sentiment expressed by the widowed Governor Israel Pickens of Alabama, who viewed his children as "now my only objects of affectionate concern and the very trouble they afford me is perhaps at this moment a blessing, as they furnish subjects of attention both to my body and mind." Unlike Pickens and many other planters, however, merchant men and women raised their children in a manner that encouraged neither aggressive, much less "ferocious," boys nor dainty ladies. Nor did they seek to crush their children's independent will. Rather parents in merchant families struggled to instill in their children self-discipline shaped by hard work and Christian morality. Parents braced for the task, in part, by adopting bourgeois familial roles.[11]

The father, as the family's presumed moral guardian, attempted to direct the intellectual and moral education of the children. Once again the example set by Isham Howze is instructive. The Mississippi merchant displayed a keen devotion to molding the consciences of his children from their infancy through adulthood. Howze's journal reveals his deep interest in the moral qualities his seven children exhibited. Despite, or perhaps because of, his own misgivings concerning his stagnant career, he wrote long passages exploring the children's character and the likely obstacles they would confront in life. If nothing else, it seemed a constructive way to employ his time behind the counter. An 1851 entry declared his eldest son, Adrian, to be Howze's "chief hope." The eighteen-year-old displayed "industry, economy, and morals," and "for his age and experience," he was "skillful and enterprizing [sic]." The discipline Adrian received as a youth had its desired effect. As a young clerk in Memphis, he avoided the temptations that appeared in a "thousand forms." Howze left similar descriptions, with differing assessments, for each of his children. He hoped his son William might some day be a "literary man," while young James, then age four, would receive a preacher's calling. Aside from their potential for marriage, little comment is offered on the prospects of his two daughters, Susan and Elizabeth. While Howze's journals disclose his own assumptions regarding what constituted virtuous character, the intent behind the observations was prescriptive.[12]

Howze filled his diaries and letters with advice to his children. This counsel assumed neither a commanding nor a supplicatory tone. The merchant suggested his children follow the moral precepts that his experience had proven sound. When they failed to observe this general code, however, Howze noted his objections and accepted their decisions. Thus he cautioned his children to "not be in haste to marry—25 or 30 years of age will be soon enough for my boys, & 20 for my daughters." When several of his children ignored this admonition and married young anyway, Howze promptly resigned himself to the new circumstances. This unarticulated philosophy of child-rearing manifested itself four years later when his son Adrian accompanied Howze's business partner to a neighborhood party—the same partner he had hoped would provide a strong moral influence on the son (see chapter 1). Isham Howze believed such activities threatened the participants with dissipation and eventual ruin. Though he penned a cool entry in his journal, the merchant permitted his son's attendance only with a prayer for the Lord's protection. In practice, the paternal regime that Howze established seems neither delinquent nor onerous.[13]

Evidence suggests that many southern merchants embraced a similar approach to child-rearing. Cushing B. Hassell also sought to teach his children through example and judicious counsel. In the early spring of 1847 the Williamston, North Carolina, merchant and father ordered a piano from the New York firm of White & Barnes. The expensive instrument in the family parlor testified to the success he enjoyed as a merchant. Yet pedagogy was the stated object behind the purchase. Hassell had obtained the piano for the edification of his daughter. Such material possessions reveal as much about Hassell's child-rearing practices as they do about any anxieties he might have felt about his status. The children of southern merchants found themselves surrounded by music and books. Parents expected their children to benefit from the lessons conveyed by this environment. Fathers and mothers employed such material objects, along with formal education, to instruct their children intellectually and morally. The discipline required in such education was explicit while its method remained benign. Hassell directed the education of his children through their environment as well as with cautionary tales from his own experiences. When the instruction failed, he accepted the outcome with the same aplomb Isham Howze exhibited. Shortly after the purchase of the piano, Hassell reluctantly allowed his children to attend a traveling circus. He declared such exhibitions frivolous yet relented in the belief that "it was well enough to gratify children with a view of [the circus] once but grown people should have better sense than to be led off so repeatedly to the gratification of a vain & idle curiosity." Such resignation to the will of children reflected a philosophy of child-rearing that revered individual volition. Merchant parents did define the parameters of their children's instruction, though. The merchant Charles Ellis Sr. wrote detailed letters to his sons when they were attending school away from home. These letters represented Ellis's attempt to make his children "real students" rather than "mere pretenders." Pages are dedicated to describing the virtues of self-discipline and those habits that a "young man that intends to exhibit any distinction in the world, and make his way to fortune & the highest honours of his country" needed to possess. Ellis was a successful Richmond merchant with a forceful personality. His letters, like those of Hassell and other merchants, reveal an appreciation for Christian morality and a belief that intellectual accomplishment served as the ultimate goal.[14]

Mothers in merchant families sought the same objectives through other means. The relations between mothers and their children demonstrated the influence of a growing national bourgeois culture. As with most southern women, the identity that women in merchant families assumed proceeded from their domestic and, more fundamentally, maternal roles. Yet while many of their southern sisters lost themselves amid obligations to children and husband, merchant mothers kept much of their personal character intact in the performance of their maternal duties. Their child-rearing practices frequently mirrored those of their husbands. Mothers taught their children discipline and personal responsibility by their own Christian example. Their child-rearing rarely depended on physical coercion. Within their domestic realm mothers instructed their children in reading, religion, and social grace. Lessons from the Bible and rules of social etiquette supplemented the more formal education of the schoolhouse. Quite often merchant women continued these lessons for financial gain when their children left the home. One such woman from a South Carolina family decided to teach guitar lessons while her children attended school. The training and interest in teaching possessed by these women distinguished them from their sisters in the planter class. While plantation mistresses like Margaret Collet of North Carolina impressed upon their daughters the "importance of education" and urged them to gain "all useful knowledge," these mothers also, as Elizabeth Fox-Genovese has argued convincingly, "firmly discouraged those daughters from becoming teachers." Driven by financial need and apparent interest, anecdotal evidence suggests daughters and wives of storekeepers often taught school for at least a few years. This in part explains their interest in teaching their children self-discipline as well as practical skills while cultivating their own personalities. Parents whose children failed to exhibit self-discipline were open to criticism. Catherine Stine, whose husband operated the Cake & Beer shop in Baltimore, Maryland, questioned the child-rearing practices of her merchant brother Samuel Aby and his wife Sarah. Writing to her mother in 1843, Stine declared her nephew Tom "one of the worst of children," a boy spoiled by Sarah, who "never pretends to correct him." Tom's reckless character is particularly apparent when compared to the behavior of his brother, Charles, whom Stine describes as a "sweet boy." Stine held her brother and particularly her sister-in-law responsible for the boy's poor conduct. The parents failed to inculcate "little Tom" with the self-discipline expected from children of their social position.[15]

Upon examination it is not surprising that merchant wives shared many bourgeois values with their husbands for they came from similar backgrounds. Like their husbands, they generally received an excellent education by the standards of antebellum southern society. Similar to the instruction that children received in nineteenth-century New England, the lessons they mastered in schoolhouses and academies across the South highlighted such Victorian ideals as self-discipline and time management. Letters that Mary Caroline Jacocks wrote from the Oxford Female Academy in Oxford, North Carolina, to her merchant brother Charles Jacocks are suggestive and typical. When relating the progress of classes, Mary devoted special attention to her marks. She excelled in most subjects, but her instructors seemed especially pleased with her self-discipline. The stock phrase "deportment very good and person neat" echoes through the evaluations that Mary Jacocks received from the academy. The experience of twelve-year-old Elizabeth Adams offers another example. In 1844 young Elizabeth, who would marry the Louisiana merchant Jean Baptiste Bres four years later, passed the winter writing essays that bore such titles as "Perseverance & Friendship" and "Neatness and Order." She believed the latter represented "two great qualities necessary in all classes of life whether it be among the rich or the poor." Elizabeth concluded her reflections on the subject by adding that her teacher "does not fail to impress it on our minds while we are young that we may grow up and be patterns of neatness and order." Securing marital and domestic happiness remained the fundamental purpose of education for young ladies in the antebellum South, but despite this conservative goal, a more

modern appreciation for self-discipline, thrift, and work figured prominently in their instruction. The bourgeois values that Mary Jacocks and
Elizabeth Adams, as well as their friends from the ranks of the planter
class, learned during their formal education they later passed on to their
own children.[16]

Compared to most antebellum southern women, mothers and daughters from merchant families enjoyed more opportunities outside the home.
As noted earlier, many women taught school for several years before mar-
rying. Little evidence suggests that merchants viewed young schoolteach-
ers as particularly attractive matches emotionally or financially; more
likely mutual regard for education and liberal capitalist values brought
teachers and merchants into the same society. Both men and women often
championed public education. While much of the planter class exhibited little interest in the movement, Jonathan Daniel Wells found that
middle-class support for public education "helped southerners from many
different professional and commercial careers to conclude their identity
differed from that of other southern whites." Once betrothed, most commercial men expected their brides to leave the schoolhouse behind, yet
this domestic ideal often collapsed before economic necessity. The money
Elizabeth Howze earned while teaching in Chulahoma, Mississippi, sustained her family during several moribund periods in her husband Isham's
mercantile career. Teaching alternately in local schoolhouses and in her
home while raising seven children proved trying. In 1852 a gloomy Isham
Howze reflected in his diary, "My poor wife has a hard time of it *with her
little school* to attend to, and her sick family upon her hands, and her husband powerless." Mothers, sisters, and daughters from merchant families
voiced similar frustrations or hopes. Martha Webb declared to her brother
Charles Jacocks that her pupils proved so "irregular" in their habits that
the only reward her four months of instruction had reaped lay in the
scholarly accomplishments of her own children. Returning to the classroom in 1851 after raising several merchant sons, Barcia Norfleet Gordon
O'Bryan worried that her small class in Franklin, Tennessee, seemed insig-
nificant, though she tried not to "despise the day of small things." These
and other women during more tranquil moments in their lives found their
classroom activities personally fulfilling.[17]

Aside from teaching and occasional work in the family store, merchant wives in urban settings busied themselves with community activities. The experience of the Ladies Benevolent Society in Wilmington,

North Carolina, is illustrative. A volunteer organization of women from mercantile, professional, and planting families, the society operated a store where gentlemen could send their clothes for mending. The "depository" also offered women instruction in proper needlework. Like working in the classroom, participation in such associations gave merchant wives opportunities to perform more public roles than most white women had in the antebellum South. In various forms, most of their social roles involved teaching, whether disseminating lessons on thrift, economy, and hard work in the classroom or in the larger community. Naturally most merchant wives, like those in planter families, subscribed to the domestic ideal. One southern newspaper plainly captured the essence of this ideal when it told women that submitting to household tasks, "however repugnant," was better than "doom[ing] yourself to a loveless home." Custom and law circumscribed the role women could play. Only sound household management and a measure of submission on the part of the wife could justify her husband's love. Despite these obstacles, merchant wives frequently employed their skills within and without the home. Their conduct reveals the growing influence that northern and European bourgeois culture had on southern life during the late antebellum period, particularly among the region's commercial classes in larger towns and cities.[18]

The influence of nineteenth-century Victorian ideals extended to sibling relationships within merchant families as well. Affection and business dictated the tone of these relationships across the Old South. Family ties proved the most enduring avenues of commercial and emotional support in an unpredictable agricultural economy. The themes of sibling love and commercial trade are intertwined in the historical record. The very discourse employed in personal letters suggests the occasional subversion of sharp distinctions between the former and latter. Letters designed to inform a loved one on a wide variety of issues made the coincidence of these subjects quite pronounced. The manner in which familial devotion and business interests shaped these sibling relationships once again affirms the impact of a commercial bourgeois culture upon the families of southern merchants.[19]

Upon receiving news of his father's death in the spring of 1853, Samuel Aby wrote a letter to his brother Charles, a midshipman then serving on the USS *Delaware*. As the family suffered a profound loss, the death of its moral patriarch, Samuel revealed to Charles that "I can hardly enjoy myself, that I shall feel all the time sad & unhappy, for really & truly did I love & respect him." He continued in this melancholy vein over several paragraphs. His solemn tone, however, was fleeting. Aby concluded his devotional epistle with a lengthy description of his business activities. He reported that the new goods he had ordered for his store had yet to arrive, but "trade with us has been very fair and prosperity [is] cheering." Resorting to a cliché suitable in light of his correspondent, Aby hoped a strong cotton crop that year would mean "fair seas ahead" for his business. Thematic juxtaposition of business and family is characteristic of merchant correspondence. Like most Southerners, from the small farmer to the largest planter, merchants passed along work-related news to their brothers and sisters. What distinguishes the correspondence of such siblings from the writings of their contemporaries is the vast number of references to sales, deal making, and general business enterprise. Details from the ledger book flourished amid paragraphs relating family gossip. Even in letters to family members with no connection to the mercantile trade, merchants dwelled upon their commercial interests.[20]

Southern merchants enjoyed sharing their business philosophies with their brothers and sisters. Throughout 1823, the Port Gibson, Mississippi, storekeeper Horace Carpenter sent money to his family in Munroe, Connecticut. The financial support seemed freely, even lovingly, given. Carpenter made no remonstrations against his family's demands but did lecture his brothers and nephews on their unsteady habits and faltering ambition. He held himself up as an example of what a "determination to succeed" could accomplish. Carpenter boasted that he never conformed to "old established opinions or customs—or shaping any conduct by any other rule, than that prompted by the monitor within." After further strong counsel, the Mississippian went on to give an account of his profits over the preceding two months. Trade advice and summaries of profit margins in family correspondence increased when more than one sibling worked in the mercantile trade. The letters passed between the Biggs brothers, Asa, Kader, Joseph, and William, all of whom operated stores in North Carolina or Mississippi, included long discussions of their businesses.[21]

Of course not all such communication glorified the profession. Edward Rumsey operated a grocery in Greenville, Kentucky, from the mid-1830s through the 1860s. When his brother James contemplated entering the mercantile trade, Edward warned him "it is a specious + delusive business and cannot succeed to any great extent, without patience, much attention + economy in all its details." Sibling devotion induced Rumsey to caution his brother against entering such a volatile career. As the letter stated, only regular habits, indeed even a bourgeois mentality, could secure prosperity for a southern merchant. It seems that by the 1850s, as the market and agricultural economy grew in Kentucky, business improved for Edward. Nevertheless no evidence suggests that James Rumsey left his teaching position in Hopkinsville, Kentucky, for a career in the mercantile trade.[22]

The ties between merchant family siblings traversed obstacles familiar to most antebellum Southerners. Religion, marriage, illness, and westward migration all mediated family relationships. Whether facing adversity or enjoying success, the correspondence between brothers and sisters in merchant families reveals confidence in specific principles. Assumptions regarding economy, discipline, and success shaped the world of these families. Siblings reflected upon these issues in their personal letters. They cultivated order in their public and private lives and expected the same from their families. The merchant home attempted to integrate emotional support with business opportunities to create a cohesive whole. The financial and psychological success of this delicate balancing act depended upon the specific characteristics of the family. Its variety of personalities and attitudes notwithstanding, the sibling correspondence of merchant families suggests that a certain bourgeois design imbued the larger merchant culture of the antebellum South.

These factors also fundamentally shaped such apparently private concerns as courting and marriage. Love and money typically dictated courting practices. Examining courtship manuals and specific encounters, the historian Steven M. Stowe found that by the 1820s, when young Southerners, particularly those with means, were entering into courtship with thoughts of eventual marriage, they placed ever greater value on personal happiness over such mundane considerations as wealth. The daughter of a Murfreesboro, Tennessee, merchant wrote in her diary a few years before the Civil War, "I don't think station always brings happiness, any more than wealth does." The courting letters and diaries from merchant families reflect this theme of romantic passion. More practical considerations influenced decisions in courtship, and wealth and social position rarely disappeared entirely from personal calculations. As with men and women from the growing northern middle classes, courtship and marriage practices in southern merchant culture attempted to reach a respectable balance between the demands of an increasingly bourgeois society and impetuous romanticism.[23]

Courting and its various rituals gave southern women a rare opportunity to realize meaningful control over their personal lives. Men from antebellum commercial families, like other southern men, generally expected deference from their wives and daughters. Southern custom and law publicly sustained their private assumptions. Courting, more specifically the practice of choosing a marital partner, represented a notable exception to this order. Women, particularly those from wealthy or established families, could exercise significant independence in rejecting or accepting suitors. As romantic ideals like affection and friendship came to shape how Southerners envisioned marriage, parents left a growing number of marital decisions in the hands of their daughters. More educated, better read, and more sophisticated than most of their southern sisters, women from merchant families wielded this fragile authority to attain, they hoped, affection and status.[24]

Cushing Hassell, a merchant and Baptist minister from Martin County, North Carolina, experienced the ultimate power a woman could wield during courtship. In 1838 the thirty-eight-year-old Hassell courted the widow Foreman for most of the year. Despite his best efforts, Foreman demurred when he proposed marriage, because she found the idea of raising his four children unbearable. Hassell pleaded with her, declaring that if she refused him he would never court again, but Foreman stood her ground. Merchants occasionally recognized their weakness vis-a-vis women during courting in quite explicit terms. When Jane Marriot seemed indifferent toward her beau Isaac Proctor during his many visits, the young storekeeper begged her not to "trifle" with his affections. He compared the tenor of their recent correspondence and found that while his letters "had breathed so much devotion," hers had "said so little." Proctor explored his pathetic situation in some detail. Jane Marriot, like the widow Foreman, had the power to accept or reject her suitor. The relative command women enjoyed while courting often proved fleeting, yet placed within a broader analysis of the language and rituals of courtship, it suggests the development of a bourgeois identity within southern antebellum merchant culture.[25]

Like the children of the southern planter class, with whom they frequently socialized, male merchants and the daughters of established commercial men sought one another's company at dances, picnics, family socials, and other social affairs that allowed young men and women to mingle in a relatively structured environment. There they remained free

to choose their company. Diaries and letters suggest that parents in mercantile families rarely directed their children to marry primarily for such
base considerations as wealth or status. To be sure, parents with means
improved the odds of a favorable match by seeing to it that their children circulated in the same society as the children of lawyers, doctors,
and planters. Yet even as parents and other family members might share,
during a courtship, any misgivings they had about an eventual match,
most relented before the desires of the interested couple. Status and wealth
continued to influence whether or not a family approved of a prospective
spouse for a son or daughter. As the antebellum period came to a close,
however, young people within merchant society increasingly sought marriages that combined practical considerations with romantic love.

The language that couples adopted during courtship and the first
years of marriage highlights the significant roles that romantic passion and
business considerations simultaneously played. Early in his long courtship, the aforementioned merchant Isaac Proctor declared that his "excess
feeling of affection" toward Jane Marriot filled him with melancholy.
Scattered in letters describing the daily activities of his store in Raleigh,
North Carolina, as well as other financial matters, he solicited Marriot's
devotion with poetry. Despite his peevish disposition, young Proctor won
the hand of his intended. Beyond mere juxtaposition of romantic affir-
mations with financial matters, young couples occasionally incorporated
mercantile subjects and language in their demonstrations of affection.[26] In
the summer of 1848, Jean Baptiste Bres, a twenty-eight-year-old French
Creole who was a partner in the New Orleans commission firm Bres,
Frellsen & Company, wrote a love letter to his seventeen-year-old fiancée,
Elizabeth Adams, who was, as noted earlier, a devotee of neatness and
order. Complimenting her upon the quality of veil she had procured for
his sister Jan, Bres playfully suggested to Adams, "I think you had better
turn your attention to the commission business and be a Commission
Merchant I think you would prosper at it." A few days later Adams ten-
derly replied that she could not decide whether to be a merchant or a
planter for she feared "that if I were Merchant the only articles I could
bargain for would be *hearts*; and as a Planter the only seeds I would sow
would be seeds of Discord." This exchange framed expressions of love
within a mercantile discourse. Bres implicitly praised Adams's shopping
expertise, a profitable skill for a businessman's wife to have, by comparing
her activity to that of a commission merchant. Adams returned the com-

pliment by suggesting that perhaps Bres and his mercantile establishment would play into her future life.

Similar language is found in courtship letters between the Marylander Benedict Semmes and Jorantha Jordan. Semmes spent 1848 and 1849 selling dry goods and wooing Jordan, the daughter of a New York congressman. While following commercial pursuits in Washington, D.C., Semmes kept Jordan informed of his activities. Like Jean Bres, Semmes blithely speculated upon the business skills of his betrothed. Concerning Jordan's neat handwriting Semmes remarked, "I have often said that you would make a capital clerk under my management you have an enquiring mind—speak *precisely*—act readily and are not Dull at figures." In the same paragraph he flirtatiously inquired if she would "show me your books" upon their next meeting. Business concerns rarely left Semmes's mind, apparently not even while writing love letters. A month before marriage he attributed a delinquent letter to the rush of business. He had penned three lines to Jordan when several "valuable" customers entered the store. Thus, he explained, "Instead of writing to you I made about $120 for you." The romantic passion that southern merchants articulated readily accommodated the language of bargains, speculations, and profits. The daily demands of their profession impressed upon them a discourse they subsequently used in many areas of their personal lives, including courtship and marriage. More fundamentally, the subjects these men and women discussed and the language they adopted while courting emanated from values that frequently deviated from the norms established by their yeoman and planter neighbors. Of course both farmers and planters on occasion mentioned business concerns in romantic letters. Emphasis upon selling goods, fashion trends, and accounting, however, distinguish the correspondence of the merchant class from that of men and women more directly tied to the land. After marriage, newlyweds continued to shape a life together that reflected the romantic ideals and materialism that initially brought so many of them together.[27]

Upon the successful culmination of courtship—marriage—men and women of the merchant class attempted to establish a respectable economic and social position. Purchasing material goods for home and family offered a means toward achieving this end, and most merchants could afford to provide their families with some degree of material comfort. In an era when the personal wealth of southern farmers ranged from a few hundred dollars for the poorest, to several thousand for the "middling" nonslaveholding yeoman farmers, to tens of thousands for affluent planters, most merchants secured enough wealth to purchase at least a limited number of material goods. In 1860 merchants in Sumter County, Alabama, reported an average of $1,246 in real wealth and another $2,900 in personal wealth. A sample of the economic backgrounds of Confederate veterans from physician and merchant families in antebellum Tennessee found a median wealth of $20,000 each. The historian T. Lloyd Benson's study of Orange County, Virginia, determined the inventory amassed by the lowliest merchant to be only $1,500, while one of the most well-to-do merchants in the county had personal wealth and inventory exceeding $78,000. My larger sample of twenty-two counties (212,971 free and slave population) from the 1850 federal census showed that 36.9 percent of commercial family heads owned real estate with an average value of $2,495 (see appendix, table 5). These figures do not include the investment that slaveholding merchants (some 20 to 25 percent) had in their chattel property (see appendix, table 6). Nationally, clerks who possessed little or no financial stake in a store could expect to earn $400 to $600 a year. Benson's study also concluded that the average retail store in 1840 represented a capital investment of $4,300. While few merchants could surround themselves with material comforts rivaling those of the region's planter class, many could expect to purchase goods beyond mere food and shelter. Even merchant families with limited means purchased luxury goods when economically feasible. The logic behind such behavior became more explicit as the antebellum period evolved. Exhibiting behavior historically associated with the northern middle classes, southern merchant families readily embraced the developing capitalist market economy.[28]

Historians disagree about the extent to which commercial relations influenced households across the antebellum South. One side in the debate includes Lewis C. Gray, Robert Fogel, Stanley Engerman, and James Oakes, who contend that the rational economic behavior of the planter class belies incompatibility between slavery and capitalism. On the other hand, such historians as Eugene D. Genovese, Steven Hahn, and Barbara Fields claim that the impact of slavery upon the political economy of the region helped produce an ideology antithetical to capitalist development and commercial penetration. In her study of the plantation household, Elizabeth Fox-Genovese maintains that slavery and staple production "established distinct limits on the penetration of market relations into the interstices of southern households." Yeoman farmers in the South remained even further removed from the forces of the market economy. According to Steven Hahn, yeomen in the Georgia up-country lived in a world where "kinship rather than the marketplace mediated most productive relations. . . . Family self-sufficiency proved the fundamental concern." Reaching a more guarded conclusion, Lacy Ford found that up-country yeoman families produced goods for the market economy but energetically sought to keep individual members from participating in the labor market. The experience of merchant households, by definition a group tied to the marketplace, receives scant attention. The material condition of these southern households reveals the cultural impact of the growing nineteenth-century commercial economy. The consumption patterns of merchant families betray aspects of their bourgeois identity.[29]

Regardless of where they lived, merchant families exhibited a growing interest in accumulating and owning material possessions. Following a pattern found in the northern United States and in western Europe, the southern merchant class attempted to define itself as belonging among the region's socioeconomic elite through possession of the appropriate goods. The physical characteristics of the home, and more importantly the items found therein, reflected the ideals of the merchant family.[30] The very quantity of possessions that merchants transported, mainly west, across the South when they relocated their business operations is itself revealing. In 1845, John Dunlap, a merchant and business agent in the Louisiana firm of Dalhonde & Grosbach, prepared to move his family from Augusta, Georgia, to New Orleans. After renting a two-story brick house in New Orleans, this moderately successful businessman wrote to his wife in Georgia asking her to send their things, including their slaves, by water. Dunlap reminded her to pack his "merchants magazines" along with the family's other books. The inventory of goods sent to their new home included a piano, bed clothing, carpets, waiters, silverware, looking glasses, and hair mattresses. John N. Johnson, whose father was a merchant in Bristol, Tennessee, lived a more sedentary life in an eight-room house with a kitchen, smokehouse, and separate brick servants' quarters. Merchants who could afford such large homes filled them with a variety of luxury goods. In 1857, the Louisville merchant John Jefferson spent twenty-three dollars for a cherry wardrobe with veneered panels. A few days later he noted in his diary that his mother purchased a solid silver soup ladle and a *porte-monnaie* (purse) for his father on his fifty-fourth birthday. Jonathan Worth, the postbellum governor of North Carolina as well as an antebellum merchant, bought his daughters silver sets and sofas in addition to such modest gifts as subscriptions to *Harper's Magazine*. On occasion Kate Carney's merchant father let her use the family carriage for shopping trips with her friends in Murfreesboro. Another merchant complained to his brother that despite suffering from "hoping [*sic*] cough," his family was still "able to eat and wear more than I am able to buy for them." Even storekeepers with little capital and less business success amassed quantities of luxury goods. Isham Howze, known to his creditors for having few assets, transported a wagonload of books, bookcases, a secretary, and other items when he moved his family from Tennessee to Mississippi in 1854. Similarly, at a time when Samuel Aby could repay his creditors a mere thirty cents on the dollar, a neighbor in Grand Gulf, Mississippi, wrote of seeing Aby's wife riding in a "splendid new carriage of the finest kind used here" with a pair of "splendid matched Roans." Accumulation of nonessential goods conferred prestige upon merchant families in the antebellum South. Even those with little means attempted to live at a material level higher than most of their neighbors.[31]

As evidenced by their fashion consciousness, merchant families believed that consumption made for a more interesting and comfortable life. The southern press reflected the allure of fashion, and large town newspapers in particular published articles describing the latest women's fashions from Paris and London. In 1851 the *Charleston Mercury* ran a lengthy story on the "fashions for November" in that city. The writer declared that "ball and evening dresses will be worn with trains" and predicted that, "regarding 'home' dresses, the deshabilles Pompadour will be much worn this winter." Indeed the pursuit of fashion on the part of Charleston's upper classes occasionally inspired the *Mercury*'s editors to satire. Thus an editorial titled "Fashions by a 'First' Hand" pronounced: "Fingers are very much worn; nearly to the bone—skirts and accounts are still very long, while bodies, particularly those that think themselves somebodies, are excessively low, with a great deal of stitliness [*sic*] and a quantity of bone about the place where the heart likely to come, if there happens to be any. In evening dress the petticoat is usually very full and the pocket often very empty. The material of the bosom is frequently glace, and covered with a transparent issues of imitation stuff, which may be seen through easily."[32]

As well as a target for such sarcasm, wealthy merchant families, particularly those living in more settled areas, represented an important market for antebellum fashion. Like many of his colleagues in the mercantile trade, the Williamston merchant Cushing Hassell ordered his personal suits directly from New York City. Women from merchant families purchased finished dresses and bolts of material inspired by the latest European fashion. Wives wrote their husbands letters detailing their latest clothing purchases, and mothers raised their children, particularly their daughters, to be consumers of fashion. Families could be quite absorbed by sartorial deliberations. In addition to teaching school and following her son's early mercantile career, Barcia Norfleet Gordon O'Bryan made sure her daughter Fannie had at least one formal dress of silk and ruffles. Virginia Leslie, from a South Carolina merchant-planter family, wrote her sister Louisa that the vogue for bonnet ribbon in 1852 required that it be quilled, "then put on under a bow, on the back of the bonnet, and brought round on each side to the top in a point." Conveniently for Louisa, dress styles had changed little from the previous year. The rationale for consumption, from silk ribbon, dresses, and parlor furnishings to such minute luxuries as gold pins, lay in the value that merchant families assigned individual items.[33]

Reaching firm conclusions about consumption patterns is impossible from the personal documents these southern families left behind, but their bourgeois purchasing habits seem to parallel those of the region's planter class, members of which enjoyed a reputation for luxury. Bertram Wyatt-Brown has asserted that hospitality and largess formed two fundamental pillars of planter culture. The historians Eugene Genovese and Raimondo Luraghi have described the "prebourgeois" consumption habits of the planter class as serving to differentiate them from the mass of southern society. Certainly a predilection for grand estates, thoroughbred horses, and other luxuries suggests that planters subscribed to an ethos of gentility and honor that distinguished them from many of their neighbors. Yet most of the goods that planters bought, and the language they employed to describe their own consumption habits, varied little from those of merchant families. Planters spent no more of their income on luxuries than did other wealthy Americans. Thus, like the wives of successful planters in the 1850s, fashionable merchants' wives wore hoop skirts "truly prodigious" in size. Reminiscent of the bonnet correspondence between the Leslie sisters, Kate Carney of Murfreesboro, Tennessee, kept a diary so she would "know how I was dressed sometimes, & how my dress was made, just to remark the change a few years will make." Planter men kept abreast of New York and European fashions as well. Historians and cultural anthropologists who study upper-class behavior have suggested that elites like these merchant and planter families acquired luxuries in part to create a barrier between themselves and the rest of society. Capacity for accumulating luxury goods determined access to privileged bourgeois circles. More fundamentally, merchant families clearly enjoyed owning luxury goods. By the 1850s merchants across the South, particularly those in larger towns, increasingly expressed themselves through the consumption of goods. Their desire to be fashionably dressed and housed in a dignified manner was not unique, for most Southerners yearned for the material rewards offered by the growing American commercial market. Yet their greater access to capital and the northern credit economy enabled an increasing number of merchant families, unlike most of their neighbors, to satisfy their bourgeois consumer appetites.[34]

The same factors that advanced bourgeois ideals within southern merchant families—close ties to the commercial market and openness to northern culture—also moderated their experience with illness. Merchants and their families typically followed the most advanced medical practices of the day. Medicine in the antebellum period, often called by historians the "heroic age of medicine," relied upon such antiphlogistic treatments as bleeding, blistering, vomiting, and sweating. For the mass of poor rural southern whites, access to professional treatment and medicine remained limited. The wealth and commercial ties merchant and planter families enjoyed, however, allowed them to partake of a wide array of treatments.

Storekeepers served as the principal distributors of patent medicines in their communities. Thus while the price of many of these nostrums, particularly those containing opium, might exceed fifty cents an ounce, wealth and reliable access to credit enabled merchants to use these medicines in treating their own families. It is hardly surprising that merchant families ingested large quantities of drugs. Isham Howze kept a ready supply of quinine, used for treating malaria, in his Mississippi home. Frequently in late summer and early fall during the first years of the 1850s his entire family lay stricken with chills, fevers, and bloody discharges. The cost for the medicine that treated the family's various afflictions drove Howze into debt, but his credit back east remained secure. After consulting many doctors concerning his own ailment, seemingly a degenerative intestinal disease, Howze attempted to sustain himself with morphine and the knowledge that "none of the professors of the healing art can do me any good." Clara Solomon, the daughter of the New Orleans merchant

Solomon Solomon, resorted to cocaine against a host of bodily ills. Young Clara's diary is replete with references to such brands as Syme's and Burnett's Cocoaine. The Solomon family developed a strong attachment to this "excellent article." On occasion merchants traveled North for treatment.[35]

In 1847, the North Carolina storekeeper and farmer Joseph Biggs took his wife with him on his annual purchasing trip to New York City so she could have a wen surgically removed. He and his wife found the constant bustle of the large city exhausting, yet like many antebellum merchants, Joseph and Elizabeth Biggs endured discomfort and expense for care they perceived to be more refined and therefore superior. The famous southern diarist Mary Boykin Chesnut revealed the experience of many planter families when she related her own dependence upon morphine to see her through headaches and depression. The medical treatment merchant families received mirrored that of the southern planter class, both generally securing more expensive and seemingly more scientific treatment than most other Southerners could afford. While wealth enabled planter families to obtain medicine and professional treatment, access to credit and goods in the North proved more critical to antebellum merchants with limited means. These commercial families distinguished themselves from their farmer neighbors with their ability to obtain the latest medical treatment of the day.[36]

Not surprisingly, the various bourgeois practices merchant families embraced, both within and without the home, and their strong ties to the growing commercial market, fundamentally shaped their view of the North. To be sure, they frequently subscribed to the derogatory stereotypes of the greedy, boorish "Yankee" commonly held by many Southerners, but this public stand was tempered by significant respect and even affection for the North and its culture. The personal documents that merchant families left behind reveal a disposition toward the North as complex as their own place within the South.[37]

The personal histories of many storekeepers provide one obvious explanation for their strong feelings for the North. A significant minority of southern merchants, estimated between 5 and 20 percent, were born and raised in a northern state. Indeed, when the Northerner Henry Benjamin Whipple toured the South during the winter of 1844, he discovered "everywhere at the south . . . energetic northerners located & successfully competing with those southerners educated & reared here . . . and in point of business talent . . . the preponderance is decidedly in favor of the north." Most of these merchants and their families readily embraced their adopted homes without relinquishing their sentimental attachment to the North. A letter written by the White County, Tennessee, merchant Tyrus Brainerd suggests the devotion many northern emigrants, particularly New Englanders, continued to have for their homes. The homesick shopkeeper declared to a friend back in Connecticut:

> New England "with all thy faults I love thee still." I love New England for her political and religious institutions for her general Intelligence and good order and believe there is no country morally and intellectually which surpasses her. Her territory is narrow her resources more husbanded and consequently age and wealth to contend with [*sic*]. Her young men must come out from her and come out with the right kind of capital business capacity which is the best kind of stock and they are sure to succeed. The honorable and profitable stations her sons occupy in every State and territory in the United States are witnesses to her moral and mental worth.[38]

Brainerd found his position in Tennessee satisfactory, but like many merchants from the North, he never forgot his home. Of course occasionally such emigrants compared their new surroundings with those they left behind in the North and found them wanting. Hailing from Maine, Ruth Ingraham, a shopkeeper in Augusta, Georgia, denounced the local "Crackers" for not celebrating Thanksgiving, but she and her family did their "best to be thankful" and enjoyed "excellent hominy" that she found to be a "good dish." Frequently a legacy of affection for the North was passed down to children born in the South. In 1856, the Charleston, South Carolina, merchant George Williams joined the New England Society, a fraternal organization for men with ties to or interests in the Northeast, though Williams's father, not he, had been born in New England. The respect Williams and many other southern-born merchants evinced toward liberal bourgeois northern culture became increasingly uncommon in the sectionalized and defensive slave South of the 1850s. Merchant sentiment went beyond employing New England tutors for the instruction of their children, a practice long embraced by the planter class; rather southern merchants attributed a dynamism to the North and its inhabitants that they felt was absent in the South.[39]

The business literature that shopkeepers most valued came from northern cities. Published in New York City, *Hunt's Merchants' Magazine and Commercial Review*, the preeminent trade journal for southern merchants and the nation at large, tended to idealize northern business practices. The magazine presented the thrifty Yankee trader as the archetypal successful businessman. A regional dependence on such commercial journals drove the southern nationalist James D. B. De Bow to develop a magazine called the *Commercial Review of the South and West* specifically for merchants and industrialists in Dixie, but the publication never seriously rivaled *Hunt's Merchants' Magazine*.[40]

Besides following business advice emanating from the North, merchants and their families regarded its cities as centers of learning and sophistication. Prosperous merchants made regular trips to northern cities to obtain goods for their stores, but merchants and their families also sought education there. William Lea, a merchant in Leasburg, North Carolina, raised his six children to take an interest in the larger world and particularly the northern United States. Upon graduating from college in 1836, Lea's youngest son, Addison, expressed his wish to complete his education with a tour of several northern cities. Despite this "anxious" desire, Addison Lea's strong religious convictions—he would later become a Methodist minister—caused him to refrain from a trip "without some other object in view than merely to satisfy a vain and idle Curiousity [*sic*]." Few children of the merchant class let religious or political views bar at least one pilgrimage to New York City, Philadelphia, or Boston. During the fall of 1859, Kate Carney's family visited New York City where they stayed at the Metropolitan, a hotel prominent in the seventeen-year-old's mind because southern men liked it "on account of [its] having colored waiters in the dining room, but white chamber maids." The "fare" in New York reminded Kate of Boston. Already a savvy traveler, she enjoyed shopping for dresses with her father in particular. The family later visited Philadelphia; Sulphur Springs, Virginia; Washington, D.C.; and other locales frequented by wealthy nineteenth-century Americans. Sometimes such trips brought merchants into contact with exotic practices they had only read about. In 1855 the Savannah merchant James Sullivan had such an experience during his trip from New York City to Niagara Falls when he witnessed "*a live Bloomer* & 2 *conspicious* [*sic*] *Negroes*" in Syracuse, New York. Sullivan expressed more curiosity than astonishment when reflecting upon this uniquely northern episode. In the end, "Yankee" periodicals and a deep respect for the cultural and economic achievements of northern cities encouraged southern shopkeepers, a class already economically dependent on the North, to reach favorable judgments regarding the character of northern men and women.[41]

Antebellum merchants, like the majority of Southerners, perceived the cultural divide between their region and the rest of the country. Most merchants would have agreed with proslavery theorist George Fitzhugh's conclusion: "Benevolence, affection, generosity, and philanthropy are equally common North and South; and only differ in their *modes of manifestation*." Northerners and Southerners alike, from Henry Adams's description of attending Harvard University with a "childlike" William Henry Fitzhugh Lee to James Henry Hammond's speeches hailing a society built upon "King Cotton," reflected upon the obvious contrast between the two regions. Yet despite the growing recognition of cultural differences between the North and South, the ties antebellum merchants created with northern society frustrated neat distinctions between the two peoples.[42]

Daniel R. Hundley's influential study *Social Relations in Our Southern States* (1860) declared the mass of southern merchants to be "cunning fellows" who, "full of their own conceit," differed "but little from any ordinary shopkeeper in New England or the North-West." Over the course of the antebellum period shopkeepers found themselves in the unenviable position of having to defend their southern identity at the same time that many of them recognized the growing number of bourgeois characteristics they shared with Northerners. A reliance upon Yankee literature, business advice, and other social affects created an intellectual debt few antebellum commercial families in the South could ignore. Not surprisingly the pressure of sustaining a regional identity while at the same time protecting cultural ties with the North produced ambivalence in merchant families. Many expressed variations on this theme in their personal writing. One merchant described a Connecticut couple he had recently met: "I like to see people saving; but there is a bitterness, sometimes, in these northerners, that I *do dislike*. These new friends of ours, seem honest and pious, and I like them much thus far." Seemingly out of habit, implications of southern cultural superiority appeared beside praise for Northerners and their mores. To be sure, most antebellum merchant families, like their planter and yeoman farmer neighbors, jealously guarded the rights and prerogatives of their region. Contrary to more extreme southern nationalists, however, these same families refrained from any outright condemnation of bourgeois culture in a North that boasted so many seemingly valuable cultural attributes.[43]

Southern merchant families displayed many of the same bourgeois practices that historians have associated with developing Victorian culture and economy in the northern United States and western Europe. Ultimately, however, the accumulation of these habits did not produce a fundamentally bourgeois merchant class. Their devotion to the conservative traditions of the Old South proved a critical barrier to the kind of intellectual transformation necessary for them to become truly bourgeois. Antebellum merchant families from across the economic spectrum, both in towns and at rural crossroads, living in the upper and lower South, shared cultural traditions antithetical to the modern bourgeois temperament that was taking root in the North. First, men from these families supported the conservative patriarchy established in southern law and custom. Second, commercial families viewed themselves and their place in society through a conservative, often evangelical Christianity that tempered their willingness to embrace liberal bourgeois practices. Evangelicalism shaped how these men and women understood not only their family roles and the place of slavery but also such abstract traditions as a southern code of honor. Finally, and most importantly, commercial families embraced the racial order of the Old South. Many merchants owned house slaves (see appendix, table 6), and the majority who did not defended the institution against attacks from northern abolitionists. At a time when an "unprecedented wave of humanitarian reform sentiment swept" through the bourgeoisie in Great Britain and the northern United States, southern merchants rejected abolitionism and other elements of the Victorian worldview. These capitalists participated in an international market. They sought its expansion in their own region, which at times put them at odds with their white neighbors. As Thomas L. Haskell and David Brion Davis, among other historians, have convincingly argued, they rejected the "new sensibility" of humanitarianism that drove the movement to end slavery in the late eighteenth and early nineteenth centuries. Instead they generally deferred to the leadership of the planter class. The example of the southern merchant complicates liberal/conservative, capitalist/precapitalist, national/regional dichotomies. Despite comparatively sophisticated bourgeois familial and commercial lives, these merchant families worked hard to sustain a southern identity.[44]

Nineteenth-century America was, by most definitions, a patriarchal society. Men, particularly fathers, were the principal authority figures in and out of the home. Traditionally husbands and fathers enjoyed control over the labor and property of their households. Yet as Mary P. Ryan, Steven Mintz, and others have noted, by the mid-nineteenth century, economic change and the rise of political liberalism in northern society had begun to weaken fathers' authority. The decline in household production and the increasingly egalitarian nature of northern families required men to rule by persuasion rather than decree. No such transformation in household relations emerged in the antebellum South. There the dominant gender ideology still placed fathers at the head of their families, while women and other dependents continued to be defined by their relationship to men. Having an agricultural economy in which the production of goods within most households remained critical, the South proved resistant to significant changes in gender relations. The social code and the isolation of farms and plantations limited the roles southern women could play. State and common law further reinforced patriarchal organization in the South. A woman's legal existence ended upon entering marriage. While women's rights in the North expanded through changes in the economy and the rise of the "cult of domesticity," these factors had limited effect in the South, where the law granted husbands full custody of children, declared that a woman's personal property belonged to her husband, and limited the availability of divorce. Like men in yeoman and planter homes across the South, husbands and fathers in merchant families expected to govern their households. The personal papers of merchant families suggest, however, that the struggle for patriarchal authority within the family and the responsibilities such power entailed often proved a sobering contest for both men and women.[45]

As the oldest son, Charles W. Jacocks wielded significant patriarchal authority over his widowed mother and younger sisters. Jacocks operated a dry-goods store in Windsor, North Carolina. When not occupied in the store, he served as clerk and master of equity in the Bertie County courts. The personal success Jacocks realized as a storekeeper, along with his position in the court, gave him numerous opportunities to exercise the kind of power successful men held in the antebellum South. Active as an agent and executor of several estates, he intimately observed how patriarchy in the South limited women's rights. Widows, among them Mary Potter of Brownsville, Tennessee, depended upon Jacocks to supervise the sale of their late husbands' estates. When the rental income from her husband's land fell short of her needs, Potter appealed to the merchant as "one that has befriended me heretofore to dispose and manage the business as your better judgment may think propper [*sic*]." Jacocks performed this and other legal tasks for Potter despite the fact she seemingly did not pay for his services. From the nature of their correspondence, one is left to conclude that Jacocks viewed Mary Potter as a woman in need. His conduct toward her reveals an important aspect of his own male identity in a patriarchal southern society. Jacocks, as well as many of his planter neighbors, helped women in need and expected deference in return. Thus when he assisted his widowed sister Martha Webb through a financial embarrassment in 1844, she thanked him in a style sure to please him. Between declarations of gratitude Webb wrote that his "fatherly caution . . . was greatfully [*sic*] received + will be strictly attended to yes. . . . I should not be deserving a place among civilized people if I did not attend closely to the advice of the only friend I have in the world." Law and custom encouraged Jacocks to take a direct interest in his sister's affairs, and in this instance Jacocks handled himself with aplomb. The growing paternal relationship between him and his sister pleased both parties.[46]

Such agreement had not always graced the Jacocks family. The frayed ties between Charles and his two other sisters, Ann Roscoe and Mary Reed, exemplified both the strength and limitations of merchant patriarchy in the antebellum South. The problem with both women, according to brother Charles, was the men in their lives. As head of the family, he required his sisters to seek his blessing before entering into marriage. Like the physician, planter, and fellow North Carolinian James Norcom, Jacocks hoped for "cheerful submission" to his will. Furthermore, after his sisters married, Jacocks expected to receive proper respect from his new brothers-in-law. In both particulars he would be disappointed.[47] By early 1833, Jacocks had become so estranged from his sister Ann that he communicated with her only through the other sister, Mary. The last recorded letter he sent to Ann pleaded with her to reconsider an impending marriage with a minister named James Bunch. Jacocks feared that by attaching herself to a man with so little public standing, his sister would meet ruin. More importantly, the merchant sought to protect the family's reputation. Jacocks pronounced Bunch to be "one of the most ignorant men in Bertie, illiterate (that is can't hardly read or write) and has several children by a former marriage." Harking back to the authority of the former patriarch, Jacocks declared that if their father were alive, "He would rather that you should be laid in the Grave among the dead. Nay, he would almost put you there himself rather than it should ever be said that a Bunch married into the Jacocks family." Jacocks concluded his threatening missive with the promise that should she go through with the marriage he would have her banished from the family. Thus ended what he described as his "*last letter of advice to a last undone sister.*" As head of the household, Charles Jacocks, a sophisticated merchant with strong economic ties to the North, expected submission from the women and other dependents in his family. But like most southern white men, he possessed only a limited amount of leverage with which to enforce his will. It seems Ann Roscoe did marry Bunch, and by all indications Jacocks held fast to his vow to terminate relations with her.[48]

His stand against Roscoe's decision failed, however, to bolster Jacocks's role as the family patriarch, for only three years later he once again faced an obstinate sibling, this time over patriarchal rights.Charles appeared to have a warm relationship with his sister Mary Reed, but after several bitter confrontations, he spurned Mary's husband, James Reed. The dispute, mediated by Jacocks's brother Jonathan, involved Reed's sale of family [Jacocks] slaves and his failure to secure an adequate home for his wife. When Charles Jacocks admonished Reed for his inability to support his sister in the style to which she was accustomed, Reed responded by publicly assailing his brother-in-law's character. Mary sided with her husband against her brother, while Jonathan Jacocks and mother Elizabeth attempted to remain neutral. During the spring of 1836 the acrimony between the respective parties increased as caustic letters passed back and forth. Eventually Jonathan Jacocks concluded that Reed had indeed pursued a course "dictated by a disposition to degrade Bro Charles."

Tension within the family further escalated when the brothers learned of their mother's plans to move in with the Reed family. Clearly Elizabeth Jacocks thought more highly of James Reed than her sons did. Jonathan Jacocks wrote his mother that he could not "trust you out of the protection of your friends with a man who I have seen myself + many of your friends have often told me does not treat you as he should." Charles and Jonathan Jacocks had firmly voiced their disapproval of James Reed and had protested their mother's relocation to his home. The former had gone even further by questioning Reed's ability to support his sister. The clash between the patriarchal dominance of Jacocks and Reed remained unresolved. While his mother and sisters did not question Charles's right to protect the family and its reputation, they did not always follow his direction—as quietly evidenced by the 1850 census, which reveals the seventy-seven-year-old Elizabeth Jacocks living in Perquimans County, North Carolina, with her daughter Mary Reed's family. Throughout it all, Jacocks continued to expect the same patriarchal rights promised all white men in the antebellum South.[49]

Isham Howze frequently reflected upon patriarchy and gender relations in his diary. Like many southern theologians and proslavery ideologues, Howze viewed patriarchy as fundamental to human nature. Undoubtedly the merchant would have agreed with the southern intellectual Thomas Roderick Dew when he wrote that a woman's "physical weakness incapacitates her for combat; her sexual organization, and that part which she takes in bringing forth and nurturing the rising generations, render her necessarily domestic in her habits." Seeking to ground his support for patriarchy on biblical teaching, Howze found the Apostle Paul's injunctions in Ephesians 5:21–22 particularly comforting. It seemed obvious to Howze that "power to decide has to be lodged somewhere in the family, and God has given it to the husband." He conceded that women could become merchants in some lines of stock, but ultimately their proper sphere was the "domestic circle." Yet Howze's views were hardly static. Amid financial difficulties and emotional upheavals he longed to "shift off my responsibility, as the head, upon my beloved wife, and let her be the head to plan and execute too." Nevertheless biblical law and social propriety sustained Howze's belief in southern patriarchy. This position appears yet more remarkable in view of his unlikely friendship with the controversial Fanny Wright.[50]

Howze met Fanny Wright during the winter of 1850 when he agreed to rent Nashoba, the two-thousand-acre farm she owned in Shelby County, Tennessee. During the late 1820s Wright had attempted to build Nashoba into a cooperative community along the lines of Robert Dale Owen's experiment in New Harmony, Indiana. Here black and white residents were to create a classless society that would break free from traditional marital and family roles. Wright declared marriage laws void in Nashoba, where "no woman can forfeit her individual rights or independent existence, and no man assert over her any rights of power whatsoever beyond what he may exercise over her free and voluntary affection." By the 1830s political, religious, and sexual scandals brought the communal experiment in western Tennessee to an end, but not before Wright had, according to the historian Barbara Taylor, become the "most notorious feminist radical in America." Howze encountered her near the end of her life.[51]

Wright posed an ideological dilemma for Howze. During their three-year acquaintance he failed to reconcile his vision of the proper Christian family with the undeniable respect he felt for his radical landlord. He confessed in his diary to loving Wright, whom he described as a "great woman" with a "fine" mind. Her failure to accept Christianity and the woman's role within the Christian family, however, made Howze fear for the state of her soul. His esteem for her led him to pray that "she may bow her knees to Jesus & yet become an advocate for that cause which she now slights." Unlike many of his Tennessee neighbors, Howze never condemned Wright nor questioned her integrity. The well-read merchant apparently enjoyed discussing philosophy and religion with her, even while he agreed with his fellow Southerners that her denunciations of traditional marriage and family life threatened community mores. He declared Wright's theories ingenious but godless. After her death in 1852, Howze frequently speculated on her eternal reward. Her good works—she "fed the hungry and clothed the naked, and had a benevolent heart"—did coincide with the southern merchant's maturing bourgeois inclinations toward benevolent associations and helping the poor. Her feminist critique of the patriarchy that Howze held dear led him to the sad conclusion that her fate rested in the hands of a Christian God "whose existence and merits she did disown." The merchant could only pray that a loving God would forgive Wright for heresies that he and his neighbors found so disturbing.[52]

The rationale that Isham Howze offered in defense of traditional patriarchal relations illustrates another check on the development of a mature bourgeois ideology among antebellum merchants, namely the influence of conservative Protestant theology. Like many nineteenth-century Americans, including most residents of the South, the mass of southern merchants considered themselves good Protestants, observing a faith grounded in Scripture and traditional Christian teaching. Mirroring denominational patterns in the midwestern United States, evidence suggests that merchants in the antebellum South belonged overwhelmingly to the Presbyterian, Methodist, and Baptist churches. By the late 1830s at least half of the South's white adult population regularly attended evangelical preaching. Seeking a personal relationship with God in Christ, merchants and their families joined the ranks of their evangelical neighbors. Even those merchants not inclined to accept conservative Protestant theology found their own families and neighbors caught in the tide of an evangelical faith that swept the antebellum South.[53]

Evangelical ministers preached a Christian message of emotional intimacy, spiritual equality, and godly self-discipline. A direct outgrowth of the revivalism of the First and Second Great Awakenings, by the 1830s the evangelical call for a "life of holiness" reached Southerners from across the social and economic spectrum. Evangelical Protestants maintained that in a world rife with sin only an emotional confrontation with Scripture and subsequent conversion could offer personal salvation to an unworthy soul. Revivalist fervor, self-debasement, and missionary zeal for a religion of the heart were certainly not unique to the South. Much of this drive for a Christian society had its roots in the eighteenth- and nineteenth-century North.[54] In New England and other northern states Presbyterian, Congregational, and Baptist ministers called for an active, intimate relationship with Christ. Alongside their search for ultimate salvation, evangelical Southerners readily embraced the patriarchy inherent in the rising "cult of domesticity"—a spiritual understanding of the family promulgated by middle-class Yankee evangelicals, in which women best served their families and their own faith by remaining in the home. In both regions evangelical Protestantism enabled poor and middling farmers to establish a more coherent identity based on religious solidarity. Northern evangelical reform influenced wealthier Southerners as well. Beginning in the 1820s and lasting through the 1850s influential southern Protestants supported such benevolent enterprises as Sabbatarianism, anti-dueling societies, and ministries to the poor. Despite the pervasive impact that northern evangelicalism had in nineteenth-century America, merchant families and their neighbors shared a distinctively southern religious sensibility.[55]

While evangelical belief led many in the North to welcome social reform imposed by the state, particularly temperance and abolitionist legislation, the ideological demands of living in the slave South resulted in a socially more conservative evangelical Protestantism. The psychological need for white Southerners to ground their peculiar institution in Scripture led them to develop a proslavery ideology that became inseparable from their religious beliefs. In his analysis of proslavery thought in eighteenth- and nineteenth-century America, Larry E. Tise has found that southern defenders of their institution girded themselves for conflict with abolitionist critics by becoming "proponents of purity in religion." From the curse of Ham and the sanction of slavery that the Apostles provide in the Epistles, conservative southern Protestants concluded that the master-slave relationship, like the patriarchal white family, had been ordained by God.[56] Although the impact of evangelicalism was much different in the South than in the North, the imperative for a genuine conversion experience did serve as an essential factor uniting all evangelicals, both North and South. Only by acknowledging personal moral corruption and attaining the "joyful release of conversion" could a Christian enter the evangelical fold and receive God's saving grace. The process of religious conversion could be immediate or take many months. Since evangelicals believed humanity entered the world spiritually dead, anyone who failed to experience a "second birth" risked ultimate damnation. Like anyone else, merchants and their families undergoing such a religious transformation found their lives profoundly changed. Indeed, many described their conversion experience as the central event of their life.[57]

During the winter of 1827, eighteen-year-old Cushing Hassell felt himself "arrested by some Supernatural power and exceedingly distressed on account of the original depravity of his heart and the consequent impure stream that were constantly issuing from this corrupt fountain." Over several months the young Tar Heel came to believe that "faith in Christ was the only medicine through which peace & pardon could flow." Hassell later recorded the date when he was saved, January 13, 1828, and when he was baptized, March 11, 1828, in his memoirs. Thus began Hassell's spiritual journey into the Baptist church. George O'Bryan experienced a similar spiritual transformation almost thirty years later while employed as a clerk in the Nashville, Tennessee, firm of Gordon & Company. The twenty-four-year-old "confessed Christ" in 1856 and joined the First Presbyterian Church of Nashville. Like Hassell, O'Bryan resolved to change his life after accepting his new faith. During his child-hood on the Georgia frontier, George Walton Williams underwent a con-version that led him into the Methodist church. Before being "born again" these and other merchants described feelings of personal unworthiness, isolation, and depravity. After conversion most claimed their new faith gave them powerful emotional support in their personal and professional lives, as well as fellowship with like-minded Christians. After publicly confessing Christ before his Baptist congregation in Houston, Texas, store clerk Constantine Perkins prayed and even cried for the conversion and salvation of his friends. Of course those who became reborn in Christ preached biblical messages to their friends and associates. Perhaps more significantly, evangelical church leaders depended upon the family to help spread the faith. This calling left merchants who were outside the evangelical community open to the entreaties of family members who had already been saved. Parents, spouses, and children, with varying success, pleaded with their merchant kin to repent and serve the Lord.[58]

In the years following his conversion experience, Cushing Hassell urged the saving grace of God upon his friends and family alike. Indeed by the end of his life he had become one of the leading ministers of the Primitive Baptist Church in Martin County, North Carolina. When not preaching to his own congregation Hassell struggled to convert his relatives, particularly his merchant cousins Asa, Kader, and Joseph Biggs. The state of cousin Asa's soul seemed to hold particular interest for the merchant-preacher. Asa Biggs also served in the North Carolina legislature during the 1840s and the U.S. Congress in the 1850s, but the prestige he enjoyed as a congressman, militia colonel, and wealthy merchant-planter did not stop the poorer Hassell from lecturing his cousin on the subject of religion. Of course Hassell prayed with Biggs and his family, and he enjoined the Biggs family to strictly follow God's "Word" while avoiding the "influence of Methodist excitement," which was then prevalent in their 1850s North Carolina neighborhood. It seems that Joseph and Kader Biggs shared their cousin's impulse to spread proper evangelical theology. Describing a favorite relative who had yet to undergo an evangelical conversion, Joseph wrote Kader, "I saw no evidence to believe he knows any thing about the grace of God in truth and as to his believing in the doctrine of Election, the Election of God, I have no idea." Regardless of place or time, evangelical families continually attempted to "save" their kin in the antebellum South.[59]

Though most evangelicals believed that genuine conversion could not be forced, the merchant Asa Runyon joined his brother in subtly pressuring his nephew to be baptized during a week-long revival held in Minerva, Kentucky. The women in the Jacocks family would have appreciated Runyon's efforts, as they similarly attempted to save the soul of the family patriarch, Charles Jacocks. Before Mary wed John Reed, she first angered her brother by joining the "despised" Methodist church. She wrote Charles letters begging him *"to turn, O turn before you die,* do not wait to grow better you may perhaps never have another opportunity if you will give your whole heart to God he will take you just as you are." Seven years after Charles received this appeal from his sister, his cousin Jane Williams was still praying for the Lord to transform his "sinful heart into holiness." No evidence indicates that Jacocks ever joined the Methodist church or any other evangelical denomination. Like many apparently religious merchants, Jacocks found himself besieged by a growing number of family members and neighbors who questioned the power of his faith. Southern merchants, whether they were Catholic, Jewish, or traditional Protestants like Jacocks and Asa Biggs, could not avoid the cultural influence of evangelical Protestantism.[60]

Southern merchants engaged in a wide range of pious duties and religious activities during the antebellum period. At the very least they and their families studied the Bible. In spite of irregular reading habits Isham Howze read the entire Bible at least six times. Aside from this near universal practice, many merchants, particularly evangelicals, assumed various positions of authority within their churches. While working as a clerk in one of his father's Louisville stores, the twenty-four-year-old John Jefferson became secretary of the Brook Street Methodist Episcopal Church Sunday School. Jefferson worked to reorganize the school and "fix things up shipshape," while his brother Lewis attempted to establish a Methodist missionary society. As a young man, the Nashville merchant Robert Stewart Hollins Sr. wrote a lengthy exegesis of the Bible. Later, as a husband and father, Hollins led his family in regular prayer and eventually assumed the position of "Ruling Elder" in the First Edgefield Presbyterian Church. His neighbor and fellow merchant George O'Bryan, who had joined the First Presbyterian Church of Nashville after his conversion in 1856, went on to serve as a deacon and superintendent of the Sunday school. As the earlier example of Cushing Hassell indicates, a number of merchants combined business and preaching. Between 1836 and 1843, William Henry Wills split his time between his store in Halifax, North Carolina, with his circuit-riding activities on behalf of the Methodist church. In addition to editing the *Methodist Protestant* and *Central Protestant* newspapers, Wills served as president of the Methodist Conference in 1849. When pastoral duty called, merchant-preachers like Wills and Hassell depended on their wives to sustain the family business in their absence. During the antebellum period financially successful merchants, including many conservative evangelicals, deftly wedded their religious values with demands imposed by the commercial market.[61]

During the nineteenth century conservative and evangelical American Protestants championed the virtues of discipline and self-denial. The business activities southern merchants and their families practiced exemplified this broad trend. Successful merchants attended their daily business with an almost religious zeal. Many believed hard work and long hours in the store to be a Christian regimen. Evangelical storekeepers assumed that men and women who did not observe this ethic risked economic and spiritual failure. The New Orleans storekeeper C. E. Catonet offered a typical explanation when he attributed his business failure to "dissipation and bad habits." Merchants kept a steady guard against moral lapses that could harm the workplace. Such a conviction explains why Cushing Hassell fired one of his clerks for enjoying too much recreation in after-hours Williamston, North Carolina. When George O'Bryan acquired his own store, he taught his clerks that "all legitimate business could be carried on successfully in the fear of God." O'Bryan's Presbyterian minister declared upon his death that the merchant's rough treatment of his employees provided the "means of saving them at a critical moment from some wrong conduct that would have ruined them both morally and materially." Despite the sometimes ribald atmosphere of the southern store, religious tracts occasionally found their way to the countertop. Isham Howze kept recent copies of the *Tennessee Baptist* newspaper in his store out of personal interest, as well as for the edification of employees and customers.[62]

As these examples suggest, southern merchants saw few contradictions between their religious values and their daily business activities. Those who gave the matter any thought generally believed Christian self-discipline improved a merchant's financial bottom line. Overall, however, business considerations could limit the influence religion had within the store as well. Notwithstanding their views on temperance, many southern merchants, including evangelicals, sold alcohol. Living with such apparent ideological contradictions proved easier over time. Merchants did occasionally comment on the discrepancy between their job as purveyors of trifling goods and Christian admonitions against self-indulgence. Isham Howze chided women who worshipped at the "shrine of fashion." He believed that before God such ornaments are of no value compared to a "meek and quiet Spirit." Of course it was the very business activities of Howze and other southern merchants that made such adornment possible.[63]

Conservative and evangelical Protestant merchants faced more serious spiritual contradictions during periods of political or economic dislocation. Atlanta merchant Samuel Richards found concentrating on religious matters difficult during the controversy surrounding the 1860 presidential election and the possibility of secession. Temporal concerns regarding the future of his Book, Music, and Fancy Store plagued Richards even during worship. On one particularly dreary October afternoon the anxious Richards wrote in his diary of being unable to enjoy church services "for thinking of 'hard times' and fearing for the future which I ought not to do." He tried to place his economic fate in God's hands but found it "very hard to keep my mind intent on divine things" when "we have a good deal of money to pay and none coming in." Comments like these are both revealing and extraordinary. Most merchants believed their business activities fit neatly within a virtuous Christian society. It required political upheaval or economic "hard times" before many reflected upon their dual identities as storekeepers and fervent Christians. When they did so, southern merchants worked hard to overlook inconsistencies within themselves.[64]

The religious views conservative and evangelical Protestant merchants held in the antebellum South resembled those of their colleagues in the North. By the mid-nineteenth century evangelical Protestantism in the northern United States began experiencing a decline in orthodox belief and an increasing fragmentation. The cumulative effect of industrialization, immigration, and family mobility changed the nature of the region's Protestantism. By contrast a religiously heterogeneous South created an atmosphere in which Roman Catholics and Jews occasionally complained of bigotry even from Episcopalians, whom one merchant described as being "nearly Methodists or nearly Presbyterians." Yet, irrespective of denominational differences, southern merchants enjoyed closer cultural ties to a growing bourgeois North than most of their neighbors. To be sure, merchants, like most Southerners, generally supported patriarchy or paternalism in the home and a conservative Protestantism rooted in Scripture. Antebellum Southerners seemed to share a religious understanding opposed to the rising tide of individualism and liberal capitalism found in the North. The degree to which merchants supported patriarchy and evangelical Protestantism distinguished them from many Northerners, but the difference was not qualitative. The factor that did fundamentally divide southern merchant families from their friends and colleagues in the North was the institution of slavery. Most southern merchants did not own slaves and even fewer entered the ranks of the region's planter class.[65] Rather the measure of the peculiar institution's influence upon merchant families lies in their daily lives. Slavery limited their commitment to liberal capitalism, evangelical Protestantism, and radical egalitarianism.[66]

The imperatives of slavery ruled antebellum southern society. Although most of the white population remained slaveless, the institution formed the region's political economy and culture. Slavery, and the plantation system that depended upon it, produced an impressive rate of economic growth over the antebellum years. At the same time, political efforts to protect slavery, as well as demands of the commercial market, created a hierarchical, agricultural society. Peter W. Bardaglio maintains that slave labor slowed the expansion of individualism in the South. As discussed in chapter 1, the slave South presented those working in the mercantile trade with unusual challenges and significant economic opportunities. Most small and middling merchants—that is, the majority of storekeepers—had a limited financial stake in the institution of slavery. Cotton factors aside, commercial men and women believed they could survive in a free labor economy just as well. What antebellum merchants feared most was instability. They wanted to work within a predictable economy that would equitably compensate their services. To this end merchants and their families embraced that pillar of the antebellum South—slavery. Their customers depended upon yearly cotton sales to pay outstanding bills. Understandably southern businessmen came to hail "King Cotton." Personally they held conflicting views on the relative merits of slavery, but in public they defended the institution as a cornerstone of their society.[67]

Environmental factors influenced how those in the mercantile trade perceived slavery. Clearly a storekeeper in southern Appalachia viewed slavery differently than a merchant operating in Natchez, Mississippi. That said, an examination of merchant diaries and correspondence suggests that by the 1840s a rough consensus had formed among them regarding slavery. Once again Isham Howze spoke for the majority of his merchant peers when he declared, "Our slaves are well-fed, and clothed, and are happy, in comparison with the poor white slave, either in Europe or in our northern states. . . . God has decreed a difference in mankind, and some men are born inferior to others, some to rule and some to be ruled." Acquainted with the work of the proslavery theorist George Fitzhugh and others, merchants used religious and naturalist principles to claim that the best society rested upon stratification and interdependence. The traditional paradigm of white over black and man over women should not be challenged. While this doctrine faced obstacles within the white merchant household, particularly from mothers and daughters influenced by the more egalitarian culture of the North, it prevailed in race relations.

Various apologies for slavery that northern and European immigrants produced after moving into the South indicates the dominance of the region's
slave order.[68]

Daniel R. Hundley astutely described this ideological transformation in *Social Relations in Our Southern States*. Echoing the sentiments
of Harriet Beecher Stowe, Hundley wrote: "When the farmer goes to live
in the North he is sure to turn abolitionist, although he may have been a
negro-trader up to that time; and so, too, when the latter directs his steps
Southwards, notwithstanding he may have been previously a constant
employee on the Underground Railroad, he immediately discovers a sweet
divinity in the peculiar institution, and no Southern overseer could expa-
tiate more eloquently on its manifold beauties than he." The experience
of the Yankee transplant Ruth Ingraham confirms Hundley's observation.
After moving from Augusta, Maine, to Augusta, Georgia, Ingraham and
her family readily adopted the mores of the slave South. Soon after establishing their dry-goods and hat store, Ingraham and her husband hired
a slave girl named Ellen to work in their home and occasionally behind
the counter at the store. Ingraham sent her sister in Maine long descriptions of slave women wearing half "turbans" and carrying baskets on their
heads. From their laughing in the streets, the Yankee merchant thought
them "the happiest class of bipeds here." After visits to local slave markets
in Augusta and across the river in Hamburg, South Carolina, Ingraham
admitted surprise at how quickly she adjusted to the constant presence
of African slaves. Initially she did not expect to be reconciled to their
"continual presence" but found "habit is everything, I expect to get along
peaceably with moskitoes [*sic*] and bed bugs even." The analogy Ingraham
used is revealing. Immigrants in the antebellum South, like their new
neighbors, came to view Africans as an inferior race naturally suited for
slavery. The exotic customs of the slaves and their "gift" for mirth and song
amused merchant families and confirmed their racist assumptions regarding the superiority of Western culture, the general perception being that
Africans, free or slave, were not dignified individuals to be taken seriously.
After two years in Georgia, Ingraham declared to her sister that if northern abolitionists could witness the treatment that her hired slave Ellen
received "they would not say so much about the galling [*sic*] chain." Over
the course of two years the Ingraham family followed a uniquely southern intellectual journey that began with their tolerating African slavery to
their defending the institution before family and friends in the North.[69]

Though economically bound to the slave system, most merchants never owned a slave. Small and middling storekeepers rarely had the financial resources to enter the master class. Those who were able to purchase slaves generally remained, by choice or circumstance, small slaveholders. The sample from the 1850 census consisting of twenty-two counties from across the South showed that slightly less than 24 percent of commercial workers owned slaves. Furthermore, these merchants, clerks, and grocers owned an average of only eight slaves each. Data from a much smaller, informal sample based on manuscripts, credit reports, and census statistics reveals that slaveholding merchants owned on average fewer than six slaves. Commercial families occupied their slaves around the home and store or hired them out in the local community. Families living in more urban areas generally needed fewer slaves than those maintaining small country farms. For example, the young slave Edward Jones remembered that the land his master, a merchant and teacher named Tom Dickerson, maintained in Hinds County, Mississippi, was "different from big places." While five adult slaves did most of the work, Jones would pick "a little cotton, and gather up brush wood for the fires" and sometimes "make a little money holding a horse for a white gentleman or taking a message for him." More typical yet was the childhood experience of Robert K. Morris. While Morris was growing up in Nashville, his merchant parents found no need to own slaves. Closer to the country in DeKalb County, Georgia, John Fite's merchant father owned eight slaves who did the plowing on his small farm while their owner did "a lot of hoeing." Inside the home Fite's mother superintended and assisted the work of the family's female slaves. Because waiting servants and house slaves might also work in the family store, merchants were very selective whenever they hired or purchased slaves. The brother of one North Carolina merchant desired a "good looking" mulatto of more than "ordinary intelligence" who could drive his horse and wait on him at work and home. Cushing Hassell, who bought and sold slaves throughout the 1840s, owned a slave named Harry who occasionally helped out in the store during the holidays and other busy periods. Like Edward Murphy in New Orleans, John Jefferson in Louisville, Kader Biggs in North Carolina, and hundreds of other merchant slaveholders, every year Hassell profited by hiring out most of his slaves. Over time such practices tended to diminish the possibility for any personal relationship between master and slave within merchant households. Rather than developing a paternalistic interest in the welfare of their slaves, many merchants and their families viewed their servants as simply another commodity to be haggled over in the marketplace. Some mercantile firms like that of J. & J. A. Lane in Vicksburg, Mississippi, even dabbled in the slave trade. For the right price, merchants sold or traded their slaves for cash, cotton, stock, and land.[70]

Numerous slaveholding merchant families subscribed to the ideal of reciprocal obligations and deference that historians now associate with paternalism. Some needed to see their slaves as subordinate creatures in need of protection and direction. References to the "white and black" family, the modern historian's favorite linguistic evidence for paternalism, are occasionally found scattered in the correspondence of antebellum merchants. Indeed, slaves themselves occasionally employed such terms. Looking back on her childhood as a slave in a merchant household in Chapel Hill, North Carolina, Mary Anngady said that black and white children played together and everyone was "one large happy family." Annette Milledge and her mother were owned by a storekeeper living near Augusta, Georgia. Interviewed about her childhood as a slave, the eighty-three-year-old woman told her interviewer, "We had anything we wanted to eat . . . Masrter [sic] had a storeroom right next to my mother's room and anything she wanted to get to cook, she would go dere [sic] and get it." Apparently the storekeeper, who originally hailed from the north but saw his son die fighting for the Confederacy, had doctors treat his slaves when they were injured or ill, took them to church, and never whipped any of them. Like many slave narratives produced long after slavery died, Milledge's account made it clear that her experience was far from pleasant. She said her master's second wife "was mean" and kept Annette's hair shaved. Because neighboring plantations often resorted to "severe" whippings, if Milledge's merchant master did keep violence to a minimum, his rule would seem all the more benevolent in comparison. Significantly, merchant-farmers and those living in rural areas embraced the language and sentiment of paternalism more than their peers in southern towns and cities. When William Wills left his North Carolina home on business, his wife Anna kept her part-time merchant, full-time farmer husband apprised of his white and black family's health. Violating North Carolina law, Jonathan Worth taught his slaves to read and write. Upon the death of his slave Harry, an emotional Cushing Hassell declared, "He was a servant greatly esteemed by the public—regarded as an honest man and a firm friend of the white man." All of these merchants owned sizable farms in addition to their stores. Commercial families living on land worked by slaves did observe something akin to a paternalistic ethos. Those who did not have cotton fields requiring labor or who lived in town rarely developed such ties. Slaves in these households are notable for their absence from family documents.[71]

The historian Steven M. Stowe has concluded that far from exposing a close paternalistic bond between master and slave, the personal papers of most planters rarely mention their slaves. Much the same can be said for the diaries and correspondence of slaveholding merchant families. The principal exception to this trend were those times that slave activity inconvenienced merchant masters. Like slaveholders throughout the antebellum South, merchants viewed slave misconduct with a coarse mixture of disbelief and cynical satisfaction. They expected more from their slaves but ultimately viewed their misbehavior as simply more evidence confirming southern white theories on black inferiority. The diary John Jefferson kept while he clerked in his Louisville dry-goods store mentions the family's slaves only when they neglected their duties. When his new cow and calf strayed off in the night, Jefferson gave a sharp rebuke to the responsible slaves for failing to exercise "prudence & discretion." Less than a week later his slave named Susan, perhaps in response to Jefferson's criticism, slipped away for several days before being apprehended. Needless to say John Jefferson did not consider Susan to be family. Isham Howze, who fancied himself a part-time planter, could not control his slaves. Time and again he found himself whipping them for "insolent language" and poor work. After one young slave stole his mule, an exasperated Howze wrote in his diary: "Would to God I could have nothing to do with slavery. Not that I believe it is sinful under our circumstances. No, I do not. To the African race I believe, with Providence of God, it has been a blessing, but I am not of the right temperament to be a slave owner. I am not rigid enough in my discipline. But I will say no more. God rules, and all his ways are just and true." Howze's sister proved little better in governing her slaves. As her trustee, Howze attempted to assist his sister in various contests with her slaves. He never successfully controlled her slaves, and he characterized this added responsibility as yet another "cross that may come upon me." Merchants like Isham Howze and John Jefferson lived in households where slaves cooked, cleaned, and labored in the fields or store. Significantly the names, demeanor, or duties of these slaves barely appeared in their correspondence. The few references to slaves involved rule-breaking and financial transactions (i.e., sales, purchases, hiring out). Howze and Jefferson made distinctions between slaves and seemed to have genuine affection for several, but apparent is the absence of emotional ties between these merchant masters and their slaves. The evidence suggests that, like the Howze and Jefferson families, few living within merchant households, either black or white, developed strong paternalistic bonds. At least a portion of the merchant class seemed to have been more willing to acknowledge, in the historian Walter Johnson's words, "that the bodies of enslaved people had a measurable monetary value, whether they were ever actually sold or not." As a class dependent upon credit, merchants understood this "chattel principle," and it was not the foundation for a close relationship between master and slave.[72]

Since commerce shaped the relationship most storekeepers had with their free neighbors, it is not surprising that trade influenced their ties with slaves as well. Many white Southerners believed that merchants traded illegally with slaves, that slaves would steal goods from their masters then surreptitiously trade the contraband with a nearby storekeeper. The transaction enabled slaves to acquire liquor while the storekeeper obtained food or other items at a steep discount. The number of local ordinances across the antebellum South banning such trade suggests it was thought either to be widespread or to be a serious threat to the planters' control over their slaves. The precise scale of such illegal trade is impossible to gauge, but clearly a percentage of storekeepers were involved in it. Based upon an analysis of the minutes of the Savannah city council, Timothy James Lockley discovered that one-fifth of the people who were granted liquor licenses before 1820 were at some time prosecuted for trading with slaves or "entertaining Negroes." Evidently commercial links between merchant and slave communities were so extensive that in 1851 the Chatham County grand jury requested that storekeepers be excluded from the ranks of local watchmen, because they "knew so many slaves personally as trading partners." Lockley, who has examined this trade in the Georgia low-country in detail, argues that by supporting it white shopkeepers implicitly rejected the authority of the planter aristocracy. At the very least, it reveals that the profit motive could lead a sizable minority of merchants to break ranks, if only temporarily, with their white neighbors. Indeed, in the Carolinas merchants often challenged mandatory participation in slave patrols, because such night work rendered them and their clerks "incompetent to the performance of their daily employments" during the day. Business considerations mattered just as much to the mercantile class as they did to the planter class, and on occasion their interests conflicted, leading to resentment within both communities. One Georgia planter noted bitterly, "Storekeepers are always ready to accommodate the slaves, who pay cash." Merchants, of course, understood this trade as a generally harmless way to supplement their bottom line. This dispute between important members of the southern white community would acquire even greater significance once the South seceded from the Union.[73]

Merchant families straddled a cultural divide between the antebellum North and South. In the South they personified the cultural influence and economic grasp of the liberal capitalist order developing in the North and in Europe. Merchant families were among the few white Southerners who experienced a physical and psychological divide between their home and their workplace. In both spheres they, like their Yankee colleagues, embraced the principles of time discipline. The manner in which parents in commercial families raised their children and related to one another suggests the growing influence of a national bourgeois culture. Furthermore, they openly admired many of the modern, bourgeois cultural practices they found when they traveled North. These same households nonetheless fully embraced conservative southern values.

The stand of merchants on religion and race typically distinguished them from their business associates in the North. Commercial development, political crises, and technology influenced the activities and positions of them and their families within the South, causing their commitment to accepted southern ideals and their embrace of a bourgeois, liberal capitalist North to ebb and flow over the course of the antebellum period. Given different circumstances these factors might naturally have led merchants to share positions of leadership with the region's planter class in a commercially mixed slave economy. Of course that was not to be. Before any such evolution could occur, secession and war destroyed the South these merchants and their families called home.

4

Secession, Merchant-Soldiers, and the Civil War, 1860–1863

The election of 1860, secession, and the rise and fall of the Confederate States of America wreaked havoc upon the lives of thousands of southern merchants and their families. War changed business patterns, threatened the safety of homes, and called men away from their families to take up arms for their new nation. This turmoil left its mark on merchant culture. Many husbands and sons never returned home from the war. Wives and daughters exercised increased authority in homes and stores. Freed slaves left merchant families and began attempting to create new lives. The Civil War brought substantive and rapid change to the United States. Its significance for the liberal capitalist culture of the southern merchant is less clear. Opportunities for trade, speculation, and investment expanded during the war, and in many ways the conflict rewarded the economic habits and values that merchants had long practiced. At the same time, as war spread misery across the South many people discussed the morality and cultural ambiguity of the mercantile trade with a contempt and anger that was absent from prewar debates. Southerners protested the outsider status of its merchant classes with renewed vigor. Rather than transforming antebellum merchant culture, war intensified tensions and habits that had long characterized the lives of southern merchants and their families.

The election of the Republican Abraham Lincoln to the presidency in 1860 precipitated the initial wave of southern state secessions. For the first time in the young country's history a sectional party, committed to at least the gradual expunging of slavery, had won the presidency. The most serious in a chain of political crises that divided southern and northern sympathies during the 1850s, Lincoln's election gave defenders of the South's "peculiar institution" sufficient cause to demand secession. South Carolina, long the most radical southern state, led the secession movement when a special convention took the state out of the Union on December 20, 1860. Six other Deep South states quickly followed suit. Representatives from the secessionist states soon met in Montgomery, Alabama, and formed the Confederate States of America. Of course not all Southerners supported the secession movement. Divisions existed between slaveholders and nonslaveholders, rich and poor, urban and rural, those advocating immediate secession, cooperationists, and those claiming the mere election of a Republican president to be insufficient cause for secession, and finally Unionists who opposed secession on patriotic and constitutional principles. Yet the rivalry of various political and economic factions notwithstanding, a widespread commitment to slavery, white supremacy, and mutual defense against a seemingly hostile antislavery majority united most white Southerners behind secession. During this tumultuous period even merchants, by now mainly ex-Whigs and often political moderates, could agree with the southern nationalist James D. B. De Bow when he declared the Republican Party to be "an active, powerful, unscrupulous organization." The more significant question for fire-eating leaders and their followers across the South was whether the region's commercial classes would take the personal economic risks and support secession despite the distinct possibility of violent conflict over seemingly abstract constitutional principles.[1]

The southern merchant community did not have a single unified position on the question of secession. This is hardly surprising when one considers the financial, geographic, and social divides among storekeepers, larger wholesalers, and regional cotton factors. Those with close ties to the region's political and cultural elite tended to embrace the secessionist cause with passion. Merchants who originally hailed from the North and still had family there generally opposed secession. The bulk of the merchant community rested somewhere between these two extremes, resisting hasty action and believing that those most responsible for the current political crisis could be found in the fanatical ranks of both the northern abolitionists and the southern fire-eaters. The political and social journey these merchants followed during the secession crisis and the early years of the Civil War, from initial ambivalence to conditional support for the Confederate cause, further demonstrates their ambiguous southern identity.

Merchants large and small privately questioned the merits of secession during the last two months of 1860. The North Carolina dry-goods merchant Jonathan Worth, a Unionist and old Whig, grew despondent

witnessing the secession of the Deep South. He blamed zealous abolitionists and secessionists for blocking political compromise and destroying
his beloved Union. A political leader, Worth opposed calling a secession
convention in 1861 and claimed that "during the canvass I had in front of
my store a large flag marked, 'United we stand and divided we fall, Union
Forever.'" Fellow North Carolinian Cushing Hassell described the United
States Congress as being in a "fog" during the crisis but also declared his
own state legislature to be "equally at fault." George Walton Williams of
South Carolina, a vehement opponent of abolitionism and the Republican
Party, stood firmly against secessionists within his state. Like thousands of
their fellow Southerners, Worth and Williams initially had serious reservations about their state's decision to leave the Union. Ultimately, however, both men joined their neighbors in supporting secession once their
home states left the Union and formed the Confederate States of America.
Reuben Clark, a clerk and partner in the Knoxville, Tennessee, firm of
Cowan and Dickinson succinctly described the predicament he and most
merchants confronted. He had personally opposed secession but had to
take sides. In the end, Clark, like Robert E. Lee, justified his support
for the Confederacy on the grounds that he "could not desert my own
people." The secession crisis forced southern merchants to reconsider their
values and political assumptions. It also made them anxious about the
economic bottom lines of their businesses.[2]

Established businessmen with trade connections around the country viewed secession as a dire threat to their economic well-being. They
adhered to the same position as was espoused by southern manufacturers,
who, according to the historian Harold S. Wilson, "maintained steady
business communications with the North" and "took a Whiggist perspective on national economic issues such as the tariff, banking, and railroad
development; and they vigorously opposed the violent rhetoric of nullification and secession." Merchants in 1860 Vicksburg, Mississippi, fit this
pattern. They had plans for new railroads, shops, and even a cotton factory.
The collapse of the Union not only jeopardized these financial designs but
also had the potential to topple whatever social influence merchants had
achieved. Even smaller storekeepers in the Deep South feared the effects of
secession upon their trade. Samuel P. Richards and his brother Jabez, both
native Englishmen, operated a Book, Music, and Fancy Store in Atlanta,
Georgia, and had little use for the political leadership that seemed to be
driving their business to financial destruction. Samuel did not hide his

contempt for outspoken secessionists, whom he described in his diary as "*professional* men and young *squirts* who have but little or nothing to lose in any event, or *politicians* who aspire to office in a Southern Confederacy." Richards found the political excitement resulted in dull business for his store and in the winter of 1860 declared secession to be a "momentous crisis" that he feared would bring "distress and ruin upon us."[3]

Businessmen living in the upper South and the border states had even greater cause to fear that secession would devastate their professional lives. Wholesale agents in that region often enjoyed a sizable trade with neighboring free states. Merchants in Lynchburg, Virginia, worried that secession would end their lucrative tobacco trade with the North. Predictably, most of them spoke on behalf of the Union. The 1860 election in Mobile, Alabama, saw the majority of residents, led by several businessmen, vote for the national Democratic candidate, Stephen Douglas. The Constitutional Union candidate, John Bell, a senator from Tennessee who was popular among cotton factors and many businessmen who had roots in the North, finished second. The Warrenton, Virginia, merchant John R. Turner certainly would have approved of Mobile's support for the Tennessean. During the fall of 1860 he and his business colleagues organized a Bell & Everett Club that met every Monday night. There men and women would listen to three or four speeches in support of the Union, the Constitution, and political moderation. As late as February 1861, businessmen in Williamston, North Carolina, voted to continue purchasing their goods from northern suppliers as long as their state remained in the Union. The availability of cheap goods took precedence over any sympathy these men shared for their fellow Southerners living in the new Confederacy. Far from unusual, such actions by the merchant class and the hypocrisy of their customers led an obviously frustrated editor of the *Federal Union* in Milledgeville, Georgia, to complain:

> While southern merchants patronize Northern houses, the North will continue to laugh at us, and continue to steal our property, whenever they can. . . . Nine-tenths of the political hotspurs of the South who are almost crazy because they can't get rid of the Union in a day, will buy goods from a merchant, if the latter gets them from Fred Douglas [*sic*], provided the merchant sells them a few cents under the other local merchants, in the place where they reside. As long as Southern men will buy of Southern mer-

chants who sell them the cheapest, it is idle to expect Southern merchants to buy their goods of Charleston houses.[4]

The editor was somewhat unusual in this case because his broadside was leveled more at the patron for undercutting southern economic independence than at the merchant. He was right to note, however, the volatile financial situation in 1860–1861. Reckoning the harmful financial effect that secession would have upon trade along the Mississippi River in general and their hometown, Louisville, Kentucky, in particular, the clerk John Jefferson and his merchant father Thomas Jefferson clung to the "Old Democratic Ship" by voting for Stephen Douglas in the national election and the Union ticket in local elections. The young clerk strongly objected to the belligerent rhetoric of fire-eaters like William L. Yancey of Alabama. The political havoc such radicals created damaged the Kentuckian's business. Even marginally successful merchants in the upper and lower South recognized the close relationship between shifting political sentiment and trade. Before secession reached what now seems its inevitable denouement in bloody war, few businessmen joined the leading ranks of states' rights and nationalist radicals across the South. Political moderation and business considerations remained the order of the day. Once a working majority of Southerners rallied behind the Confederacy in early 1861 most pragmatic merchants swiftly, if not enthusiastically, joined their ranks. Some even came to love their new nation.[5]

During the first few months of 1861 popular support for secession and the new Confederacy grew among merchants and the general population alike. Commenting upon the wild revelry in Atlanta following Georgia's secession from the Union on January 19, 1861, Samuel Richards wrote, "I cannot sympathize in such demonstrations although I have lately been obliged to think that Secession was a stern necessity for us in the present crisis." Thomas Webber, a partner in the Marshall County, Mississippi, firm of Webber & Watkins expressed the shifting views of many in the merchant class when he wrote in his diary:

> Aside from the financial troubles which trouble me, chill my very Soul and sap my life blood. The political troubles of the Country are enough to weary any man out of his life who feels and [sic] interest in the interests & welfare of his country in the good & glory of his nation. The Secession of the State of South Carolina is

a step toward breaking the proudest and most powerful nationality on the globe. I was always opposed to a dismemberment of our
government up to the election of Lincoln as our chief Magistrate
of the nation. But finding that we can have no security for our
rights and no guarantees of our freedom under his administration. I see that Secession or revolution is the only remedy.[6]

Changing nationalist rhetoric and southern pride climaxed when
Confederate forces in Charleston, South Carolina, under the command
of General P.G.T. Beauregard, bombarded Fort Sumter for two days, April
12–13, 1861. On April 14, the commander of the Federal garrison surrendered the fort. In the days immediately following the fall of Fort Sumter,
President Lincoln called upon the states to furnish troops to restore the
Union. Refusing to take up arms against their sister slave states, four more
southern states seceded and joined the Confederacy: Virginia (April 17),
Arkansas (May 6), Tennessee (May 7), and North Carolina (May 20). War
had come. More celebrations erupted across the South. Men rushed to
join the army; women began helping to organize the home front; and cautious storekeepers prepared their businesses for the inevitable disorder.[7]

Few merchants or their families proved immune to the infectious war
fever. Formerly ambivalent businessmen now railed against the "fanatical aggressors" from the North who sought to take away southern rights.
Once secession had become fact most threw their support behind a strong
new Confederacy but held out hope that war could be avoided. While visiting her sister in Yazoo County, Mississippi, Kate Carney expressed surprise and pleasure upon learning that her storekeeper father had joined a
home guard in Murfreesboro, Tennessee; she had been "afraid Pa, was still
for the Union." According to Kate, local opinion seemed to have swayed
the storekeeper: "I know from the way he writes & by him being changed,
there is an unusual amount of stir & excitement at home." Merchant-
farmer William Henry Wills and his son Richard Henry Wills both feared
the consequences of war, while emotionally preparing for its possibility.
The Wills family, from Halifax County, North Carolina, prayed for peace
and put their lives on hold when war erupted. Richard wished to marry
but concluded that taking a wife in such "troublesome times" would be
foolhardy. Similarly the outbreak of war ended the store clerk Robert
A. Grannis's futile attempts at courtship. While employed in the presti-
gious Richmond, Virginia, dry-goods firm of Kent, Paine, & Company,

Grannis had spent months attempting to win the heart of Emma Kent, the daughter of one of the firm's partners, Horace L. Kent. Once Virginia seceded from the Union and war appeared imminent, the Brooklyn, New York, native thought it best to return to the North rather than be forced to enlist in the Confederate army and fight his friends and family from back home.[8]

Many families straddling the sectional divide found themselves in similar circumstances because of the impending conflict. More so than most of their white neighbors during the secession crisis, merchant families understood the grave implications of severing political ties with the North. Obviously their economic connections to northern wholesalers and creditors directly determined their livelihood. Many had close friends and family in the North. Together they witnessed the dissolution of their world. The correspondence between brothers Daniel Hoard (D.H.) Baldwin and William Baldwin reveals how, for some, the Civil War stereotype of "brother against brother" was a painful reality. D. H. Baldwin, a cotton factor in Savannah, Georgia, had maintained close personal and economic ties with his family, particularly his brother William, back in his boyhood home near Phillipston, Massachusetts. Apparently William had a career in business as well. The two men exchanged lengthy communications on the secession crisis. Between requests to "settle up all of my present bills and be ready for any emergency," D. H. Baldwin filled letters to his brother with attacks against the Republicans and warnings about the cost of war. As well as blood, the latter included a financial price, and D.H. advised his brother to "calculate your business" on the assumption that the South would never return to the Union. Though he backed secession on the grounds that the South had to defend itself, Baldwin predicted the war would last at least three years and see "3 to 4 Millions" killed before it ended. "I know the South will not give up what they deem their rights," Baldwin wrote his brother, "and I presume the North will do all they can to win us." Debates over a "nonsensical" Republican majority, as D. H. Baldwin described Lincoln's base, roiled a merchant family in Savannah as well. Jacob L. Florance, a merchant in Philadelphia, warned his son-in-law, who owned a commodity brokerage and shipping firm in the southern city, that the "people of the south will be woefully taxed for their fun."[9]

Such instances of painful separations and shaken families occurred throughout the South during the spring of 1861. What distinguished southern merchants from their neighbors was their business activity immediately following the onset of war. Merchants and their families tirelessly worked to place their businesses on a war footing. For some this entailed a temporary pause in business until the economic and political furor generated by the collapse of the Union subsided. Most expected to continue in the mercantile trade either with their established creditors and suppliers in the North or perhaps with new southern and European firms. As practical businessmen, when merchants saw their daily sales diminish during the excitement surrounding the new Confederate government and the possibility of war in the spring of 1861, they began trying to collect the outstanding debts on their books. It seemed wise to settle old accounts before customers joined the Confederate army, relocated, or spent what hard currency they might have saved. As business declined to the point of "suspension" in Cartersville, Georgia, the storekeeper Heyman Herzberg collected bills, packed his remaining stock of merchandise, sold his house and furniture, and shipped everything to his brother-in-law in West Point, Georgia, for safekeeping. A Mississippi storekeeper complained in his diary, "It seems useless to make any effort toward business & am Selling [sic] goods enough but my debtors wont pay up at all. The present international troubles and the prospect of civil war with the north make men pocket their money and you cant persuade it out of them." Some northern-born merchants had even greater incentive to conclude their business operations as public-spirited neighbors exercised their newfound Confederate patriotism by driving Yankees out of their communities. When Lincoln called on volunteers to put down the southern rebellion, residents in towns like Williamston, North Carolina, encouraged northern merchants and teachers to return home with strong "recommendations" and written passports from the local authorities.[10]

Once war between the United States and the Confederacy seemed inevitable, northern creditors attempted to collect on the loans they had made to southern storekeepers. Wholesale firms from New York City, Philadelphia, and elsewhere wanted to settle their open accounts while normal business operations seemed to persist between the two regions. The novelist and proslavery editor John B. Jones described the remarkable scale of this activity in Richmond, Virginia. During the last week of April 1861, Jones wrote in his diary: "Today I recognize Northern merchants and Jews in the streets, busy collecting the debts due to them. The Convention [Virginia secession convention] has thrown some impediments in the way; but I hear on every hand that Southern merchants, in the absence of legal obligations, recognize the demands of honor, and are sending money North, even if it be used against us. This will not last long."[11] Evidence supports Jones's observation that merchants continued to pay their debts to northern creditors despite secession and the threat of war. Before the Civil War interrupted its credit rating activities in the South, R. G. Dun & Company continued to receive positive reports from the field regarding the financial dependability of firms in seceded states. Almost five months after Louisiana left the Union, a firm in New Orleans was deemed a "safe" and "perfectly good" risk for northern creditors. The same held true for merchants throughout the young Confederacy. During the fall of 1862 the British hardware wholesaler and creditor William Carson Corsan toured the Confederacy. From Federally occupied New Orleans, through Mobile, to Charleston and Richmond, he found "the greatest anxiety existed here that their foreign and even Northern creditors should know that they had not repudiated, and did not intend to repudiate, a single debt, but could and would pay every cent and interest." The rationale behind such behavior on the part of so many Confederate businessmen can be found in their continuing relationships with northern capital.[12]

Pragmatic merchants were reluctant to sever their financial ties with the North. Even businessmen who counted themselves among the most fervent supporters of the Confederacy refused to close the door entirely on possible economic relationships with Yankee firms. Sometimes honor, albeit a more commercially oriented version than what Bertram Wyatt-Brown and other historians have described, influenced merchants to pay their debts to northern creditors. Thomas Webber recorded in his diary that many of the "best men" in his Mississippi home did not intend to "put themselves to much trouble to pay their eastern debts." He planned not to follow this course, because, as he understood his situation, "my honor compels me to think I must act in compliance with my promise no matter to whom it is made and I am going to pay as I would if no difficulty existed." The fact that he and his partner were "selling goods Rapidly [*sic*]" to anxious customers during the secession crisis helped soften the financial blow his principled stand delivered. O. S. Baldwin showed himself to be another Confederate merchant with strong ties to the North. Despite his allegiance to the southern cause during the secession crisis, Baldwin agreed to serve as the business agent for fellow Wilmington merchant Samuel D. Allen who had returned to his home in Putnam,

Connecticut. When the Confederate government accused Allen of being an "alien enemy" and attempted to sequester his property, Baldwin fought the move in court on the grounds that only Allen's poor health, not northern sympathies, led him to leave North Carolina. Baldwin argued before Judge Asa Biggs, the brother of yet another North Carolina merchant, that a doctor's orders had sent Allen back to New England and that "since his departure sundry letters have been received from him in which he expresses his intention to return to Wilmington with the view of continuing his resident there." No evidence suggests, however, that Allen returned to Wilmington while it remained in Confederate hands. One thing is certain, Baldwin and Allen had loaned each other hundreds of dollars before the war, and they valued their economic relationship, if not their personal friendship. Baldwin's rather weak defense of Allen's hasty departure from the South suggests these ties mattered more to him than his growing loyalty to the young Confederacy. Cultural and ideological bonds between southern and northern merchants remained strong, and, after all, business was business.[13]

The case of the Atlanta merchant and Confederate blockade-runner Sidney Root is instructive. Born in Montague, Massachusetts, in 1824, Sidney Root moved to Lumpkin, Georgia, in 1844 where he worked as a clerk in his brother-in-law E. E. Rawson's store. Five years later the young entrepreneur had entered into a partnership with Rawson, and the firm of Rawson & Root began making money in the dry-goods business. By 1857 Root had amassed enough wealth to try his luck in the growing town of Atlanta, where he formed a new mercantile firm with a local businessman named John N. Beach. When war erupted in 1861, the wealth and political influence Root enjoyed made him a leading businessman in Atlanta. An old "Union man," the turbulent events of the 1850s convinced the merchant that the two sections could no longer live in harmony and that the South must secede in order to protect its interests against northern aggression. John Beach remained a firm supporter of the Union and relocated to the North for the duration of the war. All the while the partnership of Beach & Root persevered as a vital financial enterprise. Before the Union blockade of southern ports took effect, the firm had purchased and shipped $150,000 worth of goods from the North to the South. By the end of 1861, Beach had borrowed ten thousand dollars from an Augusta, Georgia, bank to open cotton trading offices in Liverpool, England, and Le Havre, France, in addition to the branches they already operated in

New York City and Atlanta. Root, who counted President Jefferson Davis and other leading Confederate officials among his personal friends, apparently saw no conflict between his economic ties to Yankeedom and his political support for the Confederacy. The Civil War dictated how Root and Beach lived; the war tested their political convictions; the war killed their friends and neighbors; but initially the war did not change the nature of their business. Wealthy southern cotton factors and middling storekeepers did not discard their liberal capitalist values during the Civil War. Rather they supported the Confederacy while still keeping an eye out for the main chance.[14]

The public roles merchants and their families undertook in the Confederacy resembled those they had typically performed during the antebellum period. Few businessmen obtained important positions in the Confederate government. Southern political leadership continued to be dominated by planters and lawyers. Merchants did, however, remain active in state and local government. The northern-born Texas merchant and farmer John Adriance, described once in a credit report as a "perfect Yankee Sharper," served as a deputy for the Confederate Commissary Department and as the Brazoria County commissioner during the war. Similarly, once Confederate authorities recognized the business acumen of the Tennessee storekeeper George O'Bryan, they transferred the private from his regiment to serve in the commissary department. North Carolinian Asa Biggs served as a Confederate judge. In central North Carolina, Jonathan Worth would serve as county commissioner for the Relief of Indigent Soldiers' Families for Randolph County. Another Tar Heel merchant, Peter Mallett, directed the North Carolina Conscript Bureau. On a more local level, before fighting actually began, Sidney Root joined the Minute Men of Fulton County (Georgia), an organization, consisting of Atlanta's political and economic elite, that promised to "stand ready" in support of the state's efforts "in asserting her independence." Root also belonged to an extralegal "committee of safety" whose goal was to rid Atlanta of individuals "hostile and dangerous to the rights and interests of the city or state." Like his colleague to the south, Cushing Hassell helped form a vigilance committee in Williamston, North Carolina. The committee, which included his cousin and fellow merchant Joseph Biggs, met regularly in the counting room of Hassell's store, where they dedicated themselves to "scrutinizing all such persons coming into this vicinity," with the idea that they would "release the same or hand them over to the proper authorities, according to their best discretion." Later in the war, the state appointed Hassell and Biggs, among others, to receive bonds and certificates from state authorities for the purposes of raising a police force, providing aid to soldiers' families, and paying for bounties, subscriptions, and transportation of volunteers.[15]

Proficient bookkeepers, entrepreneurs, and community gadabouts, it is not surprising that merchants would be drawn to such wartime occupations as commissary agents, town quartermasters, and army recruiters. Such jobs readily fit within the activities and liberal capitalist worldview these businessmen had embraced during the antebellum period. The support that merchant wives and daughters lent the Confederacy proceeded along similar lines. The Civil War drastically changed the lives of southern women. Empty vessels both legally and politically during the antebellum period, women were encouraged to view the family as the appropriate outlet for their affection and feminine influence. The dislocations of war undermined this paradigm. The work of Drew Gilpin Faust, Catherine Clinton, LeeAnn Whites, and other scholars has revealed that during the first two years of the conflict, Confederate, state, and local leaders called upon women to support the war effort in ways that ultimately politicized their traditional activities. George C. Rable has concluded that the new roles forced upon southern women led, at least temporarily, to a reign of "sexual confusion." The work women performed during the first two years of the war almost immediately began undercutting the established paternalistic order. Women in merchant families came to exemplify this trend.[16]

Patriotic women from merchant families joined their neighbors, mainly those hailing from the planter class, in forming institutions to aid the Confederate war effort and sustain the home front population. That such a devoted sisterhood should mobilize early in the war is hardly surprising since, as members of a property-holding and sometimes a slaveholding class, the wives and daughters of prosperous merchants benefited from the same social structure that sustained the planter class. Of course one of the planter class's responsibilities that did not devolve to most women in merchant families was the management of large numbers of slaves. Since most mercantile families did not own even house slaves, much less field slaves, few mistresses in commercial households were forced to become, in Drew Faust's words, "reluctant agents of power" over their slaves. Nevertheless, with this important exception, the experience of most wives and daughters in mercantile families mirrored that of the planter class. Thus the ranks of fundraising, nursing, supply, and other charitable organizations across the Confederacy, particularly in towns and cities, included dozens of wives, daughters, and sisters of established southern merchants. The managerial skills these women had gained in helping to operate stores served them well in their work with volunteer organizations. Hospitals had to be established and maintained, food and clothing collected and distributed, and money raised. Such activities fit neatly within the purview of women who had worked behind a store counter. For example, Catherine Barnes Rowland, the wife of Augusta, Georgia, cotton factor Charles Rowland, served in the local Ladies' Aid Society after her husband enlisted in the Confederate army. She also made a point of privately donating goods to needy families in and around Augusta during the war. The wife of another merchant, this time in Columbus, Georgia, incurred the displeasure of her husband when she donated his shirts to a local hospital for use as bandages. Likewise women from the professional and planting classes in Mobile, Alabama, formed the Protestant Episcopal Church Employment Society to provide sewing jobs for poor women and war widows. The members of the society applied their entrepreneurial expertise by opening a garment shop in order to sell goods directly to the public. Such charitable activities aided the war effort while simultaneously reinforcing the status of wealthy women from the planter and merchant elite.[17]

Of course public-spirited men from mercantile families lent their support to the Confederacy as well. Older merchants who wished to aid the Confederate cause and younger commercial men who did not serve in the army occasionally organized or labored alongside their wives and daughters in relief work. The wartime activities of George Walton Williams, a merchant and banker in Charleston, South Carolina, helped make him, according to his biographer, the city's "outstanding philanthropist." The influential forty-year-old, who would live until 1903, did not join the Confederate army, but he did create or join the Soldiers' Board of Relief, the Charleston Subsistence Committee, the Free Market of Charleston, and the Committee for the Procurement of Wood for the Citizens. At the same time, his wife was a member of the Ladies Clothing Association and the Ladies Auxiliary Christian Association. As did many others among the southern elite, Williams and his wife supported the Confederacy by providing supplies to victims of the war. Typically well known in their communities and proficient in obtaining goods for their own stores, orchestrating relief work for widows and orphans proved to be relatively easy for Confederate merchants. Another forty-year-old merchant, Abraham Minis, helped coordinate the activities of the Ladies Relief Society in Savannah during the fall of 1861 as that organization obtained equipment for the Oglethorpe Light Infantry stationed at Camp Lawton, Georgia. Of course some especially wealthy merchants spent considerably more money than time supporting the Confederacy. Moses Mordecai earned praise for being a "Generous and Patriotic Jew" when he donated ten thousand dollars to the South Carolina treasury shortly after his home state seceded. One savvy merchant observed that the fundamental difference between peace and wartime for a businessman was that during the latter his work on behalf of the community seemed to be "all gratis." Mordecai may well have agreed with this assessment.[18]

The precise number of mercantile men and women who joined charitable organizations across the Confederacy cannot be determined, but manuscript evidence from the period suggests that their level of participation was proportional to their presence in the general southern population. Larger towns with relatively large commercial populations saw more merchants involved with charitable and relief activities, but the trend was for planters and their families to dominate relief work in the Confederacy. While men and women from merchant families employed their commercial skills for relief work, most did not volunteer for such duty; as they had before the war, it seems they deferred to the leadership and zeal of the planter class. More often than not, men from the commercial ranks who wished to support their new government did so, like most Southerners, by joining the army. Class privilege influenced how men from mercantile families experienced life in the Confederate army. A majority of commercial men, if not many leading businessmen, joined the infantry, but their relatively high status enabled them to receive a disproportionate number of commissions as officers compared with typical Southerners, particularly those from the poorer, nonslaveowning yeoman class. Individuals from the slim ranks of avid secessionist merchants were more likely to have the necessary wealth and influence to raise and eventually command military companies. In the spring of 1861, D. G. Cowand, a merchant in Plymouth, North Carolina, began recruiting men whom he expected to command. Over several weeks Cowand organized the second company from Plymouth and became its captain. In the same state, the Fayetteville wholesale merchant Peter Mallett parlayed his antebellum commercial and political experience to become colonel of a North Carolina battalion and "Commandant of Conscripts" in his state. Of course the fortunes of war helped some individuals move rapidly up the ranks. John Fite, the son of a merchant, captained Company B of the Seventh Tennessee Infantry. After his regiment withstood several bloody engagements in northern Virginia in 1862, the onetime captain found himself a colonel. Battlefield deaths led to promotions for many commercial men.[19]

Such examples notwithstanding, the typical experience of men from commercial families conformed to that of most Confederate soldiers. They joined, fought, and often died as enlisted men. Called to protect their families and communities against the threat of Yankee barbarism, hundreds of clerks, small storekeepers, and even partners in larger commercial firms across the South joined their local regiments. Indeed, older merchants found themselves "bereft of all white male help" around the store. Edward Murphy, a forty-two-year-old widower with an eleven-year-old son, took a leave of absence from his partnership in the New Orleans firm of John I. Adams & Co. and enlisted in Company B of the Louisiana Guard. The Confederate private entrusted his share of the firm, a tidy thirty-five thousand dollars, to the care of his business partners. This pattern repeated itself across the South. In an examination of 107 company rolls representing 7 states, 28 regiments, and 9,000 private soldiers, the historian Bell Irvin Wiley counted 472 clerks and 138 merchants. Clearly many commercial men heard the call to arms. The merchant Heyman Herzberg described the war fever in Cartersville, Georgia, as "very great" and said that "every young man was expected to join some military organization." The enthusiasm in the town was such that all three merchant Herzberg brothers, though born and raised in Philadelphia, entered Confederate ranks. Patriotism and the opportunity to achieve personal glory on the battlefield inspired these merchants, their brothers, and their sons, to join the Rebel army.[20]

Charles Christopher Blacknall exemplified this commitment in the extreme. A dry-goods merchant and resort owner before the war, Major Blacknall of the Twenty-third North Carolina fervently embraced the Confederate cause and sought to make this passion his legacy to his young son Oscar, whom he affectionately called "Captain." Writing from Virginia in March 1862 to his family back home in western North Carolina, Blacknall described his expectations for a spring of hard fighting. He hoped for success in the coming campaign but tried to prepare

Oscar for the possibility that his father might die in battle. If he should be so "unfortunate" as to be killed, Blacknall wanted to leave the "best fortune" that he could hand down to his son: "that you must follow my footsteps in this respect and shoulder your musket as soon as you are large enough to carry one, and fight the Yankees to the last." Oscar was not yet a teenager. Few commercial men, civilian or military, openly expressed such devotion to the Confederacy. Perhaps they did not have to, as their sons joined the Washington Light Artillery, the First Mississippi Volunteers, and other such regiments from virtually every corner of the South. Early in the war men and boys like Oscar Blacknall felt significant pressure to enlist. At least during the first few years of the war, those belonging to merchant families, like most Southerners, publicly condemned men who shirked military duty. During the secession crisis Thomas Webber deplored his community's inability to raise a company for the home guard. He concluded reluctantly that "nothing short of the blaze and thunder of the enemy's cannon will arouse us from our lethargy." In their personal correspondence, however, these same commercial men rarely alluded to their own fears of risking life and limb in the army. Thus the manuscript evidence is scant in this regard, but in at least one instance a member of a self-styled merchant "family," a slave named Harrison Beckett, described how the patriarch's son deserted in the face of the enemy.[21]

The forty-nine slaves who labored on the plantation of the merchant-planter Iredell D. Thomas in San Augustine County, Texas, witnessed the results of unsteady martial spirit firsthand. In an interview after the war Beckett described how combat revealed the character of his old master's two sons, Iredell Jr. and James. Soon after war erupted both of the Thomas boys joined the Third Texas Cavalry. The regiment boasted over a thousand volunteers who served under the command of Brigadier General Benjamin McCulloch. Iredell and James seemed to adjust to the toil of drills and other military preparations, but combat proved to be overwhelming for one of them. Beckett remembered the surprise he felt as a young boy upon hearing his fellow slaves and the Thomas family heatedly discussing "Little Ide's" desertion from his unit. The slaves remarked that when Iredell saw the first cannon "busted" (that is, discharged—most likely at the battle of Wilson's Creek or later at Pea Ridge), he "start runnin' an' never stop 'til he git back home." Not long after his desertion a band of men swept through the plantation, and Beckett saw them "git little Ide an' take him back," where he continued to serve with his unit. Behaving more valorously than his older brother, James Thomas "didn't break de ranks" and "stood his ground," an accomplishment that surprised Beckett in light of Little Ide's experience. The Thomas brothers went on to serve in the Confederate army for the remainder of the war. Later both gained a measure of political notoriety in postwar Texas, James as a senatorial candidate in 1877 and Iredell as a leading organizer of the Ku Klux Klan in San Augustine County. No evidence indicates that either the Thomas family or Iredell's superiors in the Third Texas Cavalry publicly commented about Iredell's ignoble homeward dash, nor did his temporary absence from the ranks seem to have any negative impact on him or his family during or after the war. Iredell Thomas Jr.'s stint in the Rebel army suggests the possible frailties of even the most patriotic commercial men when confronted with their own mortality on the battlefield.[22]

The actual combat experience that merchants and their sons faced while serving in the Confederate army during the first three years of the war proved to be typical in its frenzy, violence, and horror. As fighting men, merchants typically did not distinguish themselves. When Bell Irvin Wiley described the average Rebel private as everything from "light-hearted" to "war-weary," an occasional grumbler whose resilient "cheerfulness outweighed his dejection," he could have been commenting upon the character specifically of merchant-soldiers. Once away from home, many former commercial men, particularly those who saw combat, formed strong emotional bonds with other men in the ranks, whether farmers, mechanics, or planters. As Reid Mitchell has noted, once the initial excitement of the first few months of war died away and it became evident that the conflict would be a long and bloody one, men in the field forged closer bonds with one another. Their personal roles in this cataclysmic event and in army life in general seem to have intrigued former storekeepers, factors, and peddlers. Letters the men from merchant families wrote home help shed light upon their perception of combat and the solidarity in the Confederate ranks between 1861 and 1863.[23]

Like those of many Confederate soldiers, the letters and diaries that onetime commercial men wrote tended to focus on a few broad topics, mainly the tedium of camp life, the esprit de corps of their units, and the battles they engaged in. Letters home often described the soldier's "monotonous life" of drilling and marching between engagements. For some men from commercial backgrounds service in the army presented them with the most fatiguing labor they had ever performed. The dry-goods clerk Louis Leon, a private in the Fifty-third North Carolina serving in Virginia, had to endure ribbing from his comrades when his lieutenant made him carry water rather than cut wood since he performed the latter duty like a "clerk." The *"miserable idleness"* between battles, as one merchant described it, aside from being wearisome, gave these soldiers time to judge the character of the men in their units. Most liked what they saw. While serving as an officer in the Army of Tennessee during the winter of 1862, Benedict J. Semmes of Memphis commented repeatedly upon the honorable conduct and fighting spirit of Confederate soldiers. The Kentuckians in his unit had "fine manners, and a great deal of dash." The educated, bourgeois officer was particularly impressed that some of these refined men, who played several musical instruments and sang fashionable arias in camp, could also perform the "most daring & bloody deeds, and, keep a sort of diary of the number of Yanks they have individually slain," complete with the states and regiments of those they had killed. Despite the heavy casualties that the army suffered in 1862, and notwithstanding the wound he received at the Battle of Shiloh that spring, Semmes emphasized to his wife back in Memphis the camaraderie and high morale among the troops.[24]

As a member of the Louisiana Guard serving in Virginia, Edward Murphy also grew close to the men with whom he served. Initially stationed near Norfolk, Murphy had ample opportunity to admire the tenacity of the Virginia troops in particular. He found that they did not exaggerate their bravery. Relating the various martial qualities of southern troops to a friend back in New Orleans, the merchant praised the sons of Virginia for calmly going about the business of war while soldiers from other states "eternally" boasted of their ability to whip the enemy as though "God made them courageous and none others." Like many of the letters he wrote home in 1861, Murphy ended his account with an appeal to remember him to "all the folks at the store." The following year began auspiciously with a promotion to first lieutenant for the Irish-born merchant from Louisiana. As with so many others, Murphy's good fortune did not last: he was killed on August 9, 1862, fighting beside his men at the Battle of Cedar Mountain in Virginia.[25]

Merchants who saw combat as members of the Rebel army exhibited the same virtues and limitations that most soldiers, North and South, shared during the Civil War. During the first half of the war, eager to prove their courage and to defeat the Yankees, an enemy that threatened their homes and white racial hegemony, merchant soldiers willingly risked their lives on the battlefield. So long as the southern cause seemed alive, these men expressed few regrets over the hardships they endured. Some believed that the ordeal of war could fortify the individual and release his best qualities. This outlook extended at times to their families back home. Most would have agreed with the sentiments of one former storekeeper who wrote his mother, "I cannot see why those at home should not be willing to make some sacrifice while we who are in the army, make all, both of comfort and ease and frequently life itself." Indeed, men from numerous mercantile families paid for their support to the Confederacy with their lives.[26]

No accurate calculation can be made of the number of merchants who died fighting in the Confederate army during the first three years of the war, but nothing suggests that the mortality rate among commercial men deviated from the overall average of Confederate forces as a whole—about one in three men in uniform died. By 1863 numerous mercantile families, like their neighbors, had been scarred by war. The military experience of the Howze brothers from Mississippi is instructive.[27] During the late antebellum period Isham R. Howze and his wife Elizabeth raised seven children in Wall Hill, Mississippi, where, as described in earlier chapters, Howze and his partner operated a dry-goods store. Though he died in 1857, the thoughtful and self-conscious Howze, a man who once declared himself "too small to attract any notice," raised four boys who all eventually served in the Rebel army. Soon after the war erupted, the oldest son, twenty-nine-year-old George Adrian Howze, enlisted in the Forty-second Mississippi and left his wife, his home, and his clerking position in a Memphis wholesale firm when his regiment joined the Army of Northern Virginia in June of 1862. It seems Adrian Howze made a fine soldier as he rose in short order from the ranks of the enlisted to lieutenant. The young clerk also revealed himself to be a pious warrior. On May 17, 1863, shortly before the Confederate army invaded Pennsylvania, Lieutenant Howze was baptized and elected permanent secretary of his regiment's "Christian Association." Perhaps Howze's anxiety about the upcoming campaign nourished his religious awakening. If so, his worst fears were realized: the young lieutenant was killed on July 1, 1863, the first day of the Battle of Gettysburg. One of Adrian's younger brothers, William Duke Howze, served as a lieutenant in the First Mississippi. Taken prisoner when Fort Donelson fell to Union forces under General Ulysses S. Grant in 1862, twenty-three-year-old William was eventually exchanged and managed to survive the war. The third Howze brother, James Wilson, did not share such good fortune. Having enlisted in the Nineteenth Mississippi at the age of sixteen, the young soldier lost his life on June 28, 1862, fighting in the Chickahominy Swamp during the Seven Days' Battles. Finally, the youngest brother to serve, Henry LeGrand Howze, joined William's regiment, the First Mississippi, when it was reorganized in 1863, and he, like his brother, was captured by Union forces. Seized at Port Hudson in 1863, subsequently paroled and sent home, Henry was later arrested and imprisoned in Camp Chase for the duration of the war after being caught with an armed party near his home in Mississippi. The young Howze claimed that he was only hunting squirrels. By 1863 two Howze brothers had died in battle, while two others had been captured by the enemy. As will be seen in pages to come, few commercial families willingly sacrificed as much for the Confederacy as the Howzes.[28]

Crippling setbacks in the summer of 1863, with resounding defeat at Gettysburg and the loss of Vicksburg, undermined many soldiers' confidence, and those with a commercial background were no different from the mass of Confederate soldiers from the agricultural classes. Their letters home continued to resonate with patriotic and anti-Yankee sentiment, but in many cases the professions of optimism rang ever more hollow. Only days after the Rebel collapse at Vicksburg, Benedict Semmes, writing from his unit with the Army of Tennessee, told his wife "not to despair," that "I am just as sanguine as I ever was & indeed full of high hopes in spite of our recent Disaster." Semmes's confidence in the Confederacy's ultimate success offered tepid comfort to a wife and children made homeless by the war. Reuben Clark of the Fifty-ninth Tennessee was in the garrison that the Yankees captured at Vicksburg and, not surprisingly, had a different assessment of the course of the war. Though he returned to serve with his unit after his parole and exchange, Clark concluded that the "contrast was so great between their well fed and bountifully supplied army and our starved forces, that it disaffected many of our men." Months later he and other officers in the Fifty-ninth found it "impossible" to get some of the paroled men back into the army. Clark, Semmes, and other merchants who enlisted in the first months of war continued to support the Confederacy on the battlefield despite the setbacks of 1863, but as southern losses mounted during the last two years of the conflict, they increasingly sought fellow businessmen at home and in the North who would assist their families once the war ended.[29]

The experience of merchants who served in the Confederate army varied little from that of average soldiers who hailed from yeoman farmer families. While their unique commercial worldview influenced their decision to enter upon or avoid military service, once they were in the ranks, patriotism and unit loyalty typically overshadowed other considerations. The only two noteworthy exceptions to this were the tendency of former merchants to seek quartermaster positions in Confederate armies and their proclivity to speculate and trade goods between battles. The latter characteristic will be examined in chapter 5. The quartermaster and commissary departments of Confederate armies tended to draw a disproportionate number of men with commercial experience. According to the Confederate War Department the quartermaster was to provide "quarters and transportation of the army; storage and transportation for all military supplies; army clothing; camp and garrison equipage; cavalry and artillery horses; fuel; forage; straw and stationery." Most quartermasters also had responsibilities relating to the paymaster's duties. Commissary agents simply obtained and distributed food to the army. Regiments, brigades, military hospitals, and army headquarters typically each had quartermasters and commissary officers of various ranks. The diverse and unique duties required of these agents called for individuals who could be bonded and could responsibly handle public and private funds and property, who could function within an often inefficient Confederate bureaucracy and obtain enough material to supply large military units in a war-torn South. Writing to his wife, the farmer Edgeworth Bird described his duties as quartermaster with the Fifteenth Georgia as issuing "sundry things" that were charged and invoiced to him, "so I have them all to account for. Today, I believe it all right, so it is with money." It is unlikely a merchant would have to explain the process to his wife. At the same time quartermasters and commissary agents performed these duties, they also had to live with the widespread belief in the army that they exploited troops for personal profit while serving well behind the lines. Men who had operated stores in the antebellum South possessed the necessary skill, ambition, and thick hide to thrive in these positions.[30]

As a matter of stated policy the Confederacy did not explicitly recruit merchants for quartermaster and commissary positions. This said, Harold S. Wilson's study of Confederate industry found that Abraham Myers, the Confederate quartermaster general, recruited personnel from both "the old service and from the active businessmen of the South." The government did not record what their quartermasters and commissary officers had done before the war. The manuscript and newspaper records, however, show clearly that when merchants enlisted or were conscripted they often pursued and obtained these positions—Lieutenant John Zirvas Leyendecker, for instance, served as a quartermaster with the Thirty-third Texas; Benedict Semmes served as assistant quartermaster for the Army of Tennessee; and George O'Bryan became a commissary agent for his Tennessee regiment. The Richmond Clothing Bureau was administered by a former businessman, Major Richard P. Waller, who employed at least two former merchants in his office, Captain James B. Ferguson Jr. and his brother William. The former served as Abraham Myers's "principal contracting agent." In the Nashville quartermaster's depot, former merchant George Cunningham helped to outfit Albert Sidney Johnston's army, and he would later head the Atlanta depot in 1863. Former Mobile, Alabama, merchant William Anderson effectively ran the government's quartermaster depot in Memphis, Tennessee. The network employed twelve hundred manufacturing workers and spent approximately six hundred thousand dollars on supplies each month. The reason that Confederate authorities might prefer commercial men in these positions is self-evident. As one Southerner later commented about O'Bryan's promotion to the commissary department, he joined as a private, but his mercantile experience as a clerk in Nashville and his "keen business judgement" led Confederate authorities to place him where he could do the most good for the southern cause.[31]

The impetus for merchants to join the quartermaster and commissary departments is less apparent. Though direct evidence is scant, perhaps a desire to remain out of harm's way led some men to seek positions removed from action. At least that was what one commissary clerk believed. Before the war John R. Turner had been a merchant in Warrenton, Virginia. Once the Old Dominion seceded from the Union, Turner joined the Warrenton Rifles. This unit became part of the Seventeenth Virginia, in which Turner soon earned a promotion to second lieutenant. In late 1861 the regiment was camped near Centreville, Virginia, and Turner found himself courting a young woman named Sallie, who attended school in his hometown. In the letters he wrote to his sweetheart, Turner revealed his evolving views on the commissary department.

Early in the war, the merchant-cum-soldier did everything in his power to obtain a transfer to the commissary. After returning from a furlough during which he had visited Sallie, he wrote her about his attempts to find a commissary clerk's job: "It is very cold and uncomfortable in camp and will be much more so I suppose as the Winter [*sic*] advances." Much of the remainder of this letter is filled with patriotic sentiments and several pointed comments on the unchristian conduct of the Sabbath-violating cardplayers in his unit. Clearly Turner supported the war and cared about the character of his unit, but he also viewed the position of commissary clerk as more befitting someone like himself. His entreaties paid off in 1862 when Turner received an appointment as a commissary clerk in A. P. Hill's command. Over the course of 1862, Turner expressed to Sallie satisfaction with his work though he did not like many of his fellow officers. He kept his complaints to a minimum, though, and often asked about events in Sallie's life and business changes back home in Warrenton; the dissolution and formation of new mercantile partnerships still interested the commissary agent greatly. By the spring of 1863 apparent discontent with several officers in his unit as well as a newfound sense of "duty" had driven Turner to seek reassignment to a frontline unit from Warrenton. The patriotic merchant-soldier concluded that he had held "a soft place quite long enough" in the commissary service. More important still, Turner wrote, "*I am afraid my friends may think I sought the place to keep out of danger.*" During 1863 the Virginian continued to express mixed feelings about serving in the "*Bomb proof* department." The fact that Sallie need "feel no uneasiness in regards to my safety" pleased Turner, but he worried about the fate of his country and about his own manhood. In July he missed his opportunity to defend either one directly when his unit participated in the Gettysburg campaign, where Turner still saw no action. The letters to young Sallie back in Warrenton ended in 1863, but Turner continued in the commissary service for some time. Like many of his professional colleagues, Turner survived the war and commenced the mercantile trade once again, this time in Woodville, Virginia. By limiting his exposure to combat, commissary work may have challenged Turner's sense of manhood and may even have tarnished his public reputation, but the position also helped him escape death.[32]

Though initially indecisive, merchants and their families supported the Confederacy once it became a reality. Older men adjusted their business practices to new circumstances, while young men answered the call to arms. Women from commercial families joined their female neighbors from other ranks of society to support their men in the field. In most ways, the military experience of these men resembled that of any other soldier. Nevertheless, the merchant family did confront unique challenges during the war. As the conflict dragged on, the business habits and liberal capitalist worldview that helped define the merchant class proved to be of mixed value. As manufacturing increased, markets expanded and collapsed, and the speculation of all types of goods became commonplace, the influence of southern merchants grew accordingly. At the same time, their reputation as a class was ever more vilified, while their communities suffered from the devastation of a war that seemed to be closing in on them.

5

Merchants and Their Families in the Confederacy, 1861–1863

The effect of the Civil War on the southern commercial population transcended the number of merchants who served and died while fighting for the Confederacy. The war also radically altered the lives of families, friends, and business associates who lived on the home front. Confederate citizens endured material deprivation, loss of independence to a swelling state bureaucracy, and all the personal hazards associated with warfare. The conflict stretched the bonds of southern society to their breaking point. Within this maelstrom, commercial families, like their white and black neighbors, endured hardship in obtaining food, in being forced to relocate, and, of course, in losing loved ones to death in the war. When confronting these challenges and burdens, merchant families revealed the bourgeois ethos that distinguished them from the larger white southern population but not necessarily from their peers in the North.

In the face of disrupted trade, the behavior of merchants and their families during the first half of the Civil War often resembled that of commercial businessmen in the North, many of whom, particularly in eastern cities, depended upon southern trade. Nevertheless, as Sven Beckert found in New York City, "a minority of merchants . . . began to adjust themselves to the dynamics of the new age, and it was these who blossomed most during the war." John D. Rockefeller, an entrepreneur in Cleveland, Ohio, whose commercial trade boomed during the war and whose experience in certain respects paralleled that of the southern merchant class, provides a striking example. A partner in the wholesale commodity firm of Clark and Rockefeller, the young merchant, like most southern merchants, supported the broad values of the region where he lived. In 1854, Rockefeller wrote a high school essay attacking the "cruel masters" of the South, and by 1861 he was a firm supporter of abolition. At the same time, he kept his focus on the bottom line of his business—when called upon to serve in the army, Rockefeller paid a substitute three hundred dollars to go in his place. After the war he explained that military service "was simply out of the question. We were in a new business, and if I had not stayed it must have stopped—and with so many dependent upon it." This sentiment would be similarly expressed throughout the Confederacy by its merchant class. Rockefeller did support wartime charities. Even more important for his future endeavors, by 1863 government contracts and expanded trade allowed his business to increase fourfold as his firm earned a profit of seventeen thousand dollars. Government spending and the phenomenal growth of the state meant that never before "had the federal government played such an important role in domestic life." While the state had new, sometimes troubling power over their personal lives, such legislation as the Legal Tender Act (1862) and the National Currency Act (1863), by creating a national currency and stabilizing banks, generally benefited the commercial classes. Northern merchants negotiated the new economic landscape while on the lookout for the main chance. Their counterparts in the Confederacy often faced different hardships but carried themselves in a similar manner.[1]

Several policies implemented by the Confederate government had a conspicuous impact on merchant families. Conscription in particular troubled them and many of their white neighbors. Despite several notable military victories, by the spring of 1862 the South faced imminent disaster as the one-year enlistments of nearly half its troops were due to expire with few soldiers eager to reenlist. "The subject of revolunteering is the great topic in camp," wrote commissary clerk John Turner. "I hardly know what to do myself." On April 16, 1862, the Confederate Congress attempted to forestall a critical manpower shortage by enacting the first conscription law in United States history. It declared able-bodied white male citizens between the ages of eighteen and thirty-five liable to serve for three years. The act also extended the terms of one-year volunteers for another two years. Later supplementary acts advanced the eligibility age for service from thirty-five to forty-five years and sought to eliminate loopholes—particularly the hiring of substitutes—in the first act. Ultimately Confederate officials hoped the apparent shame of being drafted, combined with enlistment bonuses, would boost the number of volunteers. Nevertheless the Confederacy's continual struggle to keep men in its army, by force if necessary, inspired expressions of fear, contempt, and outrage among southern merchants and their families.[2]

Older, more established merchants, like many civilians, responded to conscription with apprehension. In Atlanta, Samuel Richards spoke for many of his colleagues when he remarked, "I dont want to go to war if I can avoid it; for if I go I fear I should be so little service and destroy my own self." Despite being an immigrant from England with family in Massachusetts, Richards defended secession and the new Confederacy as a just response to northern tyranny. This did not mean, however, that the thirty-eight-year-old merchant abandoned his "loathing and horror" of war or his sense of class privilege. He did everything in his power to avoid being thrown into the "company of such men as form the greater part of our army," where he feared that he would be "ordered about by incompetent, drunken officers." While few merchants shared Richards's squeamish elitist posture, many shared his reluctance to join the Confederate army. An occasional storekeeper needed to be embarrassed by the gift of a petticoat or pistol-whipped by a neighbor before he joined the ranks. Government conscription and community pressure tested the patriotism of would-be soldiers like Samuel Richards. The steps he and other merchants took to avoid service betray their conditional support for the Confederacy.[3]

Men from business families employed a variety of tactics to escape serving in the army. A respected merchant, Cushing B. Hassell managed to obtain a medical exemption for his twenty-one-year-old son Sylvester on the grounds that he suffered from consumption. The ailment presumably prevented the young man from serving in the army but did not stop the family doctor from prescribing a vigorous regimen of horseback riding for treatment. By 1864, Sylvester Hassell was teaching fourteen pupils at the Williamston Academy. He earned $86.90 for five months of work. If a medical excuse could not be had, it behooved the cautious businessman to purchase a substitute or to find employment in one of the work categories exempted from the draft. Heyman Herzberg, a merchant in north Georgia, purchased a substitute after his discharge from the army, though he still avoided the local provost marshal, who apparently sent all able-bodied men to the army regardless of their exempt status. Family ties helped David Worth avoid conscription in North Carolina when his father Jonathan Worth, a wealthy merchant and later the postwar governor of the state, managed to place the thirty-year-old in the position of state salt commissioner. The exemption that accompanied the job proved valuable to David when the law was passed in 1863 prohibiting him from continuing to pay a substitute to do his military service for him. Likewise, a position in city government and an appointment to direct soldier relief in his hometown of Charleston, South Carolina, provided an exemption for merchant George Walton Williams. A storekeeper and his son in Eagles Nest, Tennessee, procured exemption papers from the Confederate Nitre and Mining Bureau because they manufactured gunpowder for the government. When options of this sort were unavailable, some storekeepers, for instance the Texan Bart DeWitt, decided to escape the draft by joining a local militia unit. These units offered refuge for many young men, especially in Georgia and other states where the governor reserved his militia from conscription. These examples suggest that merchants interested more in business than in fighting could avoid serving in the Confederate army.[4]

The wartime example of Samuel Richards forcefully illustrates how a persistent storekeeper could exploit his skill and connections to escape conscription. Following the passage of the Confederacy's first draft legislation in April 1862, Richards and his brother Jabez, who was also his business partner, utilized every means possible to avoid conscription. Both men joined the local militia so they would not be eligible for service in the army. Like Heyman Herzberg, Richards was often reluctant to walk about the streets of Atlanta for fear of meeting officers who were "taking up the conscripts vigorously." By 1863, Samuel and Jabez had secured part-time jobs at a local newspaper called *The Soldiers Friend*—with perhaps unintentional irony, given the fact that draft laws exempted newspaper publishers and editors from army service. When this plan also failed, the Richards brothers had to resort to obtaining substitutes to fill their positions in the army. When the government no longer accepted substitutes a disgusted Samuel spewed, "This is what I call a grand Government Swindle." Despite the Richardses' apprehension, the army never conscripted them. Samuel and Jabez advocated the War between the States as long as their business wasn't harmed and they didn't have to carry any rifles. Wealth and business skill allowed the Richards brothers to escape military service until Sherman ended the war for Atlanta.[5]

Numerous government decrees besides the conscription law upset the lives of civilian merchants and their families. Like most white citizens of the Confederate States of America, merchants had to pay higher taxes during the war. On top of their regular taxes, by 1863 retail, wholesale, and commission merchants annually paid as much as two hundred dollars in "war taxes." A portion of this tax was levied on inventory in stores and warehouses—drafters of the tax hoped that, in addition to raising desperately needed revenue, this measure would discourage hoarding and speculation. A woman from South Carolina hailed the bill as a necessary measure to "make extortioners disgorge their accumulation for the benefit of the public." Predictably, some storekeepers complained that they could not sell much of this stock because of the war, and hence it should not be included under the war tax. Such protests went unheeded. When one Atlanta merchant refused to pay the war tax, the local tax collector declared him disloyal, closed his store, and sold his stock to pay what he owed. A few merchants even objected to their business losses when the Confederate government ordered their stores closed during days of public thanksgiving and fasting. Samuel Richards made it a point to be found behind his store counter on such days "with the door closed but not *fastened.*" Merchants on the southern home front denounced certain Confederate regulations, but these decrees did not fundamentally alter their commercial activity or the lives of their families. Indeed, most storekeepers found adapting to wartime business conditions easier than negotiating the upheaval that the conflict visited upon friends and family. These wounds proved more difficult to salve.[6]

The Civil War often generated ideological and physical rifts in commercial families. Like many others in the South, some of these families found themselves split along sectional lines. The occasional storekeeper on the Confederate home front lamented the fact that his father, mother, or siblings living in the North supported a bloody war upon southern rights. Conflicting allegiances within merchant families, though relatively infrequent, at times did weaken the ties of affection and obligation that had held them together before the war. Southern families threatened by or living under Federal occupation often suffered the most obvious discord. Murfreesboro, Tennessee, where Kate Carney's father operated a profitable store, was under Federal control as early as the spring of 1862. While Confederate forces would recapture the town for a short period in 1863, it would be dominated by Union troops for the remainder of the war. One of the many features of life under occupation that disgusted the nineteen-year-old Carney was the steady stream of old friends and family members who took the oath of allegiance to the United States. Whether such individuals took the oath out of conviction or because Federal forces required them to do it in order to conduct business, Carney labeled them all "detestable." Her father's business partner took the oath in May of 1862 along with several of her family's friends. Most shocking to Kate, however, was when her own brother took the oath and left the Confederate army, presumably after being captured. Upon hearing the news, Kate wrote in her diary, "Why didn't he die, before returning to bring eternal disgrace on the family." Later, after he returned to Murfreesboro looking "as well as ever," Kate noted angrily: "I hope he will regret taking the oath, I wish there was no blood in his veins that is in mine." The fact that her father refused to take the oath in 1862, while her friends' fathers and her very own brother did, severed many of the "intimate" ties she cherished from before the war. Business families who had no northern relatives, or households simply too committed, or too pragmatic, to be divided over politics, faced a more familiar plight: separation. The vagaries of war—battles, Federal raids, personal displacement—frequently limited or interrupted communication and personal contact between members of southern merchant families.[7]

As the war dragged on, invading Federal armies and the threat of nearby battles destroyed any sense of order that southern civilians may have had. Within this maelstrom, commercial families suffered along with their neighbors. Living in Martin County in eastern North Carolina, Cushing Hassell and his family quickly found how Federal raids eclipsed the rhythms of their daily lives in Williamston. Personal contact between friends and family diminished as Union forces wreaked havoc in their county. A licensed mail contractor for the Confederacy, who sold all types of goods, including gunpowder and shotguns, to the government, Hassell weathered the first Union raid of Williamston in July 1862. None of the three hundred soldiers who had arrived on Federal gunboats robbed the merchant's home or store. Nevertheless dozens of the family's neighbors fled their homes, many not to return for several years. The Hassell family lamented the disintegration of their southern community but thanked God for hearing their "prayers in behalf of Williamston & Martin County . . . that the enemy had as yet done the inhabitants very little damage."[8]

By November of 1862 the family's prayers were apparently no longer being answered. Once again Federal forces entered Williamston, this time sacking the town and plundering the Hassell home. The commercial family lost an estimated twenty thousand dollars in property. More personally distressing, Cushing Hassell, fearing arrest for his mercantile and militia activities, left his wife Martha, a native New Yorker, and his children to maintain their home in Williamston while he stayed with friends in central

North Carolina. The raid separated the Hassell family for several months in 1863, during which time Cushing and Martha communicated little. By 1864 the family had reunited, but repeated incursions of Union forces led the merchant to conclude, "Never were a premises put in worse plight by man & beast than these had been by the abolition forces." The Hassells' plight was repeated among commercial families across the Confederacy. The circumstances of war often tore these families apart—husbands forced to live temporarily in tents, wives staying with distant relatives, children sent away to schools in more protected settings. Such dislocations and separations had severe consequences for merchant families. On a basic level, these families, like other Southerners on the home front, expended more time and energy simply sustaining their material needs.[9]

The level of material wealth and even opulence that many commercial families had enjoyed in the antebellum South proved difficult to maintain during the Civil War. Warring armies, the Union naval blockade, and other factors threatened even the wealthiest southern merchants with relative economic deprivation. Like their neighbors, commercial families found meat, salt, and cloth increasingly difficult to obtain in the war-torn Confederacy. When these staples were available, their inflated price often depleted family budgets. For example, the high cost of bread and its impact on her family mortified the New Orleans teenager Clara Solomon. As early as July 1861 her father Solomon Solomon, a merchant and later sutler for the Army of Northern Virginia, owed more than fifty dollars to the local baker. The debt altered the behavior of the Solomon household as the family patriarch went to lengths to evade the baker, who apparently threatened to take Solomon to court if he did not meet his financial obligations. At one point Solomon dared not eat dinner with his family lest the baker choose that time to call and seek payment. Young Clara declared the entire affair "shameful" and hoped "Pa will be able to pacify him." Shortly after the embarrassing dinner episode Solomon paid the family's debt to the baker. Bills paid late, if at all, and obligations unmet—such was life on the Confederate home front.[10]

Bart DeWitt and his family in San Antonio, Texas, certainly learned how the exigencies of war could rapidly change a household's material circumstances. Like the Solomon family's store, which had the advantage of being located in the substantial commercial market in New Orleans, the modest but steady retail activity DeWitt had conducted in the late 1850s floundered during the first year of war. Having a family to support, the merchant scrambled to find work as a bookkeeper with the mercantile firm of Sweet & Lacoste. DeWitt quickly realized that the forty dollars he earned each month would not keep his "head above water." Though he supplemented his income with minor speculations in bacon and land and a "little store" of his own, DeWitt and his family still found it necessary to restrain their bourgeois appetites. They let their servant go and curtailed family purchases. DeWitt's wife wore the same bonnet for three years, and he went without a winter coat. DeWitt wrote to a colleague in Laredo that, while many of their friends continued to attend musical performances at the casino and fundraisers for Confederate soldiers, "we can stay at home and my fiddle take the place of an Orchestra and my little family does the part of the Audience, so we go on." The merchant detailed the small afflictions that his family had to bear so that his friend "may know extravagance has not been our motto." Like most struggling families, the DeWitts managed to secure basic items to sustain their household, but obtaining such luxury goods as bonnets, books, and wine proved more challenging. This said, it is important to note that many, perhaps most, storekeepers and their families were able to sustain their standard of living during wartime better than the average farm family in the Confederacy.[11]

The consumption of goods helped southern merchant families define themselves in the antebellum and Confederate periods. Their morale often rose and fell in relation to the availability of certain products. The primary difference between average white Southerners and commercial families was the latter's greater ability to satisfy their material wants. Studies of the Chattahoochee Valley and elsewhere reveal that leisure and consumption rates remained much more stable for the upper classes than for poorer yeomen. The evidence merchant families on the Confederate home front left behind, regardless of minor regional variations, generally supports this conclusion.[12] Commercial households far removed from the ravages of the battlefield and even those overrun by Federal troops were more capable of preserving their customary standard of living. Indeed, one merchant's wife wrote her husband in the Confederate army that "the enemy behaved so well in Memphis, that one can hardly realize their presence save when necessity going down to the neighborhood of their barracks." Further correspondence and diaries left behind by merchant families in such places as Memphis and New Orleans, both captured by Union forces in the spring of 1862, allude with relative frequency to luxury items. For instance only a few weeks after New Orleans fell, young Clara Solomon had already begun adjusting to Federal occupation. True, her merchant family endured a more precarious financial existence in 1862, particularly with her sutler father far removed from home in northern Virginia, yet her mother, sister, and she still had resources to purchase fine cloth, expensive food, and cocaine for their headaches. They continued to enjoy such simple pleasures as a neighbor's informal piano recital. More than offering solace amid the trauma of war, the ability of struggling commercial families like the Solomons to purchase and surround themselves with certain luxuries reflected the enduring values of a self-styled southern bourgeoisie. As Clara described the Solomon's piano, these objects changed "the aspect of a house, & like a baby" they offered "a well-spring of joy." Even small material comforts could remind them of the relative wealth and standing they had enjoyed before the conflict. To this same end, merchant families attempted to maintain many of their social and cultural routines.[13]

Activities that had helped define bourgeois civility for antebellum Southerners, whether attending dinner parties and public lectures or reading about the latest European fashions, continued to capture the imagination of many shopkeepers and their families during the Civil War. At a time when increasing numbers of white Southerners questioned the benefits of the commercial market and even families with means struggled to survive, merchants generally remained true to their market values. Like their "social betters" in the planter class, they still could spend a good deal of time polishing their silver, purchasing calico dresses, drinking Catalonian wine, reading northern newspapers, and enjoying other luxuries when available. Though the history being made on distant battlefields governed the tenor of civilian life on the Confederate home front, many Southerners, including members of merchant families, held fast to their nascent middle-class identities and kept attuned to changing cultural trends in the North as well as across the Atlantic. By the autumn of 1863 the daily newspaper in the commercial port of Wilmington, North Carolina, ran stories bemoaning the Confederacy's military setbacks that summer at Gettysburg and Vicksburg alongside a lengthy article on the revolution in European ladies' fashions. At once the readership could learn about the consequences of Vicksburg and the fact that "no lady of *ton* [French, meaning "tone"] will dare to promenade with trailing dresses or long petticoats" in the "fashionable centres" of Europe. While editor and subscriber might disagree over the relative merits of Jefferson Davis and his administration, it appeared certain that "hoops and skirts are quite exploded in Paris." Along similar lines, in early 1863 the *Memphis Daily Appeal*—published in Jackson, Mississippi, after the Tennessee city fell to Federal forces—printed a lengthy article on Paris fashions intended "For the Ladies." The piece informed readers, perhaps refugees from northern occupation or struggling Mississippians, that "at present poplin and taffetas are the materials most in voge [*sic*] for simple toilette." Parisians also wore felt bonnets; the author noted that "a very pretty one was trimmed with a velvet curtain, the same color as the bonnet, which was drab; on the front, a full piece of velvet, ending at the sides in two bows, and fastening two ostrich feathers." These and other stories suggest that not only did some kind of a consumer ethic continue during the war, it also served as an invaluable distraction for a war-weary southern populace. This peculiar dichotomy between the material and psychological toll imposed by a bloody war and the relative persistence of bourgeois values is illustrated in the lives of merchant wives. It was they, after all, who assumed more responsibilities during the conflict, all the while remaining grounded in the liberal capitalist worldview their families shared.[14]

Wives and mothers in commercial families, like their men, typically supported the Confederate cause as long as it appeared viable. The sacrifices they made during the war reflected the ideal of the "Spartan mother" held by many white women in the South. The faithful expected a certain amount of suffering before their land would be redeemed from Yankee rule. This conviction was rooted in traditional Christian belief and predicated on eventual Confederate victory. These women considered the design for Confederate victory to be courage on the battlefield, patriotism on the home front, and fervor in prayer. Necessarily women left in southern stores cheered their brave boys in the field while directly lending their help to the Confederate cause at home. For example, the wife of South Carolina merchant George Walton Williams belonged to the Ladies Clothing Association and helped organize the Charleston Wayside Hospital and Soldiers' Depot. On the other side of the Confederacy, Jorantha Semmes, raising five children while her merchant-husband served with the Army of Tennessee, belonged to the Ladies Relief Association of Canton, Mississippi. A temporary refugee from her Memphis home, she and forty other women provided relief for sick and wounded Confederate soldiers. Kate Cumming, the daughter of a wealthy Mobile businessman, helped treat the wounded from the Battle of Shiloh in April 1862. By nursing and feeding wounded soldiers, these women from merchant families, along with their peers from the planter class, created what LeeAnn Whites has described as a "new kind of public household." Through this type of volunteer work, commercial women demonstrated their support for the men in the field and for the wider Confederate cause.[15]

Most women from merchant families, even ardent Confederate patriots, discovered that increasing responsibilities within their own households limited the amount of community work they could perform. With their husbands, sons, and brothers off serving in the army, they had to manage children, slaves, and financial matters by themselves. Furthermore, older children from mercantile families often found themselves shouldering increased responsibilities in the absence of their fathers. Clearly such duties were not limited to women and children from the commercial classes. As Drew Faust and others have convincingly argued, this dynamic repeated itself to varying degrees in white families across the South. Those features that did distinguish the experience of merchant women and children from their neighbors originated in their particular work and values.[16]

Like many wives and mothers of Confederate soldiers, women from merchant families found separation from their men to be painful. Routine family activities took on a melancholy air while men were away at war. When she was in church for the first time without her husband, Catherine Barnes Rowland, the wife of an Augusta merchant serving in the army, "saw the *vacant* place where he always sat." Describing the distress this caused her she said, "My heart was very, *very* sad, and the tears fell thick and fast, I could not keep them back in spite of all my efforts to do so." Eventually she found company and support back home with her parents. Rowland's emotional reaction was not as unusual as her flight to her parents. Most women either could not or would not leave their homes; rather they maintained their positions within their families and communities as best they could through the prolonged trial of war.[17]

In some respects wartime proved less turbulent for merchant women than for their peers in the planter class. The plantation mistress had to supervise overseers and perhaps even field slaves as well her family and house slaves. Since few commercial families belonged to the ranks of the planter class, their mothers and wives rarely faced problems with unruly male labor, such as overseers or field hands. Indeed Cushing Hassell and his family saw little immediate need to remove their handful of slaves from the North Carolina coast and the threat of Yankee raids, because they believed themselves to be "as well off without them as with them."

Women did, however, have to negotiate some customary relationships without the assistance of their husbands or fathers. Store clerks and white servants could also prove difficult to govern in the absence of traditional male authority.[18] The Solomons of New Orleans, for instance, found their Irish servant Ellen to be a regular source of trouble while the male head, Solomon Solomon, was away serving as a quartermaster with the Army of Northern Virginia. Ellen's unexcused absences and indolent behavior led Clara to remark that one should not "be too good and give too many liberties," for, "like dogs, the better you are to them, the worse they are to you." Clearly the Solomon family cared more about monitoring the level of responsibility their servant showed with her work than they had about paying their debt to the local baker. In this instance the derogatory "them," who are "like dogs," seems to embody both an ethnic and a class component. Outside New Orleans, and certainly in more rural areas, the latter theme repeated itself with some frequency while the former did not. As George Rable and other historians have noted, a South ravaged by war betrayed an economic chasm between rich and poor that stretched the "conservative vision of an organic society to the breaking point."[19]

The same conditions that could strain relations between maid and matron also forced merchant women to assume public roles tradition-ally carried out by their husbands and fathers. The responsibilities that wives, mothers, and daughters took on in business as well as within their homes highlight the changing nature of the merchant family during the Civil War. This upheaval is particularly evident in the shifting marriage roles of the period. Like white women from other classes, over time mer-chant wives increasingly assumed the public roles their husbands once held within the community. This was especially true for women whose husbands and fathers had left home. They needed a unique combination of business skills and personal flexibility to enable their families to survive the turmoil of war. Their expanded roles within both the family and com-munity at least temporarily limited the antebellum patriarchal order.

An early indication of the how the war could demand change in the lives of men and women in merchant families is suggested by an 1861 let-ter to the editor of the *Augusta Daily Chronicle & Sentinel*. Signed by "ONE WHO LOVES HER COUNTRY," it demanded, "Let two or three merchants sell out to one, and let that one employ female clerks." The patriotic author maintained that "women can measure tape and weigh sugar as well as men, and the men could in battle (what the hearts of most of our women long to assist in) defend our beloved country in this the hour of our peril." This argument involved a certain logic that practical southern merchants, at least prior to the war, would have appreciated, but most merchants would have rejected the implication that their profession did not require manliness, though shopkeepers undoubtedly did expect their wives and daughters to maintain their stores while they fought.[20]

Merchant soldiers were able to supervise closely their business affairs back home during the first months of the war. Before the war, Charles C. Blacknall and his brother established a store in Franklinton, North Carolina, and they later operated a resort named Kittrell Springs. While serving as a captain in the Twenty-third North Carolina, Blacknall frequently wrote his wife and brother concerning his business ventures. His letters in 1861 relate tales of military hardships but also find him lamenting the state of his business. Blacknall asked specific questions about the condition of stock and general business trends in the community during the "excitement" of war.[21] Less than a year later, Blacknall's control over events at home had clearly waned. He told his wife Jinny, who by then had joined his brother in running the family business, "You must consult your own notions about hiring . . . get who you want and dont let price be any consideration."[22] While Blacknall continued to ask occasionally about financial affairs in North Carolina, his interests soon became absorbed with the rigors of war and the details of tobacco speculation in the Army of Northern Virginia. Between promises to fight the Yankees to the last, Blacknall's letters described his tobacco transactions with the regimental surgeon from which he hoped to realize several thousand dollars profit. This activity proved a poor substitute for his absence from home as his wife grappled with the challenges of running Kittrell Springs. Some such realization seemed to affect Blacknall's conscience as he rationalized to Jinny, "I do not desire to speculate at all, nor will I do so upon any article of necessity, but tobacco not being such, I consider it right & proper to trade on it if I choose to do so." He sought to assuage his guilt and perhaps reinvigorate his diminishing place within the community by donating a portion of his profits for the benefit of the county's poor. Before he could accomplish this patriarchal act from afar, however, Charles Blacknall received two serious wounds that led to his death in 1864. Blacknall did fulfill the expectations of southern manhood, but his dedication to the Confederate cause forced Jinny Blacknall to assume significant responsibility for the daily operation of her husband's business. For the

Blacknalls, the war first altered and then destroyed antebellum gender roles.[23]

The marriage of Benedict and Jorantha Semmes well exemplified how the Civil War transformed the manner in which men and women understood their positions in the merchant family. As noted in previous chapters, their correspondence reveals the personal impact of the war on their relationship and the growing power of Jorantha Semmes within the relationship as she assumed responsibilities outside the traditional sphere. The Semmeses enjoyed an unusually close relationship before the war. After meeting in Washington, D.C., in 1848, Benedict and Jorantha underwent a prolonged courtship of some eighteen months before they married. The delay resulted primarily from Jorantha's initial reluctance to convert to Benedict's Roman Catholicism. Once married Jorantha quickly embraced the church and her expected domestic role, while Benedict supported his family by clerking in a local store. The Semmeses had lived in Washington, D.C., for several years when Benedict decided to explore promising business opportunities in the West by relocating his family to Memphis, Tennessee. After a friend secured a line of credit for three thousand dollars, in 1859 Benedict opened a dry-goods store in the fast-growing community on the Mississippi River. While he prepared the store for business, a task that included having the building blessed by the local priest, back in Washington, Jorantha readied the children for the move. Benedict outlined the risks of establishing a store in an unfamiliar environment and wrote his wife that business is always slow at first "especially in a place where all are comparatively new men and therefore more or less distrustful of each other." Despite these concerns, the Memphis mercantile community seems to have embraced the Semmes family, and the city offered Benedict and Jorantha Semmes opportunity for financial success, yet before the store could yield significant profits the war erupted.[24]

Upon the outbreak of hostilities, Benedict Semmes did not hesitate to come to the defense of the Confederacy. He initially joined the 154th Regiment, Tennessee Volunteers, and served for most of the war in the chief depot commissary of General Braxton Bragg's Army of Tennessee. Although separated from his family, Benedict attempted to keep a close eye on the activities of his wife and children. In her letters, Jorantha described the academic progress of their daughter Julia, who attended an Ursuline academy in South Carolina. More frequently the correspondence dwelled on the family's growing financial problems. By 1862 it seems Jorantha operated their Memphis store on a limited basis. Rather than worrying about the level of sales, Benedict was most concerned that his wares not fall into the hands of Federal forces. In April of that year Jorantha wrote her husband that she thought it wise to transport their stock southward to Canton, Mississippi. Only days before the Battle of Shiloh, where Benedict saw his first significant action, he expressed faith that Confederate forces could protect the city and advised against the removal. Jorantha remained in Memphis. Wounded in the battle, Benedict returned to Memphis long enough to sell most of the store stock and property while his family sought temporary refuge in Missouri. In June of 1862 he rejoined his unit, and Jorantha and their children returned to a then Federally occupied Memphis. Under these new and difficult circumstances Jorantha Semmes assumed increasing financial responsibility for the survival of the family.[25]

Yankee occupation in Memphis, as elsewhere across the South, proved lucrative to southern and northern traders alike. Commercial transactions, licit and illicit, flourished among merchants, speculators, and planters whose sympathies resided with opposing combatants on the battlefield. Within this unrestrained financial environment Jorantha Semmes struggled to support her family. In early June 1862 she wrote her husband that while several established businesses had yet to resume their normal flow of trade, the boatloads of provisions that arrived daily in the Mississippi River port sold "like lightning for specie." The money Jorantha made selling what stock remained from the store, combined with the rent she collected from boarders, led her to inquire whether her husband might need five hundred dollars sent to *him*. This reversal in gender roles was made even more explicit when she advised Benedict that they should invest the remainder of their income in land rather than letting it remain idle. Jorantha supplied Benedict with detailed information about her financial deals. Yet whether they related Mr. Magenary's purchase of champagne or noted Colonel Polk's payment for a demijohn of whiskey, Jorantha's letters to her husband rarely manifested a vacillating or supplicatory tone. She clearly lamented the emotional void Benedict's absence created, but she took a firm hand in managing many of the family's commercial transactions.[26]

In 1863 the survival of the Semmes family became more complicated when Jorantha and the children left Memphis to stay with her husband's relatives in Canton, Mississippi. Between 1863 and 1865, Benedict continued to write his family despite the likelihood of mail falling into Yankee hands. Here again one can detect Jorantha's practical mind as she occasionally responded in coded messages. Amid descriptions of camp life and queries about the children, Benedict regularly asked his wife about the financial condition of the family. Thus when he wanted to learn the status (case, number, signatures, and year payable) of the war bonds he had purchased early in the war, he had to write his wife. By 1864 the correspondence between the two suggests that the degree to which Benedict deferred to his wife's judgment in financial affairs reached new heights. Once after asking his wife not to accept the "miserable Trash which the Yankees call Money" for debt payments, Benedict concluded the letter by adding, "I am sure you will agree with me on reflection, but I would like to have your own views, for you sometimes see things clearer than I." Indeed, the financial ventures Jorantha initiated during these years reveal her clear head for business.[27]

During the summer of 1863, Jorantha supplemented the income of the Semmes family by bottling brandy and whiskey for sale. In one transaction alone she earned a profit of $150. As the war dragged on and Confederate losses on the battlefield mounted, Jorantha, who complained of being a "positive incumbrance" upon Benedict's relations, moved her family into a separate house. She estimated the cost for their living arrangements would be forty-eight hundred Confederate dollars a year. In order to keep her family within this budget Jorantha instituted a strict regimen of cost cutting. She made light of her efforts to Benedict with the observation that "my economy is making 'old clothes look almost as well as new.'" Though the funds Benedict sent home to support his family would prove insufficient, Jorantha expected to earn the difference by making a hat every week and selling it for fifty dollars. Through this hastily arranged cottage industry she hoped to earn two thousand dollars a year. The plan would also benefit the children by teaching them valuable work habits and merchant skills, as Jorantha planned to have her young boys "plait" and later sell the hats so they could "have the credit of the transaction." Unfortunately scant letters remain from the Semmeses' 1865 correspondence. The changing roles within this merchant marriage are readily apparent, but the success of Jorantha's business plan cannot be determined.[28]

As the Civil War dragged on, Jorantha Semmes and other merchant wives across the Confederate South became providers, decision makers, and financial protectors. Driven by necessity and perhaps encouraged by opportunity, these women adopted many "masculine" privileges traditionally held by the husband of the family. Thus the socioeconomic foundation upon which rested the gender constructs of antebellum merchant marriages experienced profound shifts during the Civil War. Merchants who avoided serving in the army enjoyed significant economic opportunities and maintained many of their patriarchal rights, but they paid for it in community outcry against profiteering merchants who shirked military duty. Merchants who did join the army found their traditional male roles transformed. Their inability to fight for their families on the battlefield while simultaneously providing for their needs at home forced merchants to surrender financial responsibility more and more to their wives. Such changes in merchant marriages during the Civil War at least temporarily shifted the nexus of power between these men and women.

At the same time that some authority shifted from husbands to wives in mercantile families, both parents had to work together to raise their children in the embattled Confederacy. The limited record these families left behind suggests that parental oversight weakened over time. Customary responsibilities and the natural order proved difficult, if not impossible, to maintain. Nevertheless, parents worked hard to keep their children's lives as normal as possible. These bourgeois parents sought particularly to preserve a measure of stability for their children in the realm of education. Separation, economic distress, sickness, and even death did not distract merchant fathers and mothers from the unwavering devotion to their children's education that they had exhibited during the antebellum period. Whether at the primary or university level, whether business, mechanical, or classical instruction, merchant families had the desire and often the means to continue their children's education, and parents continued to expect that study would impart the knowledge and values to help their children succeed in a growing commercial economy. Ironically, at the same time new textbooks printed in an independent South promoted the stereotype that "money-loving and money-making" were uniquely Yankee traits.[29]

Among numerous other storekeepers, Cushing Hassell and his wife Martha expressed few reservations about any potential conflict between their southern nationalism and their children's education. A conscientious business family and old Whigs who embraced secession only after their home state of North Carolina left the Union, what principally distinguished the Hassells from most others in the commercial trade was Cushing's second vocation as a minister in a Primitive Baptist Church.

A conservative religious leader in his community, the fact that the Williamston storekeeper raged against the Roman Catholic Church and all "Protestant Jesuits" who espoused an Arminian theological position clearly suggests that Cushing Hassell fell well short of embracing a uniform liberal capitalist ethic. This said, Hassell and his wife Martha also cultivated a healthy respect for learning and for trade in their nine children.[30] Like many in their line of work, when the war erupted the Hassells foresaw no conflict between their patriotism and a strong commitment to their children's education. Indeed, during the first year of war they had the ability to promote both ends. While two of their sons, seventeen-year-old Benjamin and twenty-one-year-old Theodore, joined the army in the summer of 1861, their middle son, eighteen-year-old Sylvester, returned to Chapel Hill where he expected to earn his degree from the University of North Carolina. Now that his other sons were off serving in the army, Cushing viewed Sylvester's five-month absence at the university as a trial. Alone with his wife and six daughters, the merchant faced, without the comfort and assistance of his sons, the very real threat Federal forces posed to his eastern North Carolina home. In August 1861 this burden grew more severe when Federal forces captured Theodore and Benjamin and sent them to a military prison on Governor's Island in New York. Within a few months Cushing and Martha Hassell realized their efforts to keep their sons nearby were futile. The machinery of war had circumscribed the life the Hassells had once known. Nevertheless, the family's efforts to maintain some form of stability during the conflict, in this case Sylvester's education, suggest the strong continuity between their antebellum and wartime cultural values.[31]

The letters that merchant-soldiers wrote home revealed a high regard for their children's education. While serving as an officer in the Twenty-third North Carolina, part of the Army of Northern Virginia, Charles Blacknall repeatedly asked his wife Jinny about the status of their children's scholarship. Despite his wartime obligations and the distance between him and his family, Blacknall devoted serious thought to his children's academic performance. In addition to the usual advice fathers wrote their children from the front, Blacknall wanted to learn about their instructors and to personally make arrangements for teaching fees. He expressed few reservations concerning his wife and brother's management of the family store and resort, but he demanded responsibility for his children's education. This attention represented more than the random inquiries of an

officer passing time between military operations. Even after being captured by Federal forces during the Chancellorsville campaign and sent to a
prison for Confederate officers on Johnson's Island in Lake Erie, Blacknall
did his best to monitor his children's education. In the autumn of 1863
the lieutenant instructed his wife from his windswept prison in Sandusky
Bay to send their son Oscar away from home to study with a Mr. Horner,
because the boy "should be afforded all opportunities for getting an education which I fear the neighborhood cannot afford." As Blacknall was
unable to personally supervise young Oscar's intellectual growth, the
choice of instructor seemed to weigh upon him. The advice and declarations of concern he expressed for his children and their schooling suggest
much about the changing nature of the merchant family during the Civil
War. Like many merchant-soldiers, Blacknall sought to preserve his traditional rights and responsibilities within the family, in this instance by
championing his children's education; at the same time the war made the
practical links between him and his family in North Carolina quite tenuous. Indeed Blacknall's recognition of this trend may have heightened his
concern for the emotional and material welfare of his family. Despite his
best efforts, ultimately he found that any continuity between the antebellum and wartime education of his children depended not upon his measures but upon those of his wife. The Blacknalls were far from alone.[32]

Letters between Benedict Semmes and his wife Jorantha further disclose how the responsibilities for training children of the merchant class
fell increasingly to mothers. While Semmes fought, his wife raised their
growing family—six children by war's end—first in Memphis and later
in Corinth, Mississippi. When eleven-year-old Mary and nine-year-old
Joseph needed to enter upon an education suitable for the children of
a successful merchant, much of this responsibility devolved to Jorantha
Semmes. As revealed in the family's correspondence, after Benedict joined
the 154th Tennessee, Jorantha controlled the flow of information within
the family. She had to send him news of young Julia's progress at the
Ursuline Academy in South Carolina. It was from his wife that the merchant-
soldier learned his daughter had excelled in all her subjects except gram-
mar, for it seems he received few letters from his children while he served
in the Confederate army. Later in the war Benedict could still pay the
$2,777 tuition and board for his daughter's education but depended on
his wife for information. Julia, now almost fourteen years old, apparently
inherited some of her parents' enterprise, for the Ursuline sisters described

her as "a child of grace" whose "precocious" mind and ambition "may lead her to study too assiduously for the strength of her body." Distance obviously prevented either parent from directly shaping their daughter's academic habits.[33]

During the war, then, fathers and husbands found themselves far removed from routine decisions regarding their children's education. Little evidence suggests that, within southern commercial families at least, letters passing between school and home found their way to the battlefield. Letters and academic reports tended to stay in the traditional channels. Thus onetime merchants like Benedict Semmes who wished to continue influencing their children's education found themselves having to issue anxious demands. When young Malcolm Semmes, for example, apparently stopped attending school late in the war, his father, by then a major in the commissary department of the Army of Tennessee, implored his wife to control the boy's behavior and enroll him in classes: "Tell him I am very much afraid he is losing valuable time and that when he does go back to school after the war he will be so far behind other boys that it will mortify him." This is not the commanding voice of a patriarch called away from the hearth, but it still carried a tone of authority. Rather than orders, Benedict Semmes offered suggestions, even pleas. Like most white southern families caught in the war, commercial families did their best to sustain their peacetime attitudes and habits. By providing their children with a strong education, parents like Benedict and Jorantha Semmes hoped to inculcate in their children their own southern bourgeois values. A measure of continuity linked the antebellum and wartime educations of the Blacknall and Semmes children. Notwithstanding the trauma of war, many children continued to attend school, albeit with their mothers assuming responsibility for their education.[34]

Battles won and lost, the death of loved ones, the destruction of property, and what happened on the battlefields in Virginia, Tennessee, and elsewhere shaped the mood on the southern home front. Likewise, the quality of life at home could temper the adulation or disappointment many soldiers felt over the outcome of battles. When merchants and their families pondered the "complexion of the strife," they usually considered the entire sweep of the war. As the conflict dragged on with no foreseeable end, storekeepers and their customers debated whether the South had to be "brought low" and "acknowledge the hand of God" before it could achieve victory over the North. Others speculated about the causes of the apparent northern impulse to "exterminate" the South. Setbacks on the battlefield and turmoil at home drove both the fire-eating Confederates and the more politically moderate variety of merchants to prayer meetings across the South. Business as usual, in and out of the home, proved extremely difficult to maintain. The dissonance of war and the effect it had upon commercial families are readily apparent in their relationship with the region's preeminent institution: slavery.[35]

Those in the mercantile community who owned slaves learned quickly how war undermined their "peculiar institution." Specifically storekeepers who lived where the battles raged or near the seacoast found that the threat of Federal raids weakened their authority over their slaves. Any working relationship between owner and slave, much less stronger ties of paternalism, proved difficult to sustain when slaveholders had to move their "white and black" families to avoid Yankee troops. Cushing Hassell eventually sent his "chattels" to live with his friends in the "country," mainly central North Carolina, rather than run the risk that they would escape or be liberated by Union troops who were then active in eastern North Carolina. Commercial families who lived with their house slaves and merchant-soldiers who had been able to take a slave with them to the front were best able to preserve their conventional assumptions regarding slavery. Widespread, and at times apocryphal, stories of faithful servants who seemed so reassuring to planter households had parallels within the merchant community. The wartime experience and battlefield death of Lieutenant George Adrian Howze provides one such example.[36]

The son of a merchant and a store clerk himself before the war, Adrian Howze served as a second lieutenant in the Forty-second Mississippi. Part of a regiment recruited from counties in northern Mississippi, Howze's company was enlisted in Confederate service on May 14, 1861, in the town of Grenada. By the summer of 1863 the regiment was part of Brigadier General Joseph R. Davis's "Mississippi Brigade"(Henry Heth's division of A. P. Hill's corps). Before that Adrian Howze, like the rest of his unit, had yet to experience significant combat. Not until the Battle of Gettysburg did the Forty-second Mississippi receive its first lesson in warfare—shortly before dawn on July 1 just outside the small Pennsylvania town where their division clashed with Brigadier General John Buford's two brigades of Union cavalry. During the days preceding the conflict, Howze's health had been failing and at least one of his fellow officers believed him too "feeble to have been in the field." Nevertheless, its being his first fight

Howze was determined to do nothing that "might tarnish his honorable reputation," and he led his men in an advance upon Buford's troops. The fighting grew more intense over the course of the morning, both sides sustaining high casualties. Regiments slammed into each other, but gradually the Rebels started to drive the Yankees through Gettysburg and into the surrounding heights outside town. During this daylong action, probably in late morning, the advance of the Forty-second stalled against reinforced Federal positions. Just at the moment when the resolve of the Mississippi soldiers seemed to weaken and some of the men fell back, a minié ball struck and killed Adrian Howze. His body was left on the battlefield. In a ritual familiar to soldiers and to historians after them, it fell to Howze's slave Stephen to search the battlefield, find his master, and see that his remains received a proper burial.[37]

The account of Lieutenant Adrian Howze's death and burial, as related years after the war by his uncle LeGrand J. Wilson, who served as assistant surgeon in the Forty-second, highlights the role of Stephen the "faithful servant." When the first day of fighting at Gettysburg drew to a close the slave found his master's body and carried it back to the hospital. There Stephen apparently made a "rude" coffin for Howze and buried him in the Pennsylvania soil. Later the remains were exhumed and moved to Hollywood Cemetery in Richmond, Virginia. According to Wilson, his nephew lived an honorable life and died a noble death. The devotion Stephen demonstrated is crucial to this account. For Wilson it reveals the strong emotion and paternalism that invested the relationship between a southern gentleman, be he a planter or merchant, and his slave. A disinterested interpreter of this account might reach different conclusions than Wilson but nevertheless come away impressed with the magnitude of affection, or at least the sense of duty, that seems to have existed between Adrian Howze and Stephen. The connection between the two men, whether paternalistic or something yet more affected, may indicate a strong current in merchant-slave relations during the Civil War, but a dearth of relevant evidence makes this conclusion tentative. Indeed in many respects the example of Howze and Stephen is exceptional. Discord and anger rather than any enduring paternalistic ethos increasingly characterized the merchant family's relationship with the institution of slavery.[38]

Men and women from commercial families saw their hold over their slaves fade as the Civil War continued into a second and third year. Most concluded that their personal troubles were part of a broader instability in slave ownership that spread across the Confederacy. Suddenly two or more slaves conversing in a store or "whiskey shop" could assume the proportions of a conspiracy in white minds when in more peaceful times the loitering slaves might have been ignored. Clara Solomon noted in her diary how some slaves in her New Orleans neighborhood proved increasingly obstinate as the threat of Federal invasion loomed large in early 1862. Once New Orleans fell to Union forces the problems of slave management for Southerners like Solomon did not disappear. Young Clara and her merchant family worried that Union General Benjamin Butler, the commander of the occupation troops, would open the prison, releasing its largely black population. "It is this fear which alarms me," wrote Solomon. "I fear more from the negroes than Yankees & an insurrection is my continual horror." Such expressions of fear, disgust, and even anger directed at particular slaves or the institution in general regularly appear in the papers left by merchant families. Atlanta merchant Samuel Richards spoke for many when he declared, "I am disgusted with negroes and feel inclined to sell what I have." Never the paternalistic slaveholder, Richards concluded that if it were not for slavery there would be no War between the States. This said, he, like other merchant slaveholders, weighed his antipathy toward slavery against his financial welfare and decided to remain invested in the institution. Significantly, Richards and his brother Jabez increased their speculations in slaves despite Abraham Lincoln's Emancipation Proclamation and the apparent standoff on the battlefield.[39]

White Southerners with means traded numerous commodities and assets, including cotton, tobacco, Confederate bonds, and land, during the war. Not surprisingly, slaves proved to be a tempting investment for many. After major Confederate victories the price of slaves rose across the South as speculators purchased more slaves with the expectation of southern independence. Between 1863 and 1864 the top price for a slave at auction in Columbus, Georgia, rose from $3,500 to $4,700. Visiting Charleston, South Carolina, during the spring of 1863, Englishman Arthur Fremantle concluded, "A great deal of business is evidently done in buying and selling Negroes, for the papers are full of advertisements of slave auctions." Early in the war soldiers from the front wrote letters home advising their families to purchase slaves. The colonel of the Twenty-sixth North Carolina advised his father to invest all the family's money in slaves. The young officer wrote, "I would buy boys & girls from 15 to 20 years old & take care to have a majority of girls. . . . I would not be surprised to see negroes in 6 mos. after peace worth from 2 to 3000 dollars." Such thinking remained widespread even after the war turned against the Confederacy. The South Carolina entrepreneur George Walton Williams purchased one hundred slaves during the war. With the collapse of the Confederacy, Williams lost an estimated five hundred thousand U.S. dollars in his investment. Bourgeois merchants, both inside and outside the army, who had money and were on the lookout for the main chance joined this frenzy of speculation.[40]

Two storekeepers who thought they could strike it rich in slave speculation were Samuel and Jabez Richards. The brothers operated a book and "fancy good" store in wartime Atlanta. Jabez bought their first slave in July 1862 for a thousand dollars. Noting the purchase in his diary an excited Samuel declared, "I expect the *Yankees* would say that this was the worst possible investment under existing circumstances seeing that their Congress has declared the slaves of all *rebels* to be free!" A month later Samuel bought two more slaves for the inflated price of $9,250. The important point in the Richardses' slave purchases is that, while these slaves did work, they were viewed as purely a transitory investment. A number of Southerners purchased slaves late in the war as a public display of support for the institution of slavery and of the Confederacy. Samuel Richards possessed no such patriotic motives when he bought his slaves. In his own words, he wished the South victory so that "when we come to a successful end to this war negroes will command high prices as there will be so much demand for labor to raise cotton and a great many will have been taken away by the Yankees." While Confederate arms continued to triumph and slaves in the upper South escaped to Union lines the brothers expressed few misgivings about spending more than $11,300 for slaves in May 1863. Of course by this time storekeepers living in regions threatened by Federal armies found it advisable to sell or rent out their slave investments before they "went off to the Yankees." Sherman and his troops would be marching on Atlanta before the Richards brothers followed the example set by their colleagues in the upper South.[41]

The typical merchant family's relationship with their slaves and the wider institution of slavery seems to have stayed relatively unchanged during the first half of the Civil War. Of course most commercial families did not own slaves, thus as a group they were less impressed by changes in slavery than was the planter class. As the war stretched on, a number of storekeepers did voice frustration with slavery and its impact on the

South, while many other merchants, including some critics of the institution, speculated in slaves enthusiastically. Over the course of the antebellum period all kinds of merchants had engaged in similar conduct. Slavery troubled the liberal capitalist assumptions of some antebellum merchants, while virtually any enterprising storekeeper, when the opportunity arose, bought and sold slaves for financial gain. The dangers and possibilities that the Civil War brought on merely increased the criticism and the money that southern merchants directed toward slavery. The war created more opportunities for business families to invest in slaves but did not fundamentally change their unease with the peculiar institution. As important as slavery became for southern merchants, they continued to view themselves as traders not masters or would-be agrarians. Selling goods defined their economy and sustained their culture. Sales figures were one subject that Confederate merchants followed with more interest than reports from the battlefield. Storekeepers on the home front recorded, calculated, pondered, and refigured their wartime sales. Those who were away in the army wrote letters home asking their families to do likewise. Trade dictated how storekeepers viewed the war as it simultaneously shaped the way southern whites perceived their merchant neighbors.

Like the letters and journals they kept during the antebellum period, the records civilian storekeepers produced while trading in the Confederate states frequently remarked upon sales trends. Merchants analyzed their sales for signs of the war's impact on their business. The particularly industrious would compare daily, weekly, and monthly sales to totals from previous years. Location, inclement weather, inflation, and troop movements all could impact the storekeeper's bottom line. Notwithstanding the dislocation of war, during the summer of 1861 merchants typically described their sales as "pretty good" or "favorable." In Richmond, gunsmiths, hardware merchants, and saddlers carried on a brisk trade with the growing population of soldiers and government officials. Yet for every "giddy" outburst by a bullish storekeeper there were those like Charles Blacknall who remained "quite uneasy" over the future of their family's business. In general storekeepers tried to keep their composure during the initial excitement. Some determined that their monthly sales barely changed, either up or down, from the previous year. Indeed early in the war, the language and tone Confederate merchants used to describe their sales changed little from the antebellum period. Some days were "dull," others "slow," most "fair." The commercial credit reporting agency R. G. Dun &

Company, which continued to track many southern businesses, especially in the border states and in New Orleans, described mercantile operations, even those little removed from the front, in their customary terms: "doing well," "esteemed," "tolerable business," "a strong house." During the first year of war most merchants could carry on business as usual. Though they had fears about the future, storekeepers prided themselves on their ability to adapt and survive.[42]

The changes war brought in 1862 challenged this identity as some found it difficult to keep their businesses afloat, while the trade of others—usually those more removed from the fighting—thrived. The growing presence of Federal armies and an erratic flow of supplies began to take a toll on mercantile activity in the upper South. In locales threatened by Federal raids, storekeepers curtailed business or closed their doors entirely. Trade dwindled in Culpeper County, Virginia, and most merchants stopped advertising and trading as shipping goods to their embattled community became more difficult. In late May 1862, Benedict Semmes set a similar course for his family's store in Memphis. As noted earlier, while recovering from a wound he received at the Battle of Shiloh, Semmes returned to the store his wife had been running in his absence and sold all the stock. Approximately one week later Union troops occupied Memphis while the Semmes family temporarily relocated to Missouri. Early in the conflict, storekeepers who lived in Virginia, Tennessee, and other areas where Confederate and Union armies were clashing had to rely on their business savvy and personal connections to survive the war economically, while their colleagues throughout much of the Deep South found that opportunities abounded for enterprising merchants with capital and that living in the heart of the Confederacy gave them the security, for a time, to prosper during the war. Smaller operations, without credit or capital, typically "sold out their stocks and closed their doors."[43]

One way merchants could earn profits while supporting the Confederate cause was contracting with the government to manufacture supplies. For example, after A. H. DeWitt, a jeweler in Columbus, Georgia, obtained contracts with state and Confederate officials, he converted his shop into a sword factory. In the same town, Eldridge S. Greenwood and William C. Gray, who before the war had been cotton factors, hired gunsmiths and mechanics and set up a rifle factory. The large number of government contracts they held, combined with the relative safety of the south Georgia community, enabled them to enlarge their operation and eventually employ over 150 workers. Down the street from this factory the Prussian-born brothers Louis and Elias Haiman supervised the manufacture of mess kits, cups, and bayonets in their Muscogee Iron Works. The experience they had gained in their antebellum hardware store served them well during the war. The owners of the Columbus dry-goods firm Manly and Hodges utilized their business skills by purchasing several sewing machines, hiring workers, and making tents for the Confederate army and the Georgia militia. When circumstances for manufacturing appeared favorable, as they did in Columbus, merchants across the Deep South adopted a similar course. The North Carolina merchants Kader Biggs, Charles Blacknall, and Joseph Cathey rented space, sold beef, and supplied other food to Confederate forces. John Twohig in San Antonio, Texas, employed his peacetime connections to obtain government business during the war. The Confederate Nitre and Mining Bureau contracted with Twohig to purchase fifty thousand dollars' worth of cotton and transport it to Mexico, where he would trade it for the nitre that was essential to the southern war effort. It is unclear whether Twohig was able to deliver the nitre to the Naval Powder Mills near Columbia, South Carolina, but he did send hundreds of bales of cotton across the Rio Grande, a lucrative patriotic trade for the Texan. Twohig, like other merchants across the Confederacy, directed his liberal capitalist ethic toward its natural goal—making profits.[44]

Most storekeepers in the Deep South attempted to realize this end through the traditional practice of selling goods. Since extant financial records are few it is difficult to place a dollar amount on the sales of southern merchants during the Civil War, but clearly storekeepers in such lower South cities as Atlanta, Mobile, and Charleston had significant opportunities to sell a large quantity of goods at extremely high prices before Federal forces occupied their communities. The Union blockade made it difficult to obtain merchandise, but it also meant that what goods were available often fetched outrageously inflated, and hence profitable, prices. Visiting Mobile in the summer of 1862, the English businessman W. C. Corsan witnessed this dynamic up close. "The goods which were left" in the Alabama city, he said, "were being dribbled out as favour, for cash, at enormous profits, ranging from 750 to 1,500 per cent." By the fall of that year many Southerners began to feel the effects of the Union blockade, as Confederate currency depreciated, in the estimate of Harold S. Wilson, at an average rate of almost 10 percent a month. Citizens in Richmond now paid $25 for a pair of blankets that sold for $6 before the war; sheets that had cost $4 per pair in 1861 could not be had for less than $15 by September 1862. In 1863 ten pounds of bacon cost $10, and four pounds of coffee exceeded $20. That same year residents in Camden, South Carolina, had to spend $30 for a sack of flour. Such prices left storekeepers scrambling to buy, sell, and make their fortune.[45]

Heyman Herzberg did his best to earn a fortune in the wartime marketplace. The Georgia merchant-soldier obtained a general discharge from the Confederate army after serving only a few months. Apparently he smoothed the way for his hasty departure by obtaining a substitute, a man Herzberg estimated to be sixty years old, and giving his first lieutenant a lovely gold watch as a "souvenir." Days after leaving the army Herzberg returned to his Cartersville, Georgia, home where he scoured the countryside for goods to buy and later, after a considerable markup, resell. Jostling about in his buggy, the merchant traveled throughout northern Georgia and Alabama looking for goods. Upon finding suitable items for sale, Herzberg usually shipped the stock to Atlanta where goods obtained "fabulous" prices, though payment consisted mainly of depreciated state bank and Confederate notes. This lucrative trade continued throughout late 1861 and apparently into 1862. It seems that in early 1863, Herzberg even managed to slip into Alabama, head north through Tennessee and Kentucky, then east to Philadelphia, where he visited family. He then headed north to New York City, where he purchased a stock of goods that he personally smuggled through Union and Confederate lines in Virginia. By March 1863 he was back in Atlanta selling more goods at inflated prices. Finally sometime that year a scrape with Confederate authorities convinced Herzberg to conclude his purchasing trips. He described a business trip to Dadeville, Alabama, where he and his brother-in-law ran into a "burly" recruiting officer who asked them for their exemption or discharge papers. When it became obvious that neither of the merchants had their papers, the officer decided to escort them to a military camp some twenty-five miles away where they could have been released or possibly enrolled in the army. Not willing to risk the latter, the two men jumped in their buggy and made their escape while the officer chased, fired upon, and undoubtedly cursed the young businessmen. Aside from this violent run-in with the military authority, Heyman Herzberg's roving economic activities were not unusual. Merchants with capital and standing did try to keep their store a permanent fixture in their community. Again the example of Samuel Richards and his brother Jabez is illustrative.[46]

Like all southern merchants the Richards brothers complained over the impossibility of acquiring supplies at their prewar quantity and price. At the same time they reveled in the high prices they charged in their Book, Music, and Fancy Store in Atlanta. Samuel in particular, described by one family friend as "the absolute antithesis of the old Southern type," exalted over the store's profits. When in 1862 the prices of coffee, salt, and bacon began skyrocketing, Richards wrote in his diary that "if we had our whole stock in these articles our fortune would be made." In February 1863 the Richards brothers sold pens that had originally cost seventy-five cents for twenty-eight dollars apiece. Entries in Richards's diary that describe shortages and inflation are juxtaposed with accounts of record sales and profits. On February 8, 1862, he wrote that "all kinds of *foreign* goods and supplies are getting scarce and selling high," and just two weeks later he enthusiastically proclaimed "we have sold more [$210] than we ever did in one day." Samuel estimated their yearly sales for 1862 to be $45,250, of which only $1,750 was on credit and nearly paid at that. The following year the brothers totaled income separately at $38,646 in cash to Samuel and $18,506 to Jabez. Samuel did not exaggerate when he wrote "*some* of our profits are enormous truly." Even wealthy planters marveled at the scale of the mercantile trade in wartime Atlanta. Charles C. Jones Jr., a lieutenant in the Confederate army, wrote his planter father, "Atlanta exhibits more signs of life and energy than any other city in Georgia. You would be surprised at the immense quantities of sugars, tobacco, etc., etc." Regional shortages of goods and subsequent inflation had much to do with this commercial activity. The inflation created by the Union blockade proved to be a boon for the Richards brothers and many other storekeepers in the Deep South.[47]

Sales tallies in their ledgers held great promise for southern merchants between 1861 and 1863. The figures in those columns and the tidy sums found after each customer's name, however, are deceiving. A sales transaction in the Confederate South consisted of much more than merely handing an item to a customer and getting a cash payment in return. Storekeepers had to contend with numerous obstacles that tested their commercial skills. The growing presence of counterfeit money, produced by the United States government with the intention of bankrupting the Confederate economy or by private individuals for personal gain, represented a threat to the merchant's bottom line. On occasion southern banks found they had unwittingly accepted and disseminated thousands of counterfeit dollars. Collecting outstanding debts proved to be even more problematic.[48]

Debt had always been part of the landscape in southern mercantile life, but during the war the volume of debt became, according to merchant-soldier Edward Murphy, "formidable." Indeed Murphy even contemplated requesting a furlough and returning home to Louisiana in order to collect bills from wealthy planters who had fallen in arrears. Samuel Richards expressed the frustrations many storekeepers felt when he concluded, after a week of attempting to collect old debts, "It dont pay to sell on credit and have to *run* and *run* about a dozen times for a dollar or two and perhaps get nothing at last but curses." The solution for many was to sell only for cash. Plantation mistress Sarah Watkins discovered the new state of affairs when she visited the stores in nearby Carrollton, Mississippi, and found that they all demanded specie or reliable currency, meaning Federal greenbacks, for their goods. This practice was widespread and led to the sort of criticism that R. W. Patton of Florence, Alabama, leveled against the Huntsville merchant Francis Levert. When Levert refused to allow Patton to pay the principle of a loan he owed the merchant in Confederate currency Patton accused the businessman of "disparaging—indeed discrediting our Govt, by refusing to recognize the currency with which alone we can maintain our Independence." Levert defended himself against Patton's attack on the grounds that the money could not be reinvested and by noting that he did not expect the "whole debt" to be paid at that time, but when it came due he would demand specie. Levert concluded his letter by acknowledging his dependence upon the credit economy: "I have but little Real Estate—almost everything I am worth, is in investments of this sort. I can't live without them, shall I take them all in, and hide them away, thus letting my family starve?" The unyielding merchant did not allow even his own family to pay their debts to him in currency. The entrepreneur and politician Jonathan Worth was more flexible: he ordered his managers in North Carolina to accept cotton in addition to specie for goods. Such practices offered little solace for retailers left with unpaid debts in their books. As a last resort, merchants across the Confederacy took customers to court in order to collect past debts. Legal action occasionally produced ill will within the community against the merchant, but it also gave him the needed leverage to obtain payment. Confederate storekeepers expended great energy complaining about the economic impact of counterfeit currency and unpaid bills, and certainly their effect could be dramatic, but such complaints represent the lament of those who were generally making money and had assets on their books. Credit could serve them well in a cash-poor Confederacy. They had met the initial challenges of the wartime economy and had survived, even profited.[49]

The economic changes introduced by the war between 1861 and 1863, or "problems" according to the merchants themselves, had the potential to destroy or reinvigorate southern businesses. This was certainly true of the southern storekeeper's greatest affliction and opportunity, the Federal blockade. Abraham Lincoln issued a proclamation of blockade against Confederate ports on April 19, 1861. The blockade required several months of operation before it could show any results and even then it remained porous. In 1863 the dollar value of Charleston's foreign trade exceeded the total that the city had reached during the last year of peace. As late as 1865 one out of two blockade-runners got past the Union ships patrolling outside Charleston and Wilmington, North Carolina. Yet as we have seen, Southerners began to feel the effects of the blockade during the spring of 1862. According to one scholar, by March 1863 inflation had so diminished the Confederate dollar that it required ten to purchase what two had bought in 1861. But the inflation and scarcity that brought suffering to most white Southerners presented their neighbors in the mercantile class with opportunities. Merchants like Heyman Herzberg who shipped goods from the country into towns and those like Samuel Richards who had ties with the owners of blockade-running ships stood to make their fortunes from the Union blockade. Their business skill and experience gave them the wherewithal to obtain scarce goods while the blockade furnished them with a ready excuse to raise their prices to incredible levels. Beyond this, merchants with sufficient capital and mettle did much more than sell goods at inflated prices; they purchased the ships that brought those goods into the Confederacy.[50]

The Federal government had an average of 150 ships patrolling for blockade-runners. For merchants, captains, and even crews, blockade-running offered great risks and rewards at once. Ships carried cargoes of guns, ammunition, clothing, medicines, salt, and numerous luxury goods from bases in Nassau, Bermuda, and Havana to such southern ports as Wilmington, Charleston, and Mobile. Once the ships were safely through, their goods would typically be placed at auction while southern cotton was loaded aboard for the return run. A successful trip could net owners tens of thousands of dollars or anywhere from a 500 to a 1,000 percent return on their initial investment. It was not unheard of for a blockade-runner to make $250,000 in a single passage. With the potential for such large profits, it is hardly surprising that smaller storekeepers like Samuel Richards purchased a thousand dollars of stock in the Wyly-Markham Company, a blockade-running firm in Atlanta, or that a far richer merchant like George Walton Williams would become an investor and director in three different blockade-running firms: the Consolidated Steam Ship Company (capitalized at $2,015,000), the Sumter Steam Ship Company, and the Calhoun Trading Company. In Atlanta alone the capital investment in shipping almost tripled from $25,000 in 1862 to $73,000 in 1864. The example of yet another merchant from this city, Sidney Root, illustrates the process through which Southerners entered the business.[51]

Before the war Sidney Root was a partner in the Atlanta cotton, banking, and dry-goods firm Beach & Root. Once the conflict erupted, Root, one of Atlanta's "most influential" men, embraced the Confederate cause with an emotional commitment that distinguished him from most of his southern colleagues. For the Atlanta businessman, blockade-running represented the most logical and profitable way to support the Confederacy. A personal friend of Jefferson Davis and a key member of the Atlanta business elite, Root anticipated his blockade-running enterprise to be a primary ingredient in his plan to increase his city's and his country's European trade. John N. Beach, Root's partner, made the effort possible when he opened an office in Liverpool, England. After the Confederate government hired the firm to serve as a cotton agent in Europe, Beach & Root opened a second office in Le Havre, France. The two men eventually brought in a third partner, E. W. Marshall, who served as the firm's connection in Charleston. The firm had access to over $150,000 in goods in the North, because Beach was a "Union man," a circumstance that seems not to have bothered Root in the least. To further expedite their operations during the war, Beach became a British subject. Beach & Root owned more than nineteen ocean steamers, which were worth, in Root's estimation, between $30,000 and $150,000 each. While on the surface Root's claims seem exaggerated, there is little doubting the large scale of his firm's blockade-running activities.[52]

Most southern merchants lacked the wealth to embark upon the kind of blockade-running trade in which Sidney Root engaged. As will be seen in chapter 6, the profits Root and others gained from blockade-running not only paid dividends but generated great tension across the Confederacy as well. Indeed, the perceived wealth and speculative enterprise of all merchants, large and small, created against them as a class a backlash that would profoundly affect their lives as the war turned against the Confederacy in 1864. While Dixie collapsed, the liberal capitalist practices southern merchants had long embraced, mainly speculation and haggling, looked increasingly unpatriotic to many white Southerners. At the same time, invading Federal armies devastated merchant families and brought most of their business activity to an end. The southern identity and bourgeois worldview of the merchant family endured their greatest challenges in the final two years of the Civil War. [53]

6

The Merchant Family and the Fall of the Confederacy, 1864–1865

The perils confronting white Southerners mounted as Confederate armies suffered reverses on the battlefield. By late 1863 what little had remained of normal existence on the southern home front had come to an end as casualties, material deprivation, and invading Federal armies challenged the faith of even the most stalwart Confederate partisan. During the travails of the final two years, often more than military success, mere survival consumed the lives of southern men and women. Merchants and their families endured many of the same hardships that afflicted their white neighbors. Their men died in battle, their homes and stores were ransacked, and those who owned slaves eventually lost them. Merchants, however, carried an additional burden, for those storekeepers who still operated during the last two years of the war faced a population that viewed them with distrust if not outright hostility. The business connections, personal backgrounds, and commercial activities that earned antebellum merchants success, and on occasion disfavor, proved even more volatile during the Civil War. The bourgeois worldview and liberal capitalist practices of the southern merchant made him the ultimate outsider in the embattled Confederacy. The conservative Christian faith and support for slavery that they shared with their white neighbors did not shield them from censure. As commercial businessmen speculated and seemed to position themselves for postwar society, some critics even questioned the commitment of the merchant class to these traditional southern values.

Colonel George Washington Lee, provost marshal for Atlanta, viewed his city's merchant community as an outright threat to the Confederate cause. He wrote the secretary of war that domestic enemies and other "debris" found a safe haven among the men and women of the commercial classes. Lee requested permission to raise more troops in order to quash the many "traitors-Swindlers-extortioners-and-counterfeiters" that operated in Atlanta. The community was also plagued by what Lee characterized as a dangerous population of "Jews, New England Yankees, and refugees shirking military duties." The colonel's caustic remarks lacked decorum, but many white Southerners concurred with him. A soldier stationed in southern Alabama declared Mobile to be "the Sodom of the South," where "people are unkind, illiberal and will take advantage of the soldiers by putting exorbitant prices on every article we want." While observing the business activities of his "Hebrew friends" in Charleston, the Englishman W. C. Corsan remembered the wildly exaggerated claim of an acquaintance from Alabama who had told him that he would "meet more Jews in Charleston than I could see in Jerusalem." Several reasons accounted for this sentiment. Inflation, shortages, and speculation, among other factors, indicated to many that the economy was spiraling out of control. As generally happens in wartime, citizens believed that people who derived unwarranted benefits from the wartime economy—and in the South during the Civil War this meant mainly the commercial classes—needed to be singled out and punished for unpatriotic behavior. It must be admitted that the stereotype of the speculative merchant, albeit exaggerated, had some basis in reality. As one Savannah resident perceptively noted in 1863, loyalty to either side had little bearing on business motivations, for "anyone who is willing to buy, keep, and resell at a profit can now grow rich; the recipe is simple—the practice successful."[1]

The high prices storekeepers could demand for their goods on the southern home front proved a mixed blessing. Obviously inflated prices resulted in greater incomes, often in depreciated Confederate dollars, for savvy businessmen. As noted in chapter 5, wealthy merchants like Sidney Root could afford to purchase stock from around the South and overseas for resale in Atlanta at a large profit. When the effectiveness of the Union blockade improved in 1863, prices for food, clothing, and especially medicine became prohibitive. For example, by the end of 1863 one ounce of quinine, if it could be found at all, cost between four hundred and six hundred dollars. Confederate, state, and local governments passed legislation that sought to eliminate the "unpatriotic and wicked" consequences of speculation, but weak law enforcement in the war-torn South made these laws, according to Georgia Governor Joseph Brown, a "dead letter." Threats of fines and confinement—authorities in Salisbury, North Carolina, placed speculators in a caboose for ten days—did little to change the dynamic of supply and demand. With some storekeepers earning more than thirty thousand Confederate dollars in 1864 and selling goods at as much as a 500 percent mark-up, Samuel Richards spoke for many when he exclaimed that money "comes in so fast that we hardly know how to dispose of it to advantage." Storekeepers with the skill, capital, and luck to survive into the second half of the war found themselves with profits to invest. Yet the fashion in which they acquired these profits did not endear them to their fellow Southerners.[2]

At the same time the war brought growing devastation to the South, moneymaking opportunities continued for merchants with capital. The high price for food encouraged some to purchase livestock and perishable foods for quick resale. By 1863 corn could be bought, stored, and later sold for double its initial price. The dislocations caused by the war could also result in profits. Merchants with larger homes and stores supplemented their incomes by taking in war refugees as boarders. At a cost of five dollars per day, a few boarders could add hundreds of dollars to a storekeeper's yearly income. Of course merchants who had converted their operations in order to make supplies for the war effort continued to produce as long as the flow of government orders and the raw materials lasted. Unfortunately for the historian, the same dislocations that created financial opportunities for the merchant class also make it impossible to determine how many individuals actually participated in these business activities. What is clear from the surviving records is that land, staple crops, bonds, and slaves were the primary areas of investment for Confederate merchants.[3]

As the relative value of most goods fluctuated with the fortunes of the war, land appeared to be a very stable investment. No matter how the war ended, the expectation was that land would continue to command a respectable price. In the meantime, storekeepers could use their investment to raise food and other more lucrative crops like cotton and tobacco. Furthermore, southern merchants, like the planter class, enjoyed the prestige that landownership carried with it. The clerk and storekeeper William Burke worked in the firm of Dillon & Briggs in Prince Edward County, Virginia, but also owned a farm in neighboring Nottoway County, where he raised potatoes, corn, and other crops with the help of at least five hired hands. On a much larger scale, the wealthy South Carolina merchant George Walton Williams purchased a hundred thousand acres of Georgia timberland at a dollar an acre, as well as half a million dollars worth of

Charleston property. Of course Williams made these investments with depreciated Confederate dollars. Similarly the merchant and blockade-runner Sidney Root invested his profits in real estate, purchasing an abandoned racetrack outside Atlanta for seventy-five thousand dollars. This trend continued through 1864 when Root attempted to transfer much of his wealth from slaves and cotton into land once he became "alarmed about the safety of Atlanta." Elsewhere in the city, the bookseller Samuel Richards spent over $8,500 for nine separate properties in 1862. He and his brother Jabez would spend their Sundays first attending church and then looking for available real estate around Atlanta. Many of these lots had houses on them or were partially improved. Over the course of the following year Richards bought three more pieces of property, including a 202-acre farm, for $15,250. Most of these purchases were made for the purpose of future resale. Aside from these land deals, Richards, like Burke, anticipated that his family would raise commercial produce on the farm. Even an apparently cautious investment like land, however, carried significant risk for southern capitalists. By 1864 Samuel and Jabez Richards's farm venture proved to be a "losing speculation." The Richards brothers typically bought city lots with little agricultural potential, and they enjoyed more success with these speculations. Unlike the Richards brothers, some merchants invested in land primarily so they could facilitate their speculation in tobacco and cotton.[4]

A brief examination of the business activities of the Richmond merchant James Thomas Butler shows how commercial agriculture and commodity speculation were closely related on the Confederate home front. A partner in the antebellum grocery firm of James T. Butler & Co., he was described in his credit report as a man of "character and standing," despite the fact that he and his partners incurred a number of bad debts. After war broke out the merchant did not close shop but left his home on West Marshall Street in Richmond and concentrated his energy on operating his plantation in nearby Caroline County. He directed his slaves and hired hands to raise tobacco, wheat, and corn for the purpose of speculation. Throughout at least the first half of the war, Butler produced large crops on his Virginia farm. If the price was right, the merchant-planter sent his crops directly to market. When he judged prices to be low, he would not hesitate to hold 2,000 bushels of wheat or 27,000 pounds of corn in storage until supplies dwindled and prices rose. The wealth he derived from commercial farming provided the basis for Butler's numerous other speculative deals. In 1861 he purchased 90,000 pounds of tobacco; a year later he and W. L. Early, a Virginia state senator, purchased another $10,000 of the valuable leaf; another year later Butler invested over $41,000 in at least 19 tobacco deals with 9 different individuals. This trend continued into 1863 when he purchased 220,000 pounds of "Carolina Sun Cured" tobacco. At a time when the Confederate government expected tobacco and cotton farmers to switch to food crops, merchant-planters like James Butler continued to grow, and indeed to speculate in, tobacco. As the experience of Reuben Clark illustrates, canny merchants did not require access to a farm, or even freedom, in order to venture into commodity trading during the Civil War.[5]

Confederate officer Reuben Clark conducted business under the most trying circumstances. A successful young merchant in Knoxville before the war, Clark entered Confederate military service as a first lieutenant in the Third Tennessee. During the war he saw action in the Vicksburg campaign, where he was eventually taken prisoner as a captain in the Fifty-ninth Tennessee. After being exchanged in September 1863, Clark fought with his unit in eastern Tennessee and in the Shenandoah Valley. During the fall of 1864, Union forces again captured Clark. This time, however, the Federal army turned Clark over to the Union provost marshal of Knoxville after William "Parsons" Brownlow, a Methodist preacher, ardent Unionist, and editor of the *Knoxville Whig and Rebel Ventilator,* convinced local leaders that the former merchant had murdered a Union officer. The charge had no foundation in truth, but Clark spent the remainder of the war in an eight-foot-square iron cage in the Knoxville County Jail. Two tasks consumed Clark's time while in jail: gaining his release and protecting the profits he made during the war speculating in land and tobacco.[6]

Soon after his confinement, U.S. Treasury authorities issued a warrant confiscating all Clark's property. The beleaguered prisoner managed to send a letter warning his business partner, George Mayo, to "protect" their mutual assets. Before Mayo could place their property solely under his name, the Federal government and hungry creditors captured the tobacco they had stored in Lynchburg, Virginia. The two lots of land they had purchased in December 1862 were also confiscated by the government. A sullen Clark blamed his careless partner and a malevolent government for leaving him "practically penniless." Cold, hungry, and in danger of being executed for a crime he did not commit, the merchant-soldier's fiscal reversals seemed to add insult to injury. Nevertheless Clark recognized the financial risks of wartime speculation. He found himself in a precarious situation, but the trade in staple crops that he transacted from behind bars was not unusual. Charles Blacknall, another merchant who conducted business while in the Confederate army, expressed the general expectations of his peers when wrote his brother, "I am sure that Tobacco will continue to rise, and if the war should close it will bring the gold immediately, which makes it a safe speculation." This temperament and the behavior it inspired appears repeatedly in the historical record that the merchant class left during the war.[7]

In addition to tobacco, merchants in and out of the army, like their neighbors in the planter class as well as some northern businessmen, speculated in the South's main cash crop, cotton. Many sought their fortunes buying, storing, and eventually selling cotton to customers in Europe and the North. The Confederate government attempted to limit the trade, with only mixed success. The lure of enormous profits attracted too many people willing to ignore both the law and financial prudence for an opportunity to strike it rich, as exemplified in the activities of the Petersburg, Virginia, merchant John William Bradbury and his cotton agent, the Columbus, Georgia, firm Charles Rogers & Company. From 1862 to early 1864 Bradbury supplemented the income he earned selling hardware by regularly speculating in cotton. He traveled to Georgia and other states, where he invested profits that he and his partners made selling hardware. Charles Rogers & Company would locate, purchase, and occasionally store the cotton for Bradbury. Surviving records indicate that Rogers & Company spent $35,489 procuring 420 bales of cotton for the Petersburg merchant and his associates. The cotton factors made their money from the purchase and storage fees they charged, while Bradbury hoped to profit from future sales in a tight cotton market. This process seems to have repeated itself in other cotton-growing regions of the South. Even in states divided by the contending armies early in the war, clever merchants speculated in cotton. The North Carolina merchant and future Reconstruction governor Jonathan Worth made most of his money during the war in cotton production and speculation. While recruiting for the Confederate army, serving as a state senator, and later functioning as the salt commissioner for Randolph County, Worth found time to accumulate a nice profit from the cotton trade. Though his dry-goods store was located in Grand Coteau, Louisiana, Eugene Petetin seems to have purchased cotton throughout his home state and Mississippi. Unfortunately for the Creole businessman, Union forces under the generals Nathaniel Banks and William Franklin confiscated thirty-two bales of his cotton in 1863.[8]

The dislocation, scarcity, and subsequent inflation that made staple crops an attractive investment for entrepreneurial Southerners during the Civil War heightened interest in other financial ventures as well. Merchants and other Southerners with the inclination and means to speculate had diverse investment options. At different times during the war, Confederate bonds, Treasury notes, corporate stock, and gold all held out the promise of significant financial returns. Early in the war the hardnosed storekeeper Samuel Richards purchased one thousand dollars of stock in the Confederate Insurance Company. A year later he bought six thousand dollars in government bonds at 8 percent interest. As late as 1864, Cushing Hassell and his business associates in North Carolina demonstrated their commitment to the cause by spending more than eight thousand dollars on government bonds. Obviously the appeal of government bonds and notes waned among all but the most patriotic citizens as the war turned against the Confederacy.[9]

The slave trade offered yet another alternative for investors. Victories in the field and the expectation of ultimate Confederate independence drove an active wartime trade in slaves. Naturally with their wealth and experience the planter class took the lead in this commercial enterprise. Surging prices in the first half of the war encouraged many planter families to purchase more slaves. Even a middling farmer such as the Virginian Daniel Cobb, who worked eleven slaves on his land in Southampton County, spent $2,480 for a slave boy in 1863. When afforded the opportunity, merchants who had owned slaves prior to the war, as well as those who had not previously participated in this trade, purchased slaves. Experienced merchant slaveholders like Cushing Hassell invested money in slaves early in the war only to sell them later, before they "went off to the Yankees." Regarding the value of his family's assets, Charles Blacknall concluded that the high "prices of negroes is more surprising than anything else." The mercenary quality of this particular wartime speculation can be seen in the designs of Samuel and Jabez Richards.[10] During the antebellum period the Richards brothers did not own slaves and generally regretted the institution's harmful influence upon the South. Their position changed during the war once they became convinced that they could strike it rich through slave speculation. Jabez bought their first slave in July 1862 for a thousand dollars.

A month later Samuel purchased two more slaves for the inflated price of $9,250. As noted in chapter 5, the important point in the Richardses' slave purchases is that the slaves, though they did work, were viewed as a transitory investment. Samuel wished the South victory, among other reasons, so that "when we come to a successful end to this war negroes will command high prices as there will be so much demand for labor to raise cotton and a great many will have been taken away by the Yankees." The merchant's lust for profits outweighed his personal disgust "with negroes" and his regret that "this cruel war should be waged for them!" Like so many other participants in this wartime trade, by late 1864 the Atlanta storekeeper said that he and his brother wished they had "the value of our city lots and negroes in gold at this juncture." Nevertheless, that the Richardses overcame their repugnance and speculated in slaves demonstrates the perseverance of their calculating business mentality during the war.[11]

The broader economic context of these speculations, whether in land, staple crops, bonds, or slaves, must not be forgotten. The widespread issuance of Treasury and state notes, counterfeiting, and an increasingly effective Union blockade created unprecedented inflation across the Confederacy. One historian has estimated that by early 1864 forty-six dollars was required to buy what one dollar had bought three years earlier. This inflation rate more than doubled again during the last year of the war. Thus by 1864 many Southerners paid thirty dollars for a pair of shoes—when they were available at all—four dollars for a pound of butter, and two dollars for a dozen eggs. Shad from a river in eastern North Carolina cost locals four dollars each. Working behind a store counter in such a tumultuous environment, especially during the final two years of the war, proved to be a mixed blessing. The minority of storekeepers who could keep their stores open and stocked made great profits, albeit in inflated currency. Merchants accustomed to modest business before the war saw their sales exceed five hundred dollars a day and tens of thousands of dollars a year. Merchants who owned blockade-runners, such as Sidney Root in Atlanta and James H. Taylor in Augusta, faced even greater financial risks and rewards. These entrepreneurs continued to subscribe to a worldview and to exhibit habits they had learned in the antebellum commercial economy. The constancy of their values is not surprising, nor were their practices unique: at least when it came to cotton and other staple crops, the zeal for speculation among a segment of the planter class matched and even surpassed that of southern merchants. Nevertheless newspapers, politicians, and public opinion perceived the commercial activities of the merchant class to be of a different order. This verdict and its political, moral, and financial ramifications assumed dimensions that surprised even the most experienced storekeepers.[12]

The destruction the white population endured in the final two years of the Civil War weakened the already uncertain position of the mercantile class in southern society (see chapter 2). Some individuals publicly acknowledged the important contribution that merchants made to the Confederate war effort. After all, those who remained in operation provided goods to consumers, shipped supplies through the Union blockade, and on occasion invested their wealth in government bonds. Even so, most white Southerners viewed their merchant neighbors with a mixture of horror and contempt. As the war continued, the flow of abuse that wealthy storekeepers received, from soldier and civilian alike, deepened the familiar channels made during the antebellum period. With few exceptions the merchant class was judged to be rapacious, unpatriotic, and alien, and even its few defenders often based their arguments on the grounds that merchants were no greedier than anyone else. The Confederate Congressman Louis T. Wigfall famously articulated this position on the floor of the Senate when he pronounced: "Talk of speculators, extortioners and Dutch Jews! The farmers have been the worst. . . . Of late a wild spirit of speculation has seized upon the people which bid[s] fair to work our ruin." Similarly an "Observer," writing to the *Galveston Weekly News* in the summer of 1863, noted that many in Brownsville and elsewhere in Texas "abuse[d]" traders for hoarding specie, "but if the truth were not so unpalatable, it might be whispered that the planters are not totally free from this sin (if sin it be)." Such rare public support had little effect. As the war turned against the Confederacy, the liberal capitalist values of the merchant class seemed traitorous and, predictably, "Jewish" to a population looking for scapegoats.[13]

The relationship between white Southerners and their local merchants was strained from the onset of the war. In 1861, R. H. May, the mayor of Augusta, spoke for many leaders across the Confederacy when he put the commercial population on notice with his ominous declaration that "all our citizens should make sacrifices for the common good, and not that advantage should be taken of those least able to suffer, I sincerely trust that while these troublesome times shall exist, our merchants and traders will be satisfied (as they were before) with *living wages*." The clergy echoed the pleas and veiled threats made by Confederate political leaders. Zealous ministers preached that, aside from being personally debasing, "extortion" threatened to bring God's wrath down on the Confederacy. To the pressure exerted by government and religion, the press added its own weighty voice.[14] Published criticism of the mercantile community grew during the war but, at least initially, did not always attempt to draw blood. Occasionally newspapers printed moral tales with messages apparently calculated to restrain the commercial excesses of the merchant class. One particularly didactic story entitled "More Blessed to Give than Receive" in an 1862 edition of the *Wilmington Daily Journal* depicted a noble Christian merchant who forgave the thousand-dollar debt of a poor widow and her daughter. Aside from the eternal reward the businessman's act merited, the author had the poor but upright mother and daughter proclaim, "How much we love and reverence him whenever we think or speak of him, or ever hear him spoken of! . . . He has bound two hearts to him forever." At the end of the day the mother's every thought "was a prayer calling down blessings upon the good rich man." Surrounded by his bronze statuary, marble floors, and luxurious carpets, the merchant rests, strengthened in reputation and closer to salvation. The article's tone mirrored that of the community at large, for early in the war much of the public criticism leveled against storekeepers was mild. Storekeepers who found their activities publicly challenged, men like Oliver Chappel in Macon, Georgia, who was accused of sharing sympathy with the enemy, could dismiss such gossip as the jealous grumbling of disagreeable neighbors. In 1861, when social relations on the Confederate home front were still relatively composed, a businessman could afford to remain indifferent to such reprimands. As the war dragged on, the defensive posture of the merchant class increased proportionally to the public censure they received.[15]

Rising prices and material shortages invited a wide range of white Southerners to attack retail operators as a class. By 1863 newspaper editorials accused men "to the manner born," "dishonest men," and "big merchants" of employing the "laws of trade" as a mere pretense to gouge the last nickel from the soldier's family. A letter from William Poole to the editor of the *Montgomery Daily Advertiser & Register* forcefully articulates themes found in many southern newspapers by 1863. Poole wrote:

I think it the duty of every patriot in the land, especially those gallant spirits that constitute our armies, to discountenance and frown upon the obnoxious and most contemptible of all our enemies—the *extortioner*. He is, undoubtedly, our most dangerous foe, far surpassing the Yankee in unmitigated deeds of villainy. Living, as he does, in our midst, extending the hand of welcome to those that he is depriving of the actual necessaries of life, and feigning good wishes and friendly feelings for the success of the good cause in which we are engaged, he is straining every nerve, is using every means in his power to effect contrary results. . . . It behooves all—more especially the soldier—to guard against the moneyed wolf, the man without patriotism, without principle, nay destitute of the slightest feeling. . . . Instead of buying his goods, or recognising him in any way that one friend would another, we must totally deb [*sic*] him from society.[16]

Many white Southerners shared William Poole's anger. Those living in towns saw food supplies dwindle and costs rise as Union armies destroyed supply lines and occupied more Confederate territory. When the civilian population gained only minimal relief from the activities of blockade-runners and the Confederate authorities, many, like Poole, began equating speculators with the larger Yankee threat. The editor of the *Milledgeville Federal Union* implied that speculation was pathological when he informed his readers that the "disposition to speculate" was "a species of Yankee trick that assorts with the noble cause in which the country is engaged." Stories of greedy merchants, some undoubtedly exaggerated for effect, spread across the South. For example, after a woman reportedly asked her storekeeper how she could afford to feed her family of seven children when flour cost seventy dollars a barrel, the callous merchant answered, "I don't know, madam, unless you eat your children." Whether an illustration of malevolence or an unfortunate attempt at Swiftian humor, such comments bolstered the conclusion that storekeepers held values alien to southern people and their cause.[17]

A vocal minority of the southern population further concluded that the most egregious agents of extortion were an alien race entirely—Jews. Despite the fact that the overwhelming majority of the southern merchant population was Christian, it had often been characterized as disproportionately Jewish during the antebellum period (see chapter 2). The anti-Semitic stereotype climaxed during the last half of the Civil War. The Jewish storekeeper, an outsider in the South, offered a convenient scapegoat for the economic collapse on the home front. Editors raged against "heartless Shylocks" whose brutal commercial practices had "coined their fortunes out of the blood of the brave and the sufferings of penury." Newspapers debated whether Jews were responsible for the "deepening horrors" of war and the likelihood that the public would be forced to "take the remedy in its own hands." Along the same lines, W. A. Lewis, a frequent correspondent for the *Southern Watchman* in Athens, Georgia, wrote that business in Savannah "is in the hands, and conducted principally, by cadaverous looking, cushion-footed Jews, that infest and have cursed every hamlet, village, town, and city in the land." What particularly galled Lewis was his belief that "they refuse to shoulder their muskets and fight in defence of the invaded South." As for charitable giving, Lewis concluded that Jews were "as clear of it as a dog of a soul." In the Confederate Congress the irascible Henry Foote stated that, in Richmond, Jews accounted for "four out of five of the tradesmen in our principal thoroughfares." A prominent Virginian told the congressman that, if the present state of affairs continued, the end of the war would "find nearly all the property of the Confederacy in the hands of Jewish Shylocks." This public debate mirrored the personal views of many white Southerners. Emma Holmes complained to her diary about the exorbitant prices of auctioned goods in Charleston. She blamed the Jews for "outbidding all others" and setting up their "little shops" and leaving her unable to obtain a toothbrush for less than two dollars. The War Department clerk John Beauchamp Jones frequently vented anger in his diary against Jewish merchants, a race that had "no nationality," for depleting the Confederacy: "All wars are harvests for them. It has been so from the day of their dispersion." Most Southerners did not share the passion of Jones's antipathy for Jews in particular or for merchants in general. Nevertheless, a small number of people did lash out against the dire circumstances in which they found themselves, and the merchant class, Jews and gentiles alike, provided a ready target.[18]

Bands of white Southerners, and an occasional individual, attempted to end by direct action what they judged to be the oppressive commercial activities of the merchant class. Though planters speculated during the war, they rarely if ever confronted an angry mob, while enough storekeepers faced such treatment as to provide an example for the rest of their colleagues in the Confederacy. Unlawful mob actions could be planned or relatively spontaneous, conducted with the support of the community or socially illegitimate. In any case, when mobs forcibly removed a storekeeper, broke into a shop, or had other skirmishes with merchants, it highlighted the growing desperation of the former and the marginal position of the latter.[19] Gangs rationalized their attacks on local shopkeepers with the claim that they were defending the community. Early in the war Isaac Harman, a Jewish merchant in Greene County, Georgia, raised his prices only to have ten Mercer University students beat him outside his store. Harman deserved the punishment, according to the students, for exploiting his neighbors. The merchant and his Jewish partners filed assault charges against the students and theft charges against another, but these acts failed to win the support of their community, where they had operated for years. By 1862, Harman and his partners lost most of their business and eventually left the area. Assaults like this one and simple break-ins increased during the war. After three robberies on one October evening in 1862 the editor of the *Wilmington Daily Journal* admonished his readers, "This is a very wrong proceeding. . . . If it is necessary to resort to such measures for food, it must be done *legally.*" The editor implied that the government or, at the very least, community leaders should confiscate necessary goods from storekeepers. That same month a store in Richmond lost more than eight thousand dollars in goods during a robbery. From his government office Jones observed, "Prejudice is very strong against the extortionists, and I apprehend there will be many scenes of violence this winter." The war clerk's assessment proved correct. From 1863 until the end of the war food riots erupted in cities across the South, including Atlanta, Augusta, Columbus, Macon, and Savannah, Georgia; Salisbury and High Point, North Carolina; Mobile, Alabama; and Richmond, Virginia. In Columbus an "immense" crowd of women "helped themselves" to the stores of Gans & Co. and were moving on a shop operated by the Waltzfelder family before authorities stopped them. Both operations were owned by Jewish merchants. Remarking upon the participation of 150 Savannah women in a bread riot, the *Raleigh Weekly Conservative* noted, "Riots of this nature are becoming very common in many sections of the Confederacy—entirely too much so for the good of our cause." The *Memphis Daily Appeal* criticized the participants of the notorious 1863 Richmond bread riot, labeled a "woman's riot" by the paper, for hypocrisy. The apparent instigator of the riot, a forty-year-old huckster named Mary, came in for particular condemnation. The paper noted that the "Amazonian huckster" had been "arranging" the riot for some time, all the while she personally speculated in food goods. Even so the editor did not defend the merchant targets of Mary and her cohorts. If angry letters to the editor and occasional public insults failed to remind storekeepers of their tenuous place in the Confederacy, a hungry mob of hatchet-wielding women tended to drive the point home.[20]

Merchants would retaliate against specific violations of their person or property by filing criminal or civil charges, but little suggests that they believed it wise to respond to the steady vitriol they endured. When they did reply, merchants attributed high prices and scarcity to conditions of the market. Commercial businessmen, large and small, blamed the Federal blockade for creating the scarcity that raised inflation in the Confederacy. George Walton Williams and others tried to appease public outrage by describing the great cost to merchants of acquiring stock. Along the same lines, an Augusta merchant argued that higher prices were merely the "natural workings" of the marketplace. Storekeepers supported this contention by pointing to the southern farmer's disposition to "speculate"—that is, to hoard—his crops when the market did not offer him a satisfactory price. Though they downplayed the scale of their wartime profits and investments, merchants who made this argument were fundamentally correct. Upheavals in the supply of goods did shrink the market, but by 1864 particulars of economic theory, no matter how rational, did not win the opinion of distressed soldiers and their families. When all else failed, storekeepers with any wit emphasized their support for the failing Confederate cause. Sympathizing with veterans, or better yet being a veteran, could create goodwill with neighbors. Veteran William Perry returned to Montgomery, Alabama, and began selling confectioneries in January 1865. A historian of Civil War Montgomery found that Perry's boast of "service on the field since the war commenced" won him great customer loyalty. Another storekeeper in the Alabama town, Samuel Wreford, operated the One-Armed Man's Dry Goods Store. Even as Union forces closed upon the city, the one-armed man, feeling "cool and collected," kept his store open for business. All merchants needed the one-armed storekeeper's composure in order to successfully buy, sell, speculate, and then defend their reputation in an embattled Confederacy.[21]

Throughout the conflict, the military experience of commercial men who served in the Confederate army mirrored that of their white neighbors, regardless of class or occupation (see chapter 4). While some commercial men may have received at the onset of the war more then their share of ridicule for being soft or having poor eyesight—undoubtedly from reading their ledgers and keeping their books—after several years of bloodshed those in the ranks had become veterans as tough as any of their comrades. Hard fighting, mounting casualities, and eventual despair framed the last eighteen months of the war. Business activity and the liberal capitalist values that defined so many of these merchant-soldiers waned with the splintering Confederacy. Even some merchants and their family members fighting in the ranks came to reject the commercial activities of the businessmen in their midst—the sutlers. In the summer of 1863 Lieutenant Usher Bonney, the son of a South Carolina merchant, wrote his family that the inflated prices and shoddy goods sold by "hawk visaged" sutlers in his camp made them the "vultures of the army." Even in the relative safety of his camp near Fredericksburg, Virginia, Bonney found himself far removed from his father's store in Camden. For him, as for others hailing from the merchant class, it was left to the families on the home front and the ranks of the civilian businessmen to maintain the commercial ties that would enable the southern business community to rebuild after the war.[22]

The surviving diaries and letters that merchant-soldiers wrote during the final two years of the war suggest their increasingly desperate plight. Indeed the very paucity of these records reveals how death and imprisonment had thinned their ranks since the beginning of the war. By early 1864 only sixteen of the original company of sixty men that Louis Leon had served with in the Fifty-third North Carolina remained. The lonely soldier had to exchange letters with a Union picket to learn about the circumstances of his parents, who lived in New York. A one-time clerk serving in the Army of Northern Virginia, hoping for a respite from the carnage he faced, asked for the hand of his sweetheart back in Tennessee. He described his love in poetic terms, then declared, "I wish to go home—and it is in your power to give Me a furlough." The letter failed in its mission. As large sections of the Confederacy fell to Union forces the government called upon reservists and wounded soldiers to fill the depleted ranks. On May 21, 1864, Virginia reservist James Thomas Butler received orders to march to Richmond. At the same time, Confederate and Federal armies clashed near his Caroline County farm during the Battle of North Anna. Soldiers who still fought during the last months of the war suffered; nevertheless they considered themselves fortunate to be free and alive.[23]

Like their comrades in arms, southern soldiers from commercial backgrounds ran an increased risk of capture during the final two years of the Civil War. Over the course of the war, Union armies captured well over 214,000 southern soldiers. By 1865 approximately 12 percent of that population had died while in northern prisons. Merchants who found themselves in one of these prisons described a wide variety of conditions to their families back home. An officer in the Twenty-third North Carolina, Charles Blacknall was captured by Federal forces at the Battle of Gettysburg and sent to a prison for Confederate officers on Johnson's Island in Lake Erie. Blacknall found conditions there quite decent. He wrote his wife Jinny, "Reports that have been circulated in the South in regard to 'Yankee Cruelty' to prisoners &c&c. are all false." Blacknall added, "We receive quite as much kindness as we show to prisoners ourselves." Of course the letter might have been calculated to ease the mind of his troubled wife. Six months later the one-time merchant and resort proprietor was exchanged and returned to command with his unit near Petersburg, Virginia. Unfortunately for historians, most prisoners of war did not write letters home or keep diaries. Louis Leon and his brother Morris's feelings about being captured at the Battle of the Wilderness in May 1864 must remain a mystery. It is probably safe to assume, however, that the six months he spent in the infamous Union prison in Elmira, New York, proved difficult. Leon took the oath of allegiance to the Federal government and was released in April 1865. As noted earlier, the Confederate officer Reuben Clark endured in a Knoxville cage an extraordinary imprisonment, which he later characterized as "bitter and vindictive beyond measure." Unlike many of his fellow soldiers, however, Clark lived to tell of his experience.[24]

The case of Charles Blacknall exhibits the relative danger of fighting compared with continued imprisonment. His confinement was onerous but ultimately may have saved him from death in the Army of Northern Virginia. Had he stayed in prison, perhaps he would have survived the war, but after his exchange and return to command, Blacknall suffered an ankle wound at the Third Battle of Winchester in September 1864, and even amputation did not save the North Carolinian from dying of gangrene. Thus his wife and children joined the ranks of merchant families devastated by the war. William Henry Wills, a onetime merchant in Halifax, North Carolina, and an active Methodist preacher, lost his son George, a member of the Forty-third North Carolina, in the same campaign where Blacknall was wounded. An army chaplain informed the elderly merchant-farmer of his loss and counseled that the "decided Christian character and piety of George assures us that Your loss is his eternal gain." Reflecting upon the death of his son, Wills wrote in his diary, "Thy Will Be done." In a less sublime exchange of tidings, Reuben Clark, secure in his Knoxville cage, heard of his brother's death from a terse note passed to him by a prison guard. Most Southerners learned of a family member's death in the way that William Wills did, by official army communiqué or the letter of a friend. Mississippian Elizabeth Wilson Howze, widow of the storekeeper Isham Howze and the mother of another merchant, had lost two sons by 1864. At home in North Carolina, Cushing Hassell received the news of his son Theodore's death. Only days before the war ended the twenty-five-year-old had been killed in fighting near Goldsboro, not far from his home. Such causalities of war forever transformed families like the Hassells, Howzes, and Blacknalls.[25]

The last two years of the Civil War did prove to be the great equalizer for Confederate soldiers who saw action on the battlefield. The experience of most soldiers from commercial backgrounds resembled that of any other southern man. Merchant-soldiers may have been making postwar business plans, but they did not have time or desire to describe them in writing while giving their last measure to ward off invading Yankees. By this stage of the war, the center of mercantile activity shifted away from the decreasing number of blockade-runners and storekeepers behind Confederate lines toward the families of merchants living under Union occupation. According to some observers, the former group had come to consist mainly of "loafers" sitting in their stores ducking the call to arms. Back home on furlough in January 1864, one Confederate officer found the local store full of commercial men and other shirkers, who were complaining "that the country is totally ruined," while at the same time designing measures to "avoid taking the field." The officer "razzed" these "worthless cowards" but acknowledged their skill in making "as much money as they can out of the necessities of the people and the wives of the poor soldiers." Merchants and their families traded goods between the Union and Confederacy, reestablished economic ties with northern mercantile houses, and began laying the foundation for a postwar commercial economy in the South.[26]

The commercial activities of southern storekeepers who managed to survive the first three years of the war largely collapsed by late 1864. Civilians either could no longer profitably stock their stores or were at least temporarily forced out of business by invading Union armies. The

Atlanta merchants Sidney Root and Samuel Richards saw their business operations close once Federal troops under William T. Sherman captured their city in September 1864. Though both men had made tremendous profits during the first three years of the war—the former as a blockade-runner and the latter as a book and paper merchant—by 1865 they had suffered large financial losses. Root and his partners lost their investments in twenty or more blockade-running ships, thirteen buildings in Atlanta, and a net loss in cotton holdings estimated at the astronomical sum of $1.7 million in greenbacks. Desperate Confederate soldiers sacked Richards's store on July 22, 1864, and later in the year Yankees and the local populace plundered the store a second time. Samuel described the second break-in as a "scene that would have required the pencil of Hogarth to Portray." The bookseller was most distressed by the fact that the robbery erupted "before our eyes by men who *looked* like gentlemen!" Richards added, "Of course their looks belied their character." Following the destruction of Atlanta, both men journeyed North and lived in temporary exile in New York City until the end of the war. This story of ruin, evacuation, temporary relocation, and eventual revival played itself out across the South.[27]

Commercial families endured a multitude of losses, financial and emotional, during the last days of the war. Aside from the destruction wrought by battles and invading armies, institutions that merchants had long known, if not always embraced, disintegrated. Slavery's demise, for example, disturbed a number of merchants. Like their planter neighbors, merchant families lost their slaves with the arrival of Union troops. As Federal forces neared their home in Mississippi, Benedict Semmes implicitly acknowledged the breakdown of paternalism when he implored his wife Jorantha to "*trust nothing whatever to any of the Negroes.*" Mary Anngady, slave to a general merchant in Chapel Hill, North Carolina, remembered that Yankee troops looked for her master's hidden silver, plundered his store, and gave her father a portion of the merchant's food. She and her family were free to go, though they remained with the "white folks" for a time. Cushing Hassell's account of the conduct of his slaves at war's end resembles the descriptions written by the planter class. The merchant claimed to have kept his slaves well fed, clothed, and together. At the commencement of hostilities, Hassell promised them that if they would "stick" to him they would be supported and "happy." Despite this paternal interest, several months before the war ended three of his male slaves left to join the Union army in eastern North Carolina, and Hassell sold a female slave before she had an opportunity to flee. The fact that Hassell both owned slaves and fancied himself a paternal master made him an oddity among his fellow retail businessmen. The shock and disappointment he expressed at his slaves' behavior is less peculiar. Storekeepers frequently heaped scorn upon the African-American population, both slave and free, whom they blamed for causing the white South's woes. In the fall of 1865 one South Carolina merchant wrote in a pleading letter to his onetime northern wholesaler that the seventeen slaves he lost with emancipation would have been enough to pay his outstanding prewar debts with the New York City firm.[28]

As the case of Jorantha Semmes shows, southern merchants or their family members who were able to save a portion of their inventory could continue to ply their trade under Federal occupation. Don Doyle's analysis of several southern cities during and after the Civil War revealed that entrepreneurial businessmen in Nashville and elsewhere could make a tidy profit by conducting business with leaders of the occupying forces. The lingering effect of strong Unionist sentiment in Nashville from before the war apparently smoothed the economic transition from Confederate to Federal control. The implications for many local merchants were significant since they could participate in the million-dollar commodity trade conducted in that city during 1864–1865. Once Federal troops arrived, commercial men who had gone into manufacturing during the war also exhibited adaptability to the new order. After the Confederacy collapsed, manufacturers displayed "undisguised haste" in their willingness to take President Andrew Johnson's prescribed oath and receive a pardon. Harold S. Wilson's analysis of these petitions led him to conclude that most of these businessmen "revealed a sincere, emotional desire to establish a commercial reunion with the North." This rush to begin the "romance of reunion" suggests the ambivalent feelings many southern businessmen had had about the conflict since before secession. Of course the small number of southern merchants who could prove themselves to have been Unionists throughout the war reveled in Confederate defeat and hoped the sacrifices they made would be rewarded by the United States.[29]

People in Columbus, Georgia, considered the trader and teamster Thomas Hogan to be a rank Unionist and Yankee sympathizer. Not only had he opposed secession; the old Whig had declared publicly that the "damned Democrats caused the war." During the war "nine-tenths" of the community would not speak to him. One of his few friends, a lukewarm

Confederate physician named John E. Bacon, told government investigators after the war: "You can get five hundred men to testify to his loyalty to the United States government during the war and curse him while giving their testimony." His neighbors did not threaten him with physical abuse, but their disapprobation and disdain injured his "business and social relations." The fact that his son had served in the Confederate army undoubtedly helped him. Nevertheless Hogan's economic woes continued for four years, until Federal forces entered Columbus in the final days of the war. True to his convictions, Hogan supplied the Federals with three thousand pounds of fodder, and these same troops apparently helped themselves to one of his mules. Following the war, the Southern Claims Commission, established by the U.S. government to compensate southern Unionists for supplies that had been confiscated or furnished to the army during the war, reimbursed Hogan for his losses. He received only a portion of what he asked for, but in a short time his thirty-year-old son James had taken over and expanded the family mercantile business. James became a businessman and assistant postmaster in the New South.[30]

John A. Cherry, another Unionist merchant, did not enjoy such postwar success. Cherry operated a dry-goods store and grocery in Williamston, a river city in eastern North Carolina. There he, along with his wife Nancy, sold goods and earned a reputation as a "loyal man" to the United States. On at least one occasion Cherry called a neighbor a "Damn fool" for joining the Confederate army. More proactively, when Federal gunboats approached the town in 1862 Cherry walked down to the wharf, unfurled his U.S. flag and "invited the Federals to come ashore." When Union troops under the command of General John Gray Foster eventually did enter Williamston, Cherry took the oath of allegiance and provided his new northern friends with livestock, food, salt, and brandy. Even after the Federals left and Confederate forces returned, Cherry on at least one occasion "hoisted" his U.S. flag on his house. Not surprisingly Confederate troops "came very near shooting" Cherry over the incident. Government records do not reveal why Cherry escaped official punishment or extralegal reprisals, but the fact that he was described in documents as a sickly, childless, "cripple" suggests the community viewed him as more pathetic than threatening. The Southern Claims Commission determined Cherry to be a loyal citizen and compensated him $817 after the war for the supplies he gave Foster's men. The goodwill Cherry had earned with the authorities in Washington, D.C., might have helped him recover his economic position following the war had he not died in 1866. His widow, Nancy Cherry, carried on after the war without her "loyal man."[31]

The cases of Thomas Hogan and John Cherry indicate that a small percentage of southern merchants may have been favorably positioned to reopen contacts with northern creditors and wholesalers after the war. This said, the records of the Southern Claims Commission do not indicate more Unionist sentiment within the merchant class than either their planter or yeoman farmer neighbors displayed. While privately merchants may have been ambivalent about secession and quick to embrace the postwar order, in public most swam in the stream of popular opinion. The material and psychological ruin that so many white Southerners sustained between 1861 and 1865 forever transformed the region. The once dominant planter class had to redefine itself in an attempt to regain political and economic control. White farmers regrouped and toiled for a measure of economic security. Freedmen tested their new political rights. Amid this turbulence thousands of Southerners barely managed to eke out an existence. As historians of the New South have noted, the mercantile class not only adapted to the postwar economy; it helped to create it. Storekeepers with business experience from the antebellum and Confederate South laid the foundation for this success. Indeed young merchants, both in and out of the Confederate army, and their families began planning for their postwar careers during the final months of the conflict when the end could be foreseen.

Southern merchants living in communities behind Union lines revived their business operations at the earliest possible moment. Jean Baptiste Bres of Louisiana, for example, resumed his speculations in cotton, whiskey, and other goods after he took a loyalty oath to the United States on June 8, 1864. In the last year of the war the entrepreneurial Bres obtained passes from the provost marshal general to conduct business in Saint Louis, Missouri; Cairo, Illinois; and New York City. Following the war Bres drew upon his wartime business experience to obtain a position as a cotton agent for Allen Greene & Son. Two weeks after the fall of Charleston and one month before Robert E. Lee's surrender, George Walton Williams took the oath of allegiance and later made the effort to seek a personal pardon from the president because his worth exceeded twenty thousand dollars. During the process Williams, arguing for a rejuvenated South, wrote, "We shall have no more use for nullification or secession in this day and generation." Along similar lines after the Union army occupied Atlanta,

Samuel Richards and Sidney Root both temporarily relocated to New York City, where they began their economic recovery. Having obtained a line of credit in New York City, Richards returned to Atlanta in August 1865 and reopened his bookstore. In 1866, a local Dun & Co. agent reported Richards's firm as coming through the war "without sustaining much loss" and having "considerable means left." The storekeeper thrived in the New South. The destruction of the Confederacy left Sidney Root much more disillusioned. For several years after the war the old blockade-runner avoided a permanent homecoming to Atlanta. By 1878, however, Root moved back home to take a position as general superintendent with Chamberlain, Boynton & Company. The Camden, South Carolina, store-keeper Eli Bonney offered to pay his northern wholesaler/creditors fifty cents on the dollar for the principal of his prewar debt so he could have "matters settled" and "try & rise once more and commence my old busi-ness again." He promised his northern connections that his new business would be a "cash system"—indicating that they would be paid in a timely matter. Bonney invited his old associates to visit his community and verify his circumstances for themselves.[32]

Merchants who did not have the desire or opportunity to travel North often looked to their families for business assistance. John S. West, a part-ner in a Buckingham County, Virginia, dry-goods firm, made sure that his family would maintain a foothold in commercial trade. Despite numerous obstacles, West managed to keep his firm open throughout most of the war. More important, as one of his sons served in the Confederate army, he sent another to serve as a clerk with the Richmond tobacco firm Neal Brothers & Company. There the young man learned the habits that would sustain the family firm in the coming years. The apprentice clerk wrote his family in February 1865 about his efforts to "do my duty in every respect both to my maker & employers" while "trying too to save all the money I can." Following the war he returned to the family firm and employed his skills and values to sustain what one observer called "one of the most thriving firms" in the county. As described in chapter 5, Benedict Semmes depended upon his wife Jorantha to maintain the family through retail activity while he served as a soldier in the commissary department. The economic role she assumed continued until Benedict rejoined his family in 1865. In a matter of weeks the Semmeses returned to Memphis where Benedict reopened Semmes & Company, a wine and liquor firm. As with West's store, the early success of Semmes & Company after the war rested in part upon the wartime activities of Semmes's family, particularly the labor of his wife.[33]

The destruction wrought by the final two years of the Civil War forced hundreds of merchants and their families to suspend business, relocate, and bury their dead. The business so many storekeepers had conducted during the first half of the war disappeared. Merchants who did continue to sell goods came under increased attack from a white southern population exhausted by war and speculation. The commercial population, with their liberal capitalist practices, habits, and bourgeois mien, suffered greatly but ultimately survived the collapse of the Old South. Their staying power can be in part attributed to the tenacious spirit they shared with their southern neighbors. On a practical level, the business ties that the vast majority of these storekeepers had enjoyed with commercial wholesalers in the North during the antebellum period were critical in their effort to reestablish themselves after the war. That northern and southern merchants held so many views in common facilitated the transition. Perhaps more fundamentally, merchant families recovered financially and psychologically in the New South because they had never enjoyed a conventional home in an antebellum South dominated by the planter class.

Conclusion

Merchant Culture in the
Slave South and Beyond

It is sad to think how things are changing. In another generation or two, this beautiful country of ours will have lost its distinctive civilization and become no better than a nation of Yankee shopkeepers.

—Eliza Frances Andrews, July 27, 1865

The appearance of a purely trading class will have of itself no revolutionary significance; . . . its rise will exert a much less fundamental influence on the economic pattern of society than will the appearance of a class of capitalists whose fortunes are intimately linked with industry; . . . while a ruling class, whether of slave-owners or feudal lords, may take to trading or enter into a close alliance with traders, a merchant class . . . is unlikely to strive to become a dominant class in quite that radical and exclusive sense.

—Maurice Dobb, *Studies in the Development of Capitalism*

Becoming Bourgeois: Merchant Culture in the South, 1820–1865 has investigated two related questions in the history of the antebellum and Confederate South. First, what identities and roles did merchants embrace in that society? Second, what do the activities and popular images of the merchant class reveal about the nature of southern society as a whole? Answering the first question required piecing together disparate fragments that were left behind by the overlooked men and women of the merchant class. What emerges from the historical record are the stories of people who shared a cosmopolitan worldview that emphasized a strong commitment to liberal capitalism, Whig politics, close family ties, a Protestant work ethic, and white supremacy. These findings suggest areas for further investigation. Recent scholarship on the American middle class in the nine-

203

teenth century has advanced our knowledge of this surprisingly neglected group, but much work, particularly in southern archives, remains to be done. Examining merchant culture and how that culture was perceived by outsiders helps advance our understanding of the nineteenth-century South in general. The complex nature of the slave South and its political economy, the essence of my second question, has for decades elicited conflicting interpretations from historians.[1]

The image of an agrarian, economically underdeveloped, even anticapitalist South has long been a staple in American thought. John Taylor of Caroline celebrated it, Hinton Rowan Helper deplored it, and H. L. Mencken jeered it. Historians have long debated the degree to which capitalism penetrated the slave South. During the past forty years, perhaps the historian with the most to say on the point has been Eugene Genovese. Beginning with his first study, *The Political Economy of Slavery* (1965), and further developing his theories in several other of his influential works, Genovese has maintained that the hegemonic class in the antebellum South, the slaveholders, were fundamentally noncommercial, perhaps even acommercial; they were rarely interested in money for its own sake; and they participated in a slave system that proved unprofitable for individual owners as well as for the southern economy as a whole. Furthermore, the paternalism that Genovese sees as defining the master-slave relationship assaulted the slave's personality while allowing many of them an overlooked measure of cultural breathing space. Based in part upon the theoretical work of Karl Marx, Antonio Gramsci, Maurice Dobb, and others, Genovese's interpretation of the slave South has won many supporters within the historical profession. Others have found his argument less convincing. A number of historians and economists—Robert W. Fogel, Stanley L. Engerman, and James Oakes being among the most vocal— have found slaveholders to have been profit-driven capitalists much like any businessman in Europe or the northern United States. Over the years numerous academics, many bringing fresh insight, have weighed in on this question. The preponderance of studies on the planter class, however, have deflected scholarly attention from those other segments of the white population that also influenced the southern economy.[2]

Examining the political economy of the slave South through the historical prism of the planter class makes sense. After all, they more than anyone else ruled the "Cotton Kingdom." Nevertheless, as I have attempted to illustrate, the merchant class proved to be instrumental "retainers" in this imagined realm. Over time these commercial servants exerted ever greater influence, until the economic transformation occurring in the antebellum South—greatly hastened by the Civil War—made businessmen the masters in the New South. Their retail operations, connections to northern wholesale firms, and business savvy helped build a relatively sophisticated, viable southern economy. Most historians have overlooked their cultural and economic influence within the Old South, because they have implicitly accepted significant aspects of the Marxist historical paradigm developed by Eugene Genovese. On this point Maurice Dobb is instructive, for his work fundamentally influenced Genovese. According to Dobb, merchant capital in Europe was merely a "parasite on the old order" before manufacturing and commercial interests produced a "mature" capitalism by changing the mode of production and thus creating a large class of wage laborers. Building and improving upon this theoretical assumption, Genovese concluded that George Fitzhugh and other defenders of the slave South created a "world in which the fundamental social relations remained nonbourgeois." Scholars who have taken exception to this conclusion have responded to Genovese by delineating bourgeois characteristics of the planter class rather than by investigating the element within southern society that most fervently embraced the bourgeois culture of the North and of western Europe: the merchant class.[3]

Once it is understood, the historical experience of the merchant class in the slave South suggests that the opposing interpretations of the "South-as-non-capitalist" and the "South-as-capitalist" schools may be too overdrawn to adequately explain the complex economic and cultural habits of most white Southerners. As we have seen, in many ways merchants and their families best exemplified the divide between liberal capitalist and conservative agrarian values, for it was they, more than most of their neighbors, who had the ability to participate in an increasingly commercial, bourgeois United States. Given the opportunity after the Civil War, many other Southerners, white and black, followed their example.[4]

Naturally this conclusion leads to a related, and seemingly interminable, debate among historians of the nineteenth-century South about the extent to which the New South that arose from the ashes of the Civil War was actually new. While consideration of this question dates from the late nineteenth century, the most influential statement on the subject is C. Vann Woodward's classic *Origins of the New South, 1877–1913* (1951). Arguing for social, political, and economic discontinuity between the Old and New South, Woodward generally agreed with a Mississippi planter whom he quoted as describing a new order in which the "Negro and poor white men of the country made nothing; the factors and the country merchant were the divinities presiding over the agricultural interests . . . ; the landowners were out in the cold ignored even by their tenants." This is far from a transformed society in which the mudsill is on top. Over the years, detractors have taken Woodward to task for exaggerating the importance of regional class divisions while at the same time failing to give due emphasis to the overwhelming impact of race in the South. These historians typically emphasize how labor controls and political influence enabled planter rule to persist in the South long after the war. Still others, notably Gavin Wright, have written that the question of continuity versus change in the nineteenth-century South is essentially unanswerable, an intellectual dead end. Despite such skepticism, a glance at the expanding historiography and the continuing fascination in the broader popular culture with the nineteenth-century South reveals clearly that the issue of continuity versus change will not, and probably should not, disappear anytime soon.[5]

Uncovering the historical experience of the southern merchant class will certainly not end the debate that C. Vann Woodward helped frame more than half a century ago. That slaves gained their freedom while the planter class attempted to reestablish its political-economic position without its traditional labor source seems a more fruitful avenue of investigation for historians interested in comparing southern society before and after the war. What a survey of the merchant class does suggest is that the culture and political economy of the nineteenth-century South was much more complex than previously thought. Both before and during the Civil War, the southern merchant class staked out a middle ground between a bourgeois North and more conservative South, indicating a degree of cultural continuity over the course of the nineteenth century. Lacy K. Ford, Don H. Doyle, David Lee Carlton, and other historians of the postwar South have produced excellent studies revealing how the scale of urbanization and industrialization increased in the South during the late nineteenth and early twentieth centuries. This growth, accompanied by political changes on a state level, enabled the merchant class to come into its own. Between 1880 and 1910 the number of Southerners living in villages and towns increased by five million, while the number of stores exceeded 150,000—or 144 stores per county—by 1900. Retail commercialism, particularly advertising, loomed ever larger in the world of average folk. Clearly the New South "creed" was real. Yet, as I hope this study has described, the worldview that produced this creed had its prophets long before the war. Indeed, some of the antebellum and wartime merchants examined in this work helped to build the New South.[6]

Those storekeepers who survived the war, reopened their stores, and managed to pay off their share of the estimated $150 million debt owed to northern wholesalers, often expanded their mercantile operations to include basic manufacturing, advertising, and retail. For example, a year after the Civil War ended, the Nashville storekeeper George O'Bryan and his brothers began manufacturing the Duckhead brand of clothing, which is still being sold across the South 140 years later. After obtaining stock from his business connections in New York City, Cushing Hassell sold more than ten thousand dollars in goods during the summer of 1865. Four years after the war, as Atlanta rose from the ashes, Samuel Richards found his bookstore "overrun with trade" as the result of vigorous advertising and ruthless business methods against his competitors. In 1876 the Confederate veteran Daniel Hoard Baldwin reestablished himself in Savannah as a cotton factor, having spent a decade in New York City as a commission merchant. Benedict Semmes, who had been promoted to a major in the final months of the war, returned home to Memphis, Tennessee. Welcoming him was his wife Jorantha, who had done so much to keep their four children safe and their finances solvent. Benedict and his sons reestablished their commercial operation, selling mainly liquor, while Jorantha went on to give birth to three more children. The Semmeses' store grew into one of the largest establishments of its kind in Memphis. Though the manuscript record largely ends with the war, no doubt from time to time Benedict continued to rely upon Jorantha's shrewd head for business. While the commercial classes expanded their activity, they became sizable landlords as well. In Rome, Georgia, Reuben Clark built a large estate named Bell Vue after making a small fortune in the dry-goods business. The economic growth that these personal stories represent changed the South. By the 1890s successful merchants had the fortune to boast, "I could make money rapidly," and the hubris to assert, "I never loved money for its own sake." The extent of such rhetoric and the economic activity that supported it was greater but not qualitatively different than in the past.[7]

This final point is crucial to appreciating the question of continuity/

discontinuity between the Old and New South. As Michael O'Brien and others have noted, Woodward's description of a postwar South that broke from the past rested heavily upon the premise of southern distinctiveness, that the nineteenth-century South had deviated from mainstream American experience. The institution of slavery, and later the rise of enforced segregation under Jim Crow, did distinguish the South, yet the members of its influential merchant class had much in common with their counterparts in the North throughout the nineteenth century. The contours of their bourgeois profiles fell along the same lines, and the end of slavery removed one of the few rifts between these regional allies. Following the war, southern merchants could embrace the same goals as "bourgeois" New York businessmen, who, in the words of one scholar, sought "to restore the political economy that they [the South] had left behind in 1861, save for slavery." The sectional divide in the experience of northern and southern merchants, who though small in number were economically powerful, was not significant. As they negotiated between the two regions, one wonders how much real difference they would have perceived between the Old and New South once tenant farming and the Jim Crow laws replaced slavery.[8]

Americans who lived to see the war end, along with historians who followed them, have often described it as a conflict between two competing systems. A conservative, slaveholding, agrarian South fought and lost to a liberal, free labor, capitalist North. As Eliza Andrews bitterly remarked in the summer of 1865, it would be only a matter of time before her South became a "nation of Yankee shopkeepers." Clearly this "Georgia Girl" viewed merchant capital as a threat to her beloved South's traditional culture and economy. What might she have made of Dobb's conclusions on this issue? Important features that had made the South distinctive, such as African slavery and the social and economic control of the planter class, had undergone a revolution. Nevertheless, white Southerners in 1865—as well as many scholars of the War between the States and the American South since then—underestimated the economic continuity that bound the antebellum, Confederate, and postbellum South into a commercial whole. The business activity of southern merchants and their families before and during the Civil War was nothing new nor did it end with Lee's surrender at Appomattox. Their influence and commercial habits reveal that the South of George Fitzhugh and young Eliza Andrews was on its way to becoming a nation of shopkeepers well before its cause was lost.

Appendix

Table 1. Population Sample of Southern Commercial Classes, 1850

	Commercial Population in County	Percent of Overall County Free Population (Including Families)
Lowndes County (AL)	209	3.45
Washington County (AL)	13	1.10
Alachua County (FL)	17	1.00
Leon County (FL)	201	6.20
Putnam County (FL)	27	5.60
Clarke County (GA)	299	4.90
Emanuel County (GA)	3	0.08
Gwinnett County (GA)	119	1.30
Wayne County (GA)	5	0.45
Concordia Parish (LA)	4	0.48
West Feliciana Parish (LA)	156	6.30
Terrebonne Parish (LA)	102	3.00
Davidson County (NC)	82	0.66
Martin County (NC)	88	1.80
Williamsburg County (SC)	70	1.80
Hardeman County (TN)	191	1.80
McMinn County (TN)	148	1.20
McNairy County (TN)	167	1.50
Panola County (TX)	34	1.30
Rusk County (TX)	186	3.10
Grayson County (VA)	56	0.90
Southampton County (VA)	85	1.10
Total	*2,262*	*2.20*

1.8% (rounded average taken from total free population of all 22 counties: 123,223)

Overall Profile: States=9; Counties=22; Free population=123,223 (57.9%);
Slave population=89,748 (42.1%); Total population=212,971

Table 2. Occupation Profile of Southern Commercial Classes, 1850

	Total No. Commercial Workers (Com. Pop.)	No. Merchants, Grocers, Etc. (% Com. Pop.)	No. Clerks (% Com. Pop.)	No. Peddlers, Hucksters, Etc. (% Com. Pop.)
Lowndes County	76	44 (57.9%)	29 (38.2%)	3 (3.9%)
Washington County	5	4 (75.0%)	0 (0.0%)	1 (25.0%)
Alachua County	11	5 (45.5%)	6 (54.5%)	0 (0.0%)
Leon County	86	41 (47.6%)	44 (51.2%)	1 (1.2%)
Putnam County	8	6 (75.0%)	2 (25.0%)	0 (0.0%)
Clarke County	109	61 (56.0%)	46 (42.2%)	2 (1.8%)
Emanuel County	3	3 (100.0%)	0 (0.0%)	0 (0.0%)
Gwinnett County	24	19 (79.2%)	2 (8.3%)	3 (12.5%)
Wayne County	1	1 (100.0%)	0 (0.0%)	0 (0.0%)
Concordia Parish	3	2 (66.7%)	1 (33.3%)	0 (0.0%)
W. Feliciana Parish	58	37 (63.8%)	21 (36.2%)	0 (0.0%)
Terrebonne Parish	32	24 (75.0%)	8 (25.0%)	0 (0.0%)
Davidson County	21	10 (47.6%)	10 (47.6%)	1 (4.8%)
Martin County	25	18 (72.0%)	7 (28.0%)	0 (0.0%)
Williamsburg County	20	17 (85.0%)	3 (15.0%)	0 (0.0%)
Hardeman County	71	41 (57.8%)	26 (36.6%)	4 (5.6%)
McMinn County	49	34 (69.4%)	15 (30.6%)	0 (0.0%)
McNairy County	50	36 (72.0%)	14 (28.0%)	0 (0.0%)
Panola County	13	8 (61.5%)	5 (38.5%)	0 (0.0%)
Rusk County	58	41 (70.7%)	17 (29.3%)	0 (0.0%)
Grayson County	17	9 (52.9%)	8 (47.1%)	0 (0.0%)
Southampton County	41	17 (41.5%)	24 (58.5%)	0 (0.0%)
Total/Average Percent	*781*	*478 (61.2%)*	*288 (36.9%)*	*15 (1.9%)*

Table 3. Age and Gender Profile of Southern Commercial Classes, 1850

	Number/Percent of Male Commercial Population		Number/Percent of Female Commercial Population		Average Age of Merchant/ Grocer	Average Age of Clerk	Average Age of Peddler
Lowndes County	75	(98.7%)	1	(1.3%)	33.2	25.5	25.0
Washington County	4	(100.0%)	0		27.3	—	60.0
Alachua County	11	(100.0%)	0		31.8	26.0	—
Leon County	87	(100.0%)	0		35.6	24.4	30.0
Putnam County	8	(100.0%)	0		30.3	20.5	—
Clarke County	107	(98.2%)	2	(1.8%)	33.2	24.4	40.0
Emanuel County	3	(100.0%)	0		28.3	—	—
Gwinnett County	24	(100.0%)	0		34.3	23.5	32.0
Wayne County	1	(100.0%)	0		40.0	—	—
Concordia Parish	3	(100.0%)	0		51.0	20.0	—
W. Feliciana Parish	57	(98.3%)	1	(1.7%)	38.5	25.5	—
Terrebonne Parish	32	(100.0%)	0		34.5	25.9	—
Davidson County	21	(100.0%)	0		40.7	22.3	24.0
Martin County	25	(100.0%)	0		31.7	18.6	—
Williamsburg County	20	(100.0%)	0		33.1	24.6	—
Hardeman County	71	(100.0%)	0		32.4	22.6	21.7
McMinn County	48	(98.0%)	1	(2.0%)	34.4	22.3	—
McNairy County	50	(100.0%)	0		31.4	22.5	—
Panola County	13	(100.0%)	0		30.4	23.8	—
Rusk County	58	(100.0%)	0		33.5	26.8	—
Grayson County	17	(100.0%)	0		41.1	23.0	—
Southampton County	41	(100.0%)	0		32.8	22.9	—
Total/Average Percent	776	(99.3%)	5	(0.7%)	34.5	23.4	33.2

Table 4. Place of Origin of Southern Commercial Classes, 1850

	Home State	Slave State	the North	Europe	Elsewhere	
		Number/Percent of Commercial Workers Who Came from				
Lowndes County	9 (11.8%)	44 (57.9%)	15 (19.7%)	8 (10.5%)	0	
Washington County	2 (50.0%)	2 (50.0%)	0 (0.0%)	0 (0.0%)	0	
Alachua County	3 (27.3%)	5 (45.5%)	2 (18.2%)	1 (9.1%)	0	
Leon County	8 (9.2%)	55 (63.2%)	16 (18.4%)	6 (6.9%)	2	(2.3%)
Putnam County	2 (25.0%)	4 (50.0%)	1 (12.5%)	1 (12.5%)	0	
Clarke County	70 (64.2%)	17 (15.6%)	15 (13.8%)	6 (5.5%)	1	(0.92%)
Emanuel County	2 (66.7%)	0 (0.0%)	0 (0.0%)	1 (33.3%)	0	
Gwinnett County	15 (62.5%)	7 (29.2%)	2 (8.3%)	0 (0.0%)	0	
Wayne County	0 (0.0%)	0 (0.0%)	1(100.0%)	0 (0.0%)	0	
Concordia Parish	0 (0.0%)	2 (66.7%)	0 (0.0%)	1 (33.3%)	0	
W. Feliciana Parish	14 (24.1%)	10 (17.2%)	6 (10.3%)	28 (48.3%)	0	
Terrebonne Parish	6 (18.7%)	2 (6.3%)	1 (3.1%)	21 (65.6%)	2	(6.3%)
Davidson County	19 (90.4%)	1 (4.8%)	1 (4.8%)	0 (0.0%)	0	
Martin County	22 (88.0%)	1 (4.0%)	0 (0.0%)	2 (8.0%)	0	
Williamsburg County	14 (70.0%)	2 (10.0%)	1 (5.0%)	3 (15.0%)	0	
Hardeman County	28 (39.4%)	37 (52.1%)	2 (2.8%)	3 (4.2%)	1	(1.4%)
McMinn County	35 (71.4%)	9 (18.4%)	2 (4.1%)	3 (6.1%)	0	
McNairy County	27 (54.0%)	23 (46.0%)	0 (0.0%)	0 (0.0%)	0	
Panola County	0 (0.0%)	10 (76.9%)	1 (7.7%)	2 (15.4%)	0	
Rusk County	1 (1.7%)	43 (74.1%)	6 (10.3%)	5 (8.6%)	3	(5.2%)
Grayson County	15 (88.2%)	1 (5.9%)	1 (5.9%)	0 (0.0%)	0	
Southampton County	39 (95.1%)	2 (4.9%)	0 (0.0%)	0 (0.0%)	0	
Total/Average Percent	*331 (42.4%)*	*277 (35.5%)*	*73 (9.3%)*	*91 (11.7%)*	*9*	*(1.1%)*

Table 5. Residence, Family Size, and Real Estate Holdings of Southern Commercial Classes, 1850

	Average Size of Families (No. Persons)	Percent of Merchants with Clerks Living in Their Homes	No./Percent of Merchants Living with Their Farm Families	No./Percent of Merchants Owning Real Estate	Average Value of Merchant-Owned Real Estate
Lowndes County	3.9	14.3%	1 (1.3%)	28 (36.8%)	$2,361
Washington County	3.6	0.0%	0	2 (50.0%)	$62.50
Alachua County	5.0	9.1%	0	4 (36.4%)	$1,275
Leon County	4.2	35.7%	0	23 (26.4%)	$5,593
Putnam County	3.0	33.3%	1 (12.5%)	3 (37.5%)	$1,866
Clarke County	4.8	16.4%	3 (2.7%)	34 (31.2%)	$4,080
Emanuel County	—	0.0%	0	1 (33.3%)	$150
Gwinnett County	5.3	10.5%	4 (16.7%)	15 (62.5%)	$1,486
Wayne County	5.0	0.0%	0	1(100.0%)	$2,000
Concordia Parish	—	50.0%	0	0	$0
W. Feliciana Parish	4.1	21.6%	0	18 (31.0%)	$3,642
Terrebonne Parish	4.6	16.7%	1 (3.1%)	11 (34.4%)	$2,591
Davidson County	4.8	50.0%	1 (4.8%)	9 (42.8%)	$2,928
Martin County	3.9	16.7%	1 (4%)	9 (36.0%)	$3,133
Williamsburg County	4.3	5.0%	2 (10.0%)	9 (45.0%)	$2,203
Hardeman County	4.0	19.5%	3 (4.2%)	24 (33.8%)	$6,814
McMinn County	5.2	23.5%	2 (4.1%)	22 (44.9%)	$3,824
McNairy County	5.5	8.3%	3 (6.0%)	25 (50.0%)	$1,754
Panola County	4.0	0.0%	0	3 (23.1%)	$2,173
Rusk County	4.9	12.2%	0	30 (51.7%)	$2,569
Grayson County	5.2	22.2%	0	6 (35.3%)	$3,771
Southampton County	4.0	52.9%	0	11 (26.8%)	$1,625
Total/Average Percent (taken from 781 total)	*4.5*	*23.2%*	*2.8%*	*36.9%*	*$2,542*

Table 6. Slavery and the Southern Commercial Classes, 1850

	No./Percent of Merchants Owning Slaves	No./Percent of Clerks Owning Slaves	No./Percent of All Commercial Workers Owning Slaves	Percent of County's Slaves Owned by Commercial Workers	Average No. of Slaves per Commercial Worker
Lowndes County	23 (52.3%)	3 (10.3%)	26 (34.2%)	1.4%	7.7
Washington County	1 (33.3%)	0	1 (25.0%)	0.06%	1.0
Alachua County	1 (20.0%)	0	1 (9.1%)	0.33%	3.0
Leon County	12 (28.6%)	6 (13.6%)	18 (20.7%)	1.2%	5.4
Putnam County	1 (16.7%)	0	1 (12.5%)	7.8%	16.0
Clarke County	26 (42.6%)	8 (17.4%)	34 (31.2%)	3.9%	6.4
Emanuel County	0	0	0	0	—
Gwinnett County	8 (42.1%)	0	8 (33.3%)	3.8%	10.8
Wayne County	1(100.0%)	0	1(100.0%)	1.2%	5.0
Concordia Parish	0	0	0	0	—
W. Feliciana Parish	2 (5.4%)	0	2 (3.4%)	0.30%	15.0
Terrebonne Parish	5 (21.0%)	1 (12.5%)	6 (18.75%)	1.1%	7.7
Davidson County	4 (40.0%)	1 (10.0%)	5 (23.8%)	1.2%	7.0
Martin County	9 (50.0%)	1 (14.3%)	10 (40.0%)	2.3%	7.8
Williamsburg County	8 (47.1%)	0	8 (40.0%)	1.6%	17.3
Hardeman County	12 (29.3%)	0	12 (16.9%)	3.1%	18.4
McMinn County	13 (38.2%)	3 (20.0%)	16 (32.6%)	3.1%	3.0
McNairy County	16 (44.4%)	0	16 (32.0%)	5.7%	5.7
Panola County	2 (25.0%)	0	2 (15.4%)	0.42%	2.5
Rusk County	12 (29.3%)	1 (5.9%)	13 (22.4%)	2.6%	4.3
Grayson County	4 (44.4%)	0	4 (23.5%)	4.6%	5.7
Southampton County	3 (17.6%)	1 (4.2%)	4 (9.7%)	0.62%	9.0
Total/Average Percent	163 (20.9%)	25 (3.2%)	188 (23.7%)	2.3%	7.9

Notes

Introduction

1. Jorantha Semmes to Benedict Semmes, June 21, 1862, Benedict Joseph Semmes Papers, SHC.

2. Evidence that women actively or implicitly undercut the Confederate war effort is shown in Escott, *Many Excellent People*, 23, 67; Bynum, *Unruly Women*; and Faust, *Mothers of Invention*, 37, 238–44.

3. Jorantha Semmes to Benedict Semmes, June 13 and July 15, 1862; Benedict Semmes to Jorantha Semmes, July 17, 1864, Benedict Joseph Semmes Papers, SHC.

4. Genovese, *Political Economy of Slavery*, 160–65.

5. Hundley, *Social Relations in Our Southern States*, 101–2; Sidney Root, "Memorandum of My Life, 1893," AHC. Surprisingly little has been written on the public image of merchants in nineteenth-century American culture, particularly in the South; see Leach, *Land of Desire*, 116–17, 122–30.

My research suggests that southern newspapers frequently depicted merchants as greedy and unprincipled; see *Carolina Watchman* (Salisbury, N.C.), November 10, 1832; *Edenton Sentinel and Albemarle Intelligencer*, May 1, 1841; *Augusta Daily Chronicle & Sentinel*, October 19, 1852; *Wilmington Daily Journal*, September 19 and October 9, 1854; *Greenville Mountaineer*, November 29, 1855. During the Civil War many newspapers attacked merchants for speculating in foodstuffs and war material. This popular discontent over merchant speculation figured prominently in southern food riots during the war. Two good descriptions of such riots can be found in McPherson, *Battle Cry of Freedom*, 617–19; and Thomas, *Confederate Nation*, 201–6.

6. Beckert, *Monied Metropolis*, 8. In an insightful survey of the historiography on the American middle class, the historian Robert D. Johnston acknowledges Alan Brinkley, Christopher Lasch, and others for moving "away from considering 'the middle class' as one monolithic entity. Analytically . . . this very well might be the most important lesson we are currently learning—that the study of *the* American middle class can proceed only by denying the essence and unity of the very subject under consideration"; see Johnston, "Conclusion: Historians and the American Middle Class," in Bledstein and Johnston, eds., *Middling Sorts*, 305–6. Jonathan Daniel Wells's analysis of a broader southern middle class includes an

excellent summary regarding the difficulties in defining such a class in the ante-bellum South; see Wells, *Origins of the Southern Middle Class*, 7–12.

7. Gay, *Schnitzler's Century*, 26, 32–33; Barzun, *From Dawn to Decadence*; Hunt, *Middling Sort*; Leach, *Land of Desire*; Schama, *Embarrassment of Riches*; Fox and Lears, eds., *Culture of Consumption*.

8. William Faulkner, *The Hamlet* (New York: Random House, 1940); T. S. Stribling, *The Store* (Garden City, N.Y.: Doubleday, Doran, 1932).

9. For a more detailed examination of popular depictions of the merchant class in antebellum southern literature, see Byrne, "Merchant in Antebellum Southern Literature."

10. McVeagh, *Tradefull Merchants*, 1–2, 4, 16–19, 138; Watts, *Businessman in American Literature*, 1–5, 37–39; Price, *Stories with a Moral*, 64–65, 70; Longstreet, *Georgia Scenes*, 53–56; King, *Augustus Baldwin Longstreet*, 10–27, 74–75; Simms, *Guy Rivers*, 52–53; Edgar Allan Poe, *The Complete Works of Edgar Allan Poe* (New York: AMS Press, 1965), 123. For an early yet still influential discussion of the Other in world history, see Edward W. Said, *Orientalism* (New York: Pantheon Books, 1978). Popular depictions of merchants and their stores as disruptive forces in southern communities can be found in American film as well. In addition to other screen adaptations of Faulkner's work, see *The Long, Hot Summer* (Beverly Hills, Calif.: Twentieth Century Fox, 1958), based on *The Hamlet*. Hollywood has often depicted the southern store as an arena where tra-ditional religious and social values are challenged. It is hardly surprising that Scarlett O'Hara builds wealth in postwar Atlanta as the hard-bargaining wife, and later widow, of a lumber dealer; see *Gone with the Wind* (Culver City, Calif.: Metro-Goldwyn-Mayer, 1939). Alvin York first examines and eventually rede-fines his pacifist religious beliefs while discussing the nature of war with the local storekeeper; see *Sergeant York* (Hollywood, Calif.: Warner Brothers, 1941).

11. Doyle, *New Men, New Cities*, 87.

12. Doyle, *New Men, New Cities*, 89–90; Hundley, *Social Relations in Our Southern States*; Olmsted, *Cotton Kingdom*; Gregg, *Essays on Domestic Industry*.

13. Wells, *Origins of the Southern Middle Class*, 7–13, 172–85, 209. For a discussion of southern occupations and jobs found within the Commerce, Professions, and Factory/Manual Labor categories, see Huston, *Calculating the Value of the Union*.

14. Ford, "Rednecks and Merchants"; Escott, *Many Excellent People*; Tullos, *Habits of Industry*.

15. Those who have argued that slaveholding planters dominated the Old South include Phillips, "The Origin and Growth of the Southern Black Belts"; Gray, *History of Agriculture*, vol. 1, 444–45, 474, 532–37; and Dodd, *Cotton Kingdom*, 24–47. Eugene D. Genovese describes the social and political hege-mony of the planter class in *Political Economy of Slavery*, 160–75. See also Fox-

Genovese and Genovese, *Fruits of Merchant Capital*; Davis, *Problem of Slavery in Western Culture*; Kolchin, *American Slavery*; Wright, *Old South, New South*. James Oakes challenges this static view of the planter class and its control of the South in *Ruling Race* and *Slavery and Freedom*. The economic and cultural roles of the planter family in southern society continued to be debated in Stowe, *Intimacy and Power in the Old South*; Kenzer, *Kinship and Neighborhood*; and Burton, *In My Father's House*. Challenging many of the conclusions of Bertram Wyatt-Brown and others, Jeffrey Robert Young in *Domesticating Slavery* makes a strong argument that the domestic ideals within planter families in Georgia and South Carolina had much more in common with the domestic, often bourgeois values typically embraced in the antebellum North. Even studies that emphasize the contradictory nature of yeoman politics acknowledge the dominance of the southern planter class; see Harris, *Plain Folk and Gentry*; Ford, *Origins of Southern Radicalism*; and McCurry, *Masters of Small Worlds*.

16. Atherton, *Southern Country Store*, 12–28, 35–55. Frank L. Owsley's classic study *Plain Folk of the Old South* discounts the primacy of the southern planter elite and argues that the mass of Southerners were essentially middle class in orientation. See also the work of Owsley's students Blanche H. Clark, *The Tennessee Yeomen*, and Herbert Weaver, *Mississippi Farmers*. For a brief summary of how the merchant was viewed in southern society, see Ronald L. F. Davis, "The Southern Merchant: A Perennial Source of Discontent," in Fraser and Moore, eds., *Southern Enigma*.

17. Clark, *Pills, Petticoats, and Plows*, 12–15.

18. The historiography on the political economy of the antebellum South is quite large. See Elizabeth Fox-Genovese and Eugene D. Genovese's *Fruits of Merchant Capital*, as well as Eugene D. Genovese's *Political Economy of Slavery* (1965), *World the Slaveholders Made* (1969), and *Roll, Jordan, Roll* (1974). Each of Genovese's three books places special, but successively less, emphasis on the precapitalist nature of the southern economy. Several excellent studies that build upon or challenge Genovese's analysis include Woodman, *King Cotton & His Retainers*, 150–64, 290–96; Wright, *Political Economy of the Cotton South*, 43–88; and Wright, *Old South, New South*, 10–14. See also Ransom, *Conflict and Compromise*; Fogel and Engerman, *Time on the Cross*; Oakes, *Ruling Race*; Oakes, *Slavery and Freedom*; Shore, *Southern Capitalists*; Siegel, *Roots of Southern Distinctiveness*; Levine, *Half Slave and Half Free*; and Egnal, *Divergent Paths*. These broad overviews of the antebellum southern economy build upon such older studies as Lewis Cecil Gray's now seminal work *History of Agriculture in the Southern United States to 1860*. Also see the influential, though dated, works of Ulrich Bonnell Phillips, *American Negro Slavery* and *Slave Economy of the Old South*. For a recent synthesis on intellectual life in the Old South that includes excellent analysis of the political economy as well, see Michael O'Brien's magisterial study *Conjectures of Order* (2004).

More recent examinations of the antebellum economy concentrate upon regions within the South; see Coclanis, *Shadow of a Dream*; Waterhouse, *New World Gentry*; Klein, *Unification of a Slave State*; and Dunaway, *First American Frontier*, 5–12. Dunaway's study challenges historians who have argued that the South maintained a "moral economy" largely unscathed by market relations before the war; see Hahn, *Roots of Southern Populism*; and McCurry, *Masters of Small Worlds*. The intellectual origins of this debate can be found in articles on households in early American society; see Merrill, "Cash Is Good to Eat"; and Henretta, "Families and Farms."

The past twenty-five years have witnessed a tremendous increase in the number of historical studies written about nineteenth-century southern communities; see Hahn, *Roots of Southern Populism*; McCurry, *Masters of Small Worlds*; Harris, *Plain Folk and Gentry*, 5–35; Burton, *In My Father's House*, 7–10, 57; Kenzer, *Kinship and Neighborhood*, 20, 32–38; Cecil-Fronsman, *Common Whites*, 36–37, 165; Morris, *Becoming Southern*; Bryant, *How Curious a Land*; Kimball, *American City, Southern Place*. Historians have also begun to explore the impact of the Civil War upon southern communities; see Ash, *When the Yankees Came*; Durrill, *War of Another Kind*; Mohr, *On the Threshold of Freedom*; Fields, *Slavery and Freedom on the Middle Ground*; Paludan, *Victims*; and McPherson, *Battle Cry of Freedom*. Several essays in Catherine Clinton and Nina Silber's *Divided Houses* have proven instrumental in explaining the impact of the Civil War upon the household.

For various discussions of gender relations within the nineteenth-century family, some of which attempt broad syntheses, see Wyatt-Brown, *Southern Honor*; Clinton, *Plantation Mistress*; Cashin, *Family Venture*; Ownby, *Subduing Satan*; and Stowe, *Intimacy and Power in the Old South*; also see Taylor, *Cavalier and Yankee*. For a more general theoretical work on gender, see Lorber, *Paradoxes of Gender*. Important works on female culture within the northern middle class include Welter, "The Cult of True Womanhood"; Cott, *Bonds of Womanhood*; and Lebsock, *Free Women of Petersburg*, xix, 110–50. See also Hewitt, "Beyond the Search for Sisterhood"; DuBois, *Feminism and Suffrage*; and more recently Sklar, "The Historical Foundations of Women's Power in the Creation of the American Welfare State." Studies that explore women's roles and patriarchy in the nineteenth-century South include: Friedman, *Enclosed Garden*; Clinton, *Plantation Mistress*; Bynum, *Unruly Women*; Fox-Genovese, *Within the Plantation Household*; Cashin, *Our Common Affairs*; and the more recent works: Faust, *Mothers of Invention*; and Edwards, *Scarlett Doesn't Live Here Anymore*. For the physical world of southern women, see McMillen, *Motherhood in the Old South*. Margaret Ripley Wolfe offers an excellent overview of this literature in *Daughters of Canaan*.

In contrast to the abundant literature on antebellum households, few studies have focused upon the household in the Confederate South. Insightful studies do include Wiley, *Confederate Women*; Clinton, *Other Civil War*; Rable, *Civil Wars*; Faust, "Altars of Sacrifice"; and Faust, *Mothers of Invention*, 50–60. Many recent monographs on the white family in the antebellum and Confederate South draw their inspiration from influential studies on the slave family; see Blassingame, *Slave Community*; Rawick, *From Sundown to Sunup*; Genovese, *Roll, Jordan, Roll*; Gutman, *Black Family in Slavery and Freedom*; and Levine, *Black Culture and Black Consciousness*.

19. When contemplating the scale of this study, I was impressed with the tremendous insight of numerous studies of slavery, the planter class, and yeoman society, among others that have discussed these critical subjects from a broad perspective encompassing the entire South. Once again, the historian Peter Gay's work on bourgeois society in nineteenth-century Europe is instructive. He found that the "Victorian bourgeoisie was sizable, diverse, and deeply fissured"; thus any study of this group's "shared family traits" necessarily depends upon a certain number of cautious generalizations. See *Schnitzler's Century*, 4–5.

20. See Byrne, "Rebellion and Retail."

1. Merchant Culture and the Political Economy of the Old South

1. My discussion of "worldview" borrows from Peter Kolchin's discussion of the subject in *Unfree Labor*, 240. Another insightful discussion of worldview and its differences from a more concrete ideology can be found in Bowman, *Masters & Lords*, 83–87. For a useful discussion of the cultural ties between northern and southern professionals/merchants, see Wells, *Origins of the Southern Middle Class*, 19–66.

2. Jefferson, *Notes on the State of Virginia*, 172; Peterson, *Thomas Jefferson and the New Nation*, 729. Jefferson was far from alone in his conclusions regarding merchants or, more broadly, the commercial ethic and regionalism in the United States. Surveying antebellum literature on the subject, Susan-Mary Grant has found the common theme to be: "The North represented the corruption that accompanied progress; the South represented the agrarian ideals of the past and was the repository of all the social virtues"; see Grant, *North Over South*, 38–39.

3. Doerflinger, *Vigorous Spirit of Enterprise*, 17–18; Doyle, *New Men, New Cities*, 5. For the sake of economy and variety I frequently use the terms "merchant" and "commercial" interchangeably when discussing all classifications of businessmen and businesswomen employed in the South.

4. Earle, *Making of the English Middle Class*, 5; Lawrence E. Klein, "Politeness for Plebes: Consumption and Social Identity in Early Eighteenth-Century England," in Bermingham and Brewer, eds., *Consumption of Culture*, 363–64; Peter Gay, *Bourgeois Experience*, vol. 1, 30–31, 43, 67; Egnal, *Divergent Paths*, 64–66.

5. Kennedy, *Population of the United States in 1860*, 668–69.

6. I selected the twenty-two counties in my sample of the 1850 census primarily because they provide a representative cross section of the region. The sample includes a total population of 212,971 people—123,223 who were free and 89,748 who were slaves. The sample includes rural counties, from various geographic regions, with relatively small free and slave populations: Washington County (Ala.), Putnam County (Fla.), Wayne County (Ga.), Panola County (Tex.); counties that boasted significant staple agriculture and large slave populations: Lowndes County (Ala.), Concordia Parish (La.), West Feliciana Parish (La.), Terrebonne Parish (La.), Williamsburg County (S.C.), Southampton County (Va.); and counties with an often more balanced economy with sizable free, and occasionally large slave, populations: Clarke County (Ga.), Emanuel County (Ga.), Gwinnett County (Ga.), Davidson County (N.C.), Martin County (N.C.), Hardeman County (Tenn.), McMinn County (Tenn.), McNairy County (Tenn.), Rusk County (Tex.), Grayson County (Va.). This sample attempts to account for the antebellum South's unique regional diversity by including counties from the Black Belt, upcountry and mountainous areas, the Piedmont, and the coast. The availability of records, primarily the necessity to obtain both free and slave schedules for each county, also influenced the makeup of the sample. Since no counties in this sample contained a major city, in order to round out a profile of the southern antebellum merchant I have relied upon city and business directories in addition to several excellent secondary sources that have examined the region's few large cities in detail. Finally, few of the more than one hundred merchants and their families whom I uncovered in the manuscript sources hailed from counties in this sample. Additional research in the census records often helped add valuable information regarding these merchants.

7. Suarez, "Bargains, Bills, and Bankruptcies," 190; Tolbert, *Constructing Townscapes*, 49; Cecil-Fronsman, *Common Whites*, 99; Manuscript Census, Buckingham County, Virginia, 1850; *Seventh Census of the United States: 1850* (Washington: Robert Armstrong, Public Printer, 1853), cvi, 256; Kyriakoudes, "Plantation to Town," 49–50. The total number of commercial workers (merchants, storekeepers, grocers, clerks, hucksters, peddlers, liquor dealers) found in the census schedules taken in these counties was 790 (8 being categorized as miscellaneous), and the total commercial household population was 2,262. The free population numbered 123,223, while the slave population was 89,748, for a total population of 212,971. Each of the twenty-two counties was chosen on the basis of its general economic, geographic, and demographic correspondence to the South as a whole. Thus in the survey are rural, urban, poor, rich, low-country, mountainous, Upper South, and Deep South counties.

8. Greb, "Charleston, South Carolina, Merchants," 26; Bancroft, *Census of the City of Savannah*, 7–16; Manuscript Census, Dinwiddie County, Virginia,

1860; *Williams' Atlanta Directory*, 11, 35–149. In 1850, Buckingham County had twenty-three heads of commercial households with an average size of six persons, while Dinwiddie County had 261 heads of commercial households averaging five members each. Those employed in commercial fields who were not heads of households—typically living with family members or as boarders—were counted individually. Regarding the relative stability of the commercial populations in these two Virginia counties, a close analysis of the 1850 and 1860 census schedules for both indicates a persistence rate of 22 percent in Buckingham and 16 percent in Dinwiddie. When only the same surname is carried over from the 1850 census to the 1860 census, suggesting family continuity in the merchant profession, persistence rates rose to 39 percent in Buckingham County and 31 percent in Dinwiddie County. This finding supports Gregory Allen Greb's study of Charleston, South Carolina, in which he discovered that the persistence rates for the city's merchant population never dropped below 47 percent between 1840 and 1859. He concluded that those who failed to appear in more than one census moved out of the city and that no more than 4 percent of this population entered other occupations; see Greb, "Charleston, South Carolina, Merchants," 30. For comparative purposes these statistics do not include barbers, barkeepers, druggists, tailors, and seamstresses.

9. Suarez, "Bargains, Bills, and Bankruptcies," 205; Sellers, *Market Revolution*, 392; Ford, *Origins of Southern Radicalism*, 77–84, 237; Bryant, *How Curious a Land*, 18–20; Eaton, *History of the Old South*, 400–405; Fox-Genovese and Genovese, *Fruits of Merchant Capital*, 17–50; Woodman, *King Cotton & His Retainers*, 193–4; Oakes, *Ruling Race*, 93; Oakes, *Slavery and Freedom*, 52, 102. For an informative, if at times exaggerated, analysis of middle-class influence in the Old South, see Wells, *Origins of the Southern Middle Class*, 207–34.

10. *Nashville Whig*, April 22, 1826; Grant, *North Over South*, 44; *Charleston Mercury*, October 12, 1852; Atherton, *Frontier Merchant in Mid-America*, 80–81, 93–94; *Vicksburg Register*, November 10, 1836; *New Orleans Daily Picayune*, January 17, 1851. For an analysis of merchant economic boosterism in antebellum Texas, see Summers, "Public Policy and Economic Growth in Antebellum Texas," 127–45; for Louisville, see Burckin, "Formation and Growth of an Urban Middle Class," 9. For a general description of the economic role that urban communities played in the antebellum South, see Doyle, *New Men, New Cities*, 5–6.

11. Wells, *Origins of the Southern Middle Class*, 22; Whipple, *Bishop Whipple's Southern Diary*, 91. In 1850, 94 percent of the merchants working in rural Buckingham County, Virginia, were born in the state. The same census reported that 80 percent of the merchants employed in more urban Dinwiddie County were also native-born Virginians. This pattern generally held true throughout the South. Seemingly the only exceptions were such newly settled frontier states as Arkansas and Texas, and more cosmopolitan cities such as New Orleans and

Savannah, Georgia, the latter of which in 1848 reported only 25 percent of the commercial classes being originally from Georgia. See Manuscript Census, Buckingham County, Virginia, 1850; Manuscript Census, Dinwiddie County, Virginia, 1850; Bancroft, *Census of the City of Savannah*, 7–14; *Williams' Atlanta Directory*, 35–149; *Nashville, State of Tennessee, and General Commercial Directory*, 35–55, 78–79, 88–91. For a discussion of free black, and perhaps slave, hucksters, see Lockley, *Lines in the Sand*, 67–75; Berlin, *Many Thousands Gone*, 337.

12. Biographical information and introduction, Aby Family Papers, MDAH; Kader Biggs Papers, NCSA; Clark, *Valleys of the Shadow*, xix–xx, 119–20 (n. 2); Jefferson biography and coversheet, John F. Jefferson Papers, FCHS; Blacknall memoirs and introductory material, Oscar W. Blacknall Papers, NCSA. Suzanne L. Summers's analysis of merchants in Houston and Galveston found that "a sizable portion in each city had at least one blood relative or in-law working in commerce." In Houston, 85 percent of those merchants with identifiable backgrounds had at least one family member in trade, while in Galveston, 56 percent of the merchants were related to someone in commerce; see Summers, "The Geographic and Social Origins of Antebellum Merchants in Houston and Galveston."

13. Howze Journal, September 28, 1853, Howze (Isham Robertson) and Family Papers, MDAH; George H. Shelton to John Benson, December 26, 1847, John Benson Papers, SHC. Thomas Potter to Charles Jacocks, February 5, 1832, Charles W. Jacocks Papers, NCSA; *Journal of Commerce*, quoted in the *Carolina Watchman* (Salisbury, N.C.), June 21, 1839; Morris, *Becoming Southern*, 122. Licensing requirements for peddlers varied across the southern states, but Georgia acted typically when in 1840 it required that all peddlers purchase a twelve-month license for fifty-seven dollars, allowing them to sell "any kind of goods, wares, and merchandize" anywhere in the state; see *Milledgeville Federal Union*, February 4, 1840.

14. Duerr Diary, June 23, July 2, and December 31, 1843; Mary Duerr to Christian Duerr, August 1, 1843; Christian Duerr to Mary Duerr, August 21, 1843; Christian Friedrich Duerr Papers, CAH; Manuscript Census, Harris County, Texas, 1850. The best study of the strain that westward migration put on southern families is Joan E. Cashin's *Family Venture*; see also Frank Owsley's *Plain Folk of the Old South*, 74–76. John Mack Faragher's monograph *Sugar Creek: Life on the Illinois Prairie* examines the impact of migration and subsequent community development in a northern setting.

15. Benedict Joseph Semmes Papers, SHC; Semmes Family Papers, TSLA; Howze Journal, introduction and miscellaneous papers, Howze (Isham Robertson) and Family Papers, MDAH.

16. Wyatt-Brown, *Southern Honor*, 214–17; Beckert, *Monied Metropolis*, 35. The R. G. Dun & Company records consist of confidential handwritten credit reports written by investigators the firm hired for the period 1841–1881. That

Dun & Co. could establish such a far-flung, profitable information network suggests the increasing growth and sophistication of commercial trade in both the northern and southern states by the middle of the nineteenth century.

17. In my sample of thirty-three entries, three make definite reference to the financial backing of a parent or spouse. William Biggs, Mississippi, vol. 21, p. 97, R. G. Dun & Company Reports, HGSB; Horace Carpenter, Mississippi, vol. 6, p. 177, R. G. Dun & Company Reports, HGSB; Horace Carpenter to Philinia Carpenter, October 4, 1825, Carpenter Family Papers, TSLA; Samuel H. Aby to Jonas (the name of the addressee is not entirely clear) Aby, January 3, 1842, Aby Family Papers, MDAH; Francis Levert to Dr. Robert W. Withers, January 14, 1845, Levert Family Papers, SHC.

18. *New Orleans Daily Picayune*, October 5, 1859; Byrne, "Merchant in Antebellum Southern Literature," 18–47, 113–22; Atherton, "Problem of Credit Rating in the Ante-Bellum South," 534; George H. Shelton to John Benson, December 26, 1847, John Benson Papers, SHC; Muckleroy and G. B. Holyard to John Adriance, May 30, 1846, John Adriance Papers, CAH. In another example, one David Brewster of Laurel, Kentucky, asked the merchant Thomas Howard for "a few goods about the amount you once told me you started on," later adding, "Excuse my plane way of Riting. . . . You were very Rich and me in moderate circumstances"; David Brewster to Thomas Howard, November 8, 1838, FCHS.

19. Tadman, *Speculators and Slaves*, 54; Greenberg, *Honor & Slavery*, 51–86; Bryant, *How Curious a Land*, 50; McCurry, *Masters of Small Worlds*, 64, 96–104; Wyatt-Brown, *Southern Honor*, 345–46; Woodman, *King Cotton & His Retainers*, 38–42; Gray, *History of Agriculture*, vol. 2, 411–15, 430–32, 456; Lawrence E. Klein, "Politeness for Plebes: Consumption and Social Identity in Early Eighteenth-Century England," in Bermingham and Brewer, eds., *The Consumption of Culture*, 373.

20. Sellers, *Market Revolution*, 267–68. Agencies like Dun & Co. relied on lawyers who would charge nothing for the initial investigation with the promise that, if a merchant failed to pay his debt to a northern wholesaler, the lawyer would gain that wholesaler as a client, and would of course receive a commission, in any subsequent lawsuits. Atherton, "Problem of Credit Rating in the Ante-Bellum South," 534, 542–45, 551; Atherton, *Southern Country Store*, 128; Pease and Pease, *Ladies, Women, & Wenches*, 17; Ditz, "Shipwrecked," 54–58, 67; Mississippi, vol. 6, p. 137, Tennessee, vol. 21, p. 10, R. G. Dun & Company Reports, HGSB; Suarez, "Bargains, Bills, and Bankruptcies," 197.

21. Edward Murphy to Josephine Cross Murphy, April 21, 1849, Murphy Family Papers, HNOC; Louisiana, vol. 6, p. 176, R. G. Dun & Company Reports, HGSB; Howze Journal, January 17, 1853, Howze (Isham Robertson) and Family Papers, MDAH.

22. Thomas C. McDowell to Francis Levert, April 22, 1848; Francis Levert to Henry Levert, January 24, 1847; Levert Family Papers, SHC.

23. Harris, *Plain Folk and Gentry*, 97, 99; Atherton, "Problem of Credit Rating in the Ante-Bellum South," 534; Jonathan Worth to James Williams, November 16, 1853, Jonathan Worth Papers, NCSA; Bolton, *Poor Whites of the Antebellum South*, 26.

24. *Nashville Republican and State Gazette*, March 29, 1833; *Central Monitor* (Murfreesboro, Tenn.), January 18, 1834.

25. All of the merchants I have investigated in both manuscript collections and credit reports were engaged in business partnerships with one or more parties. Of course wholly independent merchants did operate in the antebellum South, but their numbers remained quite low. Escott, *Many Excellent People*, 5; Faust, *James Henry Hammond and the Old South*, 111.

26. Atherton, *Frontier Merchant in Mid-America*, 120–21; Coulter, *George Walton Williams*, 47; Perry & Somervell partnership agreement, May 7, 1833, Perry (James Franklin and Stephen Samuel) Papers, CAH; Haden E. Stone & Co. partnership agreement, January 2, 1852, Edward S. Haydon Papers, KHS.

27. Howze Journal, July 21, 1853, June 5, 1854, February 22, 1855, Howze (Isham Robertson) and Family Papers, MDAH; Mississippi, vol. 15, p. 19, R. G. Dun & Company Reports, HGSB.

28. Hassell Diary and Autobiography, 1837–1838, Introduction, Cushing B. Hassell Papers, SHC. Of course a tremendous range of issues caused discord within southern business partnerships. John Dunlap's experience in 1844 at a New Orleans firm was typical. He complained to his wife Beatrice in Augusta, Georgia, that his partners lacked industrious habits and business acumen, thus making his job much more difficult. Contrasting business conduct and personal values left many partners divided and estranged from each other (see chapter 3); John Dunlap to Beatrice Dunlap, November 6 and 10, 1844, Dunlap Correspondence, HTML.

29. Atherton, *Southern Country Store*, 57–61, 321. Atherton estimated at least a third of all western storekeepers traveled to the East for goods. My informal sample suggests even higher rates for southern merchants. See Atherton, *Frontier Merchant in Mid-America*, 69–71; Horace Carpenter to William Carpenter, September 5, 1822, Carpenter Family Papers, TSLA; Benjamin Smith to Abram Barnes, October 5, 1816, Barnes-Willis Family Papers, CAH; Hassell Diary, March 6 to April 1, 1848, Cushing B. Hassell Papers, SHC; Drayage and Insurance Receipt, October 21, 1830, Perry (James Franklin and Stephen Samuel) Papers, CAH. Of course one must remember that the Commercial Convention movement called for direct trade between Europe and the South, thus they would tend to inflate the cost of purchasing goods in the North; see Gadsden, *Minutes of the Proceedings of the Third Commercial Convention*, 15.

30. Not surprisingly the rising tide of sectionalism after 1850 prompted many southern leaders to call for the region's business community to end its trade with the North; see *Richmond Republican,* quoted in *Charleston Mercury,* March 27, 1850, February 28, 1851; *Richmond Enquirer,* September 27, 1851, August 6, 1855; *Winnsboro Register,* quoted in *Charleston Mercury,* September 5, 1853. Surviving manuscript evidence suggests that merchants themselves rarely dwelled upon the political implications that their purchasing junkets held for the South. New Orleans served as a primary distribution point for groceries and other perishable items. See, for example, Anton F. Wulff to John Leyendecker, June 5, 1856, John Zirvas Leyendecker Papers, CAH; Business Receipts, August 1815, George Wood Meriwether Papers, FCHS; *Weekly Raleigh Register, and North Carolina Gazette,* January 22, 1851; Robert Crawford to the firm of Beardslee & Adriance, November 27, 1837, John Adriance Papers, CAH.

31. Howze Journal, March 13, 1857, Howze (Isham Robertson) and Family Papers, MDAH; Bonney Diary, September 27, 1837, Eli Whitney Bonney Papers, PL.

32. Lydia Adriance to John Adriance, August 10, 1850, John Adriance Papers, CAH; July 15, 1849, September 22, 1850, Constantine Osborne Perkins Papers, VHS; Horace Carpenter to William and Charity Carpenter, September 23, 1822, Carpenter Family Papers, TSLA. Some merchants avoided long absences from their families by taking their wives and children with them. This practice prevented the strain of absence on familial relations but also shaped these families in unique ways. See Samuel Aby to Charles Aby, July 31, 1853, Aby Family Papers, MDAH.

33. Edward Murphy to Josephine Murphy, July 20, 1852, Murphy Family Papers, HNOC.

34. The average age of clerks in this sample is 23.4 compared to 34.5 for their merchant/grocer employers and neighbors (see appendix, tables 2 and 3). All of the clerks in this sample from the 1850 census were recorded as white males.

35. Tolbert, *Constructing Townscapes,* 50–54; Hassell Diary, April 22, 1850, Cushing B. Hassell Papers, SHC; *Williams' Atlanta Directory,* 57; Manuscript Census, Buckingham County, Virginia, 1860; Manuscript Census, Dinwiddie County, Virginia, 1860; James Sullivan Diary, November 15, 1855, Hynes-Sullivan Papers, GHS; Lockley, *Lines in the Sand,* 30. Lockley suggests that an "overwhelming need for paid work" drove whites to accept the same pay as their African American coworkers in King's store. While data about stores that employed white and free black clerks is scant, the level of fairness when it came to pay in King's store seems rare and may reveal more about this storekeeper's personal values than about the dearth of wage work in Darien.

36. Scott, *Random Recollections of a Long Life,* 19; Eaton, *History of the Old South,* 237; Kolchin, *American Slavery,* 36–37; Faust, *James Henry Hammond and*

the Old South, 125; Ryan, *Cradle of the Middle Class*, 165–79; see also Johnson, *Shopkeeper's Millennium*.

37. *Nashville Republican and State Gazette*, December 26, 1832; R. A. Howard to Major O. Evans, January 3, 1853, John Zirvas Leyendecker Papers, CAH; Grays Firm to A. Barnes and Linton, August 17, 1824, Barnes-Willis Family Papers, CAH; Memis Timlin to Robert Collins, April 18, 1860, Henry Patillo Farrow Papers, HL; B. W. MaCrae to A. Amelia MaCrae, February 5, 1851, B. W. MaCrae Correspondence, TSLA; Grannis Diary, January 1, 1859, January 21, 1860, Robert A. Grannis Diary, VHS.

38. Tolbert, *Constructing Townscapes*, 62; George O'Bryan to Barcia Norfleet Gordon O'Bryan, May 1 and September 9, 1851, O'Bryan Family Collection, TSLA; Carney Diary, January 14, 1859, Kate S. Carney Diary, SHC.

39. William Biggs to Kader Biggs, April 29, 1842, Kader Biggs Papers, NCSA; George O'Bryan to Barcia Norfleet Gordon O'Bryan, June 12, 1851, O'Bryan Family Collection, TSLA; Grannis Diary, September 22–30, November 26, December 28, 1858, Robert A. Grannis Diary, VHS; Carney Diary, March 26, 1859, Kate S. Carney Diary, SHC.

2. The Antebellum Merchant in Southern Society

1. *Richmond Enquirer*, November 30, 1855.

2. Earle, *Making of the English Middle Class*, 138; Atherton, *Southern Country Store*, 145–47, 170; Kenzer, *Kinship and Neighborhood*, 38.

3. Richards Diary, October 24, 1860, Samuel P. Richards Papers, AHC; Grannis Diary, April 11, 1860, Robert A. Grannis Diary, VHS.

4. Kentucky, vol. 24, p. 177, North Carolina, vol. 15, p. 70, R. G. Dun & Company Reports, HGSB; Jefferson Diary, February 16 and August 17, 1857, June 24, 1858, July 14 and August 4, 1859, John F. Jefferson Papers, FCHS; Hassell Diary, June 27, 1848, July 31, 1849, January 31, 1850, Cushing B. Hassell Papers, SHC; Bart DeWitt to John Leyendecker, August 20, 1859, John Zirvas Leyendecker Papers, CAH.

5. Jefferson Diary, August 4 and September 29, 1859, John F. Jefferson Papers, FCHS. The per capita income figure is for the entire population, free and slave. The national per capita income for the same year was $128. See Fogel and Engerman, *Time on the Cross*, 247–50; see also Soltow, *Men and Wealth in the United States*; Hassell Diary, July 1, 1850, December 31, 1858, Cushing B. Hassell Papers, SHC.

6. Georgia, vol. 9, R. G. Dun & Company Reports, HGSB. On movement in and out of the planter class, see Oakes, *Ruling Race*, 67–68, 229–32; Campbell, "Intermittent Slave Ownership," 15–23; Wiener, *Social Origins of the New South*.

7. Lewis Atherton has estimated that between 60 and 75 percent of all sales in the antebellum South were on credit. He also estimated a 20 percent failure rate for loan repayment over the same period; see Atherton, *Southern Country Store*, 54; Ford, *Origins of Southern Radicalism*, 91; Virginia, vol. 7, p. 600, R. G. Dun & Company Reports, HGSB; William Agee to John West, March 17 and 22, 1858, J. S. West & Co. account book, January 1, 1861, West Family Papers, VHS; Bailey, ed., *Patriarch; or, Family Library Magazine*, 214. Steven Tripp has attributed the reluctance that merchant's felt in accepting credit to their lack of appreciation for the "social value of casual credit and debt networks"; see Tripp, *Yankee Town, Southern City*, 30. I suggest that more base economic motives encouraged merchants to avoid credit sales when possible, mainly the risk that customers would fail to pay their store accounts.

8. George H. Shelton to John Benson, November 5, 1856, John Benson Papers, SHC. Shelton would also remark when high prices for cotton, twelve to fourteen cents per pound, made it more likely that "farmers will be able to pay up" (January 24, 1851). William Agee to John West, March 17, 1858, West Family Papers, VHS; Webber Diary, January 2, 1861, Thomas B. Webber Diary, PL; *Nashville Republican & State Gazette*, March 29, 1833; Tripp, *Yankee Town, Southern City*, 39; Mayer & Gentry to Elliott & Clarke, December 7, 1838, Stephen Elliott Papers, PL; Dupre, *Transforming the Cotton Frontier*, 53.

9. Rhea & McCrabb to Preston & Son, November 3, 1826, Robert Preston to James D. Rhea, February 13, 1829, Preston & Son to Whitehall, Jaudon & Co., December 29, 1830, Preston Family Papers, VHS; Boyer, ed., *Chancery Court Records of McMinn County, Tennessee*, 53–54.

10. Samuel H. Aby to his parents (Middletown, Virginia), November 18, 1840, Aby Family Papers, MDAH; Bonney Diary, January 30, 1837, Eli Whitney Bonney Papers, PL; Benedict Semmes to Jorantha Semmes, October 9 and 23, 1857, Benedict Joseph Semmes Papers, SHC.

11. Atherton, *Southern Country Store*, 54; Jonathan Worth to "D Brother," August 28, 1853, Jonathan Worth Papers, NCSA; Zuber, *Jonathan Worth*, 65; Bolton, *Poor Whites of the Antebellum South*, 25; George Barron to John Barron, June 16, 1845, George Barron Papers, KHS. For a cogent analysis of the ties between debt payment and time consciousness, see Smith, *Mastered by the Clock*, 100–110.

12. O'Brien, *Conjectures of Order*, vol. 2, 862, 877–932. For influential, and often opposing, analyses of the Old South's political economy, among many other fine studies see Genovese, *Political Economy of Slavery*; Fogel and Engerman, *Time on the Cross*; Oakes, *Ruling Race* and *Slavery and Freedom*. For an overview on this topic, see Smith, *Debating Slavery*.

13. Important works in the historiographic debate over classical republicanism and liberalism include J. G. A. Pocock, *The Machiavellian Moment: Florentine*

Political Thought and the Atlantic Republican Tradition (Princeton: Princeton University Press, 1975); Lance Banning, *The Jeffersonian Persuasion: Evolution of a Party Ideology* (Ithaca: Cornell University Press, 1978); Joyce O. Appleby, *Capitalism and a New Social Order: The Republican Vision of the 1790s* (New York: New York University Press, 1984). For a more recent assessment of this controversy, see Ashworth, *Slavery, Capitalism, and Politics* (1995), 302–64. For a discussion of a liberal capitalist ethic among another important segment of the southern business classes, slave traders, see Tadman, *Speculators and Slaves*, 200.

14. *Nashville Whig*, January 14, 1838; Click, *Spirit of the Times*, 28, 73–77; *Charleston Mercury*, November 13, 1852, May 23, 1853; *Richmond Enquirer*, June 9, 1854; Order of Odd Fellows membership certificate, Friendship Lodge No. 27, Henry Farrow, July 1856, Henry Patillo Farrow Papers, HL; *Williams' Atlanta Directory*, 31; Agricultural Society membership certificate, Brazoria County, Texas, September 5, 1855, John Adriance Papers, CAH; Burckin, "Formation and Growth of an Urban Middle Class," 9; Pease and Pease, *Ladies, Women, & Wenches*, 123. For a review of women's charitable activities during the nineteenth century, see Smith, *Ladies of the Leisure Class*, 130–40; Rable, *Civil Wars*, 15–16. For a useful discussion of the southern middle class and the Whig Party, see Wells, *Origins of the Southern Middle Class*, 136–61.

15. While few historians have investigated popular party affiliations across the South during the Jacksonian era, evidence suggests that merchants overwhelmingly belonged to the Whig Party. Using an informal sample of frontier merchants that included Texas, Arkansas, and several northern states, Lewis E. Atherton determined that 70 percent of all merchants belonged to the Whig Party; see *Frontier Merchant in Mid-America*, 33–34. My own sample of more than 75 merchants taken from manuscript evidence produced a similar statistic (over 60 percent), but the politics of several merchants could not be determined. Watson, *Liberty and Power*, 211–12; Oakes, *Slavery and Freedom*, 123; Ashworth, *Slavery, Capitalism, and Politics*, 365; Atherton, *Southern Country Store*, 203; Thornton, *Politics and Power in a Slave Society*, 35–50.

16. Jonathan Jacocks to Charles Jacocks, February 26 and March 14, 1834, Charles W. Jacocks Papers, NCSA.

17. Jonathan Jacocks to Charles Jacocks, November 20, 1834, Charles W. Jacocks Papers, NCSA. Jacocks frequently referred to Martin Van Buren and Andrew Jackson as self-proclaimed "Kings" in his correspondence with his brother.

18. Zuber, *Jonathan Worth*, 37–40; John Burbidge to Rosina Mix, May 7, 1839, Rosina Mix Papers, SHC; Gadsden, *Minutes of the Proceedings of the Third Commercial Convention*, 3–10; John M. Sacher, "Sudden Collapse of the Louisiana Whig Party," 226. Asa Biggs, a member of a large North Carolina mercantile family, is an excellent example of a strong states' rights, commercially

oriented leader in his state's Democratic Party. A strong supporter of Andrew Jackson, Biggs vilified local Whigs all the while supporting internal improvements and other policies that would have warmed the heart of Henry Clay; see Asa Biggs to Kader Biggs, December 12 and 24, 1844, Kader Biggs Papers, NCSA; *Wilmington Daily Journal*, July 1, 1853; James Evans to brother, November 7, 1840, James Evans Papers, SHC.

19. Zuber, *Jonathan Worth*, 37–40; Ford, *Origins of Southern Radicalism*, 207–8; Howze Journal, July 1851, Howze (Isham Robertson) and Family Papers, MDAH.

20. Hassell Diary, November 4, 1856, Cushing B. Hassell Papers, SHC. More work needs to be completed on southern voting patterns, but Jonathan M. Bryant revealed in his 1996 study of Green County, Georgia, that the county's merchants and planter-businessmen led the county to give 68 percent of its vote to John Bell; see *How Curious a Land*, 59; Thornton, *Politics and Power in a Slave Society*, 426–42; Buenger, *Secession and the Union in Texas*, 135–38. Marc Egnal has offered a provocative, if not entirely satisfactory, explanation for the failure of a diversified southern economy in *Divergent Paths*, 60–70 in particular. Laurence Shore's *Southern Capitalists* and Bateman and Weiss's *Deplorable Scarcity* have also explored the limitations of the southern economy. On the subject of the vitality and diversity of the southern economy, I tend to be more reserved than Jonathan Daniel Wells, who contends that the 1850s were "a decade of transformative growth, a time of dizzying change"; see *Origins of the Southern Middle Class*, 174.

21. *Greenville Mountaineer*, November 29, 1855.

22. Kenzer, *Kinship and Neighborhood*, 20, 37–38; Sutherland, *Seasons of War*, 7–9; Archibald Trawick, "An Old Time Drummer Talks About the Grocery Business, 1846–1946," paper read before the Tennessee Historical Society on January 14, 1947, Archibald Trawick Papers, TSLA; Grannis Diary, December 1 and 2, 1858, Robert A. Grannis Diary, VHS; Scott, *Random Recollections of a Long Life*, 13, 19–20; Hassell Diary, July 11, 1848, October 30, 1850, Cushing B. Hassell Papers, SHC; Ingraham, *The South-West, by a Yankee*, vol. 2, 29; Rawick, ed., *The American Slave*, vol. 16, p. 66. For further analyses of antebellum stores and their function as community focal points, see Morris, *Becoming Southern*, 110–14; Harris, *Plain Folk and Gentry*, 119.

23. *Nashville Whig*, January 4, 1828; *Mobile Commercial Register and Patriot*, November 4, 1840; *Georgia Telegram* (Macon), August 7, 1855.

24. Bart DeWitt to John Leyendecker, June 27, 1857, John Zirvas Leyendecker Papers, CAH; Jefferson Diary, April 1, 1857, John F. Jefferson Papers, FCHS; Jorantha Jordan to Benedict Semmes, October 10, 1848, Benedict Joseph Semmes Papers, SHC; Tolbert, *Constructing Townscapes*, 58; Samuel L. Lewis to Milo Lewis, Milo Lewis Papers, PL. Lewis served as a wholesale merchant to ped-

dlers as well as being a retailer himself. See also Rose, *Victorian America and the Civil War*, 1–3, 71–77.

25. *Caddo Gazette*, February 11, 1846 (the italics are the author's). Whipple, *Bishop Whipple's Southern Diary*, 76; Olmsted, *Journey in the Seaboard Slave States*, 138–39; Atherton, *Southern Country Store*, 47; Atherton, *Frontier Merchant in Mid-America*, 54; *People's Press and Wilmington Advertiser*, October 15, 1834; *Richmond Enquirer*, March 8, 1851; Byrne, "Merchant in Antebellum Southern Literature," 33–45.

26. Rawick, *American Slave*, supp. 2, vol. 2, pt. 1, p. 228. McWhiney, *Cracker Culture*, 260; Schwaab, ed., *Travels in the Old South*, vol. 2, 330; Startup, *Root of All Evil*, 57. On class alliances and social cohesion in the antebellum South, see Kenzer, *Kinship and Neighborhood*, 29; Harris, *Plain Folk and Gentry*, 119–20; Fox-Genovese and Genovese, *Fruits of Merchant Capital*, 5–8. For an account of divisions and social distance within southern society, see Oakes, *Slavery and Freedom*, 80–136; and, more recently, Williams, *Rich Man's War* (1998). As noted earlier, in my sample federal census records from twenty-two counties across the South less than 10 percent of the merchant population hailed from northern states.

27. Barrow, *Plantation Life in the Florida Parishes of Louisiana*, 108; *Macon Georgia Telegraph*, November 29, 1842; Dimond and Hattaway, eds., *Letters from Forest Place*, 112. See also Greb, "Charleston, South Carolina, Merchants," 37; Ronald L. F. Davis, "The Southern Merchant: A Perennial Source of Discontent," in Fraser and Moore, eds., *Southern Enigma*, 133–39, 170; Baptist, "Accidental Ethnography in an Antebellum Southern Newspaper," 1373; Sellers, *Market Revolution*, 237. Larger cotton and sugar planters usually conducted the bulk of their business through factors in larger cities, but many supplemented their trade with local storekeepers; see Gray, *History of Agriculture*, vol. 2, 706–13; Woodman, *King Cotton & His Retainers*, 6–26, 115–20, 152–64; Ford, *Origins of Southern Radicalism*, 88; Roeder, "New Orleans Merchants," 222–38. For examples of planter-merchant conflict and the dominance of the former, see Bryant, *How Curious a Land*, 10, 49; Bailey, *Class and Tennessee's Confederate Generation*, 33. Jacqueline Jones has offered a succinct analysis of merchant-slave trade in the antebellum South in *American Work*, 200–202; also see Sutherland, *Seasons of War*, 23. Like all respectable southern newspapers the *Richmond Enquirer* strongly criticized trade between slaves and merchants without the master's permission. For an amusing account of how such trade could destroy a merchant's reputation, see the *Richmond Enquirer*, November 26, 1853.

28. Morris, *Becoming Southern*, 161; John Burbidge to Rosina Mix, February 24, 1841, Rosina Mix Papers, SHC.

29. Byrne, "Merchant in Antebellum Southern Literature," 35–39. See also Frank J. Byrne, "The Literary Shaping of Confederate Identity: Daniel R.

Hundley and John Beauchamp Jones in Peace and War," in Gordon and Inscoe, eds., *Inside the Confederate Nation*. Census figures show that in 1850, Dinwiddie County, Virginia, urban and relatively cosmopolitan by rural southern standards, boasted well over four hundred practicing merchants, more than 80 percent of whom were born in the South while 3 percent hailed from the North and some-what in excess of 12 percent from Europe. By 1860 the percentage of native-born Southerners in the county dipped to 77 while 5 percent had migrated from the North and almost 17 percent from Europe; see Manuscript Census, Dinwiddie County, Virginia, 1850, 1860. Not surprisingly the figures for native-born Southerners rose for rural counties. Over 90 percent of the merchants living in Buckingham County, Virginia, were born in the state, while only one northerner (1.7 percent) and three Europeans (5.1 percent) plied their trade there in 1860; see Manuscript Census, Buckingham County, Virginia, 1860. It is difficult to determine the number of Jewish merchants who lived in the South, but with the exception of those living in larger cities like New Orleans and Savannah, most appear to have been first-generation European or northern immigrants.

30. *Charleston Mercury*, October 7 and 9, 1854.

31. Bleser, ed., *Secret and Sacred*, 94.

32. Bleser, ed., *Secret and Sacred*, 95; *Charleston Mercury*, October 10 and 12, 1854. Mordecai was one of three powerful spokesmen for Charleston's com-mercial interests in the legislature, the others being Thomas Bennett Jr. and Ker Boyce; see Greb, "Charleston, South Carolina, Merchants," 57–58.

33. Carl R. Osthaus, *Partisans of the Southern Press*, 3–10; Burton, *In My Father's House*, 68. See also Stem, *Tar Heel Press*. The historical literature on North and South Carolina is large. A brief listing of several studies for each state suggests the volume of the historiography. North Carolina: Watson, *Independent People*; Censer, *North Carolina Planters and Their Children*; Escott, *Many Excellent People*; Kenzer, *Kinship and Neighborhood*; Tullos, *Habits of Industry*; Bynum, *Unruly Women*; Cecil-Fronsman, *Common Whites*. South Carolina: Burton, *In My Father's House*; Ford, *Origins of Southern Radicalism*; O'Brien and Moltke-Hansen, eds., *Intellectual Life in Antebellum Charleston*; Coclanis, *Shadow of a Dream*; McCurry, *Masters of Small Worlds*.

34. On divisions within Carolina society, see Burton, *In My Father's House*; Ford, *Origins of Southern Radicalism*; Cecil-Fronsman, *Common Whites*; Lefler and Newsome, *North Carolina*. For an insightful analysis of merchant self-con-struction see Ditz, "Shipwrecked," 51–57.

35. Ronald L. F. Davis, "The Southern Merchant: A Perennial Source of Discontent," in Fraser and Moore, eds., *Southern Enigma*, 131–33; Earle, *Making of the English Middle Class*, 34; Hundley, *Social Relations in Our Southern States*, 103.

36. Lefler and Newsome, *North Carolina*, 110, 365–66; *Carolina Watchman*,

November 10, 1832; Hundley, *Social Relations in Our Southern States*, 101; *Greenville Mountaineer*, November 29, 1855. Comic accounts of merchant duplicity seem rather common in antebellum newspapers. A small notice in the *Federal Union*, published in Milledgeville, Georgia, is illustrative. Under the headline "*Mourning*" it recounts a "wag" in a Louisville store who, "after having his bales and boxes driven from the side walk by authorities, suspended his many colored remnants from the windows in the upper story—and as a mark of respect for the sudden disappearance of their companions, covered each fabric with a piece of crepe. In three days the fellow's store was overrun with customers"; see *Federal Union*, February 18, 1840.

37. Osthaus, *Partisans of the Southern Press*, 78–79; *Charleston Mercury*, March 27, 1850, February 28, 1851; Gray, *History of Agriculture*, vol. 2, 931; Ronald L. F. Davis, "The Southern Merchant," in Fraser and Moore, eds., *Southern Enigma*, 133; Woodman, *King Cotton & His Retainers*, 169–73.

38. *People's Press and Wilmington Advertiser*, October 15, 1834.

39. *Edenton Sentinel and Albemarle Intelligencer*, May 1, 1841.

40. *Wilmington Daily Journal*, September 19 and October 9, 1854. On merchant control of local markets in North Carolina, see Cecil-Fronsman, *Common Whites*, 36–37; Kenzer, *Kinship and Neighborhood*, 37–38.

41. *Carolina Watchman*, May 22, 1846, November 25, 1847; Startup, *Root of All Evil*, 13, 127–135. Startup argues persuasively that northern ministers, like their southern brethren, made the same condemnation of greed and consumption.

42. Byrne, "Merchant in Antebellum Southern Literature," 35–36.

43. *Carolina Watchman*, October 4, 1838; *Charleston Mercury*, August 5, 1853.

44. *Carolina Watchman*, July 1, 1843, May 11, 1844.

45. *Wilmington Daily Journal*, October 3, 1851, March 25, 1854; *Charleston Mercury*, October 12, 1852; John A. B. Fitzgerald to Joseph Cathey, January 12, 1854, Joseph Cathey Papers, NCSA. In 1802 merchants in Savannah, Georgia, repackaged cotton that entered the city in order to detect false packing and thereby protect the reputation (and price) of Georgia cotton. Similar activities were occasionally attempted elsewhere in the South; see Gray, *History of Agriculture*, vol. 2, 706.

46. *Weekly Raleigh Register*, January 19, 1853. Newspapers from across the South routinely highlighted the many benefits of advertisements to merchants and customers alike. For example, the October 31, 1845, edition of the *Vicksburg Sentinel* included the following passage: "Let our readers examine the advertisements and mark them. Nothing is truer than that advertisers are the men who sell bargains." See also Presbrey, *History and Development of Advertising*, 202–10; Pope, *Making of Modern Advertising*, 5.

47. Augst, *Clerk's Tale*, 49; Smith, "Old South Time in Comparative Perspective," 1448–52; Atherton, *Southern Country Store*, 66.

48. *Charleston Mercury*, January 8, 1850, July 17, 1854.

49. Mallett credit reports, 1846, Peter Mallett Papers, SHC; Atherton, *Southern Country Store*, 181.

50. Hassell Diary, Cushing B. Hassell Papers, SHC; Joseph Biggs to Kader Biggs, October 23, 1843, Kader Biggs Papers, NCSA; John Burbidge to Rosina Mix, November 27, 1837, Rosina Mix Papers, SHC.

51. Jonathan Worth to Simson Colton, August 30, 1853, Jonathan Worth Papers, NCSA; Hassell Diary, March 15 and November 1, 1847, Cushing Hassell Papers, SHC; Letter, August 30, 1853, Joseph Cathey Papers, NCSA. For a thoughtful analysis of support for public education and reform within the southern middle class, see Wells, *Origins of the Southern Middle Class*, 10–11, 133–50.

52. *Charleston Mercury*, November 13, 1852, January 7 and May 23, 1853.

53. *Carolina Watchman*, June 21, 1839; George Barron to John Barron, December 21, 1845, George Barron Papers, KHS.

54. *Carolina Watchman*, May 12, 1838; *Greenville Mountaineer*, May 30, 1835, April 26, 1850; *Charleston Mercury*, November 25, 1851, June 10 and 14, 1853.

55. On the relationship between work and time see E. P. Thompson's seminal essay "Time, Work-Discipline, and Industrial Capitalism" (1967), reprinted in his *Customs in Common*, 352–70. On planter culture and refinement, see Wyatt-Brown, *Southern Honor*; Stowe, *Intimacy and Power in the Old South*; Fox-Genovese, *Within the Plantation Household*.

3. The Merchant Family in the Antebellum South

1. There is a large and growing literature on the culture of the white family in the antebellum South. The dynamics of the planter family are explored in: Young, *Domesticating Slavery*; Cashin, *Family Venture*; Fox-Genovese, *Within the Plantation Household*; Stowe, *Intimacy and Power in the Old South*; Burton, *In My Father's House*; Censer, *North Carolina Planters and Their Children*; Lewis, *Pursuit of Happiness*; and Wyatt-Brown, *Southern Honor*. The experience of yeoman families in the antebellum South and beyond is analyzed in McCurry, *Masters of Small Worlds*; Cecil-Fronsman, *Common Whites*; Tullos, *Habits of Industry*; Ford, *Origins of Southern Radicalism*; Escott, *Many Excellent People*. On the relationship between the planter and business classes in the Old South, see Doyle, *New Men, New Cities*, 7–8. For a collection of insightful essays on the familial and economic lives of working women, see Delfino and Gillespie, eds., *Neither Lady nor Slave*.

2. Censer, *North Carolina Planters and Their Children*, 72; Young, *Domesticating*

Slavery, 148–49; Stephanie Cole, "White Women, of Middle Age, Would Be Preferred: Children's Nurses in the Old South," in Delfino and Gillespie, eds., *Neither Lady nor Slave*, 75–78, 81; Wells, *Origins of the Southern Middle Class*, 47; Fox-Genovese, *Within the Plantation Household*, 62–65. See also Rose, *Victorian America and the Civil War*, 146, 179; Mintz, *Prison of Expectations*, 13–20. In certain respects, many marriages within commercial households mirrored that of William and Elizabeth Wirt as described by Anya Jabour in *Marriage in the Early Republic: Elizabeth and William Wirt and the Companionate Ideal*. The cultivated and prominent Virginia couple shared cultural ties to the Old South as well as to the Northeast. Thus, according to Jabour, they "felt both the tension between mutual love and increasingly demarcated gender roles commonly associated with the urban Northeast and the contest between new ideals of companionate marriage and the patriarchal ideals that many scholars argue still flourished in the South," 3.

3. No historical works have examined the views of antebellum merchants on race, gender relations, or religion. One of the best studies of merchant life, Lewis E. Atherton's *The Southern Country Store, 1800–1860*, focuses on business activities. In more general studies of antebellum southern history, white racism and the ideology of slavery is explored in Jordan, *White Over Black*; Faust, ed., *Ideology of Slavery*; Tise, *Proslavery*. Elements of southern white patriarchy are examined in Clinton, *Plantation Mistress*; Wyatt-Brown, *Southern Honor*; Lebsock, *Free Women of Petersburg*; Fox-Genovese, *Within the Plantation Household*; McCurry, *Masters of Small Worlds*; Faust, *Mothers of Invention*; Cashin, ed., *Our Common Affairs*. Wyatt-Brown, Clinton, Fox-Genovese, and McCurry, among others, have found more evidence of patriarchy in southern marriages than Censer, Lebsock, Jabour, et al. A recent study of evangelical Christianity in the Old South is Christine Leigh Heyrman's *Southern Cross*. See also Boles, *Great Revival*; Mathews, *Religion in the Old South*; Hill, ed., *Religion in the Southern States*.

4. Isham Howze Journal, June 20, 1854, Howze (Isham Robertson) and Family Papers, MDAH; Samuel H. Aby to parents, October 19, 1847, Aby Family Papers, MDAH.

5. Atherton, *Southern Country Store*, 52–55. For the influence of northern Victorian culture in the antebellum South, see Wells, *Origins of the Southern Middle Class*, 17–66; Wyatt-Brown, *Southern Honor*, 23. The vast majority of merchants, grocers, hucksters, and most other retail operators across the antebellum South were men (see appendix, table 3). Smaller storeowners would often have their store or storehouse on the same lot as their house. In these cases it is unclear how much husbands and wives saw of each other or how much work the women performed in the store. For examples in McMinn County, Tennessee, see *Chancery Court Records of McMinn County, Tennessee*, 37–38.

6. Lebsock, *Free Women of Petersburg*, 180–81; Barbara J. Howe, "Patient

Laborers: Women at Work in the Formal Economy of West(ern) Virginia," in Delfino and Gillespie, eds., *Neither Lady nor Slave*, 121–51; Timothy J. Lockley, "Spheres of Influence: Working White and Black Women in Antebellum Savannah," in Delfino and Gillespie, eds., *Neither Lady nor Slave*, 110; Wells, *Origins of the Southern Middle Class*, 112–13.

7. Sidney Root, "Memorandum of My Life, 1893," Sidney Root Papers, AHC; John Burbidge to Rosina Mix, February 24, 1841, Rosina Mix Papers, SHC.

8. Brown, *Modernization*, 135–44; Smith, "Old South Time in Comparative Perspective," 1447–48; Smith, *Mastered by the Clock*, 69–128. For an influential analysis of the relationship between time and work, see E. P. Thompson's classic article "Time, Work-Discipline, and Industrial Capitalism," in his *Customs in Common*.

9. Bailey, *Class and Tennessee's Confederate Generation*, 33.

10. For an enlightening analysis of comparable activities among merchant wives in Europe, see Smith, *Ladies of the Leisure Class*, 4–6. A useful, though overstated, account of the business roles of antebellum merchant wives is offered in Wyatt-Brown, *Southern Honor*, 214–15. More recently (1997) Mark Smith has suggested that the manner in which southern women ran their households revealed the influence of a northern bourgeois economy; see *Mastered by the Clock*, 62. To a significant degree, the marital relations within southern merchant families followed the national nineteenth-century pattern described by E. Anthony Rotundo: "Man's primacy in the home was modified and circumscribed but not denied. All parties recognized the man as head of the household—and one dimension of his power was his dominion over his wife"; in *American Manhood: Transformations in Masculinity from the Revolution to the Modern Era* (New York: Basic Books, 1993), 140.

11. Lewis, *Pursuit of Happiness*, 174–210. Pickens is quoted in Wyatt-Brown, *Southern Honor*, 137. Bertram Wyatt-Brown asserts that southern parents, particularly those from the ranks of the planter class, followed a policy of "bemused indulgence" with their children that eventually led to aggressive young boys; see *Southern Honor*, 138–43. This conclusion varies from that of Dickson D. Bruce Jr., who maintained that southern child-rearing practices tended toward repression and denial; see *Violence and Culture in the Antebellum South*, 44–56; Mintz, *Prison of Expectations*, 13–20; Rose, *Victorian America and the Civil War*, 146; Ryan, *Cradle of the Middle Class*, 155–78. See also Greven, *Protestant Temperament*, 99, 268–91.

12. Howze Journal, 1851, Howze (Isham Robertson) and Family Papers, MDAH; Wilson, *The Confederate Soldier*, 206.

13. Howze Journal, February 22, 1855, Howze (Isham Robertson) and Family Papers, MDAH.

14. Hassell Diary, March 17 and April 8, 1847, Cushing B. Hassell Papers,

SHC; Charles Ellis Sr. to Charles Ellis Jr., May 20, 1832, Munford-Ellis Family Papers, PL. Ellis would frequently pit one of his children against another in order to inspire, or perhaps shame, each child to do his or her best. In a March 9, 1832, letter to his son Charles Jr., Ellis wrote, "Your Brother Thos studied for weeks together before his examination 20 & sometime 21 hours out of the 24. Your sister Elizabeth has commenced Latin & I have no doubt will make good progress." Members of the planter class often followed similar practices with their children. Jane Turner Censer found that the planter class in North Carolina "urged self-control as well as thrift and industriousness upon its offspring"; see *North Carolina Planters and Their Children*, 51. Censer's conclusion differs from those found in the work of Bertram Wyatt-Brown and others.

15. Mattie C. Tennent to Anna Louisa Lesley, January 23, 1847, Norris and Thomson Family Papers, SCL; Censer, *North Carolina Planters and Their Children*, 42; Fox-Genovese, *Within the Plantation Household*, 46; Catherine Stine to Sarah Aby, October 22, 1843, Aby Family Papers, MDAH; Mintz, *Prison of Expectations*, 10–12. For a useful examination of southern education on a local level, see Stevenson, *Life in Black and White*, 124–32.

16. Mary Caroline Jacocks to Charles W. Jacocks, May 8, 1824, Charles W. Jacocks Papers, NCSA; Elizabeth Adams essays, January 23, 1844, Bres Family Papers, HTML; Wolfe, *Daughters of Canaan*, 95; Rable, *Civil Wars*, 20–22; Farnham, *Education of the Southern Belle*, 68–93. Daughters of planters would often receive similar lectures on the importance of self-discipline from their families. For example, Sarah E. Watkins of Carroll County, Mississippi, wrote her daughter Letitia, attending school in Columbia, Tennessee, the following: "Do my dear child try and learn as fast as you can. Do not speak ill of your teachers, be very respectful to them and you will gain their esteem. Do not be ill-natured to your schoolmates and do not say any thing against one girl to another"; see Dimond and Hattaway, eds., *Letters from Forest Place*, 13–14. Typically the evidence suggests that merchant families emphasized the need for industry and discipline more regularly and with greater urgency than did planter families.

17. Wells, *Origins of the Southern Middle Class*, 150; Howze Journal, July 8, 1852, Howze (Isham Robertson) and Family Papers, MDAH; Martha Webb to Charles Jacocks, July 9, 1844, Charles W. Jacocks Papers, NCSA; Barcia Norfleet Gordon O'Bryan to Fannie O'Bryan, March 12, 1851, O'Bryan Family Collection, TSLA.

18. *Wilmington Daily Journal*, January 31, 1855; *Nashville Republican and State Gazette*, January 29, 1860; Bardaglio, *Reconstructing the Household*, 30–35; Smith, *Ladies of the Leisure Class*, 80–100. For a discussion of the influence of bourgeois discourse in the southern slaveholding family, see Elizabeth Fox-Genovese, "Family and Female Identity in the Antebellum South: Sarah Gayle and Her Family," in Bleser, ed., *In Joy and in Sorrow*, 20–25.

19. Mintz, *Prison of Expectations*, 145–50.

20. Samuel Aby to Charles Aby, April 19, 1853, Aby Family Papers, MDAH.

21. Horace Carpenter to Philinia Carpenter, December 14, 1823, Carpenter Family Papers, TSLA. Virtually every letter in the extensive correspondence among the Biggs brothers touches upon some business concern; for two examples, see William Biggs to Joseph Biggs, October 24, 1841, William Biggs to Kader Biggs, October 28, 1841, Kader Biggs Papers, NCSA.

22. Edward Rumsey to James D. Rumsey, December 1835, Edward Rumsey Papers, KHS.

23. Stowe, *Intimacy and Power in the Old South*, 50–65; Carney Diary, January 1859, Kate S. Carney Diary, SHC; Rose, *Victorian America and the Civil War*, 150–60. In opposition to Stowe, Wyatt-Brown, Fox-Genovese, and others, Karen Lystra has argued that economic and family concerns played secondary roles to romantic love in nineteenth-century American courtship practices; see Lystra, *Searching the Heart*, 7–9, 123–55. For a discussion of courtship practices in another western context, see Earle, *Making of the English Middle Class*, 180–200.

24. Fox-Genovese, *Within the Plantation Household*, 207–10; Brown, *Good Wives*, 254–60; Wyatt-Brown, *Southern Honor*, 199–205; Lebsock, *Free Women of Petersburg*, 20–30; Bynum, *Unruly Women*, 2, 16, 35–61.

25. Hassell Diary, September 20, 1848, Cushing B. Hassell Papers, SHC; Isaac Proctor to Jane Marriott, October 5, 1852, Jennie Marriott Proctor Papers, NCSA.

26. Isaac Proctor to Jane Marriott, June 11, 1848, Jennie Mariott Proctor Papers, NCSA.

27. J. B. Bres to Elizabeth Adams, August 2, 1848, Elizabeth Adams to J. B. Bres, August 6, 1848, Bres Family Papers, HTML; Louisiana, vol. 11, p. 312, R. G. Dun & Company Reports, HGSB; Manuscript Census, Orleans Parish, Louisiana, 1850; Benedict Semmes to Jorantha Jordan, September 24, 1848, March 14, 1849, Benedict Joseph Semmes Papers, SHC; Stevenson, *Life in Black and White*, 57–60.

28. Kyriakoudes, "Plantation to Town," 58; Bailey, *Class and Tennessee's Confederate Generation*, 21. Bailey's results approximate my own findings derived from manuscript and credit report records. This financial data, unfortunately available for only sixteen antebellum merchants in my records, shows an average real wealth of $15,195 for the years between 1846 and 1861. This average includes two merchants who were reported as having virtually no assets or wealth. T. Lloyd Benson, "The Plain Folk of Orange: Land, Work, and Society on the Eve of the Civil War," in Ayers and Willis, eds., *Edge of the South*, 64; Theodore F. Marburg, "Income Originating in Trade, 1799–1869," in Conference on

Research in Income and Wealth, *Trends in the American Economy in the Nineteenth Century*, vol. 24, 321. The question surrounding the wages that clerks received is still unanswered. While most were paid, it seems some clerks served apprenticeships that gave them little more than room and board; see Atherton, *Southern Country Store*, 207.

29. Lewis C. Gray, *History of Agriculture*; Fogel and Engerman, *Time on the Cross*; Oakes, *Ruling Race*; Genovese, *Political Economy of Slavery* and *Roll, Jordan, Roll*; Fields, *Slavery and Freedom on the Middle Ground*; Fox-Genovese, *Within the Plantation Household*, 89; Hahn, *Roots of Southern Populism*, 29; Ford, *Origins of Southern Radicalism*, 84–85.

30. Several excellent studies of European bourgeois consumption patterns include Ann Bermingham, introduction to Bermingham and Brewer, eds., *Consumption of Culture*, 1–20; Victoria de Grazia, "Changing Consumption Regimes: Introduction," in de Grazia and Furlough, eds., *Sex of Things*, 11–24; Leora Auslander, "The Gendering of Consumer Practices in Nineteenth-Century France," in de Grazia and Furlough, eds., *Sex of Things*, 79–112; Lears, *No Place of Grace*, 30–40.

31. John Dunlap to Beatrice Dunlap, February 16, 1845, Dunlap Correspondence, HTML; Louisiana, vol. 9, p. 68, R. G. Dun & Company Reports, HGSB; Bailey, *Class and Tennessee's Confederate Generation*, 23; Jefferson Diary, March 11 and 16, 1857, John F. Jefferson Papers, FCHS; Zuber, *Jonathan Worth*, 84; Carney Diary, January 1, 1859, Kate S. Carney Diary, SHC; Charles Ellis Sr. to Powhatan Ellis, January 17, 1822, Munford-Ellis Family Papers, PL; Hassell Diary, March 17, 1847, Cushing B. Hassell Papers, SHC; Howze Journal, January, March 13, 1854, Howze (Isham Robertson) and Family Papers, MDAH; Mississippi, vol. 15, p. 19, R. G. Dun & Company Reports, HGSB; Mississippi, vol. 6, p. 137, R. G. Dun & Company Reports, HGSB.

32. *Charleston Mercury*, November 25, 1851, June 10, 1853.

33. Hassell Diary, September 29, 1847, Cushing B. Hassell Papers, SHC; Jorantha Semmes to Benedict Semmes, August 29, 1859, Benedict Joseph Semmes Papers, SHC; Barcia Norfleet Gordon O'Bryan to Fannie O'Bryan, April 15, 1852, O'Bryan Family Collection, TSLA; Virginia Leslie to Louisa Leslie, October 28, 1852, Norris and Thomson Family Papers, SCL.

34. Wyatt-Brown, *Southern Honor*, 330–40; Genovese, *Political Economy of Slavery*, 18, 130, 158; Luraghi, *Rise and Fall of the Plantation South*, 74; Gallman, "Slavery and Southern Economic Growth"; Ford, *Origins of Southern Radicalism*, 63–65; Faust, *Mothers of Invention*, 220–40; Fox-Genovese, *Within the Plantation Household*, 127–28; Halttunen, *Confidence Men and Painted Women*, 62–82; Leora Auslander, "The Gendering of Consumer Practices in Nineteenth-Century France," in de Grazia and Furlough, eds., *Sex of Things*, 83.

35. Duffy, "Medical Practice in the Ante Bellum South," 61–65; McMillen,

Motherhood in the Old South, 12–15; James Harvey Young, "Patent Medicines: An Element in Southern Distinctiveness?" in Savitt and Young, eds., *Disease and Distinctiveness in the American South*, 159; Howze Journal, June 28, July 13, October 5, 1853, March 17, 1854, February 28, 1857, Howze (Isham Robertson) and Family Papers, MDAH; Solomon, *Civil War Diary of Clara Solomon*, 106, 110, 164.

36. Joseph Biggs to Kader Biggs, December 10, 1847, Kader Biggs Papers, NCSA; Chesnut, *Mary Chesnut's Civil War*, 247, 285–86, 344, 765–66.

37. For a thoughtful analysis of southern interest in the antebellum North, see Wells, *Origins of the Southern Middle Class*, 41–66.

38. Tyrus Brainerd to Samuel Arnold Haddam, January 14, 1838, Tyrus Brainerd Correspondence, TSLA.

39. Predictably rural counties had fewer merchants hailing from the North than more urban counties. For example, in 1850 rural Buckingham County, Virginia, had only one northern transplant (1.9 percent of the county's mercantile population) in its merchant community, while more settled Dinwiddie County, Virginia, was home to 16 northerners (3.7 percent) and an impressive 54 European storekeepers (12.6 percent); see Manuscript Census, Buckingham and Dinwiddie counties, Virginia, 1850. Kyriakoudes, "Plantation to Town," 49–50, 61; Cecil-Fronsman, *Common Whites*, 99–100; Whipple, *Bishop Whipple's Southern Diary*, 73; Ruth Ingraham and Mary Leonard to Susan Fisher, November 24, 1839, Susan Fisher Papers, SHC; Coulter, *George Walton Williams*, 47. The Biggs brothers, like many merchants, hired northern instructors; see Asa Biggs to Kader Biggs, March 5, 1847, Kader Biggs Papers, NCSA. On the increasing ideological divide between the North and South, see Genovese, *World the Slaveholders Made*, 65, 99, 102, 122; Walther, *Fire-Eaters*, 85–87, 201, 224–30, 273–87.

40. Walther, *Fire-Eaters*, 199–201.

41. Addison Lea to William Lea, May 21, 1836, Lea Family Papers, SHC; Carney Diary, August and September 1859, September 16, 1859, Kate S. Carney Diary, SHC; James Sullivan Diary, September 1, 1855, Hynes-Sullivan Papers, GHS. A "Bloomer" was a woman who advocated dress reform by abandoning restrictive clothing in favor of shorter skirts and knee-length undergarments. Sullivan's reference to "conspicious Negroes" is not clear but probably meant that their dress or decorum suggested an assertiveness off-putting to the merchant. On southern reading patterns, see Oakes, *Slavery and Freedom*, 40–42; Stowe, *Intimacy and Power in the Old South*, 52–88.

42. Fitzhugh, *Cannibals All!*, 188; Adams, *Education of Henry Adams*, 57; Bleser, ed., *Secret and Sacred*, 272–73.

43. Hundley, *Social Relations in Our Southern States*, 102. For an exploration of community resentment against the merchant class, see Ronald L. F. Davis, "The Southern Merchant: A Perennial Source of Discontent," in Fraser and

Moore, eds., *Southern Enigma*, 139; Howze Journal, February 28, 1857, Howze (Isham Robertson) and Family Papers, MDAH.

44. Haskell, "Capitalism and the Origins of the Humanitarian Sensibility," 339–45.

45. Here I am following Judith Lorber's definition of patriarchy as basically "the process, structure, and ideology of women's subordination"; see Lorber, *Paradoxes of Gender*, 3. Mintz, *Prison of Expectations*, 60–62; Ryan, *Cradle of the Middle Class*, 31–43, 53–59, 73–75; Ginzberg, *Women and the Work of Benevolence*, chapter 5; Rose, *Victorian America and the Civil War*, 145–92; Brown, *Good Wives*, 4–5; Whites, *Civil War as a Crisis in Gender*, 75; McCurry, *Masters of Small Worlds*, 56–61; Cashin, ed., *Our Common Affairs*, 10–22; Cashin, *Family Venture*, 20–26; Wolfe, *Daughters of Canaan*, 62, 76; Fox-Genovese, *Within the Plantation Household*, 63–64, 286, 370; Stowe, *Intimacy and Power in the Old South*, 191, 238; Lebsock, *Free Women of Petersburg*, 15–21; Wyatt-Brown, *Southern Honor*, 62–87, 195–200, 254–91; Bardaglio, *Reconstructing the Household*, 27, 34–35, 80–93; James W. Ely Jr. and David J. Bodenhamer, "Regionalism and the Legal History of the South," in Bodenhamer and Ely, eds., *Ambivalent Legacy*, 10–12; Bynum, *Unruly Women*, 59–87. Jane Turner Censer disputes the existence of southern patriarchy altogether; see *North Carolina Planters and Their Children*, 60–70, 130–200.

46. Mary Potter to Charles Jacocks, March 27, 1827, Martha Webb to Charles Jacocks, July 9, 1844, December 11, 1844, Charles W. Jacocks Papers, NCSA.

47. Norcom is quoted in Wyatt-Brown, *Southern Honor*, 207.

48. Charles Jacocks to Mary Reed, April 23, 1833, Charles W. Jacocks Papers, NCSA.

49. Jonathan Jacocks to Charles Jacocks, February 1 and 3, 1836, March 20, 1836, Jonathan Jacocks to Elizabeth Jacocks, February 21, 1836, Charles W. Jacocks Papers, NCSA; Manuscript Census, Perquimans County, North Carolina, 1850.

50. Dew is quoted in Fox-Genovese, *Within the Plantation Household*, 198; Howze Journal, August 11, 1850, August 8, 1851, November 3, 1852, March 20, 1853, Howze (Isham Robertson) and Family Papers, MDAH.

51. Howze Journal, introduction, Howze (Isham Robertson) and Family Papers, MDAH; Taylor, *Eve and the New Jerusalem*, 66–67.

52. Howze Journal, August 1, 1851, April 13, 1853, Howze (Isham Robertson) and Family Papers, MDAH.

53. Atherton, *Frontier Merchant in Mid-America*, 37. For scholarship on southern Protestantism in general, and evangelicalism in particular, see Mathews, *Religion in the Old South*; Boles, *Great Revival*; Hill, ed., *Religion in the Southern States*; Friedman, *Enclosed Garden*; Calhoon, *Evangelicals and Conservatives in the Early South*; Eugene D. Genovese and Elizabeth Fox-Genovese, "The Religious Ideals of Southern Slave Society," in Bartley, ed., *Evolution of Southern Culture*;

Tise, *Proslavery*. More recent works on the subject include W. Reginald Ward's transatlantic study *The Protestant Evangelical Awakening* (1992); Stephanie McCurry's *Masters of Small Worlds* (1995); and Christine Leigh Heyrman's important work *Southern Cross* (1997), 1–10.

54. Heyrman, *Southern Cross*, 19, 158–59, 191–92; Mathews, *Religion in the Old South*, xv–xvi, 41–62; McCurry, *Masters of Small Worlds*, 136–39.

55. Mathews, *Religion in the Old South*, xv–xvi, 189–205; Wayne Mixon, "Georgia," in Hill, ed., *Religion in the Southern States*, 85; Wells, *Origins of the Southern Middle Class*, 80–85; Lewis, *Pursuit of Happiness*, 20–22. For further discussion of northern evangelicalism, see Ryan, *Cradle of the Middle Class*, 60–104; Rose, *Victorian America and the Civil War*, 20–30; Greven, *Protestant Temperament*, 13–71, 151; Gay, *Bourgeois Experience*, 59.

56. Tise, *Proslavery*, 360, 116–20; Mathews, *Religion in the Old South*, 34–35, 157–75; Oakes, *Ruling Race*, 103–9.

57. Heyrman, *Southern Cross*, 4; Greven, *Protestant Temperament*, 62–64; Oakes, *Ruling Race*, 98–102.

58. Hassell Diary, 1827–1828, Cushing B. Hassell Papers, SHC; George O'Bryan obituary, 1912, O'Bryan Family Collection, TSLA; Perkins Diary, February 4, 1849, Constantine Osborne Perkins Papers, VHS; Coulter, *George Walton Williams*, 8–11; Heyrman, *Southern Cross*, 26.

59. Primitive Baptists like Hassell emphasized strong theological ties to John Calvin, particularly their views regarding God's sovereign power and predestination. Primitive Baptists also opposed the centralizing agencies and conventions found in many evangelical churches, including Baptist and Methodist; see Mathews, *Religion in the Old South*, 127–28. Hassell Diary, April 11, 1851, Cushing B. Hassell Papers, SHC. Cushing Hassell frequently denounced the Methodist church and its theology. Typical was his comment following a three-week Methodist revival in Hamilton, North Carolina, where he predicted that the participants would "to some extent quit getting drunk, gambling, swearing & the like for a few months at that place & then return to their vicious habits with renewed zeal"; see Hassell Diary, October 5, 1848, Cushing B. Hassell Papers, SHC. Joseph Biggs to Kader Biggs, December 11, 1848, Kader Biggs Papers, NCSA; Asa Runyon to Mary Burgess, February 12, 1851, Runyon Family Papers, FCHS.

60. Mary (Jacocks) Reed to Charles Jacocks, July 3, 1829, Jane B. Williams to Charles Jacocks, July 4, 1836, Charles W. Jacocks Papers, NCSA. For a discussion of family divisions caused by southern evangelical Protestantism, see Heyrman, *Southern Cross*, 129–30.

61. Howze Journal, March 12, 1857, Howze (Isham Robertson) and Family Papers, MDAH; Jefferson Diary, January 3, 1857, John F. Jefferson Papers, FCHS; Robert Stewart Hollins Sr. obituary, O'Bryan Family Collection, TSLA; George O'Bryan obituary, O'Bryan Family Collection, TSLA; William Henry

Wills to his wife, May 11, 1854, William Henry Wills Papers, SHC; Mathews, *Religion in the Old South*, 89–111; Heyrman, *Southern Cross*, 167–69, 178, 203–5; Friedman, *Enclosed Garden*, 113–18. For a comparison to the North, see Johnson, *Shopkeeper's Millennium*.

62. Greven, *Protestant Temperament*, 215; Mathews, *Religion in the Old South*, 62; C. E. Catonet to Beatrice Dunlap, June 29, 1832, Dunlap Correspondence, HTML; Hassell Diary, December 25, 1850, Cushing B. Hassell Papers, SHC; George O'Bryan obituary, O'Bryan Family Collection, TSLA; Howze Journal, March 19, 1857, Howze (Isham Robertson) and Family Papers, MDAH.

63. Howze Journal, August 11, 1850, Howze (Isham Robertson) and Family Papers, MDAH.

64. Richards Diary, October 17 and 24, 1860, Samuel P. Richards Papers, AHC. For an analysis of the contradictions between commercial trade and religious belief in American and European contexts, see Rose, *Victorian America and the Civil War*, 58; Schama, *Embarrassment of Riches*, 330–35.

65. The term "planter" refers to a landowning farmer of substantial means. The designation is usually applied to those owning twenty or more slaves.

66. Mintz, *Prison of Expectations*, 50–60; Rose, *Victorian America and the Civil War*, 41–47, 58; Lears, *No Place of Grace*, 35–40; Benedict Semmes to Jorantha Semmes, April 18, 1849, Benedict Joseph Semmes Papers, SHC; Wyatt-Brown, *Southern Honor*, 128–30; Lewis, *Pursuit of Happiness*, 51–67; Mathews, *Religion in the Old South*, 78; Eugene Genovese, "'Our Family, White and Black': Family and Household in the Southern Slaveholders' World View," in Bleser, ed., *In Joy and in Sorrow*, 72. My sample of 22 counties with a free population of 123,223 and a slave population of 89,748 showed that 188 out of 790 commercial workers owned slaves (total commercial household population 2,262). This 23.7 percent of the commercial population owned an average of approximately 8 slaves. In these 22 counties, commercial workers (storekeepers, grocers, factors, etc.) owned 2.3 percent of the slave population, while planters, farmers, and others owned approximately 98 percent of the slave population (see appendix, table 6).

67. Oakes, *Slavery and Freedom*, 92–93; Owsley, *Plain Folk of the Old South*, 8–16; Fox-Genovese and Genovese, *Fruits of Merchant Capital*, 37–40. Marc Egnal's study *Divergent Paths: How Culture and Institutions Have Shaped North American Growth* compares the development of the southern political economy with that of the northern United States and French Canada, 50–60. Oakes, *Ruling Race*, 51–67; Bardaglio, *Reconstructing the Household*, 36.

68. Hassell Journal, June 23, 1853, Hassell (Isham Robertson) and Family Papers, MDAH; Eugene Genovese, "'Our Family, White and Black': Family and Household in the Southern Slaveholders' World View," in Bleser, ed., *In Joy and in Sorrow*, 70–72; Wolfe, *Daughters of Canaan*, 77–80; McCurry, *Masters of Small Worlds*, 171–238; Rable, *Civil Wars*, 30–36.

69. Genovese, *World the Slaveholders Made*, 121; Hundley, *Social Relations in Our Southern States*, 136; Ruth Ingraham and Mary Leonard to Susan Fisher, November 24, 1839, March 29 and April 6, 1840, January 24, 1841, Susan Fisher Papers, SHC.

70. See appendix, table 6; Rawick, ed., *American Slave*, vol. 8, pt. 3, pp. 1203–6; Greb, "Charleston, South Carolina, Merchants," 28–30; Zuber, *Jonathan Worth*, 72. This is based on a small sample of twenty-five. The results do mirror those of Fred Bailey's analysis in Tennessee, which found that merchants owned a median of six slaves; see Bailey, *Class and Tennessee's Confederate Generation*, 32–33; D. Evans to James Evans, May 25, 1848, James Evans Papers, SHC; Hassell Diary, March 12, 1847, Cushing B. Hassell Papers, SHC; Edward Murphy to Josephine Cross, February 20, 1849, Murphy Family Papers, HNOC; Jefferson Diary, January 1, 1857, John F. Jefferson Papers, FCHS; L. F. (Biggs) to Kader Biggs, October 1, 1846, Kader Biggs Papers, NCSA; *Vicksburg Advocate & Register*, November 8, 1832; Oakes, *Ruling Race*, 171–73.

71. Genovese, *Roll, Jordan, Roll*, 3–7; Rawick, ed., *American Slave*, vol. 14, pt. 1, pp. 33–34, vol. 4, pt. 2, p. 435; Anna Wills to William Wills, May 1858, William Henry Wills Papers, SHC; Zuber, *Jonathan Worth*, 73–74; Hassell Diary, October 2, 1860, Cushing B. Hassell Papers, SHC.

72. Howze Journal, July 14, 1851, Howze (Isham Robertson) and Family Papers, MDAH. Of course many planters recognized the challenge of proper slave management as well. The planter Charles C. Jones wrote his son, who was completing his legal education: "I wish to make the impression upon you with the point of a diamond *that you never can succeed and attain to any eminence in your profession if you have anything at all to do with the management of Negro property. No man in any profession* within my knowledge ever has—and for the obvious reason that no man can succeed in either profession who follows *two*"; see Myers, ed., *Children of Pride*, 110 (Jones's emphasis). Stowe, *Intimacy and Power in the Old South*, xvii; Oakes, *Ruling Race*, 6–7, 27–34, 194–217; Jefferson Diary, April 23 and 25, 1857, John F. Jefferson Papers, FCHS; Howze Journal, January 25, 1854, Howze (Isham Robertson) and Family Papers, MDAH; Johnson, *Soul by Soul*, 25, 26–30.

73. Lockley, *Lines in the Sand*, 43, 76–77, 82–83; Hadden, *Slave Patrols*, 55–56; Lockley, *Lines in the Sand*, 77–78.

4. Secession, Merchant-Soldiers, and the Civil War, 1860–1863

1. Potter and Fehrenbacher, *Impending Crisis*, 442–50; Thornton, *Politics and Power in a Slave Society*, 343–461; Freehling, *Road to Disunion*, Vol. 1, *Secessionists at Bay*, 3–36; Walther, *Fire-Eaters*, 219.

2. Zuber, *Jonathan Worth*, 125; Wilson, *Confederate Industry*, 246; Hassell Diary, December 21, 1860, Cushing B. Hassell Papers, SHC; Coulter, *George Walton Williams*, 61–63; Clark, *Valleys of the Shadow*, 10.

3. Wilson, *Confederate Industry*, xxi; Morris, *Becoming Southern*, 177; Richards Diary, December 8, November 10 and 17, 1860, Samuel P. Richards Papers, AHC; Byrne, "Rebellion and Retail," 36–37.

4. *The Milledgeville Federal Union*, January 31, 1860.

5. Tripp, *Yankee Town, Southern City*, 86; Doyle, *New Men, New Cities*, 65; John R. Turner to Sallie (Turner), September 14, 1860, John R. Turner Papers, PL; Hassell Diary, February 11, 1861, Cushing B. Hassell Papers, SHC; Jefferson Diary, September 6, October 24, 1860, John F. Jefferson Papers, FCHS.

6. Webber Diary, January 6, 1861, Thomas B. Webber Diary, PL. Despite his clear commitment to the southern cause, on occasion Webber's diary continued to reveal some annoyance with political extremism in his community. On a Sunday in January 1861, Webber noted frustration with his minister: "It is seldom of late that I attend church because I have but little confidence in what I hear preached. Sectarianism *not Religion* is the Song" (Webber's emphasis). That same Webber and several other men began organizing a cavalry company in their community. Two months later Webber joined the Jeff Davis Rifles; see Webber Diary, January 20, 1861.

7. Richards Diary, January 19, 1861, Samuel P. Richards Papers, AHC; McPherson, *Battle Cry of Freedom*, 234–40.

8. Richards Diary, April 13, 1861, Samuel P. Richards Papers, AHC; Carney Diary, April 28, 1861, Kate S. Carney Diary, SHC; Richard Henry Wills to William Henry Wills, April 18, 1861, William Henry Wills Papers, SHC; Grannis Diary, April 13, 17, and 18, May 13, 1861, Robert A. Grannis Diary, VHS.

9. D. H. Baldwin to William Baldwin, November 30, 1860, April 21, 1861, Daniel Hoard Baldwin Letters, SHC; Jacob L. Florance to Abraham Minis Jr., undated, Minis Family Papers, GHS.

10. Marcus, ed., *Memoirs of American Jews*, vol. 3, 116. For an account of regional business depression attributed to the secession crisis, see Williams, *Rich Man's War*, 50–52. Webber Diary, March 18, 1861, Thomas B. Webber Diary, PL; Hassell Diary, April 22, 1861, Cushing B. Hassell Papers, SHC.

11. Jones, *Rebel War Clerk's Diary*, 10.

12. Louisiana, vol. 6, p. 176, R. G. Dun & Company Reports, HGSB. Eugene Petetin, a Frenchman who lived in Grand Coteau, likewise continued to receive a strong credit rating long after Louisiana had joined the Confederacy; see Louisiana, vol. 20, p. 7, R. G. Dun & Company Reports, HGSB. Corsan, *Two Months in the Confederate States*, 14–15, 54, 64–65. In my own informal examination of more than a hundred credit reports submitted during late 1860

through 1861, I did not find a single instance where a firm repudiated a loan to a northern creditor for political or legal reasons.

13. Webber Diary, January 3, 1861, Thomas B. Webber Diary, PL; *Confederate States v. O. S. Baldwin*, November 15, 1861(?), "Confederate Papers of the U.S. District Court for the Eastern District of North Carolina, 1861–1865," M346, Roll 1, National Archives 2, College Park, Maryland. Unlike most cases in this document, no mention is made of Biggs's judgment. The imposition of the Sequestration Act seems often to have been a complicated matter, particularly when a firm's partners lived in separate states. For example, in *Confederate States v. B. F. Grady* the defendant, a North Carolina resident, claimed he should not be forced to have any of his funds sequestered, because it was his partner, Daniel D. Orrell, not he, who had abandoned the Confederacy. Orrell had remained in New York City where their antebellum firm Orrell & Grady had opened a branch store in 1860. Apparently Orrell had sold their remaining stock on "favorable terms" and had become a "supporter of the enemy." Grady wanted the court to assist him in getting his share back plus interest. Ultimately the court decided to appoint Grady the receiver for the firm, allowing him to collect the firm's debts in the South—some eight thousand dollars. Notably absent from the court record is any discussion of the possibility that Grady and Orrell may never have severed their business connections and had in fact agreed to supervise their respective stores in New York City and Martin County, North Carolina, for the duration of the war. Such unpatriotic operations were not typical, yet as the Root example reveals, had precedent. See *Confederate States v. B. F. Grady*, 18 December 18(?), "Confederate Papers of the U.S. District Court for the Eastern District of North Carolina, 1861–1865," M346.

14. Of course the cotton trade continued to be one of the most significant areas where small storekeepers and particularly larger merchant factors had economic ties with northern firms. Because of the large volume of trade in 1860 and intermittently throughout the war, it was in this trade that southern factors frequently attempted to avoid paying northern loans. When the war ended, Southerners owed northern merchants $150 million; see Woodman, *King Cotton & His Retainers*, 205–10. Sidney Root, "Memorandum of My Life, 1893," Sidney Root Papers, AHC; McElreath, "Sidney Root: Merchant Prince and Great Citizen," 174; Byrne, "Rebellion and Retail," 32–33.

15. Biographical cover sheet, John Adriance Papers, CAH. The description "perfect Yankee Sharper," made in 1853, was intended, in this instance, as a compliment; see Texas, vol. 4, p. 140G, R. G. Dun & Company Papers, HGSB. O'Bryan obituary, O'Bryan Family Collection, TSLA; biographical cover sheet, Kader Biggs Papers, NCSA; Escott, *Many Excellent People*, 55–56; Mallett biography, Peter Mallett Papers, SHC; Cooper, *Official History of Fulton County*, 94–99; Byrne, "Rebellion and Retail," 37; McCallum, *Martin County During the Civil War*, 11–13.

246 Notes to Pages 132–136

16. Rable, *Civil Wars*, 50–51, 57, 227, 268; Cashin, ed., *Our Common Affairs*, 22; Faust, *Mothers of Invention*, 83–93, 185; Whites, *Civil War as a Crisis in Gender*, 48–54; Wolfe, *Daughters of Canaan*, 90–94; Burton, *In My Father's House*, 136; Friedman, *Enclosed Garden*, 92–96; Clinton, *Other Civil War*, 89. These and other studies suggest that the collapse of traditional gender roles during the Civil War tended to be temporary; see also Rose, *Victorian America and the Civil War*, 188–89.

17. Edwards, *Scarlett Doesn't Live Here Anymore*, 66–99; Whites, *Civil War as a Crisis in Gender*, 265 (n. 26), 50–52, 57–59, 70–71, 84–86, 90–92; Williams, *Rich Man's War*, 75; Wolfe, *Daughters of Canaan*, 89; Faust, *Mothers of Invention*, 64, 24–25, 95–98, 211; Friedman, *Enclosed Garden*, 104–8. In many respects the early wartime experience of women from commercial families, before Federal forces occupied much of the South, paralleled that of middle-class northern women; see, Jeanie Attie, "Warwork and the Crisis of Domesticity in the North," in Clinton and Silber, eds., *Divided Houses*, 247–260.

18. Coulter, *George Walton Williams*, 8–11, 76–80; Hassell Diary, December 23, 1861, Cushing B. Hassell Papers, SHC; Oglethorpe Light Infantry Testimonial, September 26, 1861, Minis Family Papers, GHS; *Milledgeville Federal Union* (the *Southern Federal Union* after Georgia seceded), January 8, 1861.

19. Bailey, *Class and Tennessee's Confederate Generation*, 79–82; Durrill, *War of Another Kind*, 36–37; Mallett biography, Peter Mallett Papers, SHC; Atherton, "Problem of Credit Rating in the Ante-Bellum South," 546; U.S. War Department, *War of the Rebellion*, ser. 1, vol. 18, pp. 115–16; ser. 1, vol. 29, pt. 2, p. 660. On the question of commercial men in the military, Don Doyle has found that "not many" of the leading men in either Atlanta or Nashville served in the Confederate army. He found that only twelve Atlanta and nine Nashville businessmen from the ranks of the elite joined the Confederate army while a handful actually served in the Union army. Doyle argues convincingly that "strong pro-Union sentiments and publicly expressed doubts about the wisdom of secession" shaped this response; see Doyle, *New Men, New Cities*, 89.

20. Hassell Diary, November 6, 1861, Cushing B. Hassell Papers, SHC; Edward Murphy to W. H. Renaud, October 14, 1861, J. I. Adams to James C. Murphy, February 22, 1864, Murphy Family Papers, HNOC; Louisiana, vol. 6, p. 176, R. G. Dun & Company Reports, HGSB; Wiley, *Life of Johnny Reb*, 330; Marcus, ed., *Memoirs of American Jews*, vol. 3, 116. Because the occupational title "clerk" subsumed many kinds of business, clerical, and governmental positions, undoubtedly men describing themselves as "clerks" on the company rolls included many individuals outside the mercantile profession. Not surprisingly, more than half of the enlistees, some fifty-six hundred, listed themselves as farmers.

21. Charles C. Blacknall to Oscar Blacknall, March 23, 1862, Oscar W. Blacknall Papers, NCSA; U.S. War Department, *War of the Rebellion*, ser. 1, vol.

51, p. 40; Wilson, *Confederate Soldier*, 193–6; Rable, *Civil Wars*, 54; Webber Diary, February 2, 1861, Thomas B. Webber Diary, PL.

22. Hale, *Third Texas Cavalry in the Civil War*, 5, 42; Rawick, *American Slave*, supp. 2, vol. 2, pt. 1, pp. 227–28; Baum, *Shattering of Texas Unionism*, 216, 284; Crocket, *Two Centuries in East Texas*, 218.

23. Wiley, *Life of Johnny Reb*, 347; Mitchell, *Civil War Soldiers*, 57–66.

24. Leon, *Diary of a Tar Heel Confederate Soldier*, 2; Webber Diary, October 2, 1861, Thomas B. Webber Diary, PL; Wiley, *Life of Johnny Reb*, 201–7; Marcus, ed., *Memoirs of American Jews*, vol. 3, 116; Benedict Semmes to Jorantha Semmes, December 7, 1862, Benedict Joseph Semmes Papers, SHC. Semmes's personal assessment of the morale of the Army of Tennessee stands in marked contrast to the accepted historical interpretation, which ties the deteriorating Confederate military situation in the west during 1862 to a significant crisis of morale in the Army of Tennessee; see Daniel, *Soldiering in the Army of Tennessee*, 127–47; Hattaway, *Shades of Blue and Gray*, 68–73.

25. Edward Murphy to W. H. Renaud, July 18, 1861, Murphy Family Papers, HNOC; Sutherland, *Seasons of War*, 134–51.

26. Mitchell, *Civil War Soldiers*, 75–78; Bruce, *Violence and Culture in the Antebellum South*, 166; Charles C. Blacknall to Caroline Howell Blacknall, May 26, 1862, Oscar W. Blacknall Papers, NCSA. Studies that offer an enlightening discussion of the mindsets and behavior of soldiers during the Civil War include: McPherson, *For Cause and Comrades*; Mitchell, *Vacant Chair*, 11–12, 28–35; Robertson, *Soldiers Blue and Gray*; Linderman, *Embattled Courage*; and of course Bell Irvin Wiley's two classic studies *The Life of Johnny Reb* (1943) and *The Life of Billy Yank* (1952).

27. Gallagher, *Confederate War*, 28–29.

28. Howze Journal, October 10, 1853, Howze (Isham Robertson) and Family Papers, MDAH; Wilson, *Confederate Soldier*, 193 (n. 1), 196 (n. 2), 206 (n. 3); Hattaway, *Shades of Blue and Gray*, 87–90. On the place of religion in the Confederate army, see McPherson, *For Cause and Comrades*, 73–76; Mitchell, *Civil War Soldiers*, 173–75.

29. Benedict Semmes to Jorantha Semmes, July 16, 1863, Benedict Joseph Semmes Papers, SHC; Clark, *Valleys of the Shadow*, 25.

30. Confederate States of America War Department, *Regulations, 1863*, 97; Bartholomees, *Buff Facings and Gilt Buttons*, 42–80; Bird, *Granite Farm Letters*, 140; Wilson, *Confederate Industry*, 8–9.

31. Wilson, *Confederate Industry*, 9–10, 22, 28–29, 99–100; Confederate order, December 1, 1864, John Zirvas Leyendecker Papers, CAH; Semmes Military Correspondence, September 30, 1863, Semmes Family Papers, TSLA; Order from Adjutant and Inspector General's Office to George O'Bryan, May 5, 1864, George O'Bryan obituary, 1912, O'Bryan Family Collection, TSLA.

32. John R. Turner to Sallie (Turner), December 1, 1861, January 26, 1862, April 4 and May 19, 1863, John R. Turner Papers, PL.

5. Merchants and Their Families in the Confederacy, 1861–1863

1. Beckert, *Monied Metropolis*, 124–27; Chernow, *Titan*, 69, 65–72; Coleberd, "John Williams: A Merchant Banker in Springfield, Illinois," 265.

2. John R. Turner to Sallie (Turner), January 26, 1862, John R. Turner Papers, PL; McPherson, *Battle Cry of Freedom*, 428–32, 603; Moore, *Conscription and Conflict in the Confederacy*, 13–16, 34–35. The Second Conscription Act, which raised the age for conscription to forty-five, passed on September 17, 1862. The Confederacy outlawed substitution entirely in December 1863 and made those individuals who had previously bought substitutes liable to conscription.

3. Richards Diary, September 24 and February 28, 1862, Samuel P. Richards Papers, AHC; Linderman, *Embattled Courage*, 87–88; *Montgomery Daily Advertiser*, May 5, 1864; Whites, *Civil War as a Crisis in Gender*, 67. Despite the obvious reluctance of many merchants to join the Confederate army, it must be remembered that most merchants, like most southern white men, enlisted and served in the war; see T. Lloyd Benson, "The Plain Folk of Orange: Land, Work, and Society on the Eve of the Civil War," in Ayers and Willis, eds., *Edge of the South*, 73–74.

4. Hassell Diary, February 24, 1864, Cushing B. Hassell Papers, SHC; McCallum, *Martin County During the Civil War*, 18; Marcus, ed., *Memoirs of American Jews*, vol. 3, 125; Zuber, *Jonathan Worth*, 173–74; Coulter, *George Walton Williams*, 64; G. W. McGee Papers, October 13, 1862, KHS. It seems many merchants had contracts with the Confederate Nitre and Mining Bureau; see the Texas merchant John Twohig's contracts of December 1863 and February 6, 1864, John Twohig Papers, CAH. Bart DeWitt to John Zirvas Leyendecker, January 10, 1864, John Zirvas Leyendecker Papers, CAH. For a list of jobs that were exempted from conscription by the Confederate government, see Moore, *Conscription and Conflict in the Confederacy*, 53–83, 122; Rable, *Civil Wars*, 76. By October of 1864 the state of Alabama had issued 4,497 exemptions to men suffering physical disabilities. This totaled nearly four times the number of exemptions for state officers (1,164); see the *Montgomery Daily Advertiser*, October 28, 1864. Ernest B. Furgurson provides a description of the demand for medical exemptions in wartime Richmond in *Ashes of Glory*, 124–25. Like David Worth, many storekeepers employed multiple strategies to evade conscription. James Thomas Butler owned a store and a farm in northern Virginia. When the substitute he purchased in 1862 no longer excused him from service in 1863, Confederate authorities ordered him to report for duty at Camp Lee in

Richmond. Butler successfully regained his exempt status by contracting with the government to supply tents to the same Confederate army that he worked so hard to avoid serving in. The exemption remained in effect until Butler fulfilled the terms of the contract; see Butler Diary, October 26, 1862, September 1863, James Thomas Butler Diary, VHS.

5. Richards Diary, August 10, 1861, November 19, 1862, March 4, August 8, and December 31, 1863, Samuel P. Richards Papers, AHC; Moore, *Conscription and Conflict in the Confederacy*, 53–57, 65–66, 73–83; Byrne, "Rebellion and Retail," 48–51.

6. *Montgomery Daily Advertiser and Register*, October 1, 1864; Holmes, *Diary of Miss Emma Holmes*, 257; Richards Diary, February 24, October 30, and November 23, 1861, March 8, 1862, Samuel P. Richards Papers, AHC; Dyer, *Secret Yankees*, 81; Hassell Diary, May 8, 1861, September 18, 1862, Cushing B. Hassell Papers, SHC.

7. Richards Diary, September 1 and 7, 1861, Samuel P. Richards Papers, AHC; Carney Diary, May 7, 27, 28, and June 15, 1862, Kate S. Carney Diary, SHC.

8. Confederate Papers Relating to Citizens or Business Firms, M346, Roll 419, May 7, October 24, and December 7, 1861, January 25, 1862, National Archives, Washington, D.C.; Hassell Diary, July 14 and 31, 1862, Cushing B. Hassell Papers, SHC.

9. Hassell Diary, July 14 and 31, November 4, 1862, November 12, 1864, Cushing B. Hassell Papers, SHC; Butler Diary, May 21 and 24, 1864, James Thomas Butler Diary, VHS.

10. Coulter, *George Walton Williams*, 66; Jones, *Rebel War Clerk's Diary*, 152, 322; Furgurson, *Ashes of Glory*, 191; Solomon, *Civil War Diary of Clara Solomon*, 81.

11. Bart DeWitt to John Zirvas Leyendecker, February 13, 1862, John Zirvas Leyendecker Papers, CAH.

12. Rable, *Civil Wars*, 95–96; Williams, *Rich Man's War*, 79–80; Blair, *Virginia's Private War*, 85–87, 109.

13. Jorantha Semmes to Benedict Semmes, June 13, 1862, Benedict Joseph Semmes Papers, SHC; Solomon, *Civil War Diary of Clara Solomon*, 255, 363.

14. Bryant, *How Curious a Land*, 74; Solomon, *Civil War Diary of Clara Solomon*, 81, 306–7; Richards Diary, July 27, 1862, October 13, 1863, Samuel P. Richards Papers, AHC; *Wilmington Daily Journal*, October 21, 1863; *Memphis Daily Appeal* (Jackson, Miss.), February 7, 1863. For an analysis of the clash between commercial capitalist and conservative agrarian values in southern society, see Tripp, *Yankee Town, Southern City*, 38–40. For a discussion of changing women's fashions in the Confederacy, see Faust, *Mothers of Invention*, 223–25.

15. Rable, *Civil Wars*, 70–72, 145; Rose, *Victorian America and the Civil War*, 19, 59; Hundley, *Social Relations in Our Southern States*, 100; Faust, *Mothers*

of Invention, 96–97, 181–85; Coulter, *George Walton Williams*, 76; Whites, *Civil War as a Crisis in Gender*, 57–59; Jorantha Semmes correspondence and receipts, 1862–1865, Benedict Joseph Semmes Papers, SHC; Lebsock, *Free Women of Petersburg*, 195–236.

16. Burton, *In My Father's House*, 135–38; Whites, *Civil War as a Crisis in Gender*, 45–55.

17. Whites, *Civil War as a Crisis in Gender*, 33.

18. Hassell Diary, November 15, 1862, Cushing B. Hassell Papers, SHC.

19. Solomon, *Civil War Diary of Clara Solomon*, 42; Rable, *Civil Wars*, 106. See Faust, "Altars of Sacrifice"; Faust, *Mothers of Invention*, 42, 56–61, 70; Fox-Genovese, *Within the Plantation Household*; Clinton, *Plantation Mistress*; Lebsock, *Free Women of Petersburg*.

20. *Augusta Daily Chronicle & Sentinel*, July 26, 1861.

21. Charles C. Blacknall to George Blacknall, September 14, 1861, Oscar W. Blacknall Papers, NCSA.

22. Charles C. Blacknall to Jinny (sometimes spelled Jinnie) Blacknall, January 5, 1862, Oscar W. Blacknall Papers, NCSA.

23. Charles C. Blacknall to Jinny Blacknall, April 3, 1863, Oscar W. Blacknall Papers, NCSA.

24. Benedict Semmes to Jorantha Semmes, September 1 and 4, 1859, Benedict Joseph Semmes Papers, SHC.

25. Jorantha Semmes to Benedict Semmes, March 6, 1862; Benedict to Jorantha, April 2, 1862; Jorantha to her mother, May 30, 1862; Benedict Joseph Semmes Papers, SHC.

26. Jorantha Semmes to her mother, May 30, 1862; Jorantha Semmes to Benedict Semmes, June 13 and 21, 1862; Benedict Joseph Semmes Papers, SHC; McPherson, *Battle Cry of Freedom*, 418–21, 620–23. For a revealing description of smuggling and its economic impact on white Southerners and of invading Federals in Georgia, see Williams, *Rich Man's War*, 102.

27. Benedict Semmes to Jorantha Semmes, July 17, 1864, Benedict Joseph Semmes Papers, SHC.

28. Jorantha Semmes to Benedict Semmes, July 15 and 20, 1863, January 23, 1865, Benedict Joseph Semmes Papers, SHC.

29. Marten, *Children's Civil War*, 58.

30. Hassell Diary, introduction, Cushing B. Hassell Papers, SHC.

31. Hassell Diary, July 17, 1861, Cushing B. Hassell Papers, SHC; Manuscript Census, Martin County, North Carolina, 1850.

32. Charles C. Blacknall to Jinny Blacknall, January 18 and October 28, 1863, Oscar W. Blacknall Papers, NCSA; U.S. War Department, *War of the Rebellion*, ser. 1, vol. 25, p. 947; ser. 1, vol. 29, p. 399. Blacknall was exchanged in March 1864; he returned to duty where he was promoted to the rank of colo-

nel and served at least for a time commanding the Twenty-third North Carolina. Planters also expressed concern about the status of their children's education. James B. Griffin, an officer in Wade Hampton's Legion and the South Carolina Reserves, directed his son Willie to be "diligent and studious" or "go to work" in the fields; see McArthur and Burton, *Gentleman and an Officer*, 151, 301–3.

33. Newman, *Maryland Semmes and Kindred Families*, 82; Benedict Semmes biographical information, Semmes Family Papers, TSLA; Jorantha Semmes to Benedict Semmes, March 6, 1862, February 2, 1864, Benedict Joseph Semmes Papers, SHC.

34. Benedict Semmes to Jorantha Semmes, August 21, 1864, Benedict Joseph Semmes Papers, SHC.

35. Hassell Diary, May 12, 1862, Cushing B. Hassell Papers, SHC; Richard Henry Wills to William Henry Wills, May 19, 1862, William Henry Wills Papers, SHC; Richards Diary, July 11, 1862, December 5, 1863, Samuel P. Richards Papers, AHC.

36. Hassell Diary, December 10, 1862, Cushing B. Hassell Papers, SHC.

37. Wilson, *Confederate Soldier*, 119, 207; Martin, *Gettysburg, July 1*, 61, 124–25; McPherson, *Battle Cry of Freedom*, 654–63; Hattaway, *Shades of Blue and Gray*, 143.

38. Wilson, *Confederate Soldier*, 119, 207.

39. Williams, *Rich Man's War*, 160; Solomon, *Civil War Diary of Clara Solomon*, 298–99, 355; Richards Diary, December 13, 1863, Samuel P. Richards Papers, AHC; see also Faust, *Mothers of Invention*, 56–61, 70.

40. Williams, *Rich Man's War*, 151; Fremantle, *Three Months in the Southern States*, 179; McPherson, *For Cause and Comrades*, 108; Coulter, *George Walton Williams*, 75.

41. Richards Diary, July 27, 1862, May 2 and 16, 1863, Samuel P. Richards Papers, AHC; Hassell Diary, October 1, 1862, Cushing B. Hassell Papers, SHC; Richard Wills slave rental contract, February 27, 1863, William Henry Wills Papers, SHC.

42. Richards Diary, March 20, 1861, Samuel P. Richards Papers, AHC; Hassell Diary, September 20, 1861, Cushing B. Hassell Papers, SHC; Furgurson, *Ashes of Glory*, 45; Sutherland, *Seasons of War*, 47; Charles C. Blacknall to George Blacknall, September 14, 1861, Oscar W. Blacknall Papers, NCSA; Thomas Jefferson, Kentucky, vol. 24, p. 177, Edward Murphy, Louisiana, vol. 6, p. 176, R. G. Dun & Company Reports, HGSB.

43. Sutherland, *Seasons of War*, 89; Jorantha Semmes to Mary Ann Jordan, May 30, 1862, Benedict Joseph Semmes Papers, SHC; Corsan, *Two Months in the Confederate States*, 53.

44. Williams, *Rich Man's War*, 67; Confederate Papers Relating to Citizens or Business Firms, M346, Roll 64, October 7, 1861, December and March 1864;

Roll 69, October 24, 1862; Roll 153, July 30, 1862, October 30, 1863, March 15 and 31, 1864; Roll 045, April 28, May 17, June 16, and September 6, 1862, August 1, 1863; National Archives, Washington, D.C.

45. Corsan, *Two Months in the Confederate States*, 53; Wilson, *Confederate Industry*, 47–48; Jones, *Rebel War Clerk's Diary*, 99, 159; Holmes, *Diary of Miss Emma Holmes*, 257.

46. Marcus, ed., *Memoirs of American Jews*, vol. 3, 115, 117–18.

47. Thornton, "Mrs. S. P. Richards," 77–78; Richards Diary, May 24, 1862, November 3, 1861, February 23, 1863, February 8 and 22, 1862, January 4, 1864, Samuel P. Richards Papers, AHC; Byrne, "Rebellion and Retail," 45; Myers, ed., *Children of Pride*, 937–38.

48. Holmes, *Diary of Miss Emma Holmes*, 194.

49. Edward Murphy to W. H. Renaud, October 22, 1861, Murphy Family Papers, HNOC; Richards Diary, September 14, 1861, Samuel P. Richards Papers, AHC; Sutherland, *Seasons of War*, 77; Dimond and Hattaway, eds., *Letters from Forest Place*, 273; Francis Levert to R. W. Patton, March 8, 1862, Levert Family Papers, SHC; Zuber, *Jonathan Worth*, 273.

50. Coulter, *George Walton Williams*, 66; McPherson, *Battle Cry of Freedom*, 313–14, 380–82.

51. McPherson, *Battle Cry of Freedom*, 378–80; Woodman, *King Cotton & His Retainers*, 218; *Charleston Mercury*, March 17, 1862; Dyer, *Secret Yankees*, 118; Coulter, *George Walton Williams*, 75; Shingleton, *Richard Peters*, 96–97.

52. Myers, ed., *Children of Pride*, 1134.

53. Sidney Root, "Memorandum of My Life, 1893," 18, Sidney Root Papers, AHC.

6. The Merchant Family and the Fall of the Confederacy, 1864–1865

1. Dyer, *Secret Yankees*, 98, 101; Webber Diary, April 2, 1861, Thomas B. Webber Diary, PL; Corsan, *Two Months in the Confederate States*, 61–62; Doerflinger, *Vigorous Spirit of Enterprise*, 197; DeCredico, *Patriotism for Profit*, 41. Of course merchants were not the only class of Southerners who speculated in goods during the Civil War. Historian Steven Elliott Tripp finds that in wartime Lynchburg, Virginia, "speculating became an especially popular sideline for virtually all citizens of property." Merchants, however, had more free capital and thus were disproportionately involved in the practice. See Tripp, *Yankee Town, Southern City*, 134.

2. Sidney Root, "Memorandum of My Life, 1893," Sidney Root Papers, AHC; Williams, *Rich Man's War*, 86–87; *Raleigh Weekly Conservative*, October 26, 1864; Richards Diary, February 23 and March 21, 1863, January 4, 1864, Samuel P. Richards Papers, AHC.

3. Richards Diary, June 27 and November 28, 1863, Samuel P. Richards Papers, AHC; Williams, *Rich Man's War*, 83–84; DeCredico, *Patriotism for Profit*, 50.

4. Burke Diary, May 7, 1863, William Floyd Burke Diary, VHS; Coulter, *George Walton Williams*, 71–73; Sidney Root, "Memorandum of My Life, 1893," AHC; Richards Diary, May 16 and 24, 1862, March 21 and April 20, 1863, March 19, 1864, Samuel P. Richards Papers, AHC.

5. Like most southern merchants during the antebellum period, James Butler changed partners fairly often, thus the name and make-up of his antebellum firms appeared in various forms: Butler & Tinsley, James T. Butler and Brother, and so forth; see Virginia, vol. 43, p. 73, R. G. Dun & Company Reports, HGSB; Butler Diary, 1861, February and October 1862, January 22, 1863, James Thomas Butler Diary, VHS; Tripp, *Yankee Town, Southern City*, 135–36.

6. Clark, *Valleys of the Shadow*, xxii–xxvi.

7. Clark, *Valleys of the Shadow*, 56–58, 79–81. No confidant determination can be made of how many merchants conducted private business while in Confederate service. Anecdotal evidence suggests that a fair number of businessmen who had positions in various quartermasters' departments engaged in personal trade on the side. For example in 1863, Philip Whitlock, a private in the Richmond Grays, purchased a tobacco shop in Richmond while still holding his quartermaster job. He and his wife ran the store for the rest of the war; see Furgurson, *Ashes of Glory*, 185; Charles Blacknall to George Blacknall, March 23, 1862, Oscar W. Blacknall Papers, NCSA.

8. Charles Rogers & Company purchase orders, February 9, 1862–January 30, 1863, John William Bradbury Papers, VHS. Storing cotton during the war cost a considerable amount over time. Bradbury and his partners paid Rogers & Company $322.11 for storing almost seventy bales of cotton in late 1863. Bradbury lost much of this investment months later when Union forces under the command of General William T. Sherman confiscated or destroyed the cotton held by Rogers & Company. Zuber, *Jonathan Worth*, 130, 168; Woodman, *King Cotton & His Retainers*, 212–15; Petetin affidavits, May–October 1863, Petetin Family Papers, HNOC.

9. By 1864 merchants hastened to sell their Treasury notes and Confederate bonds for what they could get. See William Wills to Richard Wills, February 26, 1864, William Henry Wills Papers, SHC; Richards Diary, March 1862, April 20, 1863, Samuel P. Richards Papers, AHC; Hassell Diary, February 1, 1864, Cushing B. Hassell Papers, SHC. For a description of the counterfeiting of Confederate Treasury notes, see the *Mobile Advertiser & Register*, September 12, 1862.

10. McPherson, *For Cause and Comrades*, 108; Crofts, ed., *Cobb's Ordeal*, xiii; Hassell Diary, October 1, 1862, February 3 and March 20, 1865, Cushing

B. Hassell Papers, SHC; Charles Blacknall to George Blacknall, March 23, 1862, Oscar W. Blacknall Papers, NCSA. For further discussion of the slave trade between members of the planter class during the war, see Sutherland, *Seasons of War*, 210.

11. Richards Diary, July 27, 1862, May 2 and December 13, 1863, September 9, 1864, Samuel P. Richards Papers, AHC.

12. McPherson, *Ordeal by Fire*, 199–200; DeCredico, *Patriotism for Profit*, 63; Hassell Diary, March 10, 1864, Cushing B. Hassell Papers, SHC; Rable, *Civil Wars*, 103; Mitchell, *Civil War Soldiers*, 164; Richards Diary, December 25, 1863, January 4, 1864, Samuel P. Richards Papers, AHC; *Augusta Constitutionalist*, August 6, 1864.

13. Royster, *Destructive War*, 183; *Galveston Weekly News*, July 9, 1863.

14. Whites, *Civil War as a Crisis in Gender*, 65–66; Genovese, *Consuming Fire*, 47.

15. *Wilmington Daily Journal*, July 31, 1862; Richards Diary, July 28, 1861, Samuel P. Richards Papers, AHC. See also Tripp, *Yankee Town, Southern City*, 134. Accusations of speculations and Unionist sympathy could place a merchant in a dangerous position. Neighbors accused the Atlanta dry-goods merchant Michael Myers of Unionist leanings for contributing money toward the relief of Federal prisoners and, in particular, for refusing to accept Confederate money in his store. Myers eventually issued a public statement confirming his loyalty to the Confederacy and maintaining that he owned ten thousand dollars in Treasury notes. This appeased many of his critics, but Myers remained obnoxious in the eyes of some southern patriots in Atlanta; see Dyer, *Secret Yankees*, 103.

16. *Montgomery Daily Advertiser & Register*, September 23, 1863.

17. *Montgomery Daily Advertiser & Register*, April 1, 1863; *Savannah Republican*, June 29, 1863; *Wilmington Daily Journal*, August 31, 1863; *Milledgeville Federal Union*, October 8, 1861; Clinton, *Tara Revisited*, 152–53. See also Tripp, *Yankee Town, Southern City*, 119. The childhood experience of Lucy Hall Baldwin illustrated how inflation could affect relationships within families. On one occasion in the fall of 1864, when the young girl wondered aloud what she would do with a hundred dollars, her frustrated father handed her a hundred-dollar Confederate bill and exclaimed, "There! Take it down the street and see if you can buy a stick of candy"; see Marten, *Children's Civil War*, 114. For an excellent discussion of the Confederacy's poor transportation network, poor economic policies, and their combined impact on shortages in the South, see Ball, *Financial Failure and Confederate Defeat*, 19–25.

18. *Mobile Advertiser & Register*, November 15 and December 12, 1862; *Southern Watchman*, April 30, 1862; Furgurson, *Ashes of Glory*, 191–92; Holmes, *Diary of Miss Emma Holmes*, 192; Jones, *Rebel War Clerk's Diary*, 45–46, 51–52. Don Doyle found that high prices and shortages in Mobile, Alabama, were

blamed on "foreign merchants"—the city's German Jewish businessmen; see Doyle, *New Men, New Cities*, 66. For a general treatment of this subject, see McPherson, *Battle Cry of Freedom*, 440–42.

19. For a classic discussion of crowd/mob activity, see Thompson, *Customs in Common*, 185–351.

20. Bryant, *How Curious a Land*, 72; *Weekly Columbus Enquirer*, April 21, 1863; *Wilmington Daily Journal*, October 4, 1862; *Memphis Daily Appeal* (Jackson, Miss.), April 15, 1863. The same edition of the *Daily Appeal* described the Columbus riot as well. Employing the same gendered language as he used in his description of the Richmond riot, the editor described how sixty-five "viragoes," armed with pistols and knives and led by a man known as Shanghai Brooks, robbed several stores. The editor concluded that much of the trouble was a natural result of Georgia Governor Joseph Brown's misguided impressment policy. Wilmington's being an entrepôt for blockade-runners until the last months of the war, the editor of the city's newspaper devoted much ink to lambasting the transgressions of several merchants. He singled out the Atlanta merchant Sidney Root and his blockade-runner *Kate* for special mention when it apparently carried yellow fever from an infected West Indian port to Wilmington; see the *Wilmington Daily Journal*, October 3, 1862; Jones, *Rebel War Clerk's Diary*, 104; Williams, *Rich Man's War*, 115; Furguson, *Ashes of Glory*, 194, 327; *Raleigh Weekly Conservative*, May 4, 1864; Rable, *Civil Wars*, 110.

21. Coulter, *George Walton Williams*, 71; Whites, *Civil War as a Crisis in Gender*, 68; *Wilmington Daily Journal*, July 29, 1862; Rogers, *Confederate Home Front*, 131–32; *Montgomery Daily Advertiser*, June 14, 1864, April 18, 1865.

22. Jacob L. Florance to Abraham Minis Jr., 1861, Minis Family Papers, GHS; Usher Bonney to Sue (Bonney?), July 19, 1863, Eli Whitney Bonney Papers, PL.

23. Leon, *Diary of a Confederate Soldier*, 36, 59; Letter to Fannie Aiton, March 6, 1864, Thomas Aiton Papers, SCL; Butler Diary, May 21, 1864, James Thomas Butler Diary, VHS.

24. McPherson, *Battle Cry of Freedom*, 802; Charles Blacknall to Jinny Blacknall, October 10, 1863, Oscar W. Blacknall Papers, NCSA; Leon, *Diary of a Confederate Soldier*, 63, 69–70; Clark, *Valleys of the Shadow*, 53–54.

25. Blacknall memoirs and introductory material, Oscar W. Blacknall Papers, NCSA; John Davis to William Henry Wills, September 20 and 29, 1864, William Henry Wills Papers, SHC; Clark, *Valleys of the Shadow*, 69–70; Howze biographical and introductory material, Howze (Isham Robertson) and Family Papers, MDAH; Hassell Diary, March 9, 1864, Cushing B. Hassell Papers, SHC.

26. Hundley Journal, January 25 and February 22, 1864, Daniel Hundley Papers, SHC.

27. Sidney Root, "Memorandum of My Life, 1893," 18–19, Sidney Root

Papers, AHC; Richards Diary, September 2, 1864, Samuel P. Richards Papers, AHC.

28. Benedict Semmes to Jorantha Semmes, June 7, 1863, Benedict Joseph Semmes Papers, SHC; Rawick, ed., *American Slave*, vol. 14, pt. 1, pp. 35–36; Hassell Diary, February 28, 1865, Cushing B. Hassell Papers, SHC; Eli Bonney to Messrs Converse, Harding, & Co., November 27, 1865, Eli Whitney Bonney Papers, PL. For an analysis of master-slave paternalism and its transformation during the war, see Genovese, *Roll, Jordan, Roll* and Mohr, *On the Threshold of Freedom*.

29. Doyle, *New Men, New Cities*, 25–30; Wilson, *Confederate Industry*, 244–45.

30. Thomas M. Hogan, Muscogee County, Georgia, claim 20779, "Settled Case Files for Claims Approved by the Southern Claims Commission, 1871–1880," RG 217, Records of the Accounting Officers of the Treasury Department, entry 732, National Archives, Washington, D.C.

31. Nancy Cherry, Martin County, North Carolina, claim 11449, "Settled Case Files for Claims Approved by the Southern Claims Commission, 1871–1880," National Archives, Washington, D.C.

32. Loyalty certificate, Jean Baptiste Bres to his father, July 2, 1864, Bres Family Papers, HTML; Coulter, *George Walton Williams*, 96; Richards Diary, September 9, 1864, Samuel P. Richards Papers, AHC; Georgia, vol. 71, February 3, 1866, R. G. Dun & Company Reports, HGSB; Sidney Root, "Memorandum of My Life, 1893," 18–20, Sidney Root Papers, AHC. Apparently Bres did not mourn the fall of the Confederacy. In July of 1864 the Louisiana merchant wrote that he was "glad" his son received a school holiday to celebrate the Fourth of July. Eli Bonney to Messrs Converse, Harding, & Co., November 27, 1865, Eli Whitney Bonney Papers, PL. Bonney sent several letters to various creditors in New York City, Philadelphia, and elsewhere. The letters often demonstrate the forgive-and-forget attitude that many southern white merchants embraced. Typical was a letter that Bonney began: "It has been some years since I had the pleasure of corresponding with you. Since which time exciting events have transpired. Since things have become comparatively quiet again, I have commenced a small business"; Eli Bonney to Pearson & Sallada, July 3, 1866, Eli Whitney Bonney Papers, PL.

33. John Edmund West to Sarah Agee West, February 20, 1865, West Family Papers, VHS; Virginia, vol. 7, p. 607, R. G. Dun & Company Reports, HGSB; *Business Directory of the Principal Southern Cities*, 421.

Conclusion

Epigraphs: Andrews, *War-Time Journal of a Georgia Girl*, 351; Dobb, *Studies in the Development of Capitalism*, 17.

1. Examples of recent work on middle-class culture in nineteenth-century America include: Wells, *Origins of the Southern Middle Class*; Beckert, *Monied Metropolis*; and Gilkeson, *Middle-Class Providence*.

2. For a thorough overview of this debate, see Smith, *Debating Slavery*, 1–30.

3. Dobb, *Studies in the Development of Capitalism*, 18–19, 89, 121; Genovese, *World the Slaveholders Made*, 157.

4. Smith, *Debating Slavery*, 12–13. Since the mid-1990s, a number of thoughtful studies have attempted to reconcile and bridge significant gaps in the historiography of the Old South. For examples, see Smith, *Mastered by the Clock*, and Young, *Domesticating Slavery*.

5. Woodward, *Origins of the New South*, 183–84; Harold D. Woodman, "Economic Reconstruction and the Rise of the New South, 1865–1900," in Boles and Nolen, eds., *Interpreting Southern History*, 254–72. For historians who have offered critiques of Woodward's discontinuity thesis or who have simply emphasized a general continuity from the antebellum to the postwar South, see Degler, *Place Over Time*; Bartley, *New South*; Wiener, *Social Origins of the New South*; Billings, *Planters and the Making of a "New South"*; and Wright, "Strange Career of the New Southern Economic History." Harold D. Woodman's fine overview of this debate within the historiography supports much of C. Vann Woodward's earlier analysis, albeit with certain modifications; see Woodman, "Political Economy of the New South." Two works that thoughtfully explore the continuing interest in the Old South and its legacy are Peter Applebome's *Dixie Rising: How the South Is Shaping American Values, Politics, and Culture* (New York: Times Books, 1996) and Tony Horwitz's *Confederates in the Attic: Dispatches from the Unfinished Civil War* (New York: Pantheon Books, 1998).

6. Ford, "Rednecks and Merchants"; Doyle, *New Men, New Cities*; Carlton, *Mill and Town in South Carolina*; Ayers, *Promise of the New South*, 81–92.

7. Woodman, *King Cotton & His Retainers*, 210, 245–70; O'Bryan business documents, 1866, O'Bryan Family Collection, TSLA; Hassell Diary, September 31, 1865, Cushing B. Hassell Papers, SHC; Richards Diary, January 16, 1869, Samuel P. Richards Papers, AHC; Baldwin biography, Daniel Hoard Baldwin Letters, SHC; Semmes family biography, Semmes Family Papers, TSLA; Clark, *Valleys of the Shadow*, 82; Sidney Root, "Memorandum of My Life, 1893," Sidney Root Papers, AHC. See also DeCredico, *Patriotism for Profit*, 138–40.

8. O'Brien, "C. Vann Woodward and the Burden of Southern Liberalism," quoted in Woodman, "Political Economy of the New South," 793 (n. 9); Beckert, *Monied Metropolis*, 160.

Bibliography

Primary Sources

Government Records

Confederate States of America War Department, *Regulations for the Army of the Confederate States, 1863*. Richmond, Va.: West & Johnston, 1863.

U.S. Bureau of the Census, Federal Manuscript Censuses, 1850, 1860. Population Schedules. Microfilm.

U.S. War Department. *The War of the Rebellion: A Compilation of the Official Records of the Union and Confederate Armies*. 128 vols. Washington, D.C.: Government Printing Office, 1880–1901.

National Archives and Records Administration I & II

"Confederate Papers Relating to Citizens or Business Firms," M346

"Confederate Papers of the U.S. District Court for the Eastern District of North Carolina, 1861–1865," M346

"Records of the Commissioners of Claims (Southern Claims Commission), 1871–1880," M87

"Settled Case Files for Claims Approved by the Southern Claims Commission, 1871–1880," RG 217, Entry 732

Manuscript Collections

Atlanta History Center, Atlanta, Georgia (AHC)

Samuel P. Richards Papers
Sidney Root Papers

Baker Library, Harvard University Graduate School of Business Administration, Boston, Massachusetts (HGSB)

R. G. Dun & Company Reports

Center for American History, University of Texas at Austin (CAH)

John Adriance Papers
John Thomas Brackenridge Papers

Christian Friedrich Duerr Papers
John Zirvas Leyendecker Papers
Barnes-Willis Family Papers (Natchez Trace Collection)
Jacob F. Baum Papers (Natchez Trace Collection)
Robert Cochran Papers (Natchez Trace Collection)
Charles H. Dencker Letter Book (Natchez Trace Collection)
James Campbell Wilkins Papers (Natchez Trace Collection)
Perry (James Franklin and Stephen Samuel) Papers
John Twohig Papers

Filson Club Historical Society, Louisville, Kentucky (FCHS)

Thomas C. Howard Papers
Jacob-Johnson Family Papers
John Jeremiah Jacob Papers
John F. Jefferson Papers
George Wood Meriwether Papers
Runyon Family Papers

Georgia Historical Society, Savannah, Georgia (GHS)

Hynes-Sullivan Papers
Minis Family Papers
Palmes Papers

Hargrett Library, University of Georgia, Athens, Georgia (HL)

Banks Family Papers
Henry Patillo Farrow Papers

Historic New Orleans Collection, Williams Research Center, New Orleans, Louisiana (HNOC)

Murphy Family Papers
Petetin Family Papers

Howard-Tilton Memorial Library, Tulane University, New Orleans, Louisiana (HTML)

Bres Family Papers
Dunlap Correspondence

Manuscript Division, Kentucky Historical Society, Frankfort, Kentucky (KHS)

George Barron Papers
Edward S. Haydon Papers
G. W. McGee Papers
Edward Rumsey Papers

Mississippi Department of Archives and History, Jackson, Mississippi (MDAH)

Aby Family Papers
Howze (Isham Robertson) and Family Papers

North Carolina State Archives, Raleigh, North Carolina (NCSA)

Kader Biggs Papers
Oscar W. Blacknall Papers
Joseph Cathey Papers
Charles W. Jacocks Papers
Jennie Marriott Proctor Papers
Jonathan Worth Papers

Manuscript Department, William R. Perkins Library, Duke University, Durham, North Carolina (PL)

Eli Whitney Bonney Papers
Stephen Elliott Papers
Walter Jenkins Diary
Milo Lewis Papers
Munford-Ellis Family Papers
John R. Turner Papers
Thomas B. Webber Diary

South Caroliniana Library, University of South Carolina, Columbia, South Carolina (SCL)

William Guion Childs Papers
Thomas Aiton Papers
Norris and Thomson Family Papers

Southern Historical Collection, Wilson Library, University of North Carolina at Chapel Hill (SHC)

Daniel Hoard Baldwin Letters
John Benson Papers
Kate S. Carney Diary
Chambers Family Papers
James Evans Papers
Susan Fisher Papers
Cushing B. Hassell Papers
Daniel Hundley Papers
Lea Family Papers
Levert Family Papers

Peter Mallett Papers
Rosina Mix Papers
Benedict Joseph Semmes Papers
Samuel H. Steelman Papers
James Wilson White Papers
William Henry Wills Papers

Tennessee State Library and Archives, Nashville, Tennessee (TSLA)

Tyrus Brainerd Correspondence
Carpenter Family Papers
Josiah Jeans Papers
Logue and Hamilton Account Book
B. W. MaCrae Correspondence
O'Bryan Family Collection
Jackson Pryor Papers
Semmes Family Papers
Paul Shirley Papers
Archibald Trawick Papers

Virginia Historical Society, Richmond, Virginia (VHS)

Barbour Family Papers
John William Bradbury Papers
Benjamin Brand Papers
William Floyd Burke Diary
James Thomas Butler Diary
Byrd Family Papers
Robert A. Grannis Diary
Holland Family Papers
Constantine Osborne Perkins Papers
Preston Family Papers
Preston (Robert) & Son Records
West Family Papers

Newspapers and Periodicals

Advertiser and Merchants' and Farmers' Gazette, Wilmington, North Carolina
American Banner, Edenton, North Carolina
American Beacon and Norfolk and Portsmouth Daily Advertiser, Norfolk, Virginia
Atlanta Southern Confederacy, Atlanta, Georgia
Augusta Chronicle, Augusta, Georgia
Augusta Constitutionalist, Augusta, Georgia
Augusta Daily Chronicle & Sentinel, Augusta, Georgia

Austin State Gazette, Austin, Texas
Caddo Gazette and De-Soto Intelligencer, Shreveport, Louisiana
Carolina Watchman, Salisbury, North Carolina
Central Monitor, Murfreesboro, Tennessee
Charleston Mercury, Charleston, South Carolina
De Bow's Review, New Orleans, Louisiana
Edenton Sentinel & Albemarle Intelligencer, Edenton, North Carolina
Galveston Weekly News, Galveston, Texas
Greenville Mountaineer, Greenville, South Carolina
Hunt's Merchants' Magazine and Commercial Review, New York, New York
Macon Georgia Telegraph or *Georgia Telegram*, Macon, Georgia
Memphis Daily Appeal, Jackson, Mississippi
Merchant, New Orleans, Louisiana
Milledgeville Federal Union, Milledgeville, Georgia
Mobile Advertiser & Register, Mobile, Alabama
Mobile Commercial Register and Patriot, Mobile, Alabama
Montgomery Daily Advertiser, Montgomery, Alabama
Montgomery Daily Advertiser & Register, Montgomery, Alabama
Nashville Republican & State Gazette, Nashville, Tennessee
Nashville Whig, Nashville, Tennessee
New Orleans Commercial Times, New Orleans, Louisiana
New Orleans Daily Commercial Times, New Orleans, Louisiana
New Orleans Daily Picayune, New Orleans, Louisiana
New Orleans Times-Democrat, New Orleans, Louisiana
People's Press and Wilmington Advertiser, Wilmington, North Carolina
Raleigh Register, Raleigh, North Carolina
Raleigh Weekly Conservative, Raleigh, North Carolina
Richmond Daily Dispatch, Richmond, Virginia
Richmond Enquirer, Richmond, Virginia
Richmond Whig, Richmond, Virginia
Savannah Republican, Savannah, Georgia
Savannah Weekly Republican, Savannah, Georgia
Southern Literary Journal, Charleston, South Carolina
Southern Literary Messenger, Richmond, Virginia
Southern Watchman, Athens, Georgia
Vicksburg Advocate & Register, Vicksburg, Mississippi
Vicksburg Register, Vicksburg, Mississippi
Vicksburg Sentinel, Vicksburg, Mississippi
Weekly Columbus Enquirer, Columbus, Georgia
Weekly Raleigh Register, and North Carolina Gazette, Raleigh, North Carolina
Wilmington Daily Journal, Wilmington, North Carolina

Books, Essays, Pamphlets, Reports, Speeches, Correspondence

Adams, Henry. *The Education of Henry Adams: An Autobiography.* Boston: Houghton Mifflin, 1918.

Andrews, Eliza Frances. *The War-Time Journal of a Georgia Girl, 1864–1865.* New York: D. Appleton, 1908. Reprint, Spencer Bidwell King Jr., ed. Atlanta: Cherokee, 1976.

Anonymous. "Marriage and Divorce." *Southern Quarterly Review* 26 (October 1854).

Bailey, Rufus William, ed. *The Patriarch; or, Family Library Magazine: January–December 1841.* New York: George A. Peters, 1841.

Baldwin, Joseph G. *The Flush Times of Alabama and Mississippi: A Series of Sketches.* New York: D. Appleton, 1853. Reprint, New York: Hill and Wang, 1957.

Bancroft, Joseph. *Census of the City of Savannah, Together with Statistics, Relating to the Trade, Commerce, Mechanical Arts & Health of the Same; to Which Is Added Historical Notices, and a List of the Incorporated Companies, and of the Charitable Societies.* Savannah: Edward C. Councell, 1848.

Barrow, Bennet H. *Plantation Life in the Florida Parishes of Louisiana, 1836–1846, as Reflected in the Diary of Bennet H. Barrow.* Edited by Edwin Adams Davis. New York: Columbia University Press, 1943.

Beecher, Catherine. *A Treatise on Domestic Economy, for the Use of Young Ladies at Home, and at School.* Boston: Marsh, Capan, Lyon, and Webb, 1841. Reprint, New York: Schocken, 1977.

Biggs, Asa. *Autobiography of Asa Biggs: Including a Journal of a Trip from North Carolina to New York in 1832.* Edited by R.D.W. Connor. Publications of the North Carolina Historical Commission. Raleigh: Edwards & Broughton, 1915.

Bird, Edgeworth. *The Granite Farm Letters: The Civil War Correspondence of Edgeworth & Sallie Bird.* Edited by John Rozier. Athens: University of Georgia Press, 1988.

Boyer, Reba Bayless, ed. *Chancery Court Records of McMinn County, Tennessee.* R. B. Boyer, 1980.

Bremer, Fredrika. *Homes of the New World: Impressions of America.* Translated by Mary Botham Howitt. New York: Harper & Brothers, 1853.

Business Directory of the Principal Southern Cities. With a business register of northern firms who either have already, or desire to have, business relations with the Southern states. 1866 and 1867. New York: Dunkley & Woodman, 1866.

Chesnut, Mary Boykin Miller. *Mary Chesnut's Civil War.* Edited by C. Vann Woodward. New Haven, Conn.: Yale University Press, 1981.

———. *The Private Mary Chesnut: The Unpublished Civil War Diaries.* Edited by C. Vann Woodward and Elisabeth Muhlenfeld. New York: Oxford University Press, 1984.

Childs, Arney R., ed. *Planters and Business Men: The Guignard Family of South Carolina*. Columbia: University of South Carolina Press, 1957.

Clark, Reuben G. *Valleys of the Shadow: The Memoir of Confederate Captain Reuben G. Clark, Company I, 59th Tennessee Mounted Infantry*. Edited by Willene B. Clark. Voices of the Civil War. Knoxville: University of Tennessee Press, 1994.

Cooper, Walter G. *Official History of Fulton County*. Atlanta: Walter W. Brown, 1934. Reprint, Spartanburg, S.C.: Reprint Co., 1978.

Corsan, William Carson. *Two Months in the Confederate States: An Englishman's Travels Through the South*. London: R. Bentley, 1863. Reprint, Benjamin H. Trask, ed. Baton Rouge: Louisiana State University Press, 1996.

Crofts, Daniel W., ed. *Cobb's Ordeal: The Diaries of a Virginia Farmer, 1842–1872*. Athens: University of Georgia Press, 1997.

Dawson, Francis W. *Reminiscences of Confederate Service 1861–1865*. Edited by Bell Irvin Wiley. Baton Rouge: Louisiana State University Press, 1980.

Dawson, Sarah Morgan. *The Civil War Diary of Sarah Morgan*. Edited by Charles East. Athens: University of Georgia Press, 1991.

De Bow, James D. B. *Statistical View of the United States, Being a Compendium of the Seventh Census*. Washington: Beverley Tucker, Senate Printer, 1854.

Dimond, E. Grey, and Herman Hattaway, eds. *Letters from Forest Place: A Plantation Family's Correspondence, 1846–1881*. Jackson: University Press of Mississippi, 1993.

Edmonson, Belle. *A Lost Heroine of the Confederacy: The Diaries and Letters of Belle Edmonson*. Edited by Loretta Galbraith. Jackson: University of Mississippi Press, 1991.

Featherstonhaugh, G. W. *Excursion through the Slave States*. New York: Harper & Brothers, 1844.

Fitzhugh, George. *Cannibals All! or, Slaves Without Masters*. Richmond, Va.: A. Morris, 1857. Reprint, Cambridge, Mass.: Harvard University Press, 1960.

Franklin, Benjamin. *The Way to Wealth: Advice to a Young Tradesman: Necessary Hints to Those who Would Be Rich*. Ithaca, N.Y.: Mack, Andrus, & Woodruff, 1838.

Fremantle, Arthur James Lyon. *Three Months in the Southern States: April–June, 1863*. New York: J. Bradburn, 1864. Reprint, Lincoln: University of Nebraska Press, 1991.

Gadsden, James, chairman. *Minutes of the Proceedings of the Third Commercial Convention, Held in Augusta, Georgia, in October, 1838; with the Report of the Committee on the Object of the Convention*. Augusta, Ga.: Benj. Brantly, 1838.

Gay, Mary Ann Harris. *Life in Dixie during the War: 1861–1862–1863–1864–1865*. 4th ed. Atlanta: Foote and Davies, 1901.

Gregg, William. *Essays on Domestic Industry.* Charleston, S.C.: Burgess & James, 1845. Reprint, Graniteville, S.C.: Graniteville Co., 1941.

Grisamore, Silas T. *The Civil War Reminiscences of Major Silas T. Grisamore, C.S.A.* Edited by Arthur W. Bergeron Jr. Baton Rouge: Louisiana State University Press, 1992.

Hampton, Sally Baxter. *A Divided Heart: Letters of Sally Baxter Hampton, 1853–1862.* Edited by Ann Fripp Hampton. Spartanburg, S.C.: Reprint Co., 1980.

Helper, Hinton Rowan. *The Impending Crisis of the South: How to Meet It.* New York: Burdick Bros., 1857. Reprint, George M. Fredrickson, ed. Cambridge, Mass.: Harvard University Press, 1968.

Heyward, Pauline DeCaradeuc. *A Confederate Lady Comes of Age: The Journal of Pauline DeCaradeuc Heyward, 1863–1888.* Edited by Mary D. Robertson. Women's Diaries and Letters of the Nineteenth-Century South. Columbia: University of South Carolina Press, 1992.

Holmes, Emma. *The Diary of Miss Emma Holmes, 1861–1866.* Edited by John F. Marszalek. Baton Rouge: Louisiana State University Press, 1979.

Hundley, Daniel R. *Social Relations in Our Southern States.* New York: Henry B. Price, 1860. Reprint, Baton Rouge: Louisiana State University Press, 1979.

Ingraham, Joseph Holt. *The South-West, by a Yankee.* 2 vols. Harper & Brothers, 1835. Reprint, Ann Arbor, Mich.: University Microfilms, 1966.

Jackson, Andrew. *The Papers of Andrew Jackson.* Edited by Sam B. Smith and Harriet Chappell Owsley. Knoxville: University of Tennessee Press, 1980.

Jefferson, Thomas, *Notes on the State of Virginia.* Boston: Lilly and Wait, 1832.

Jones, John B. *The City Merchant; or, The Mysterious Failure.* Philadelphia: Lippincott, Grambo, 1851.

———. *A Rebel War Clerk's Diary.* Edited by Earl Schenck Miers. New York: Sagamore Press, 1958.

Jones, Martha McDowell Buford. *Peach Leather and Rebel Gray: Bluegrass Life and the War, 1860–1865: Farm and Social Life, Famous Horses, Tragedies of War: Diary and Letters of a Confederate Wife.* Edited by Mary E. Wharton and Ellen F. Williams. Lexington, Ky.: Helicon, 1986.

Kennedy, J.C.G. *Population of the United States in 1860: Compiled from the Original Returns of the Eighth Census under the Direction of the Secretary of the Interior.* Washington, D.C.: Government Printing Office, 1864.

Le Grand, Julia. *The Journal of Julia Le Grand: New Orleans, 1862–1863.* Edited by Kate Mason Rowland and Mrs. Morris L. Croxall. Richmond, Va.: Everett Waddey, 1911.

Leon, L. *Diary of a Tar Heel Confederate Soldier.* Charlotte, N.C.: Stone Publishing Company, 1913.

Lieber, Francis. *Slavery, Plantations, and the Yeomanry.* New York: C. S. Westcott, 1863.

Longstreet, Augustus Baldwin. *Georgia Scenes Completed: A Scholarly Text.* Edited by David Rachels. Athens: University of Georgia Press, 1998.

McDonald, Cornelia Peake. *A Woman's Civil War: A Diary, with Reminiscences of the War, from March 1862.* Edited by Minrose C. Gwin. Madison: University of Wisconsin Press, 1992.

Marcus, Jacob Rader, ed. *Memoirs of American Jews, 1775–1865.* 3 vols. Philadelphia: Jewish Publication Society of America, 1955–1956.

Myers, Robert Manson, ed. *The Children of Pride: A True Story of Georgia and the Civil War.* New Haven, Conn.: Yale University Press, 1972.

The Nashville, State of Tennessee, and General Commercial Directory. Nashville: Daily American Book and Job Printing Office, 1853.

Olmsted, Frederick Law. *The Cotton Kingdom: A Traveller's Observations on Cotton and Slavery in the American Slave States.* Edited by Arthur M. Schlesinger. New York: Knopf, 1953.

———. *A Journey in the Seaboard Slave States, with Remarks on Their Economy.* New York: Dix & Edwards, 1856. Reprint, New York: Negro Universities Press, 1968.

———. *A Journey in the Back Country.* New York: Mason Brothers, 1860. Reprint, Williamstown, Mass.: Corner House, 1972.

Putnam, Sallie A. Brock. *Richmond during the War: Four Years of Personal Observation by a Richmond Lady.* New York: G. W. Carleton, 1867. Reprint, Lincoln: University of Nebraska Press, 1996.

Scott, Edwin J. *Random Recollections of a Long Life, 1806–1876.* Columbia, S.C.: Charles A. Calvo Jr., Printer, 1884.

Simms, William Gilmore. *Guy Rivers: A Tale of Georgia.* Edited by John Caldwell Guilds. Fayetteville: University of Arkansas Press, 1993.

Solomon, Clara. *The Civil War Diary of Clara Solomon: Growing Up in New Orleans, 1861–1862.* Edited by Elliott Ashkenazi. Baton Rouge: Louisiana State University Press, 1995.

Stone, Kate. *The Journal of Kate Stone, 1861–1868.* Edited by John Q. Anderson. Baton Rouge: Louisiana State University Press, 1955.

Taylor, Susie King. *A Black Woman's Civil War Memoirs: Reminiscences of My Life in Camp with the 33rd U.S. Colored Troops, Late 1st South Carolina Volunteers.* Boston: S. K. Taylor, 1902. Reprint, Patricia W. Romero, ed. New York: M. Wiener, 1988.

Trollope, Frances. *Domestic Manners of the Americans.* London: Whittaker, Treacher, 1832. Reprint, Donald Smalley, ed. Gloucester, Mass.: Peter Smith, 1974.

Weston, George M. *The Poor Whites of the South.* Washington, D.C.: Buell and Blanchard, 1856.

Whipple, Henry Benjamin. *Bishop Whipple's Southern Diary, 1843–1844.* Edited by Lester B. Shippee. Minneapolis: University of Minnesota Press, 1937.

Williams' Atlanta Directory, City Guide, and Business Mirror. Vol. 1 (1859–1860). Atlanta: M. Lynch, 1859.

Wills, William Henry. "A Southern Sulky Ride in 1837, from North Carolina to Alabama," *Publications of the Southern History Association* 6 (November 1902): 471–83.

Wilson, LeGrand James. *The Confederate Soldier.* Fayetteville, Ark.: M'Roy Print. Co., 1902. Reprint, James W. Silver, ed. Memphis: Memphis State University Press, 1973.

Secondary Sources

Books

Adler, Jeffrey S. *Yankee Merchants and the Making of the Urban West: The Rise and Fall of Antebellum St. Louis.* New York: Cambridge University Press, 1991.

Ambrose, Douglas. *Henry Hughes and Proslavery Thought in the Old South.* Baton Rouge: Louisiana State University Press, 1996.

Ash, Stephen V. *Middle Tennessee Society Transformed, 1860–1870: War and Peace in the Upper South.* Baton Rouge: Louisiana State University Press, 1988.

———. *When the Yankees Came: Conflict and Chaos in the Occupied South, 1861–1865.* Civil War America. Chapel Hill: University of North Carolina Press, 1995.

Ashworth, John. *Slavery, Capitalism, and Politics in the Antebellum Republic.* Vol. 1, *Commerce and Compromise, 1820–1850.* Cambridge: Cambridge University Press, 1995.

Atherton, Lewis E. *The Frontier Merchant in Mid-America.* Columbia: University of Missouri Studies, 1926. Reprint, Columbia: University of Missouri Press, 1971.

———. *The Southern Country Store, 1800–1860.* Baton Rouge: Louisiana State University Press, 1949.

Augst, Thomas. *The Clerk's Tale: Young Men and Moral Life in Nineteenth-Century America.* Chicago: University of Chicago Press, 2003.

Ayers, Edward L. *The Promise of the New South: Life After Reconstruction.* New York: Oxford University Press, 1992.

Ayers, Edward L., and John C. Willis, eds. *The Edge of the South: Life in Nineteenth-Century Virginia.* Charlottesville: University Press of Virginia, 1991.

Babb, Valerie. *Whiteness Visible: The Meaning of Whiteness in American Literature and Culture.* New York: New York University Press, 1998.

Bailey, Fred Arthur. *Class and Tennessee's Confederate Generation.* Fred W. Morrison

Series in Southern Studies. Chapel Hill: University of North Carolina Press, 1987.

Ball, Douglas B. *Financial Failure and Confederate Defeat.* Urbana: University of Illinois Press, 1991.

Bardaglio, Peter W. *Reconstructing the Household: Families, Sex, and the Law in the Nineteenth-Century South.* Chapel Hill: University of North Carolina Press, 1995.

Bartholomees, J. Boone, Jr. *Buff Facings and Gilt Buttons: Staff and Headquarters Operations in the Army of Northern Virginia, 1861–1865.* Columbia: University of South Carolina Press, 1998.

Bartley, Numan V. *The New South, 1945–1980.* Baton Rouge: Louisiana State University Press, 1995.

Bartley, Numan V., ed. *The Evolution of Southern Culture.* Athens: University of Georgia Press, 1988.

Barzun, Jacques. *From Dawn to Decadence: 500 Years of Western Cultural Life, 1500 to the Present.* New York: HarperCollins, 2000.

Bateman, Fred, and Thomas Joseph Weiss. *A Deplorable Scarcity: The Failure of Industrialization in the Slave Economy.* Chapel Hill: University of North Carolina Press, 1981.

Baum, Dale. *The Shattering of Texas Unionism: Politics in the Lone Star State During the Civil War Era.* Baton Rouge: Louisiana State University Press, 1998.

Beckert, Sven. *The Monied Metropolis: New York City and the Consolidation of the American Bourgeoisie, 1850–1896.* Cambridge: Cambridge University Press, 2001.

Berlin, Ira. *Many Thousands Gone: The First Two Centuries of Slavery in North America.* Cambridge, Mass.: Belknap Press of Harvard University Press, 1998.

Bermingham, Ann, and John Brewer, eds. *The Consumption of Culture 1600–1800: Image, Object, Text.* London: Routledge, 1995.

Berstein, Iver. *The New York City Draft Riots: Their Significance for American Society and Politics in the Age of the Civil War.* New York: Oxford University Press, 1990.

Billings, Dwight B., Jr. *Planters and the Making of a "New South": Class, Politics, and Development in North Carolina, 1865–1900.* Chapel Hill: University of North Carolina Press, 1979.

Blair, William. *Virginia's Private War: Feeding Body and Soul in the Confederacy, 1861–1865.* New York: Oxford University Press, 1998.

Blassingame, John W. *The Slave Community: Plantation Life in the Antebellum South.* New York: Oxford University Press, 1972.

Bledstein, Burton J., and Robert D. Johnston, eds. *The Middling Sorts: Explorations in the History of the American Middle Class.* New York: Routledge, 2001.

Bleser, Carol, ed. *In Joy and in Sorrow: Women, Family, and Marriage in the Victorian South, 1830–1900.* New York: Oxford University Press, 1991.

———. *Secret and Sacred: The Diaries of James Henry Hammond, a Southern Slaveholder.* New York: Oxford University Press, 1988.

Blumin, Stuart. *The Emergence of the Middle Class: Social Experience in the American City, 1760–1900.* New York: Cambridge University Press, 1989.

Bodenhamer, David J., and James W. Ely Jr., eds. *Ambivalent Legacy: A Legal History of the South.* Jackson: University Press of Mississippi, 1984.

Boles, John B. *The Great Revival, 1787–1805: The Origins of the Southern Evangelical Mind.* Lexington: University Press of Kentucky, 1972.

Boles, John B., and Evelyn Thomas Nolen, eds. *Interpreting Southern History: Historiographical Essays in Honor of Sanford W. Higginbotham.* Baton Rouge: Louisiana State University Press, 1987.

Bolton, Charles C. *Poor Whites of the Antebellum South: Tenants and Laborers in Central North Carolina and Northeast Mississippi.* Durham: Duke University Press, 1994.

Bowman, Shearer Davis. *Masters & Lords: Mid-19th-Century U.S. Planters and Prussian Junkers.* New York: Oxford University Press, 1993.

Boydston, Jeanne. *Home and Work: Housework, Wages, and the Ideology of Labor in the Early Republic.* New York: Oxford University Press, 1990.

Brewer, John, and Roy Porter, eds. *Consumption and the World of Goods.* London: Routledge, 1993.

Brown, Kathleen M. *Good Wives, Nasty Wenches, and Anxious Patriarchs: Gender, Race, and Power in Colonial Virginia.* Chapel Hill: Published for the Institute of Early American History and Culture by the University of North Carolina Press, 1996.

Brown, Richard D. *Modernization: The Transformation of American Life, 1600–1865.* New York: Hill and Wang, 1976.

Bruce, Dickson D., Jr. *Violence and Culture in the Antebellum South.* Austin: University of Texas Press, 1979.

Bryant, Jonathan M. *How Curious a Land: Conflict and Change in Greene County, Georgia, 1850–1885.* Fred W. Morrison Series in Southern Studies. Chapel Hill: University of North Carolina Press, 1996.

Buenger, Walter L. *Secession and the Union in Texas.* Austin: University of Texas Press, 1984.

Burton, Orville Vernon. *In My Father's House Are Many Mansions: Family and Community in Edgefield, South Carolina.* Fred W. Morrison Series in Southern Studies. Chapel Hill: University of North Carolina Press, 1985.

Burton, Orville Vernon, and Robert C. McMath, eds. *Class, Conflict, and Consensus: Antebellum Southern Community Studies.* Westport, Conn.: Greenwood Press, 1982.

Bushman, Richard L. *The Refinement of America: Persons, Houses, Cities.* New York: Knopf, 1992.

Bynum, Victoria E. *Unruly Women: The Politics of Social and Sexual Control in the Old South.* Gender and American Culture. Chapel Hill: University of North Carolina Press, 1992.

Calhoon, Robert M. *Evangelicals and Conservatives in the Early South, 1740–1861.* Columbia: University of South Carolina Press, 1988.

Calhoun, Craig, ed. *Habermas and the Public Sphere.* Cambridge, Mass.: MIT Press, 1992.

Carlton, David Lee. *Mill and Town in South Carolina, 1880–1920.* Baton Rouge: Louisiana State University Press, 1982.

Carnes, Mark C., and Clyde Griffen, eds. *Meanings for Manhood: Constructions of Masculinity in Victorian America.* Chicago: University of Chicago Press, 1990.

Cashin, Joan E. *A Family Venture: Men and Women on the Southern Frontier.* New York: Oxford University Press, 1991.

Cashin, Joan E., ed. *Our Common Affairs: Texts from Women in the Old South.* Baltimore: Johns Hopkins University Press, 1996.

Cecil-Fronsman, Bill. *Common Whites: Class and Culture in Antebellum North Carolina.* Lexington: University Press of Kentucky, 1992.

Censer, Jane Turner. *North Carolina Planters and Their Children, 1800–1860.* Baton Rouge: Louisiana State University Press, 1984.

Chernow, Ron. *Titan: The Life of John D. Rockefeller, Sr.* New York: Random House, 1998.

Clark, Blanche Henry. *The Tennessee Yeomen, 1840–1860.* Nashville: Vanderbilt University Press, 1942.

Clark, Thomas D. *Pills, Petticoats, and Plows: The Southern Country Store.* Indianapolis: Bobbs-Merrill, 1944. Reprint, Norman: University of Oklahoma Press, 1964.

Clawson, Mary Ann. *Constructing Brotherhood: Class, Gender, and Fraternalism.* Princeton: Princeton University Press, 1989.

Click, Patricia C. *The Spirit of the Times: Amusements in Nineteenth-Century Baltimore, Norfolk, and Richmond.* Charlottesville: University of Virginia Press, 1989.

Clinton, Catherine. *The Other Civil War: American Women in the Nineteenth Century.* American Century Series. New York: Hill and Wang, 1984.

———. *The Plantation Mistress: Woman's World in the Old South.* New York: Pantheon Books, 1982.

———. *Tara Revisited: Women, War & the Plantation Legend.* New York: Abbeville Press, 1995.

Clinton, Catherine, and Nina Silber, eds. *Divided Houses: Gender and the Civil War.* New York: Oxford University Press, 1992.

Coclanis, Peter A. *The Shadow of a Dream: Economic Life and Death in the South Carolina Low Country, 1670–1920.* New York: Oxford University Press, 1989.

Conference on Research in Income and Wealth. *Trends in the American Economy in the Nineteenth Century.* Vol. 24, *Studies in Income and Wealth.* Princeton: Princeton University Press, 1960.

Cott, Nancy F. *The Bonds of Womanhood: "Woman's Sphere" in New England, 1780–1835.* New Haven, Conn.: Yale University Press, 1977.

Coulter, E. Merton. *George Walton Williams: The Life of a Southern Merchant and Banker, 1820–1903.* Athens, Ga.: Hibriten Press, 1976.

Crocket, George Louis. *Two Centuries in East Texas: A History of San Augustine County and Surrounding Territory from 1685 to the Present Time.* Dallas, Tex.: Southwest Press, 1932.

Cross, Gary. *Time and Money: The Making of Consumer Culture.* New York: Routledge, 1993.

Daniel, Larry J. *Soldiering in the Army of Tennessee: A Portrait of Life in a Confederate Army.* Chapel Hill: University of North Carolina Press, 1991.

Davidoff, Leonore, and Catherine Hall. *Family Fortunes: Men and Women of the English Middle Class, 1780–1850.* Chicago: University of Chicago Press, 1987.

Davis, David Brion. *The Problem of Slavery in Western Culture.* Ithaca, N.Y.: Cornell University Press, 1966.

DeCredico, Mary A. *Patriotism for Profit: Georgia's Urban Entrepreneurs and the Confederate War Effort.* Fred W. Morrison Series in Southern Studies. Chapel Hill: University of North Carolina Press, 1990.

de Grazia, Victoria, and Ellen Furlough, eds. *The Sex of Things: Gender and Consumption in Historical Perspective.* Berkeley: University of California Press, 1996.

Degler, Carl N. *Place Over Time: The Continuity of Southern Distinctiveness.* Walter Lynwood Fleming Lectures in Southern History. Baton Rouge: Louisiana State University Press, 1977.

Delfino, Susanna, and Michele Gillespie, eds. *Neither Lady nor Slave: Working Women of the Old South.* Chapel Hill: University of North Carolina Press, 2002.

Dobb, Maurice Herbert. *Studies in the Development of Capitalism.* New York: International Publishers, 1947.

Dodd, William Edward. *The Cotton Kingdom: A Chronicle of the Old South.* New Haven, Conn.: Yale University Press, 1920.

Doerflinger, Thomas M. *A Vigorous Spirit of Enterprise: Merchants and Economic Development in Revolutionary Philadelphia.* Chapel Hill: Published for the Institute of Early American History and Culture by the University of North Carolina Press, 1986.

Dougan, Michael B. *Confederate Arkansas: The People and Policies of a Frontier State in Wartime.* Tuscaloosa: University of Alabama Press, 1976.

Douglas, Mary. *Cultural Bias.* London: Royal Anthropological Institute, 1978.

Douglas, Mary, and Baron Isherwood. *The World of Goods: Towards an Anthropology of Consumption.* New York: Basic Books, 1979. Reprint, London: Routledge, 1996.

Doyle, Don H. *New Men, New Cities, New South: Atlanta, Nashville, Charleston, Mobile, 1860–1910.* Fred W. Morrison Series in Southern Studies. Chapel Hill: University of North Carolina Press, 1990.

DuBois, Ellen Carol. *Feminism and Suffrage: The Emergence of an Independent Women's Movement in America, 1848–1869.* Ithaca, N.Y.: Cornell University Press, 1978.

Dunaway, Wilma A. *The First American Frontier: Transition to Capitalism in Southern Appalachia, 1700–1860.* Fred W. Morrison Series in Southern Studies. Chapel Hill: University of North Carolina Press, 1996.

Dupre, Daniel S. *Transforming the Cotton Frontier: Madison County, Alabama, 1800–1840.* Baton Rouge: Louisiana State University Press, 1997.

Durrill, Wayne K. *War of Another Kind: A Southern Community in the Great Rebellion.* New York: Oxford University Press, 1990.

Dyer, Thomas G. *Secret Yankees: The Union Circle in Confederate Atlanta.* Baltimore: Johns Hopkins University Press, 1999.

Earle, Peter. *The Making of the English Middle Class: Business, Society and Family Life in London, 1660–1730.* London: Methuen, 1989.

Eaton, Clement. *A History of the Old South.* New York: Macmillan, 1949.

———. *The Mind of the Old South.* Baton Rouge: Louisiana State University Press, 1967.

Edwards, Laura F. *Scarlett Doesn't Live Here Anymore: Southern Women in the Civil War Era.* Urbana: University of Illinois Press, 2000.

Egnal, Marc. *Divergent Paths: How Culture and Institutions Have Shaped North American Growth.* New York: Oxford University Press, 1996.

Epstein, Barbara Leslie. *The Politics of Domesticity: Women, Evangelism, and Temperance in Nineteenth-Century America.* Middletown, Conn.: Wesleyan University Press, 1981.

Escott, Paul D. *Many Excellent People: Power and Privilege in North Carolina, 1850–1900.* Fred W. Morrison Series in Southern Studies. Chapel Hill: University of North Carolina Press, 1985.

Ewen, Stuart. *Captains of Consciousness: Advertising and the Social Roots of the Consumer Culture.* New York: McGraw-Hill, 1976.

Faragher, John Mack. *Sugar Creek: Life on the Illinois Prairie.* New Haven, Conn.: Yale University Press, 1986.

Farnham, Christie Anne. *The Education of the Southern Belle: Higher Education and Student Socialization in the Antebellum South.* New York: New York University Press, 1994.

Faust, Drew Gilpin. *James Henry Hammond and the Old South: A Design for Mastery.* Southern Biography Series. Baton Rouge: Louisiana State University Press, 1982.

———. *Mothers of Invention: Women of the Slaveholding South in the American Civil War.* Fred W. Morrison Series in Southern Studies. Chapel Hill: University of North Carolina Press, 1996.

Faust, Drew Gilpin, ed. *The Ideology of Slavery: Proslavery Thought in the Antebellum South, 1830–1860.* Baton Rouge: Louisiana State University Press, 1981.

Fellman, Michael. *Citizen Sherman: A Life of William Tecumseh Sherman.* New York: Random House, 1995.

Fields, Barbara Jeanne. *Slavery and Freedom on the Middle Ground: Maryland during the Nineteenth Century.* New Haven, Conn.: Yale University Press, 1985.

Fogel, Robert William, and Stanley L. Engerman. *Time on the Cross: The Economics of American Negro Slavery.* 2 vols. Boston: Little, Brown, 1974.

Foner, Eric. *Reconstruction: America's Unfinished Revolution, 1863–1877.* New York: Harper & Row, 1988.

Ford, Lacy K., Jr. *Origins of Southern Radicalism: The South Carolina Upcountry, 1800–1860.* New York: Oxford University Press, 1988.

Fox, Richard Wightman, and T. J. Jackson Lears, eds. *The Culture of Consumption: Critical Essays in American History, 1880–1980.* New York: Pantheon Books, 1983.

———. *The Power of Culture: Critical Essays in American History.* Chicago: University of Chicago Press, 1993.

Fox-Genovese, Elizabeth. *Within the Plantation Household: Black and White Women of the Old South.* Chapel Hill: University of North Carolina Press, 1988.

Fox-Genovese, Elizabeth, and Eugene D. Genovese. *Fruits of Merchant Capital: Slavery and Bourgeois Property in the Rise and Expansion of Capitalism.* New York: Oxford University Press, 1983.

Fraser, Hamish W. *The Coming of the Mass Market, 1850–1914.* Hamden, Conn.: Archon Books, 1981.

Fraser, Walter J., Jr., and Winfred B. Moore Jr., eds. *The Southern Enigma: Essays on Race, Class, and Folk Culture.* Contributions in America History, no. 105. Westport, Conn.: Greenwood Press, 1983.

Fraser, Walter J., Jr., Frank Saunders Jr., and Jon A. Wakelyn, eds. *The Web of Southern Social Relations: Women, Family, and Education.* Athens: University of Georgia Press, 1985.

Freehling, William W. *The Road to Disunion.* Vol. 1, *Secessionists at Bay 1776–1854.* New York: Oxford University Press, 1990.

Friedman, Jean E. *The Enclosed Garden: Women and Community in the Evangelical South, 1830–1900*. Fred W. Morrison Series in Southern Studies. Chapel Hill: University of North Carolina Press, 1985.

Friedman, Milton, ed. *Studies in the Quantity Theory of Money*. Chicago: University of Chicago Press, 1956.

Furgurson, Ernest B. *Ashes of Glory: Richmond at War*. New York: Knopf, 1996.

Gallagher, Gary W. *The Confederate War*. Cambridge, Mass.: Harvard University Press, 1997.

Gay, Peter. *The Bourgeois Experience: Victoria to Freud*. Vol. 1, *Education of the Senses*. New York: Oxford University Press, 1984.

———. *Schnitzler's Century: The Making of Middle-Class Culture, 1815–1914*. New York: Norton, 2002.

Genovese, Eugene D. *A Consuming Fire: The Fall of the Confederacy in the Mind of the White Christian South*. Athens: University of Georgia Press, 1998.

———. *The Political Economy of Slavery: Studies in the Economy and Society of the Slave South*. New York: Pantheon Books, 1965.

———. *Roll, Jordan, Roll: The World the Slaves Made*. New York: Pantheon Books, 1974.

———. *The World the Slaveholders Made: Two Essays in Interpretation*. New York: Pantheon Books, 1969.

Gibb, James G. *The Archaeology of Wealth: Consumer Behavior in English America*. New York: Plenum Press, 1996.

Gilkeson, John S. *Middle-Class Providence, 1820–1940*. Princeton: Princeton University Press, 1986.

Gilmore, William J. *Reading Becomes a Necessity of Life: Material and Cultural Life in Rural New England, 1780–1835*. Knoxville: University of Tennessee Press, 1989.

Ginzberg, Lori D. *Women and the Work of Benevolence: Morality, Politics, and Class in the Nineteenth-Century United States*. New Haven, Conn.: Yale University Press, 1990.

Gordon, Lesley J., and John C. Inscoe, eds. *Inside the Confederate Nation: Essays in Honor of Emory M. Thomas*. Baton Rouge: Louisiana State University Press, 2005.

Gorn, Elliot J. *The Manly Art: Bare-Knuckle Prize Fighting in America*. Ithaca, N.Y.: Cornell University Press, 1986.

Grant, Susan-Mary. *North Over South: Northern Nationalism and American Identity in the Antebellum Era*. Lawrence: University Press of Kansas, 2000.

Gray, Lewis C. *History of Agriculture in the Southern United States to 1860*. 2 vols. Washington, D.C.: Carnegie Institution, 1933. Reprint, Gloucester, Mass.: Peter Smith, 1958.

Green, George D. *Finance and Economic Development in the Old South; Louisiana Banking, 1804–1861*. Stanford: Stanford University Press, 1972.

Greenberg, Kenneth S. *Honor & Slavery: Lies, Duels, Noses, Masks, Dressing as a Woman, Gifts, Strangers, Humanitarianism, Death, Slave Rebellions, the Proslavery Argument, Baseball, Hunting, and Gambling in the Old South.* Princeton: Princeton University Press, 1996.

Greven, Philip J. *The Protestant Temperament: Patterns of Child-Rearing, Religious Experience, and the Self in Early America.* New York: Knopf, 1977.

Grimsley, Mark. *The Hard Hand of War: Union Military Policy Toward Southern Civilians, 1861–1865.* New York: Cambridge University Press, 1995.

Grimsted, David. *American Mobbing, 1828–1861: Toward Civil War.* New York: Oxford University Press, 1998.

Gutman, Herbert G. *The Black Family in Slavery and Freedom, 1750–1925.* New York: Pantheon Books, 1976.

Hadden, Sally E. *Slave Patrols: Law and Violence in Virginia and the Carolinas.* Cambridge, Mass.: Harvard University Press, 2001.

Hahn, Steven. *The Roots of Southern Populism: Yeoman Farmers and the Transformation of the Georgia Upcountry, 1850–1890.* New York: Oxford University Press, 1983.

Hale, Douglas. *The Third Texas Cavalry in the Civil War.* Norman: University of Oklahoma Press, 1993.

Halttunen, Karen. *Confidence Men and Painted Women: A Study of Middle-Class Culture in America, 1830–1870.* New Haven, Conn.: Yale University Press, 1982.

Harris, J. William. *Plain Folk and Gentry in a Slave Society: White Liberty and Black Slavery in Augusta's Hinterlands.* Middletown, Conn.: Wesleyan University Press, 1985.

Harris, Leon. *Merchant Princes: An Intimate History of Jewish Families Who Built Great Department Stores.* New York: Harper & Row, 1979.

Hattaway, Herman. *Shades of Blue and Gray: An Introductory Military History of the Civil War.* Columbia: University of Missouri Press, 1997.

Hawks, Joanne V., and Sheila L. Skemp, eds. *Sex, Race, and the Role of Women in the South.* Jackson: University Press of Mississippi, 1983.

Hermann, Janet Sharp. *Joseph E. Davis: Pioneer Patriarch.* Jackson: University Press of Mississippi, 1990.

Heyrman, Christine Leigh. *Southern Cross: The Beginnings of the Bible Belt.* New York: Knopf, 1997.

Hill, Patricia Ruth. *The World Their Household: The American Woman's Foreign Mission Movement and Cultural Transformation, 1870–1920.* Ann Arbor: University of Michigan Press, 1985.

Hill, Samuel S., ed. *Religion in the Southern States: A Historical Study.* Macon, Ga.: Mercer University Press, 1983.

Hoffman, Charles, and Tess Hoffman. *North by South: The Two Lives of Richard James Arnold.* Athens: University of Georgia Press, 1988.

Horowitz, Daniel. *The Morality of Spending: Attitudes Toward the Consumer Society in America, 1875–1940*. Baltimore: Johns Hopkins University Press, 1985.

Hudson, Larry E., Jr., ed. *Working Toward Freedom: Slave Society and Domestic Economy in the American South*. Rochester, N.Y.: University of Rochester Press, 1994.

Hunt, Margaret R. *The Middling Sort: Commerce, Gender, and the Family in England, 1680–1780*. Berkeley: University of California Press, 1996.

Huston, James L. *Calculating the Value of the Union: Slavery, Property Rights, and the Economic Origins of the Civil War*. Chapel Hill: University of North Carolina Press, 2003.

Inscoe, John C. *Mountain Masters, Slavery, and the Sectional Crisis in Western North Carolina*. Knoxville: University of Tennessee Press, 1989.

Jabour, Anya. *Marriage in the Early Republic: Elizabeth and William Wirt and the Companionate Ideal*. Baltimore: Johns Hopkins University Press, 1998.

Jensen, Joan M. *Loosening the Bonds: Mid-Atlantic Farm Women, 1750–1850*. New Haven, Conn.: Yale University Press, 1986.

Johnson, Paul E. *A Shopkeeper's Millennium: Society and Revivals in Rochester, New York, 1815–1837*. New York: Hill and Wang, 1978.

Johnson, Walter. *Soul by Soul: Life Inside the Antebellum Slave Market*. Cambridge, Mass.: Harvard University Press, 1999.

Jones, Jacqueline. *American Work: Four Centuries of Black and White Labor*. New York: Norton, 1998.

———. *Labor of Love, Labor of Sorrow: Black Women, Work, and the Family from Slavery to the Present*. New York: Basic Books, 1985.

Jordan, Winthrop D. *White Over Black: American Attitudes toward the Negro, 1550–1812*. Chapel Hill: University of North Carolina Press, 1968.

Kaplan, Marion A. *The Making of a Jewish Middle Class: Women, Family, and Identity in Imperial Germany*. New York: Oxford University Press, 1991.

Kenzer, Robert C. *Kinship and Neighborhood in a Southern Community: Orange County, North Carolina, 1849–1881*. Knoxville: University of Tennessee Press, 1987.

Kilbourne, Richard Holcombe. *Debt, Investment, Slaves: Credit Relations in East Feliciana Parish, Louisiana, 1825–1885*. Tuscaloosa: University of Alabama Press, 1995.

Kimball, Gregg D. *American City, Southern Place: A Cultural History of Antebellum Richmond*. Athens: University of Georgia Press, 2000.

King, Kimball. *Augustus Baldwin Longstreet*. Boston: Twayne, 1984.

Klein, Rachel N. *Unification of a Slave State: The Rise of the Planter Class in the South Carolina Backcountry, 1760–1808*. Chapel Hill: University of North Carolina Press, 1990.

Kolchin, Peter. *American Slavery, 1619–1877*. New York: Hill and Wang, 1993.

————. *Unfree Labor: American Slavery and Russian Serfdom*. Cambridge, Mass.: Harvard University Press, 1987.

Leach, William. *Land of Desire: Merchants, Power, and the Rise of a New American Culture*. New York: Vintage Books, 1993.

Lears, T. J. Jackson. *No Place of Grace: Antimodernism and the Transformation of American Culture, 1880–1920*. New York: Pantheon Books, 1981. Reprint, Chicago: University of Chicago Press, 1994.

Lebsock, Suzanne. *The Free Women of Petersburg: Status and Culture in a Southern Town, 1784–1860*. New York: Norton, 1984.

Lee, Martyn J. *Consumer Culture Reborn: The Cultural Politics of Consumption*. New York: Routledge, 1993.

Lefler, Hugh Talmage, and Albert Ray Newsome. *North Carolina: The History of a Southern State*. 3rd ed. Chapel Hill: University of North Carolina Press, 1973.

Levine, Bruce C. *Half Slave and Half Free: The Roots of Civil War*. New York: Hill and Wang, 1992.

Levine, David. *Family Formation in the Age of Nascent Capitalism*. New York: Academic Press, 1977.

Levine, Lawrence W. *Black Culture and Black Consciousness: Afro-American Folk Thought from Slavery to Freedom*. New York: Oxford University Press, 1977.

Lewis, Jan. *The Pursuit of Happiness: Family and Values in Jefferson's Virginia*. Cambridge: Cambridge University Press, 1983.

Linderman, Gerald F. *Embattled Courage: The Experience of Combat in the American Civil War*. New York: Free Press, 1987.

Lockley, Timothy James. *Lines in the Sand: Race and Class in Lowcountry Georgia, 1750–1860*. Athens: University of Georgia Press, 2001.

Lorber, Judith. *Paradoxes of Gender*. New Haven, Conn.: Yale University Press, 1994.

Luraghi, Raimondo. *The Rise and Fall of the Plantation South*. New York: Near Viewpoints, 1978.

Lystra, Karen. *Searching the Heart: Women, Men, and Romantic Love in Nineteenth-Century America*. New York: Oxford University Press, 1989.

Marten, James. *The Children's Civil War*. Chapel Hill: University of North Carolina Press, 1998.

Martin, David G. *Gettysburg, July 1*. Conshohocken, Pa.: Combined Books, 1996.

Massey, Mary Elizabeth. *Refugee Life in the Confederacy*. Baton Rouge: Louisiana State University Press, 1964.

Mathews, Donald G. *Religion in the Old South*. Chicago: University of Chicago Press, 1977.

McArthur, Judith N., and Orville Vernon Burton. *A Gentleman and an Officer: A*

Military and Social History of James B. Griffin's Civil War. New York: Oxford University Press, 1996.

McCallum, James H. *Martin County during the Civil War*. Williamston, N.C.: Enterprise, 1971.

McCracken, Grant David. *Culture and Consumption: New Approaches to the Symbolic Character of Consumer Goods and Activities*. Bloomington: Indiana University Press, 1988.

McCurry, Stephanie. *Masters of Small Worlds: Yeoman Households, Gender Relations, and the Political Culture of the Antebellum South Carolina Low Country*. New York: Oxford University Press, 1995.

McKendrik, Neil, and J. H. Plumb. *The Birth of Consumer Society: The Commercialization of Eighteenth-Century England*. Bloomington: University of Indiana Press, 1982.

McMillen, Sally G. *Motherhood in the Old South: Pregnancy, Childbirth, and Infant Rearing*. Baton Rouge: Louisiana State University Press, 1990.

McPherson, James M. *Battle Cry of Freedom: The Civil War Era*. Oxford History of the United States, vol. 6. New York: Oxford University Press, 1988.

————. *For Cause and Comrades: Why Men Fought in the Civil War*. New York: Oxford University Press, 1997.

————. *Ordeal by Fire: The Civil War and Reconstruction*. New York: Knopf, 1982.

McVeagh, John. *Tradefull Merchants: The Portrayal of the Capitalist in Literature*. London: Routledge & Kegan Paul, 1981.

McWhiney, Grady. *Cracker Culture: Celtic Ways in the Old South*. University, Ala.: University of Alabama Press, 1988.

Mintz, Steven. *A Prison of Expectations: The Family in Victorian Culture*. New York: New York University Press, 1983.

Mitchell, Reid. *Civil War Soldiers*. New York: Viking, 1988.

————. *The Vacant Chair: The Northern Soldier Leaves Home*. New York: Oxford University Press, 1993.

Mohr, Clarence L. *On the Threshold of Freedom: Masters and Slaves in Civil War Georgia*. Athens: University of Georgia Press, 1986.

Moore, Albert Burton. *Conscription and Conflict in the Confederacy*. New York: Macmillan, 1924. Reprint, New York: Hillary House, 1963.

Moore, Winifred B., Jr., and Joseph F. Tripp, eds. *Developing Dixie: Modernization in a Traditional Society*. Westport, Conn.: Greenwood Press, 1988.

Morris, Christopher. *Becoming Southern: The Evolution of a Way of Life, Warren County and Vicksburg, Mississippi, 1770–1860*. New York: Oxford University Press, 1995.

Morris, Roy, Jr. *Ambrose Bierce: Alone in Bad Company*. New York: Crown, 1995.

Newman, Harry Wright. *The Maryland Semmes and Kindred Families*. Baltimore: Maryland Historical Society, 1956.

Oakes, James. *The Ruling Race: A History of American Slaveholders*. New York: Knopf, 1982.

———. *Slavery and Freedom: An Interpretation of the Old South*. New York: Knopf, 1990.

O'Brien, Michael. *Conjectures of Order: Intellectual Life and the American South, 1810–1860*. 2 vols. Chapel Hill: University of North Carolina Press, 2004.

O'Brien, Michael, ed. *An Evening When Alone: Four Journals of Single Women in the South, 1827–67*. Charlottesville: Published for the Southern Texts Society by the University Press of Virginia, 1993.

O'Brien, Michael, and David Moltke-Hansen, eds., *Intellectual Life in Antebellum Charleston*. Knoxville: University of Tennessee Press, 1988.

Osthaus, Carl R. *Partisans of the Southern Press: Editorial Spokesmen of the Nineteenth Century*. Lexington: University Press of Kentucky, 1994.

Ownby, Ted. *Subduing Satan: Religion, Recreation, and Manhood in the Rural South, 1865–1920*. Chapel Hill: University of North Carolina Press, 1990.

Owsley, Frank L. *Plain Folk of the Old South*. Baton Rouge: Louisiana State University Press, 1949.

Paludan, Phillip S. *Victims: A True Story of the Civil War*. Knoxville: University of Tennessee Press, 1981.

Pease, Jane H., and William H. Pease. *Ladies, Women, and Wenches: Choice and Constraint in Antebellum Charleston and Boston*. Chapel Hill: University of North Carolina Press, 1990.

Peters, J. S., and W. F. Stinespring. *An Economic and Social Survey of Rockingham County*. Charlottesville: University of Virginia, 1924.

Peterson, Merrill D. *Thomas Jefferson and the New Nation: A Biography*. New York: Oxford University Press, 1970.

Phillips, Ulrich Bonnell. *American Negro Slavery: A Survey of the Supply, Employment and Control of Negro Labor as Determined by the Plantation Regime*. New York: D. Appleton, 1918. Reprint, Baton Rouge: Louisiana State University Press, 1969.

———. *Life and Labor in the Old South*. Boston: Little, Brown, 1929.

———. *The Slave Economy of the Old South: Selected Essays in Economic and Social History*. Baton Rouge: Louisiana State University Press, 1968.

Pope, Daniel. *The Making of Modern Advertising*. New York: Basic Books, 1983.

Potter, David M., and Don E. Fehrenbacher. *The Impending Crisis, 1848–1861*. New York: Harper & Row, 1976.

Presbrey, Frank. *The History and Development of Advertising*. Garden City, N.Y.: Doubleday, Doran, 1929.

Price, Michael E. *Stories with a Moral: Literature and Society in Nineteenth-Century Georgia.* Athens: University of Georgia Press, 2000.

Rable, George C. *Civil Wars: Women and the Crisis of Southern Nationalism.* Women in American History. Urbana: University of Illinois Press, 1989.

Ransom, Roger L. *Conflict and Compromise: The Political Economy of Slavery, Emancipation, and the American Civil War.* Cambridge: Cambridge University Press, 1989.

Rawick, George P. *From Sundown to Sunup: The Making of the Black Community.* Vol. 1 of *The American Slave: A Composite Autobiography.* Westport, Conn.: Greenwood, 1972.

Rawick, George P., ed. *The American Slave: A Composite Autobiography.* Multiple vols. Westport, Conn.: Greenwood, 1972.

Reader, W. J. *Professional Men: The Rise of the Professional Classes in Nineteenth-Century England.* London: Weidenfeld & Nicolson, 1966.

Robertson, James I., Jr. *Soldiers Blue and Gray.* Columbia: University of South Carolina Press, 1988.

Rogers, William Warren, Jr. *Confederate Home Front: Montgomery during the Civil War.* Tuscaloosa: University of Alabama Press, 1999.

Rose, Anne C. *Victorian America and the Civil War.* New York: Cambridge University Press, 1992.

Royster, Charles. *The Destructive War: William Tecumseh Sherman, Stonewall Jackson, and the Americans.* New York: Knopf, 1991.

Ruggles, Steven. *Prolonged Connections: The Rise of the Extended Family in Nineteenth-Century England and America.* Social Demography. Madison: University of Wisconsin Press, 1987.

Rutman, Darrett Bruce, and Anita Rutman. *Small Worlds, Large Questions: Explorations in Early American Social History, 1600–1850.* Charlottesville: University Press of Virginia, 1994.

Ryan, Mary P. *Cradle of the Middle Class: The Family in Oneida County, New York, 1790–1865.* Cambridge: Cambridge University Press, 1981.

Savitt, Todd L., and James Harvey Young, eds. *Disease and Distinctiveness in the American South.* Knoxville: University of Tennessee Press, 1988.

Schama, Simon. *The Embarrassment of Riches: An Interpretation of Dutch Culture in the Golden Age.* New York: Knopf, 1987.

Schwaab, Eugene L., ed. *Travels in the Old South: Selected from Periodicals of the Times.* 2 vols. Lexington: University Press of Kentucky, 1973.

Schweikart, Larry. *Banking in the American South from the Age of Jackson to Reconstruction.* Baton Rouge: Louisiana State University Press, 1987.

Scott, Anne Firor. *The Southern Lady: From Pedestal to Politics, 1830–1930.* Chicago: University of Chicago Press, 1970.

Sellers, Charles. *The Market Revolution: Jacksonian America, 1815–1846.* New York: Oxford University Press, 1991.

Shammas, Carole. *The Pre-Industrial Consumer in England and America*. Oxford: Clarendon Press, 1990.

Shingleton, Royce. *Richard Peters: Champion of the New South*. Macon, Ga.: Mercer University Press, 1985.

Shore, Laurence. *Southern Capitalists: The Ideological Leadership of an Elite, 1832–1885*. Chapel Hill: University of North Carolina Press, 1986.

Siegel, Frederick F. *The Roots of Southern Distinctiveness: Tobacco and Society in Danville, Virginia, 1780–1865*. Chapel Hill: University of North Carolina Press, 1987.

Skipper, Ottis C. *J. D. B. De Bow: Magazinist of the Old South*. Athens: University of Georgia Press, 1958.

Sklar, Kathryn Kish. "The Historical Foundations of Women's Power in the Creation of the American Welfare State, 1830–1930." In *Mothers of a New World: Maternalist Politics and the Origins of Welfare States*, edited by Seth Koven and Sonya Michel, 51–53. New York: Routledge, 1993.

Smith, Bonnie G. *Ladies of the Leisure Class: The Bourgeoises of Northern France in the Nineteenth Century*. Princeton: Princeton University Press, 1981.

Smith, Mark M. *Debating Slavery: Economy and Society in the Antebellum American South*. New Studies in Economic and Social History. Cambridge: Cambridge University Press, 1998.

———. *Mastered by the Clock: Time, Slavery, and Freedom in the American South*. Fred W. Morrison Series in Southern Studies. Chapel Hill: University of North Carolina Press, 1997.

Smith-Rosenberg, Carroll. *Disorderly Conduct: Visions of Gender in Victorian America*. New York: Oxford University Press, 1985.

Soltow, Lee. *Men and Wealth in the United States, 1850–1870*. New Haven, Conn.: Yale University Press, 1975.

Spencer, Warren F. *Raphael Semmes: The Philosophical Mariner*. Tuscaloosa: University of Alabama Press, 1997.

Stansell, Christine. *City of Women: Sex and Class in New York, 1789–1860*. New York: Knopf, 1986.

Startup, Kenneth Moore. *The Root of All Evil: The Protestant Clergy and the Economic Mind of the Old South*. Athens: University of Georgia Press, 1997.

Stem, Thad, Jr. *The Tar Heel Press*. Charlotte: North Carolina Press Association, 1973.

Sterkx, H. E. *Partners in Rebellion: Alabama Women During the Civil War*. Rutherford, N.J.: Fairleigh Dickinson University Press, 1970.

Stevenson, Brenda E. *Life in Black and White: Family and Community in the Slave South*. New York: Oxford University Press, 1996.

Stowe, Steven M. *Intimacy and Power in the Old South: Ritual in the Lives of the Planters*. New Studies in American Intellectual and Cultural History. Baltimore: Johns Hopkins University Press, 1987.

Strasser, Susan. *Satisfaction Guaranteed: The Making of the American Mass Market.* New York: Pantheon Books, 1989.

Sutherland, Daniel E. *The Expansion of Everyday Life, 1860–1876.* New York: Harper & Row, 1989.

———. *Seasons of War: The Ordeal of a Confederate Community, 1861–1865.* New York: Free Press, 1995.

Tadman, Michael. *Speculators and Slaves: Masters, Traders, and Slaves in the Old South.* Madison: University of Wisconsin Press, 1989.

Taylor, Alan. *William Cooper's Town: Power and Persuasion on the Frontier of the Early American Republic.* New York: Knopf, 1995.

Taylor, Barbara. *Eve and the New Jerusalem: Socialism and Feminism in the Nineteenth Century.* New York, Pantheon Books, 1983.

Taylor, William R. *Cavalier and Yankee: The Old South and American National Character.* New York: George Braziller, 1961.

Thomas, Emory M. *The Confederate Nation, 1861–1865.* New York: Harper & Row, 1979.

Thompson, E. P. *Customs in Common.* New York: New Press, 1991.

Thornton, J. Mills, III. *Politics and Power in a Slave Society: Alabama, 1800–1860.* Baton Rouge: Louisiana State University Press, 1978.

Tise, Larry E. *Proslavery: A History of the Defense of Slavery in America, 1701–1840.* Athens: University of Georgia Press, 1987.

Tolbert, Lisa C. *Constructing Townscapes: Space and Society in Antebellum Tennessee.* Chapel Hill: University of North Carolina Press, 1999.

Tripp, Steven Elliott. *Yankee Town, Southern City: Race and Class Relations in Civil War Lynchburg.* New York: New York University Press, 1997.

Tullos, Allen. *Habits of Industry: White Culture and the Transformation of the Carolina Piedmont.* Chapel Hill: University of North Carolina Press, 1989.

Usner, Daniel H. Jr. *Indians, Settlers, and Slaves in a Frontier Exchange Economy.* Chapel Hill: University of North Carolina Press, 1992.

Walther, Eric H. *The Fire-Eaters.* Baton Rouge: Louisiana State University Press, 1992.

Ward, W. Reginald. *The Protestant Evangelical Awakening.* Cambridge: Cambridge University Press, 1992.

Waterhouse, Richard. *A New World Gentry: The Making of a Merchant and Planter Class in South Carolina, 1670–1770.* New York: Garland Publishing, 1989.

Watson, Harry L. *An Independent People: The Way We Lived in North Carolina, 1770–1820.* Chapel Hill: University of North Carolina Press, 1983.

———. *Liberty and Power: The Politics of Jacksonian America.* New York: Hill and Wang, 1990.

Watts, Emily Stipes. *The Businessman in American Literature.* Athens: University of Georgia Press, 1982.

Weaver, Herbert. *Mississippi Farmers, 1850–1860.* Nashville: Vanderbilt University Press, 1945.

Wells, Jonathan Daniel. *The Origins of the Southern Middle Class, 1800–1861.* Chapel Hill: University of North Carolina Press, 2004.

Wender, Herbert. *Southern Commercial Conventions, 1837–1859.* Baltimore: Johns Hopkins University Press, 1959.

Whites, LeeAnn. *The Civil War as a Crisis in Gender: Augusta, Georgia, 1860–1890.* Athens: University of Georgia Press, 1995.

Whitney, Walton. *France at the Crystal Palace: Bourgeois Taste and Artisan Manufacture in the Nineteenth Century.* Berkeley: University of California Press, 1992.

Wiener, Jonathan M. *Social Origins of the New South: Alabama, 1860–1885.* Baton Rouge: Louisiana State University Press, 1978.

Wiley, Bell Irvin. *Confederate Women.* Contributions in American History, no. 38. Westport, Conn.: Greenwood Press, 1975.

———. *The Life of Billy Yank: The Common Soldier of the Union.* Indianapolis: Bobbs-Merrill, 1952.

———. *The Life of Johnny Reb: The Common Soldier of the Confederacy.* Indianapolis: Bobbs-Merrill, 1943.

Williams, David. *Rich Man's War: Class, Caste, and Confederate Defeat in the Lower Chattahoochee Valley.* Athens: University of Georgia Press, 1998.

Williams, Rosalind. *Dream Worlds: Mass Consumption in Late-Nineteenth-Century France.* Berkeley: University of California Press, 1982.

———. *Notes on the Underground: An Essay on Technology, Society, and the Imagination.* Cambridge, Mass.: MIT Press, 1990.

Wilson, Charles Reagan, ed. *Religion in the South.* Jackson: University Press of Mississippi, 1985.

Wilson, Harold S. *Confederate Industry: Manufacturers and Quartermasters in the Civil War.* Jackson: University Press of Mississippi, 2002.

Wolfe, Margaret Ripley. *Daughters of Canaan: A Saga of Southern Women.* New Perspectives on the South. Lexington: University Press of Kentucky, 1995.

Woloch, Nancy. *Women and the American Experience.* New York: Knopf, 1984.

Woodman, Harold D. *King Cotton & His Retainers: Financing & Marketing the Cotton Crop of the South, 1800–1925.* Lexington: University of Kentucky Press, 1968.

Woodward, C. Vann. *Origins of the New South, 1877–1913.* Baton Rouge: Louisiana State University Press, 1951.

Wright, Gavin. *Old South, New South: Revolutions in the Southern Economy since the Civil War.* New York: Basic Books, 1986.

———. *The Political Economy of the Cotton South: Households, Markets, and Wealth in the Nineteenth Century.* New York: Norton, 1978.

Wyatt-Brown, Bertram. *Southern Honor: Ethics and Behavior in the Old South.* New York: Oxford University Press, 1982.

Young, Jeffrey Robert. *Domesticating Slavery: The Master Class in Georgia and South Carolina, 1670–1837.* Chapel Hill: University of North Carolina Press, 1999.

Zuber, Richard L. *Jonathan Worth: A Biography of a Southern Unionist.* Chapel Hill: University of North Carolina Press, 1965.

Articles and Dissertations

Amos, Harriet E. "'City Belles': Images and Realities of the Lives of White Women in Antebellum Mobile." *Alabama Review* 24 (January 1981).

Atherton, Lewis E. "The Problem of Credit Rating in the Ante-Bellum South." *Journal of Southern History* 12 (November 1946): 534–56.

Auman, William T. "Neighbor Against Neighbor: The Inner Civil War in North Carolina." *North Carolina Historical Review* 61 (1984): 60–90.

Bailey, Fred A. "Class and Tennessee's Confederate Generation." *Journal of Southern History* 51 (February 1985): 30–60.

Baptist, Edward E. "Accidental Ethnography in an Antebellum Southern Newspaper: Snell's Homecoming Festival." *Journal of American History* 84 (March 1998): 1355–83.

Barney, William L. "Patterns of Crisis: Alabama White Families and Social Change, 1850–1870." *Sociology and Social Research* 63 (April 1979): 524–43.

Burckin, Alexander Irwin. "The Formation and Growth of an Urban Middle Class: Power and Conflict in Louisville, Kentucky, 1828–1861." Ph.D. diss., University of California at Irvine, 1993.

Byrne, Frank J. "Becoming Bourgeois: Merchant Culture in the Antebellum and Confederate South." Ph.D. diss., Ohio State University, 2000.

———. "The Merchant in Antebellum Southern Literature and Society." *American Nineteenth Century History* 6 (March 2005): 33–55.

———. "Rebellion and Retail: A Tale of Two Merchants in Confederate Atlanta." *Georgia Historical Quarterly* 79 (spring 1995): 30–56.

Campbell, Randolph B. "Intermittent Slave Ownership: Texas as a Test Case." *Journal of Southern History* 51 (February 1985): 15–23.

———. "Planters and Plain Folk: Harrison County, Texas, as a Test Case, 1850–1860." *Journal of Southern History* 40 (August 1974): 369–98.

Clark, Christopher. "Household Economy, Market Exchange and the Rise of Capitalism in the Connecticut Valley, 1800–1860." *Journal of Social History* 13 (winter 1979): 19–89.

Cole, Arthur. "The Tempo of Mercantile Life in Colonial America." *Business History Review* (autumn 1959): 277–99.

Coleberd, Robert E., Jr. "John Williams: A Merchant Banker in Springfield, Illinois." *Agricultural History* 42 (1968): 259–65.

Ditz, Toby L. "Shipwrecked; or, Masculinity Imperiled: Mercantile Representations of Failure and the Gendered Self in Eighteenth-Century Philadelphia." *Journal of American History* 81 (June 1994): 50–80.

Duffy, John. "Medical Practice in the Ante Bellum South." *Journal of Southern History* 25 (February 1959): 53–72.

Escott, Paul D. "Yeoman Independence and the Market: Social Status and Economic Development in Antebellum North Carolina." *North Carolina Historical Review* 61 (1989): 275–300.

Faust, Drew Gilpin. "Altars of Sacrifice: Confederate Women and the Narratives of War." *Journal of American History* 76 (March 1990): 1200–1228.

Ford, Lacy K. "Rednecks and Merchants: Economic Development and Social Tensions in the South Carolina Upcountry, 1865–1900." *Journal of American History* 71 (September 1984): 294–318.

Fuller, Justin. "Alabama Business Leaders: 1865–1900." *Alabama Review* 16 (1963): 279–86.

Gallman, Robert E. "Slavery and Southern Economic Growth." *Southern Economic Journal* 45 (April 1979): 1007–22.

Greb, Gregory Allen. "Charleston, South Carolina, Merchants, 1815–1860: Urban Leadership in the Antebellum South." Ph.D. diss., University of California at San Diego, 1978.

Hagler, D. Harland. "The Ideal Woman in the Antebellum South: Lady or Farmwife." *Journal of Southern History* 46 (August 1980): 405–18.

Haskell, Thomas L. "Capitalism and the Origins of the Humanitarian Sensibility, Part 1." *American Historical Review* 90 (April 1985): 339–61.

Henretta, James A. "Families and Farms: *Mentalité* in Pre-Industrial America." *William and Mary Quarterly*, 3rd series, 35 (January 1978): 3–32.

Hewitt, Nancy. "Beyond the Search for Sisterhood: American Women's History in the 1980s." *Social History* 10 (October 1985): 290–321.

Huffman, Frank J., Jr. "Town and Country in the South, 1850–1880: A Comparison of Urban and Rural Social Structures." *South Atlantic Quarterly* 76 (summer 1977): 366–81.

Johnson, Michael P. "Planters and Patriarchy: Charleston, 1800–1860." *Journal of Southern History* 46 (February 1980): 45–72.

Kyriakoudes, Louis. "Plantation to Town: Merchants and the Rise of Towns in Alabama, 1860–1900." M.A. thesis, Vanderbilt University, 1988.

Levy, Babette. "Early Puritanism in the Southern and Island Colonies." *Proceedings of the American Antiquarian Society* 70 (April–October 1960).

Lockley, Timothy J. "Trading Encounters between Non-Elite Whites and

African Americans in Savannah, 1790–1860." *Journal of Southern History* 66 (February 2000): 25–48.

McCurry, Stephanie. "The Two Faces of Republicanism: Gender and Proslavery Politics in Antebellum South Carolina." *Journal of American History* 78 (March 1992): 1245–64.

McElreath, Walter. "Sidney Root: Merchant Prince and Great Citizen." *Atlanta Historical Bulletin* 7 (October 1944): 171–83.

Merrill, Michael. "Cash Is Good to Eat: Self-Sufficiency and Exchange in the Rural Economy of the United States." *Radical History Review* 4 (winter 1977): 42–71.

Morgan, Edmund. "The Puritan Ethic and the American Revolution." *William & Mary Quarterly* 24 (January 1967): 3–43.

O'Brien, Michael. "C. Vann Woodward and the Burden of Southern Liberalism." *American Historical Review* 78 (June 1973): 589–604.

Pessen, Edward. "How Different from Each Other Were the Antebellum North and South?" *American Historical Review* 85 (December 1980): 1119–49.

Phillips, Ulrich B. "The Origin and Growth of the Southern Black Belts." *American Historical Review* 11 (July 1906): 798–816.

Roeder, Robert E. "New Orleans Merchants, 1790–1837." Ph.D. diss., Harvard University, 1959.

Roediger, Dave. "Slavery and Capitalism." *In These Times* 26 (January–February 1983): 20–23.

Sacher, John M. "The Sudden Collapse of the Louisiana Whig Party." *Journal of Southern History* 65 (May 1999): 221–48.

Seidell, Kathryn L. "The Southern Belle as an Antebellum Ideal." *Southern Quarterly* 15 (July 1977).

Smith, Mark M. "Old South Time in Comparative Perspective." *American Historical Review* 101 (December 1996): 1432–69.

Somers, Dale A. "New Orleans at War: A Merchant's View." *Louisiana History* 14 (winter 1973): 49–68.

Suarez, Raleigh A. "Bargains, Bills, and Bankruptcies: Business Activity in the Rural Antebellum South." *Louisiana History* 7 (summer 1966): 189–206.

Summers, Suzanne L. "The Geographic and Social Origins of Antebellum Merchants in Houston and Galveston, Texas, 1836–1860." *Essays in Economic and Business History* 15 (1997): 95–107.

———. "Public Policy and Economic Growth in Antebellum Texas: The Role of Houston-Galveston Merchants." *Essays in Economic and Business History* 16 (1998): 127–45.

Temperly, Howard. "Capitalism, Slavery and Ideology." *Past and Present* 75 (May 1977): 94–118.

Thornton, Ella Mae. "Mrs. S. P. Richards." *Atlanta Historical Bulletin* 3 (December 1937).

Thorp, Daniel B. "Doing Business in the Backcountry: Retail Trade in Colonial Rowan County, North Carolina." *William & Mary Quarterly* 48 (July 1991): 387–408.

Welter, Barbara. "The Cult of True Womanhood: 1820–1860." *American Quarterly* 18 (summer 1966): 151–74.

Woodman, Harold D. "The Political Economy of the New South: Retrospects and Prospects." *Journal of Southern History* 67 (November 2001): 789–810.

Wright, Gavin. "The Strange Career of the New Southern Economic History." *Reviews in American History* 10 (December 1982): 164–80.

Zipf, Karin L. "'The WHITES shall rule the land or die': Gender, Race, and Class in North Carolina Reconstruction Politics." *Journal of Southern History* 65 (August 1999): 499–534.

Index

Aby, Samuel, 20, 24, 28, 47, 80, 85, 87, 95
Aby, Thomas, 20
Adams, Elizabeth, 85–86, 91
Adriance, John, 26, 35, 131
Adriance, Lydia, 35–36
Alabama, 25; commercial population in, 16. *See also specific towns and cities*
Alachua County, Fla., 209–14 (appendix)
Annapolis, Md., 55
Anngady, Mary, 117, 196
Arkansas, 55–56, 126, 221 (n. 11)
Atherton, Lewis E., 9, 10, 30
Atlanta, Ga.: 19, 37, 43, 81, 123, 125, 130–31, 147–48, 168, 171–73, 176, 179–80, 191, 196, 200, 207, 254 (n. 15); size of commercial population within, 16
Augusta, Ga., 29, 34, 94, 99, 115, 117, 133, 155, 186–87, 191–92
Augusta Daily Chronicle & Sentinel, 156

Baldwin, Daniel Hoard (D.H.), 127, 207
Baldwin, Joseph G., 25
Baldwin, O. S., 129–30
Baldwin, William, 127
Baltimore, Md., 2, 18, 33, 50, 69, 85
Baptist Church, 90, 107–10, 112, 161, 241 (n. 59)
Beach, John N., 37, 130–31, 176

Beckert, Sven, 3, 24, 145
Beckett, Harrison, 136
Biggs, Asa, 20, 55, 88, 110–11, 130–31, 228 (n. 18)
Biggs, Joseph, 20, 71, 88, 98, 110, 131
Biggs, Kader, 20, 24, 88, 110, 116, 171
Biggs, William, 20, 24, 39, 88
Blacknall, Charles Christopher, 20, 135–36, 157–58, 162–64, 169, 171, 184–85, 194–95, 250 (n. 32)
Blacknall, Jinny, 157, 162, 194
Bonney, Eli, 35, 47, 200, 256 (n. 32)
Bonney, Usher, 193,
boosterism, 34, 50; and competition between southern cities, 69. *See also* merchants: boosterism
bourgeois values, 4–6, 15, 77, 79, 86–89, 97, 154, 203–8; definition of, 2–3, 219 (n. 19). *See also* merchants: commercial values of
Bradbury, John William, 184, 253 (n. 8)
Brainerd, Tyrus, 99
Bres, Jean Baptiste, 85, 91–92, 199, 256 (n. 32)
Brown, Joseph, 180, 255 (n. 20)
Brownlow, William, 183
Brownsville, Tx., 187
Bunch, James, 104–5
Burbidge, John, 52, 60, 72, 81
Burke, William, 181–82

Ingraham, Ruth, 99, 115

Jackson, Andrew, 51, 228 (nn. 17, 18)
Jacocks, Charles W., 51–52, 85–86, 103–6, 110–11, 228 (n. 17)
Jacocks, Mary Caroline, 85
Jefferson, John F., 20, 24, 43–44, 57, 94, 111, 116, 118–19, 125
Jefferson, Thomas, 14
Jewish merchants. *See* merchants: within southern Jewish community; stereotypes of
Jones, John Beauchamp, 61, 128–29, 190–91

Kent, Horace, 40
Kiger, Basil, 60
Kentucky, 31, 48, 88–89, 110. *See also specific towns and cities*

Lea, William, 100
Leasburg, N.C., 100
Leon County, Fla., 209–14 (appendix)
Leon, Louis, 138, 193–94
Levert, Francis, 25, 28–29, 174
Leyendecker, John Zirvas, 142
Lincoln, Abraham, 121, 126–27, 128, 167, 175
Longstreet, Augustus Baldwin, 5, 61
Louisiana, 28; rural commercial culture in, 16. *See also specific towns and cities*
Louisville, Ky., 20, 24, 34, 43, 50, 57, 111, 118, 125, 232 (n. 36)
Lowndes County, Ala., 209–14 (appendix)
Lumpkin, Ga., 130
Lynchburg, Va., 46, 124, 183, 252 (n. 1)

Macon, Ga., 58–60, 188, 191
Mallett, Peter, 71, 131, 134
marketing: clothing/fashion, 74–75
Marriot, Jane, 90–91
Martin County, N.C., 209–14 (appendix)
Massachusetts, 127, 130, 147
McDuffie, George, 18
McMinn County, Tenn., 209–14 (appendix)
McNairy County, Tenn., 209–14 (appendix)
Memphis, Tenn., 1, 23, 82, 142, 152, 158–59, 170, 200
Memphis Daily Appeal, 154, 191
mercantile library associations, 50, 72–73
mercantile licenses, 22, 49
merchants: birthplace of, 18–19, 61, 88, 98–99; blockade-running of, 130–31, 175–77; boosterism of, 34, 50; and business partnerships, 20, 25–33, 40, 130, 135, 143, 224 (nn. 25, 28); business practices (general) of, 1–2, 14–15, 17, 26, 42–43, 80; child-rearing practices of, 81–85, 135–36; as distinct class, 2–3, 6–7, 14; clerking experiences of, 20, 38–40; commercial values of, 2, 26, 42, 44, 70–71, 75, 77, 81, 87, 94, 97, 112, 131, 141, 153, 201–8; competition between, 22; conservatism of, 79, 102–20; consumption patterns of, 93–97, 153–54; courting practices of, 89–92, 142; and credit; 21, 24–26, 29–30, 45–47, 71, 128–30, 197, 200–201; criticism of, 2, 41–42, 54, 56–59, 62–65, 118–20; criticism of Confederacy by, 149–50;